WEST-E / PRAXIS II

0014

Elementary Education

Teacher Certification Exam

By: Sharon Wynne, M.S
Southern Connecticut State University

"And, while there's no reason yet to panic, I think it's only prudent that we make preparations to panic."

XAMonline, INC.

Boston

W9-BMO-149

Library of Congress Cataloging-in-Publication Data

Wynne, Sharon A.
    WEST-E / PRAXIS II Elementary Education 0014: Teacher Certification / Sharon A. Wynne.
    -2nd ed. ISBN 978-1-58197-558-1
    1. WEST-E / PRAXIS II Elementary Education 0014.   2. Study Guides.
    3. WEST   4. Teachers' Certification & Licensure.   5. Careers

Disclaimer:
The opinions expressed in this publication are the sole works of XAMonline and were created independently from the National Education Association, Educational Testing Service, or any State Department of Education, National Evaluation Systems or other testing affiliates.

Between the time of publication and printing, state specific standards as well as testing formats and website information may change that is not included in part or in whole within this product. Sample test questions are developed by XAMonline and reflect similar content as on real tests; however, they are not former tests. XAMonline assembles content that aligns with state standards but makes no claims nor guarantees teacher candidates a passing score. Numerical scores are determined by testing companies such as NES or ETS and then are compared with individual state standards. A passing score varies from state to state.

Printed in the United States of America   œ-1

WEST-E/PRAXIS II: Elementary Education 0014
ISBN: 978-1-58197-558-1

TEACHER CERTIFICATION STUDY GUIDE

Project Manager:	Sharon Wynne, MS
Project Coordinator:	Victoria Anderson, MS
Content Coordinators/Authors:	Rennell Brunclik, BS
	Susan Andres, MS
	Frances Stanford, MS
	Natalie Arnett, BS
	Janis Petersen, PhD
	David White, MS
	Ted Purinton, PhD
	Christina Forsyth, MS
	Barbara Casey, PhD
	Kelley Eldredge, MS
	Vickie Pittard, MS
	James Stark, MS
	Don Rogerson, BS
	Michele Di Amico, BS
Sample test:	Shelley Wake, MS
	Deborah Harbin, MS
	Christina Godard, BS
	Kim Putney, BS
	Carol Moore, BS
	Vickie Pittard, MS
Editors: Managing	Dr. Harte Weiner, PhD
Proof reader	Heather Sugioka, MS
	Cathi Evans, AA
	Beth Anderson, PhD
	Donna Quesinberry; MS
	Paul Giacomelli, MS
	Vickie Pittard, MS
	Mary Arena, BS
	Christina Forsyth, MS
	Don Rogerson, BS
	Bonnie Snyder, PhD
	Jane Carter, MS
	Deborah Harbin, MS
Copy editor	Tamara Brewer, MS
Sample test	Christina Forsyth, MS
Pre-Flight	Mary Collins, BS
Production	David Aronson
Graphic Artist	Jenna Hamilton

Table of Contents

DOMAIN I.   **LANGUAGE ARTS**

COMPETENCY 1.0   **UNDERSTANDING LITERATURE**

Skill 1.1   Narratives 1

Skill 1.2   Nonfiction 1

Skill 1.3   Poetry 4

Skill 1.4   Resource and research material 7

COMPETENCY 2.0   **TEXT STRUCTURES AND ORGANIZATION FOR READING AND WRITING**

Skill 2.1   Structure 9

Skill 2.2   Patterns of organization 13

COMPETENCY 3.0   **LITERACY ACQUISITION AND READING INSTRUCTION**

Skill 3.1   Foundations of literacy and reading instruction 15

Skill 3.2   Children's literature 18

Skill 3.3   Strategies for word recognition 24

Skill 3.4   Strategies for comprehension 26

COMPETENCY 4.0   LANGUAGE IN WRITING

Skill 4.1   Components of language in writing including the elements of grammar and usage 39

Skill 4.2   Syntax, sentence types 49

Skill 4.3   Orthography and morphology..50

Skill 4.4   Semantics..52

Skill 4.5   Vocabulary in context 53

Skill 4.6   Figurative language..54

Skill 4.7   Social, cultural, and historical influences of language 56

COMPETENCY 5.0   COMMUNICATION SKILLS

Skill 5.1   Processes of communication as reflected in the stages of writing development..59

Skill 5.2   Stages of the writing process 61

Skill 5.3   Spelling development 66

Skill 5.4   Aspects of speaking and listening 67

DOMAIN II.   **MATHEMATICS**

COMPETENCY 6.0   CRITICAL THINKING

Skill 6.1   Deductive reasoning 73

Skill 6.2   Inductive reasoning 73

Skill 6.3   Adaptive reasoning 74

Skill 6.4   Problem analysis 75

COMPETENCY 7.0   NUMBER SENSE AND NUMERATION

Skill 7.1   Meaning and use of numbers 80

Skill 7.2   The standard algorithms for the four basic operations 80

Skill 7.3   Appropriate computation strategies and reasonableness of results 81

Skill 7.4   Methods of mathematical investigation 82

Skill 7.5   Number patterns 84

Skill 7.6   Place value 85

Skill 7.7   Equivalence 87

Skill 7.8   Factors and multiples 88

Skill 7.9   Ratio, proportion, percent 89

Skill 7.10   Representations 91

Skill 7.11   Calculator strategies 92

Skill 7.12   Number lines 92

COMPETENCY 8.0   ALGEBRAIC CONCEPTS

Skill 8.1   Algebraic methods and representations 93

Skill 8.2   Associative, commutative, and distributive properties 94

Skill 8.3   Additive and multiplicative inverses 96

Skill 8.4   Function machines 97

Skill 8.5   The special properties of zero and one 97

Skill 8.6   Equalities and inequalities, patterns, and algebraic formulas 98

COMPETENCY 9.0   INFORMAL GEOMETRY AND MEASUREMENT

Skill 9.1   Pure and real-world properties and relationships in figures
                 and shapes in two and three dimensions 103

Skill 9.2   Pythagorean theorem 105

Skill 9.3   Transformations 109

Skill 9.4   Geometric models 112

Skill 9.5   Nets 113

Skill 9.6   Standard units of measurement 114

Skill 9.7   Coordinate graphing 120

Skill 9.8   Perimeter, area, volume 121

Skill 9.9   Rates 127

Skill 9.10   Angles 129

Skill 9.11   Money, temperature, time 130

COMPETENCY 10.0   DATA ORGANIZATION AND INTERPRETATION

Skill 10.1   Visual displays of quantitative information 131

Skill 10.2   Simple probability 134

Skill 10.3   Outcomes 134

Skill 10.4   Events 135

Skill 10.5   Sample spaces 136

Skill 10.6   Counting techniques 137

Skill 10.7   Tree diagrams 139

Skill 10.8   Combinations 139

Skill 10.9   Permutations 139

Skill 10.10   Mean, median, mode 141

DOMAIN III.   SOCIAL STUDIES

COMPETENCY 11.0   GEOGRAPHY

Skill 11.1   The world in spatial terms...144

Skill 11.2   Places and regions...146

Skill 11.3   Physical and human systems...150

Skill 11.4   Environment and society 152

Skill 11.5   Uses of geography 153

COMPETENCY 12.0   WORLD HISTORY

Skill 12.1   Prehistory and early civilizations 155

Skill 12.2   Classical civilizations..160

Skill 12.3   The rise of non-European civilizations..162

Skill 12.4   Cross-cultural comparisons 166

Skill 12.5   The rise and expansion of Europe..167

Skill 12.6   Twentieth-century developments and transformations 169

COMPETENCY 13.0   UNITED STATES HISTORY

Skill 13.1   European exploration and colonization...171

Skill 13.2   The American Revolution and the founding of the nation..................173

Skill 13.3   Growth and expansion of the Republic...175

Skill 13.4   Twentieth-century developments and transformations 185

COMPETENCY 14.0 POLITICAL SCIENCE

Skill 14.1 The nature and purpose of government 191

Skill 14.2 The forms of government 192

Skill 14.3 The United States Constitution 194

Skill 14.4 The rights and responsibilities of citizens 198

Skill 14.5 State and local government 198

COMPETENCY 15.0 ANTHROPOLOGY, SOCIOLOGY, AND PSYCHOLOGY

Skill 15.1 Kinship patterns, social institutions, social stratification, and cultural changes 200

Skill 15.2 Socialization and acculturation, ethnic groups and societal change, and stereotypes and biases 202

Skill 15.3 Human development and growth, human behavior, and gender roles and differences 203

COMPETENCY 16.0 ECONOMICS

Skill 16.1 Key terms and major concepts of the economic market 205

Skill 16.2 The individual and the market 205

Skill 16.3 Economics' effect on population and resources 206

Skill 16.4 Government's role in economics and economics' impact on government 207

Skill 16.5 Economic systems 208

Skill 16.6 Impact of technological developments on the economy 209

Skill 16.7 International economics 211

DOMAIN IV.   SCIENCE

COMPETENCY 17.0   EARTH SCIENCE

Skill 17.1   The structure of the earth system 213

Skill 17.2   Processes of the earth system 215

Skill 17.3   Earth history 221

Skill 17.4   Earth and universe 224

COMPETENCY 18.0   LIFE SCIENCE

Skill 18.1   The structure and function of living systems 232

Skill 18.2   Reproduction and heredity 239

Skill 18.3   Regulation and behavior 245

Skill 18.4   Biological evolution 246

Skill 18.5   Interdependence of organisms 247

COMPETENCY 19.0   PHYSICAL SCIENCE

Skill 19.1   The structure and properties of matter 250

Skill 19.2   Energy 255

Skill 19.3   Interactions of energy and matter 259

COMPETENCY 20.0   SCIENCE AS INQUIRY

Skill 20.1   Appropriate questioning techniques 263

Skill 20.2   Planning and conducting simple investigations 264

Skill 20.3   Gathering data with the tools of science to organize and use data to draw reasonable conclusions 265

COMPETENCY 21.0   SCIENCE IN PERSONAL AND SOCIAL PERSPECTIVES

Skill 21.1   Personal health 266

Skill 21.2   Science, Technology and Society 266

COMPETENCY 22.0   HISTORY AND THE NATURE OF SCIENCE

Skill 22.1   Science as a human endeavor 267

Skill 22.2   Historical perspectives in science...267

Skill 22.3   Science as a process 268

Skill 22.4   Science as a career..271

COMPETENCY 23.0   UNIFYING PROCESSES

Skill 23.1   Systems, order, and organization...274

Skill 23.2   Structure and function models...275

Skill 23.3   Changes over time 276

Skill 23.4   Cycles...276

Skill 23.5   Equilibrium..278

Pre-test 279

Answer Key: Pre-test..302

Rationales with Sample Questions: Pre-test......................................303

Sample Test..346

Rigor Table 375

Answer Key 376

Rationales with Sample Questions 377

Great Study and Testing Tips!

What to study in order to prepare for the subject assessments is the focus of this study guide, but equally important is *how* you study.

You can increase your chances of truly mastering the information by taking some simple but effective steps.

Study Tips:

1. Some foods aid the learning process. Foods such as milk, nuts, seeds, rice, and oats help your study efforts by releasing natural memory enhancers called CCKs (*cholecystokinin*) composed of *tryptophan*, *choline*, and *phenylalanine*. All of these chemicals enhance the neurotransmitters associated with memory. Before studying, try a light, protein-rich meal of eggs, turkey, and fish. All of these foods release the memory enhancing chemicals. The better the connections, the more you comprehend.

Likewise, before you take a test, stick to a light snack of energy boosting and relaxing foods. A glass of milk, a piece of fruit, or some peanuts will release various memory-boosting chemicals and help you to relax and focus on the subject at hand.

2. Learn to take great notes. A by-product of our modern culture is that we have grown accustomed to getting our information in short doses (e.g., TV news sound bites or newspaper articles styled after USA Today).

Consequently, we've subconsciously trained ourselves to assimilate information in neat little packages. If your notes are scrawled all over the paper, it fragments the flow of the information. Strive for clarity. Newspapers use a standard format to achieve clarity. Your notes can be much clearer through the use of proper formatting. A very effective format is called the *"Cornell Method."*

> Take a sheet of loose-leaf lined notebook paper and draw a line all the way down the paper about 1-2" from the left-hand edge.
>
> Draw another line across the width of the paper about 1-2" up from the bottom. Repeat this process on the reverse side of the page.

Look at the highly effective result. You have ample room for notes, a left hand margin for special emphasis items or inserting supplementary data from the textbook, a large area at the bottom for a brief summary, and a little rectangular space for just about anything you want.

3. <u>**Get the concept then the details.**</u> Too often we focus on the details and don't gather an understanding of the concept. However, if you simply memorize only dates, places, or names, you may well miss the whole point of the subject.

A key way to understand things is to put them in your own words. If you are working from a textbook, automatically summarize each paragraph in your mind. If you are outlining text, don't simply copy the author's words.

Rephrase them in your own words. You remember your own thoughts and words much better than someone else's, and subconsciously tend to associate the important details with the core concepts.

4. <u>**Ask Why?**</u> Pull apart written material paragraph by paragraph and don't forget the captions under the illustrations.

Example: If the heading is "Stream Erosion," flip it around to read "Why do streams erode?" Then answer the questions.

If you train your mind to think in a series of questions and answers, not only will you learn more, but it will also help to lessen test anxiety because you are used to answering questions.

5. <u>**Read for reinforcement and future needs.**</u> Even if you only have 10 minutes, put your notes or a book in your hand. Your mind is similar to a computer; you have to input data in order to have it processed. *By reading, you are creating the neural connections for future retrieval.* The more times you read something, the more you reinforce the learning of ideas.

Even if you don't fully understand something on the first pass, *your mind stores much of the material for later recall.*

6. <u>**Relax to learn; go into exile.**</u> Our bodies respond to an inner clock called biorhythms. Burning the midnight oil works well for some people, but not everyone.

If possible, set aside a particular place to study that is free of distractions. Shut off the television, cell phone, and pager and exile your friends and family during your study period.

If you really are bothered by silence, try background music. Light classical music at a low volume has been shown to aid in concentration over other types of music. Music that evokes pleasant emotions without lyrics is highly suggested. Try just about anything by Mozart. It relaxes you.

7. <u>Use arrows not highlighters</u>. At best, it's difficult to read a page full of yellow, pink, blue, and green streaks. Try staring at a neon sign for a while and you'll soon see that the horde of colors obscure the message.

A quick note, a brief dash of color, an underline, or an arrow pointing to a particular passage is much clearer than a horde of highlighted words.

8. <u>Budget your study time</u>. Although you shouldn't ignore any of the material, *allocate your available study time in the same ratio that topics may appear on the test.*

By setting your personal study topics in much the same way that the test will be patterned, you will be better equipped to answer all of the test questions.

Testing Tips:

1. Get smart, play dumb. *Don't read anything into the question.* Don't make an assumption that the test writer is looking for something else than what is asked. Stick to the question as written and don't read extra things into it.

2. Read the question and all the choices *twice* before answering the question. You may miss something by not carefully reading and re-reading both the question and the answers.

If you really don't have a clue as to the right answer, leave it blank on the first time through. Go on to the other questions, as they may provide a clue as to how to answer the skipped questions.

If later on, you still can't answer the skipped ones . . . *Guess.* The only penalty for guessing is that you *might* get it wrong. Only one thing is certain; if you don't put anything down, you will get it wrong!

3. Turn the question into a statement. Look at the way the questions are worded. The syntax of the question usually provides a clue. Does it seem more familiar as a statement rather than as a question? Does it sound strange?

By turning a question into a statement, you may be able to spot if an answer sounds right, and it may also trigger memories of material you have read.

4. Look for hidden clues. It's actually very difficult to compose multiple-foil (choice) questions without giving away part of the answer in the options presented.

In most multiple-choice questions you can often readily eliminate one or two of the potential answers. This leaves you with only two real possibilities; automatically, your odds go to Fifty-Fifty for very little work.

5. Trust your instincts. For every fact that you have read, you subconsciously retain something of that knowledge. On questions that you aren't really certain about, go with your basic instincts. *Your first impression on how to answer a question is usually correct.*

6. Mark your answers directly on the test booklet. Don't bother trying to fill in the optical scan sheet on the first pass through the test.

Just be very careful not to mismark your answers when you eventually transcribe them to the scan sheet.

7. Watch the clock! You have a set amount of time to answer the questions. Don't get bogged down trying to answer a single question at the expense of ten questions you can more readily answer.

DOMAIN I.   LANGUAGE ARTS

COMPETENCY 1.0   UNDERSTANDING LITERATURE

Skill 1.1   Narratives

Narratives can be defined as interpretive stories that are historically and/or culturally based. When narratives are orally presented, they often take on the unique flavor and characteristic of the content. For example, slave narratives are often told in the "voice" and persona of nineteenth century slaves.

Organizationally, narratives are chronological; however, various disruptions in time-sequence can occur—sometimes very suddenly. Narratives can also get side-tracked based on the specific content.

A common type of narrative is the short story. Typically, a short story is a terse narrative with less developmental background about its characters than its longer narrative counterparts. A short story may include description, author's point-of-view, and tone. Poe emphasized that a successful short story should create one focused impact. Considered among the great short story writers are Hemingway, Faulkner, Twain, Joyce, O'Connor, de Maupassant, Saki, Poe, and Pushkin.

Other common types of narratives include legends, memoirs, and folk tales.

Skill 1.2   Nonfiction

Students often misrepresent the differences between fiction and nonfiction. They mistakenly believe that stories are always examples of fiction. The simple truth is that stories are both fiction and nonfiction. The primary difference is that fiction is imaginary, and nonfiction is generally true (or an opinion). It is harder for students to understand that non-fiction entails an enormous range of material from textbooks to true stories and newspaper articles to speeches. Fiction, on the other hand, is fairly simple—imaginary stories, novels, etc. But it is also important for students to understand that most of fiction throughout history has been based on true events. In other words, authors use their own life experiences to help them to create works of fiction.

The artistry in telling a story to convey a point is important in understanding fiction. When students see that an author's choice in a work of fiction is for the sole purpose of conveying a viewpoint, they can make better sense of the specific details.

Realizing what is truth and what is perspective is important in understanding nonfiction. Often, a nonfiction writer will present an opinion, and that opinion is very different from a truth. Knowing the difference between the two is very crucial.

In comparing fiction to nonfiction, students need to learn about the conventions of each. In fiction, students can generally expect to find plot, characters, setting, and themes. In nonfiction, students may find a plot, characters, settings, and themes, but they will also experience interpretations, opinions, theories, research, and other elements.

Overall, students can begin to see patterns that identify fiction from nonfiction. Often, the more fanciful or unrealistic a text or story is, the more likely it is fiction.

Nonfiction comes in a variety of styles. While many students simplify nonfiction as being true (as opposed to fiction, which is make-believe), nonfiction is much more deep than that. The following are various types of nonfiction; students should be exposed to all of these.

- *Informational texts:* These types of books explain concepts or phenomena. An informational text might explain the history of a state or the idea of photosynthesis. These types of text are usually based on research.
- *Newspaper articles:* These short texts rely completely on factual information and are presented in a very straightforward, sometimes choppy manner. The purpose of these texts is to present information to readers in a quick and efficient manner.
- *Essays:* Usually, essays take an opinion (whether it is about a concept, a work of literature, a person, or an event) and describe how the opinion was arrived at or why the opinion is a good one.
- *Biographies:* These texts explain the lives of individuals. They are usually based on extensive research.
- *Memoirs:* In a way, a memoir like an autobiography, but they tend to be based on a specific idea, concept, issue, or event in life. For example, most presidents of the United States write memoirs about their time in office.
- *Letters:* When letters are read and analyzed in the classroom, students are generally studying the writer's style or the writer's true, deep-down opinions and feelings about certain events. Often, students will find letters of famous individuals in history reprinted in textbooks.
- *Journals:* Similar to letters, journals present very personal ideas. When available (as most people rarely want their journals published),they give students the opportunity to see peoples' thought processes about various events or issues.

The key in teaching students about nonfiction is to expose them to a variety of types and to discuss how those types are similar and different from one another. The key is exposure. Students may not get the opportunity to know about these types of literature in a deep and analytical sense unless they get the chance to read them and study them academically in the classroom.

In both fiction and nonfiction, authors portray ideas in very subtle ways through their skillful use of language. Style, tone, and point-of-view are the most basic of ways in which authors do this.

Style is the artful adaptation of language to meet various purposes. Authors can modify their word choice, sentence structure, and organization in order to convey certain ideas. For example, an author may write on a topic (such as the environment) in many different styles. In an academic style, the author uses long, complex sentences, advanced vocabulary, and very structured paragraphing. However, in an informal explanation in a popular magazine, the author may use a conversational tone in which simple words and simple sentence structures are utilized.

Tone is the attitude an author takes toward his or her subject. That tone is exemplified in the language of the text. For example, consider the topic of the environment. One author may dismiss the idea of global warming; the tone may be one of derision against environmentalists. A reader might notice this through the style (such as word choice), the details the author decides to present, and the order in which the details are presented. Another author may be angry about global warming and therefore use harsh words and other tones that indicate anger. Finally, yet another author may not care one bit about the issue of the environment either in a positive or negative light. Let's say this author is a comedian who likes to poke fun at political activists. His or her tone may be humorous; therefore, he or she will adjust the language used accordingly. In this example, all types of tones are about the same subject—they simply reveal, through language, different opinions and attitudes about the subject.

Finally, **point-of-view** is perspective. While most of us think of point-of-view in terms of first or third person in fiction (or even the points-of-view of various characters in stories), point-of-view also helps to explain much of language and the presentation of ideas in nonfiction texts. The above environmentalism example proves this. Three points-of-view are represented, and each creates a different style of language.

Students need to learn that language and text are changed dramatically by tone, style, and point-of-view. They can practice these concepts in everything they read. Doing so takes little time for each nonfiction or fiction text students read in class, and it goes a long way in helping them to comprehend text at a more advanced level.

Skill 1.3   Poetry

People read poetry for many reasons, and they are often the very same reasons poets would give for writing it. Just the feel and sounds of the words that are turned by the artistic hands and mind of a poet into a satisfying and sometimes delightful experience is a good reason to read a poem. Good poetry constantly surprises.

The major purpose a writer of poetry has for creating his or her works of art is the sharing of an experience, a feeling, or an emotion; this is also the reason a reader turns to poetry rather than prose. Reading poetry is often a search for variety, joy, and satisfaction.

There is another important reason that poets create and that readers are drawn to their poems: they are interpreters of life. Poets feel deeply the things that others feel or even things that may be overlooked by others. Poets also have the skill and inspiration to recreate those feelings and interpret them in such a way that understanding and insight may come from the experience. They often bring understanding to life's big (or even not-so-big) questions.

Children can respond to poetry at very early stages. Elementary students are at the stage where the sounds of unusual words intrigue and entertain them. They are also very open to emotional meanings of passages. Teaching poetry to fifth graders can be an important introduction to seeking for meaning in literature. If a fifth grader enjoys reading poetry both silently and aloud, a habit may be formed that will last a lifetime.

When we speak of **structure** with regard to poetry, we usually mean one of three things:

1) The pattern of the sound and rhythm

It helps to know the background of this peculiarity of poetry. History was passed down in oral form almost exclusively until the invention of the printing press; it was often set to music. A rhymed story is much easier to commit to memory, and adding a tune makes it even easier to remember. Therefore, it is not surprising that much of the earliest literature—epics, odes, etc., are rhymed and were probably sung.

When we speak of the pattern of sound and rhythm, we are referring to two things: verse form and stanza form. The **verse form** is the rhythmic pattern of a single verse. An example is any meter; blank verse, for instance, is iambic pentameter. A **stanza** is a group of a certain number of verses (lines) having a rhyme scheme. If the poem is written, there is usually white space between the verses (although a short poem may be only one stanza). If the poem is spoken, there will be a pause between stanzas.

2) The visible shape it takes

In the seventeenth century, some poets shaped their poems on the page to reflect the theme. A good example is George Herbert's *Easter Wings*. Since that time, poets have occasionally played with this device; however, it is generally viewed as nothing more than a demonstration of ingenuity. The rhythm, effect, and meaning are often sacrificed by being forced into the visual contours of the poem's shape.

3) Rhyme and free verse

Poets also use devices that will underscore the meanings of their poems to establish form. A very common one is alliteration. When the poem is read (which poetry is usually intended to be), the repetition of a sound may not only underscore the meaning, it may also add pleasure to the reading.

Following a strict rhyming pattern can add intensity to the meaning of the poem in the hands of a skilled and creative poet. On the other hand, the meaning can be drowned out by the steady beat-beat-beat of it. Shakespeare very skillfully used the regularity of rhyme in his poetry, breaking the rhythm at certain points to very effectively underscore a point. For example, in Sonnet #130, "My mistress' eyes are nothing like the sun," the rhythm is primarily iambic pentameter. It lulls the reader (or listener) to accept that this poet is following the standard conventions for love poetry, which in that day reliably used rhyme and more often than not iambic pentameter to express feelings of romantic love along conventional lines. However, in Sonnet #130, the last two lines sharply break from the monotonous pattern, forcing reader or speaker to pause:

> And yet, by heaven, I think my love as rare
> As any she belied with false compare

Shakespeare's purpose is clear: he is not writing a conventional love poem; the object of his love is not the red-and-white conventional woman written about in other poems of the period. This is a good example of a poet using form to underscore meaning.

Poets eventually began to feel constricted by the rhyming conventions and began to break away and make new rules for poetry. When poetry was only rhymed, it was easy to define it. When free verse, or poetry written in a flexible form, came upon the scene in France in the 1880s, it quickly began to influence English-language poets such as T. S. Eliot, whose memorable poem, "The Wasteland," had an alarming but desolate message for the modern world. It is impossible to imagine that it could have been written in the soothing, lulling rhymed verse of previous periods.

Those who first began writing in free verse in English were responding to the influence of the French *vers libre.* However, it should be noted that free verse could also be loosely applied to the poetry of Walt Whitman, writing in the mid-nineteenth century, as can be seen in the first stanza of "Son of Myself."

> I celebrate myself, and sing myself,
> And what I assume you shall assume,
> For every atom belonging to me as good belongs to you.

When poetry was no longer defined as a piece of writing arranged in verses that had a rhyme-scheme of some sort, distinguishing poetry from prose became a point of discussion. Merriam Webster's *Encyclopedia of Literature* defines poetry as "writing that formulates a concentrated imaginative awareness of experience in language chosen and arranged to create a specific emotional response through its meaning, sound and rhythm."

A poet chooses the form of poetry deliberately, based upon the emotional response he or she hopes to evoke and the meaning he or she wishes to convey. Robert Frost, a twentieth-century poet who chose to use conventional rhyming verse to make his point, is a memorable and often-quoted modern poet. Who can forget his closing lines in "Stopping by Woods"?

> And miles to go before I sleep,
> And miles to go before I sleep.

There are a number of literary techniques that make an appearance in poetry of all forms. It is important to understand the different mechanisms that poets use in order to fully understand the meaning of the poem. These include:

Slant Rhyme - This occurs when a rhyme is not exact; oftentimes, the final consonant sounds are the same, but the vowels are different. It occurs frequently in Irish, Welsh, and Icelandic verse. Examples include "green" and "gone," "that" and "hit," and "ill" and "shell."

Alliteration - Alliteration occurs when the initial sounds of a word, beginning either with a consonant or a vowel, are repeated in close succession. Examples include "Athena" and "Apollo," "Nate never knows," and "people who pen poetry." The function of alliteration, like rhyme, might be to accentuate the beauty of language in a given context, or to unite words or concepts through a kind of repetition. Alliteration, like rhyme, can follow specific patterns. Sometimes the similar-sounding consonants aren't always the initial ones (although they are generally the stressed syllables). Alliteration is less common than rhyme, but because it is less common, it can call attention to a word or line in a poem that might not have the same emphasis otherwise.

Assonance - As alliteration typically occurs at the beginning of a word, and rhyme occurs at the end, assonance takes the middle territory. Assonance occurs when the vowel sound within a word matches the same sound in a nearby word, but the surrounding consonant sounds are different. "Tune" and "June" are rhymes; "tune" and "food" are assonant. The function of assonance is frequently the same as end rhyme or alliteration: all serve to give a sense of continuity or fluidity to the verse. Assonance is often especially effective when rhyme is absent, as it gives the poet more flexibility and it is not typically used as part of a predetermined pattern. Like alliteration, it does not so much determine the structure or form of a poem; rather, it is ornamental.

Onomatopoeia - These are words used to evoke meaning by their sounds. The early Batman series used *pow*, *zap*, *whop*, *zonk*, and *eek* in an onomatopoetic way.

Rhythm - In poetry, this refers to the recurrence of stresses at equal intervals. A stress (accent) is a greater amount of force given to one syllable in speaking than that which is given to another. For example, we put the stress on the first syllable of such words as father, mother, daughter, and children. The unstressed or unaccented syllable is sometimes called a slack syllable. All English words carry at least one stress (except articles and some prepositions such as by, from, at, etc.). Indicating where stresses occur is called scansion, or scanning. Very little is gained in understanding a poem or in making a statement about it by merely scanning it. The pattern of the rhythm—the meter—should be analyzed in terms of its overall relationship to the message and impression of the poem.

Skill 1.4 Resource and research material

Locating information for research projects and compiling research sources using both print and electronic resources is vital in the construction of written documents. The resources that are available in today's school communities include a large database of Internet resources and World Wide Web access that provide individual navigation for print and electronic information. Research sources include traditional commercial databases and The Electronic Library, both of which can be used to print and cite a diversity of informational resources.

One vital aspect of the research process includes learning to analyze the applicability and validity of the massive amounts of information in cyberspace. Verifying and evaluating electronic resources are just two parts of the process of sorting through downloaded hardcopies or electronic databases. In using a diversity of research sources, the user must be able to discern authentic sources of information from the mass collections of websites and information databases available.

In primary research, selecting a topic and setting up an outline for research information are the most important steps. They should precede using the secondary research of both print and electronic resources. Using conceptual Venn diagrams to center the topic and brainstorm the peripheral information pertaining to the topic will clarify the purpose of the research.

There are two aspect of the secondary research: using print sources and using electronic research tools. Print sources provide guides on locating specific or general information resources. Libraries have floors or designated areas dedicated to the collection of encyclopedias, specific resource manuals, card catalogs, and periodical indexes that provide information on the projected topic. Electronic research tools includes a listing of the latest and most effective search engines like Google, Microsoft, AOL, Infotrac, and Yahoo to find the topic of research, along with peripheral support information. Electronic databases that contain extensive resources will assist the user in selecting resources, choosing effective keywords, and constructing search strategies. The world of electronic research opens up a global library of resources for both print and electronic information.

Major online services such as Microsoft, Prodigy, and CompuServe provide users with information on specialized information that is either free or has a minimal charge assessed for that specific service or website. Online resources teach effective ways to bookmark sites of interest and to cut and paste relevant information onto word documents for citation and reference.

Bookmarking favorite Internet searches that contain correct sources for reference can save a lot of research time. On AOL, bookmarking is known as "Favorites"; with one click of the mouse, a user can type in the URL on the browser's location bar to create instant access to that location. Netscape uses the terminology of "bookmarks" to save browser locations for future research.

Online search engines and web portals create avenues of navigating the World Wide Web. Web portals provide linkages to other websites and are typically subdivided into other categories for searching. Portals are also specific to certain audience interests that index parts of the web. Search engines can provide additional strategic site searches.

Students should be taught about plagiarizing sources directly from the World Wide Web without attribution. This is a difficult concept for elementary-aged students to grasp. If the teacher does not attend to teaching at least a basic notion of "giving credit" to sources, he or she can expect student reports to be nothing more than cut and paste essays written by someone other than the typical fourth grader handing in the material.

COMPETENCY 2.0   TEXT STRUCTURES AND ORGANIZATION FOR READING AND WRITING

Skill 2.1   Structure

If there are two words synonymous with reading comprehension as far as the balanced literacy approach is concerned, they would be "Constructing Meaning." Cooper, Taberski, Strickland, and other theorists and classroom teachers conceptualize the reader as one who creates (constructs) a specific meaning based on both clues in the text and his or her own prior knowledge.

According to the leading theorists, comprehension for balanced literacy is a strategic process. The reader interacts with the text and brings his or her prior knowledge and experience to it. Writing is complementary to reading and is a mutually integrative and supportive parallel process. Hence, the division of literacy learning into reading workshops and writing workshops, with the same anchor "readings" or books being used for both, is particularly effective in teaching students.

Consider the sentence, "The test booklet was white with black print, but very scary looking."

According to the idea of constructing meaning as one reads the sentence above, readers' personal schemata (generic information stored in the mind) of tests will be activated by the author's ideas that tests are scary. The readers will remember emotions experienced during testing in themselves or in other people and use this information to comprehend the author's statement. Therefore, the ultimate meaning a reader derives from the page results from the interaction of the reader's own experiences with the ideas the author presents. The reader constructs a meaning that reflects the author's intent and also the reader's response to that intent.

It is also to be remembered that readings are generally fairly lengthy passages, comprised of paragraphs, which in turn are comprised of more than one sentence. With each successive sentence, and every new paragraph, the reader refocuses. The schemata are reconsidered, and a new meaning is constructed.

The purpose of reading is to convert visual images (the letters and words) into a message. Pronouncing the words is not enough; the reader must be able to extract the meaning of the text. When people read, they utilize four sources of background information to comprehend the meaning behind the literal text (Reid, pp.166-171). These are:

1. *Word Knowledge:* This is information about words and letters. One's knowledge about word meanings is *lexical knowledge*—a sort of dictionary. Knowledge about spelling patterns and pronunciations is *orthographic knowledge.* Poor readers do not develop a high level of automaticity in using orthographic knowledge to identify words and to decode unfamiliar words.

2. *Syntax and Contextual Information:* When children encounter unknown words in a sentence, they rely on their background knowledge to choose a word that makes sense. Errors of younger children, therefore, are often substitutions of words in the same syntactic class. Poor readers often fail to make use of context clues to help them identify words or activate the background knowledge that would help them with comprehension. Poor readers also process sentences word by word, instead of by "chunking" phrases and clauses. This tendency results in a slow pace that focuses on the decoding rather than comprehension. Poor readers also have problems answering wh- (who, what, where, when, why) questions as a result of these problems with syntax.

3. *Semantic Knowledge:* This encompasses the reader's background knowledge about a topic, which is combined with the text information as the reader tries to comprehend the material. New information is compared to the background information and incorporated into the reader's schema. Poor readers have problems with using their background knowledge, especially with passages that require inference or cause-and-effect.

4. *Text Organization:* Good readers are able to differentiate types of text structure (e.g., story narrative, exposition, compare-contrast, or time sequence). They use their knowledge of text to build expectations and to construct a framework of ideas on which to build meaning. Poor readers may not be able to differentiate types of text and miss important ideas. They may also miss these same important ideas and details by concentrating on lesser or irrelevant details.

Research on reading development has yielded information on the behaviors and habits of good readers versus poor readers. Some of the characteristics of good readers:
- They think about the information that they will read in the text, formulate questions that they predict will be answered in the text, and confirm those predictions from the information in the text.
- When faced with unfamiliar words, they attempt to pronounce them using analogies to familiar words.
- Before reading, good readers establish a purpose for reading, anticipate possible text structure, choose a reading strategy, and make predictions about what will be in the reading.
- As they read, good readers test and confirm their predictions, go back when something does not make sense, and make new predictions.

The point of comprehension instruction is not necessarily to focus only on the text(s) that students are using at the very moment of instruction, but rather to help them learn the strategies that they can use independently with any other text.

Some of the most common methods of teaching instruction are as follows:

- Summarization: This is where, either in writing or verbally, students go over the main point of the text, along with strategically chosen details that highlight the main point. This is not the same as paraphrasing, which is saying the same thing in different words. Teaching students how to summarize is very important, as it will help them look for the most critical areas in fiction and nonfiction. For example, in nonfiction, it will help them to distinguish between main arguments and examples. In fiction, it helps students to learn how to focus on the main characters and events in order to distinguish those from the lesser characters and events.

- Question answering: While this tends to be over-used in many classrooms, it is still a valid method of teaching students to comprehend. As the name implies, students answer questions regarding a text—either out loud, in small groups, or individually on paper. The best questions are those that cause students to have to think about the text (rather than just find an answer within the text).

- Question generating: This is the opposite of question answering, although students can later be asked to answer their own questions or the questions of peer students. In general, students should constantly question texts as they read. This is important because it causes students to become more critical readers. To teach students to generate questions helps them to learn the types of questions they can ask, and it gets them thinking about how best to be critical of texts.

- Graphic organizers: Graphic organizers are graphical representations of content within a text. For example, Venn Diagrams can be used to highlight the differences between two characters in a novel or two similar political concepts in a Social Studies textbook. A teacher can also use flow-charts with students to demonstrate the steps in a process (for example, the steps of setting up a science experiment or the chronological events of a story). Semantic organizers are similar in that they graphically display information. However, unlike flow-charts, semantic organizers usually focus on words or concepts. For example, a word web can help students to make sense of a word by mapping from the central word all the similar and related concepts to that word.

- Text structure: Many times in nonfiction (particularly in textbooks), and sometimes in fiction, text structures will give important clues to readers about what to look for. Students may not know how to make sense of all the types of headings in a textbook. For example, they may not realize that the side-bar story about a character in history is not the main text on a particular page in the history textbook. Teaching students how to interpret text structures gives them tools in which to tackle other similar texts. The most common text structures are comparison-contrast, cause-and-effect, chronological, and enumeration.

- Monitoring comprehension: Students need to be aware of their comprehension, or lack of it, in particular texts. Thus, it is important to teach students what to do when text suddenly stops making sense. For example, students can go back and re-read the description of a character, or they can go back to the table of contents or the first paragraph of a chapter to see where they are headed.

- Textual marking: This is where students interact with the text as they read. For example, armed with sticky notes, students can insert questions or comments regarding specific sentences or paragraphs within the text. This helps students to focus on the importance of the small things, particularly when they are reading larger works (such as young adult novels in middle school). It also gives students a reference point on which to go back into the text when they need to review something.

- Discussion: Small group or whole-class discussions stimulate thoughts about texts; they also give students a larger picture of the impact of those texts. More specifically, teachers can strategically encourage students to discuss concepts related to the text. Doing so helps students to learn to consider texts within larger societal and social concepts. Teachers can also encourage students to provide personal opinions in discussion. By listening to various students' opinions, all students in a class will better see the wide range of possible interpretations and thoughts regarding one text.

Many people mistakenly believe that the terms "research-based," "research-validated," or "evidence-based" relate mainly to specific programs, such as early reading textbook programs. While research does validate the efficacy of some of these programs, additional research has been conducted to test the effectiveness of other instructional strategies. On the subject of reading, many of these strategies have been documented in the report from the National Reading Panel (2000).

However, just because a strategy has not been validated as effective by research does not necessarily mean that it is not effective with certain students in certain situations. The number of strategies available far outweigh researchers' abilities to test their effectiveness. Some of the strategies listed above have been validated by rigorous research, while others have been shown consistently to help improve students' reading abilities in localized situations. There is simply not enough space to list all the strategies that have been proven effective; it is best to be aware that the above strategies are very commonly cited ones that work in a variety of situations.

Skill 2.2   Patterns of organization

Reading an essay should not take extraordinary effort for anyone. This is particularly true if the concepts are not too complex; reading an essay should not require extensive re-reading. The ideas should be clear and straightforward.

Anyone who has tried to write an essay knows that this sounds much easier than it really is! So how do teachers actually help students to become proficient at writing multi-paragraph essays in ways that allow them to clearly communicate their ideas? The trick is to help them to understand that various conventions of writing serve the purpose of making comprehension easier for readers. Those conventions include 1) good paragraphing; 2) transitions between paragraphs, ideas, and sentences; 3) topic sentences; 4) concluding sentences; 5) appropriate vocabulary; and 6) sufficient context.

1)   Good paragraphing entails dividing up ideas into bite-sized chunks. A good paragraph typically includes a topic sentence that explains the content of the paragraph. A good paragraph also includes a sufficient explanation of that topic sentence. Thus, if a topic sentence suggests that the paragraph will be about the causes of the Civil War, the rest of the paragraph should actually explain specific causes of the Civil War.

2)   As writers transition from one paragraph to another—or from one sentence to another—they will usually provide transitional phrases that give sign-posts to readers about what is coming next. Words like "however," "furthermore," "although," and "likewise," are good ways of communicating intention to readers. When ideas are thrown together on a page, it is hard to tell what the writer is actually doing with those ideas. Therefore, students need to become familiar with using transitional phrases.

3)   As mentioned above, topic sentences are used at the beginning of paragraphs to provide structure for the information that the paragraph will contain. Topic sentences help both readers and writers in communicating and understanding.

4) Concluding sentences are often unnecessary; however, when done right, they provide a nice "farewell" or closing to a piece of writing. Students should be warned to not always use concluding sentences in paragraphs to avoid overexposure. However, they should also be alerted to their potential benefits.

5) When writers use appropriate vocabulary, they are sensitive to the audience and the purpose of what they are writing. For example, if writing an essay on a scientific concept to a group of non-scientists, it would not be a good idea to use specialized vocabulary to explain concepts. However, if writing for a group of scientists, not using that vocabulary may cause the writer to appear less credible. Vocabulary depends on what the writer intends with the piece of writing. Therefore, students need to learn early on that all writing has a purpose and that because of that purpose, good writers will make conscious decisions about how to arrange their texts, which words to use, and which examples and metaphors to include.

6) When writers provide sufficient context, they ensure that readers do not have to extensively question the text to figure out what is going on. Again, this has a lot to do with knowing the audience. Using the scientific concept example from above, the writer would need to provide more context if the audience were a group of non-scientists than if the audience were scientists. In other words, it would be necessary to provide more background so that the non-scientists could understand the basic concepts.

COMPETENCY 3.0   LITERACY ACQUISITION AND READING INSTRUCTION

Skill 3.1   Foundations of literacy and reading instruction

When students practice fluency, they practice reading connected pieces of text. In other words, instead of looking at a word as just a word, they might read a sentence straight through. The point of this is that in order for the student to comprehend what he or she is reading, it is necessary to be able to "fluently" piece words in a sentence together. If a student is NOT fluent in reading, he or she sounds each letter or word out slowly and pays more attention to the phonics of each word. A fluent reader is more likely to read a sentence out loud using appropriate intonations.

The best way to test for fluency is to have a student read something out loud, preferably a few sentences in a row. Most students just learning to read will probably not be very fluent right away; with practice, they will increase their fluency. Even though fluency is not the same as comprehension, it is said that fluency is a good predictor of comprehension. Think about it: if a student is focusing too much on sounding out each word, he or she is not going to be paying attention to the meaning.

During the preschool years, children acquire cognitive skills in oral language that they apply later on to reading comprehension. Reading aloud to young children is one of the most important things that an adult can do because they are teaching children how to monitor, question, predict, and confirm what they hear in stories. Reid (1988) described three metalinguistic abilities that young children acquire through early involvement in reading activities:

1. *Word consciousness.* Children who have access to books can first understand the story through the pictures. Gradually, they begin to realize the connection between the spoken words and the printed words. The beginning of letter and word discrimination begins in the early years.

2. *Language and conventions of print.* During this early stage, children learn the way to hold a book, where to begin to read, left to right tracking, and how to continue from one line to another.

3. *Functions of print.* Children discover that print can be used for a variety of purposes and functions, including entertainment and information.

The typical variation in literacy backgrounds that children bring to reading can make teaching more difficult. Oftentimes, a teacher has to choose between focusing on the learning needs of a few students at the expense of the group, or focusing on the group at the risk of leaving some students behind academically. This situation is particularly critical for diverse learners who have gaps in their literacy knowledge.

Areas of Emerging Evidence

Experiences with print (through reading and writing) help preschool children to develop an understanding of the conventions, purpose, and functions of print. Children learn about print from a variety of sources, and in the process, they come to realize that print carries a story. They also learn how text is structured visually (e.g., in English, the text begins at the top of the page, moves from left to right, and carries over to the next page when it is turned). While knowledge about the conventions of print enables children to understand the physical structure of language, the conceptual knowledge that printed words convey a message also helps children to bridge the gap between oral and written language.

Phonological awareness and letter recognition contribute to initial reading acquisition by helping children to develop efficient word recognition strategies (e.g., detecting pronunciations and storing associations in memory). Phonological awareness and knowledge of print-speech relations play an important role in facilitating reading acquisition. Therefore, phonological awareness instruction should be an integral component of early reading programs. Within the emergent literacy research, viewpoints diverge on whether acquisition of phonological awareness and letter recognition are preconditions of literacy acquisition or whether they develop interdependently with literacy activities such as story reading and writing.

Storybook reading affects children's knowledge about, strategies for, and attitudes towards reading. Of all the strategies intended to promote growth in literacy acquisition, none is as commonly practiced, nor as strongly supported across the emergent literacy literature, as storybook reading. Children in different social and cultural groups have differing degrees of access to storybook reading. For example, it is not unusual for a teacher to have students who have experienced thousands of hours of story reading time along with other students who have had little or no such exposure.

Theories of Language Development

Learning Approach

Early theories of language development were formulated from learning theory research. The assumption was that language development evolved from learning the rules of language structures and applying them through imitation and reinforcement. This approach also assumed that linguistic, cognitive, and social developments were independent of each other. Thus, children were expected to learn language from patterning after adults who spoke and wrote Standard English. No allowance was made for communication through child jargon, idiomatic expressions, or grammatical and mechanical errors resulting from too strict adherence to the rules of inflection (*childs* instead of *children*) or conjugation (*runned* instead of *ran*). No association was made between physical and operational development and language mastery.

Linguistic Approach

Studies spearheaded by Noam Chomsky in the 1950s formulated the theory that language ability is innate and develops through natural human maturation as environmental stimuli trigger the acquisition of syntactical structures appropriate to each exposure level. The assumption of a hierarchy of syntax downplayed the significance of semantics. Because of the complexity of syntax and the relative speed with which children acquire language, linguists attributed language development to biological rather than cognitive or social influences.

Cognitive Approach

Researchers in the 1970s proposed that language knowledge derives from both syntactic and semantic structures. Drawing on the studies of Piaget and other cognitive learning theorists, supporters of the cognitive approach maintained that children acquire knowledge of linguistic structures after they have acquired the cognitive structures necessary to process language. For example, joining words for specific meaning necessitates sensory motor intelligence. The child must be able to coordinate movement and recognize objects before he or she can identify words to name the objects or word groups to describe the actions of these objects. Children must have developed the mental abilities for organizing concepts as well as performing concrete operations, predicting outcomes, and theorizing before they can assimilate and verbalize complex sentence structures, choose vocabulary for particular nuances of meaning, and examine semantic structures for tone and manipulative effect.

Sociocognitive Approach

Other theorists in the 1970s proposed that language development results from sociolinguistic competence. This theory finds that the different aspects of linguistic, cognitive, and social knowledge are interactive elements of total human development. Emphasis on verbal communication as the medium for language expression resulted in the inclusion of speech activities in most language arts curricula.

Unlike previous approaches, the sociocognitive allows that determining the appropriateness of language in given situations for specific listeners is as important as understanding semantic and syntactic structures. By engaging in conversation, children at all stages of development have opportunities to test their language skills, receive feedback, and make modifications. As a social activity, conversation is as structured by social order as grammar is structured by the rules of syntax. Conversation satisfies the learner's need to be heard, to be understood, and to influence others. Thus, his or her choices of vocabulary, tone, and content are dictated by the ability to assess the linguistic knowledge of his or her listeners. The learner is constantly applying cognitive skills in using language as a form of social interaction. Although the capacity to acquire language is inborn, a child would not pass beyond grunts and gestures without an environment in which to practice language.

Of course, the varying degrees of environmental stimuli to which children are exposed at all age levels create a slower or faster development of language. Some children are prepared to articulate concepts and recognize symbolism by the time they enter fifth grade, either because they have been exposed to challenging reading and conversations with well-spoken adults at home, or in their social groups. Others are still trying to master the sight recognition skills and are not yet ready to combine words in complex patterns.

Skill 3.2   Children's Literature

The major literary genres in adult literature include allegory, ballad, drama, epic, epistle, essay, fable, novel, poem, romance, and the short story. They are detailed below.

Allegory: A story in verse or prose with characters that represent virtues and vices. There are two meanings: symbolic and literal. John Bunyan's *The Pilgrim's Progress* is the most renowned of this genre.

Ballad: An *in medias res* story that is told or sung—usually in verse—and accompanied by music. Literary devices found in ballads include the refrain (repeated section) and incremental repetition (anaphora) for effect. Earliest forms were anonymous folk ballads. Later forms include Coleridge's Romantic masterpiece, "The Rime of the Ancient Mariner."

Drama: Plays (comedy, modern, or tragedy) that are typically performed in five acts. Traditionalists and neoclassicists adhere to Aristotle's unities of time, place, and action. Plot development is advanced through dialogue. Literary devices include asides, soliloquies, and the chorus, which represents public opinion. Considered by many to be the greatest of all dramatists/playwrights is William Shakespeare. Other dramaturges include Ibsen, Williams, Miller, Shaw, Stoppard, Racine, Moliére, Sophocles, Aeschylus, Euripides, and Aristophanes.

Epic: A long poem usually of book length that reflects values inherent in the generative society. Epic devices include an invocation to a Muse for inspiration, an overall purpose for writing, universal setting, a protagonist and antagonist who possess supernatural strength and acumen, and interventions of a God or the gods. Comparatively, there are few epics in literature: Homer's *Iliad* and *Odyssey*, Virgil's *Aeneid*, Milton's *Paradise Lost*, Spenser's *The Fairie Queene*, Barrett Browning's *Aurora Leigh*, and Pope's mock-epic, *The Rape of the Lock*.

Epistle: A letter that is not always originally intended for public distribution, but due to the fame of the sender and/or recipient, one that becomes public domain. For example, Paul wrote epistles that were later placed in the Bible.

Essay: Typically, a limited length prose work focusing on a topic and propounding a definite point-of-view and authoritative tone. Great essayists include Carlyle, Lamb, DeQuincy, Emerson, and Montaigne (who is credited with defining this genre).

Fable: A terse tale offering up a moral or exemplum. Chaucer's "The Nun's Priest's Tale" is a fine example of a *bete fabliau* (or beast fable) in which animals speak and act characteristically human, illustrating human foibles.

Legend: A traditional narrative or collection of related narratives, popularly regarded as historically factual but actually a mixture of fact and fiction.

Myth: Stories that are more or less universally shared within a culture to explain its history and traditions.

Novel: The longest form of fictional prose containing a variety of characterizations, settings, local color, and regionalism. Most have complex plots, expanded description, and attention to detail. Some of the great novelists include Austen, the Brontës, Twain, Tolstoy, Hugo, Hardy, Dickens, Hawthorne, Forster, and Flaubert.

Poem: The only requirement for a poem is rhythm. Sub-genres include fixed types of literature such as the sonnet, elegy, ode, pastoral, and villanelle. Unfixed types of literature include blank verse and dramatic monologue.

Romance: A highly imaginative tale set in a fantastical realm that deals with the conflicts between heroes, villains, and/or monsters. "The Knight's Tale" from Chaucer's *Canterbury Tales*, *Sir Gawain and the Green Knight,* and Keats' "The Eve of St. Agnes" are prime representatives.

Short Story: A concise narrative that has less background than a novel, but that typically includes many of the same plot developments and techniques. As mentioned before, some of the most notable short story writers include Hemingway, Faulkner, Twain, Joyce, Jackson, O'Connor, de Maupassant, Saki, Poe, and Pushkin.

Children's Literature

Children's literature is a genre of its own. Although it can share some of the same characteristics of adult literature, it emerged as a distinct and independent form in the second half of the eighteenth century. *The Visible World in Pictures* by John Amos Comenius, a Czech educator, was one of the first printed works in existence as well as the first picture book. After its publication, educators acknowledged that children are different from adults in many respects for the first time.

Modern educators acknowledge that introducing elementary students to a wide range of reading experiences plays an important role in their mental, social, and psychological development. Some of the most common forms of literature written specifically for children include:

Traditional Literature: Traditional literature opens up a world where right wins out over wrong, where hard work and perseverance are rewarded, and where helpless victims find vindication. These worthwhile values are ones that children identify with even as early as kindergarten.

In traditional literature, children are introduced to fanciful beings, humans with exaggerated powers, talking animals, and heroes that will inspire them. For younger elementary children, these stories in Big Book format are ideal for providing predictable and repetitive elements that are easily grasped.

Folktales/Fairy Tales: Adventures of animals or humans and the supernatural typically characterize these stories. The hero is usually on a quest aided by other-worldly helpers. More often than not, the story focuses on good and evil and reward and punishment. Some examples of folktales and fairy tales include: *The Three Bears, Little Red Riding Hood, Snow White, Sleeping Beauty, Puss-in-Boots, Rapunzel,* and *Rumpelstiltskin.*

Fables: Animals that act like humans are featured in these stories; the animals usually reveal human foibles or teach a lesson. Example: *Aesop's Fables.*

Myths: These stories about events from the earliest times, such as the origin of the world, are often considered true among various societies.

Legends: These are similar to myths except that they tend to deal with events that happened more recently. Example: Arthurian legends.

Tall tales: These are purposely exaggerated accounts of individuals with superhuman strength. Examples: Paul Bunyan, John Henry, and Pecos Bill.

Modern Fantasy: Many of the themes found in these stories are similar to those in traditional literature. The stories start out based in reality, which makes it easier for the reader to suspend disbelief and enter into worlds of unreality. Little people live in the walls in *The Borrowers,* and time travel is possible in *The Trolley to Yesterday.*

Including some fantasy tales in the curriculum often helps elementary-grade children to develop their senses of imagination. The stories typically appeal to ideals of justice and issues having to do with good and evil; because children tend to identify with the characters, the message is more likely to be retained.

Science Fiction: Robots, spacecraft, mystery, and civilizations from other ages often appear in these stories. Most presume advances in science on other planets or in a future time. Most children like these stories because of their interest in space and the "what if" aspect of the stories. Examples: *Outer Space and All That Junk* and *A Wrinkle in Time.*

Modern Realistic Fiction: These stories are about real problems that real children face. By finding that their hopes and fears are shared by others, young children can find insight into their own problems. Young readers also tend to experience a broadening of interests as the result of this kind of reading. It is good for them to know that a child can be brave and intelligent and can solve difficult problems.

Historical Fiction: This type of literature provides the opportunity to introduce younger children to history in a beneficial way. *Rifles for Watie* is an example of this kind of story. Presented in a historically-accurate setting, it's about a sixteen year old boy who serves in the Union army. He experiences great hardships but discovers that his enemy is an admirable human being.

Biography: Reading about inventors, explorers, scientists, political and religious leaders, social reformers, artists, sports figures, doctors, teachers, writers, and war heroes helps children to see that one person can make a difference. They also open new vistas for children to think about when they choose a future occupation.

Informational Books: These are ways to learn more about something that children are interested in or something that they know little about. Encyclopedias are good resources, of course, but a book like *Polar Wildlife* by Kamini Khanduri also shows pictures and facts that will capture the imaginations of young children.

Preadolescent and Adolescent Literature

The social changes of post-World War II significantly affected adolescent literature. The Civil Rights movement, feminism, the protest of the Vietnam Conflict, and issues surrounding homelessness, neglect, teen pregnancy, drugs, and violence bred a new vein of contemporary fiction that helps adolescents to understand and cope with the world they live in.

Popular books for preadolescents often focus on establishing relationships with members of the opposite sex (Sweet Valley High series) and learning to cope with changing bodies, personalities, or life situations (Judy Blume's *Are You There, God? It's Me, Margaret*).

Adolescents are typically interested in the fantasy and science fiction genres as well as popular juvenile fiction. Even today, middle school students still read the *Little House on the Prairie* series and the mysteries of the Hardy boys and Nancy Drew. Teens value the works of Emily and Charlotte Brontë, Willa Cather, Jack London, William Shakespeare, and Mark Twain as much as those of the more modern Piers Anthony, S.E. Hinton, Madeleine L'Engle, Stephen King, and J.R.R. Tolkien.

Older adolescents typically enjoy the writers in these genres.

1. Fantasy: Piers Anthony, Ursula LeGuin, Ann McCaffrey
2. Horror: V.C. Andrews, Stephen King
3. Juvenile fiction: Judy Blume, Robert Cormier, Rosa Guy, Virginia Hamilton, S.E. Hinton, M.E. Kerr, Harry Mazer, Norma Fox Mazer, Richard Newton Peck, Cynthia Voight, and Paul Zindel.
4. Science fiction: Isaac Asimov, Ray Bradbury, Arthur C. Clarke, Frank Herbert, Larry Niven, H.G. Wells.

These classic and contemporary works combine the characteristics of multiple theories. As eleven to twelve year olds function at the concrete operations stage (Piaget), are of the "good person" orientation (Kohlberg), depend on external rewards (Bandura), and exhibit all five needs from Maslow's hierarchy, they should appreciate the following titles, grouped by reading level.

Note that these titles are cited for interest at this particular grade level, and do not reflect high-interest titles for older readers who do not read at grade level. Some high interest titles will be cited later.

Reading level 6.0 to 6.9

Barrett, William. *Lilies of the Field*
Cormier, Robert. *Other Bells for Us to Ring*
Dahl, Roald. *Danny, Champion of the World; Charlie and the Chocolate Factory*
Lindgren, Astrid. *Pippi Longstocking*
Lindbergh, Anne. *Three Lives to Live*
Lowry, Lois. *Rabble Starkey*
Naylor, Phyllis. *The Year of the Gopher; Reluctantly Alice*
Peck, Robert Newton. *Arly*
Speare, Elizabeth. *The Witch of Blackbird Pond*
Sleator, William. *The Boy Who Reversed Himself*

Most seventh and eight grade students, according to learning theory, are still functioning cognitively, psychologically, and morally as sixth graders. As these are not inflexible standards, there are some twelve and thirteen year olds who are much more mature socially, intellectually, and physically than the younger children who share the same school. They are becoming concerned with establishing individual and peer group identities that present conflicts with breaking from authority and the rigidity of rules. Some at this age are still tied firmly to the family and its expectations, while others identify more with those their own age or older.

Enrichment reading for this group must help them to cope with life's rapid changes and/or provide escape; thus, it must be either realistic or fantastic depending on the child's needs. Adventures and mysteries (the Hardy Boys and Nancy Drew series) are still popular today. Preteens also become more interested in biographies of contemporary figures rather than legendary figures of the past.

Reading level 7.0 to 7.9

Armstrong, William. *Sounder*
Bagnold, Enid. *National Velvet*
Barrie, James. *Peter Pan*
London, Jack. *White Fang; Call of the Wild*
Lowry, Lois. *Taking Care of Terrific*
McCaffrey, Anne. The *Dragonsinger* series
Montgomery, L. M. *Anne of Green Gables* and sequels
Steinbeck, John. *The Pearl*
Tolkien, J. R. R. *The Hobbit*
Zindel, Paul. *The Pigman*

Reading level 8.0 to 8.9

Cormier, Robert. *I Am the Cheese*
McCullers, Carson. *The Member of the Wedding*
North, Sterling. *Rascal*
Twain, Mark. *The Adventures of Tom Sawyer*
Zindel, Paul. *My Darling , My Hamburger*

Skill 3.3   Strategies for word recognition

Phonics

As opposed to phonemic awareness, the study of phonics must be done with the eyes open. It is the connection between the sounds and letters on a page. In other words, students learning phonics might see the word "bad" and sound each letter out slowly until they recognize that they just said the word.

Phonological awareness means the ability of the reader to recognize the sounds of spoken language. This recognition includes how these sounds can be blended together, segmented (divided up), and manipulated (switched around). This type of awareness then leads to phonics, which is a method for teaching children to read. It helps them to "sound out words."

Development of phonological skills may begin during the pre-K years. Indeed, by the age of five, a child who has been exposed to rhyme can typically recognize another rhyme. Such a child can demonstrate phonological awareness by filling in the missing rhyming word in a familiar rhyme or rhymed picture book. It isn't unheard of for children to surprise their parents by filling in missing rhymes in a familiar nursery rhyme book at the age of four or even earlier.

Children are taught phonological awareness when they are taught the sounds made by the letters, the sounds made by various combinations of letters, and the ability to recognize individual sounds in words.

Phonological awareness skills include:

I.   Rhyming and syllabification
2.   Blending sounds into words (such as pic-tur-bo-k)
3.   Identifying the beginning or starting sounds of words and the ending or closing sounds of words
4.   Breaking words down into sounds (also called "segmenting" words)
5.   Recognizing small words contained in bigger words by removing starting sounds (hear to ear)

Decoding, Word Recognition, and Spelling

Word analysis (a.k.a. phonics or decoding) is the process readers use to figure out unfamiliar words based on written patterns. **Word recognition** is the process of automatically determining the pronunciation and some degree of the meaning of an unknown word. In other words, fluent readers recognize most written words easily and correctly, without consciously decoding or breaking them down.

To **decode** means to change communication signals into messages. Reading comprehension requires that the reader learn the code within which a message is written and be able to decode it to get the message. **Encoding** involves changing a message into symbols. Examples include encoding oral language into writing (spelling), encoding an idea into words, or encoding a mathematical or physical idea into appropriate mathematical symbols.

Although effective reading comprehension requires identifying words automatically (Adams, 1990, Perfetti, 1985), children do not have to be able to identify every single word or know the exact meaning of the every word in a text to understand it. Indeed, Nagy (1988) says that children can read a work with a high level of comprehension even if they do not fully know as many as 15 percent of the words within a given text. Children develop the ability to decode and recognize words automatically. They then can extend their ability to decode to multi-syllabic words.

Spelling instruction should include learning the words that are misspelled in daily writing, generalizing spelling knowledge, and mastering objectives in progressive phases of development. The developmental stages of spelling are as follows:

1) *Pre-phonemic spelling*—Children know that letters stand for a message, but they do not know the relationship between spelling and pronunciation.

2) *Early phonemic spelling*—Children are beginning to understand spelling. They usually write the beginning letter correctly, with the rest of the word being comprised of consonants or long vowels.

3) *Letter-name spelling*—Children spell some words consistently and correctly. The student is developing a sight vocabulary and a stable understanding of letters as representations of sounds. Long vowels are usually used accurately, but silent vowels are omitted. Unknown words are spelled by the child attempting to match the name of the letter to the sound.

4) *Transitional spelling*—This phase is typically entered in late elementary school. Short vowel sounds are mastered and some spelling rules are known. They are developing a sense of correct and incorrect spellings.

5) *Derivational spelling*—This is usually reached from high school to adulthood. This is the stage where spelling rules are being mastered.

How Words are Built

Knowledge of how words are built can help students with basic and more advanced decoding. A **root word** is the primary base of a word. A **prefix** is the affix (a morpheme that attaches to a base word) that is placed at the start of a root word, but that can't make a word on its own. Examples of prefixes include re-, pre-, and un-. A **suffix** follows the root word to which it attaches and appears at the end of the word. Examples of suffixes include –s, -es, -ed, -ly, and –tion. In the word unlikely, "un" is a prefix, "like" is the root work, and "ly" is a suffix.

Skill 3.4   Strategies for comprehension

Main Idea

A **topic** of a paragraph or story is what the paragraph or story is about. The **main idea** of a paragraph or story states the important idea(s) that the author wants the reader to know about a given topic. The topic and main idea of a paragraph or story are sometimes directly stated; however, there are times when the topic and main idea are not directly stated but simply implied.

Look at this paragraph:

> Henry Ford was an inventor who developed the first affordable automobile. The cars that were being built before Mr. Ford created his Model-T were very expensive. Only rich people could afford to have cars.

The topic of this paragraph is cars. The main idea is that Henry Ford built the first affordable automobile.

Readers can find the main ideas by looking at the way in which paragraphs are written. A paragraph is a group of sentences about one main idea. Paragraphs usually have two types of sentences: a topic sentence, which contains the main idea, and two or more detail sentences which support, prove, provide more information, explain, or give examples.

The **topic sentence** indicates what the passage is about. It is the subject of that portion of the narrative. The ability to identify the topic sentence in a passage will enable the student to focus on the concept being discussed and to better comprehend the information provided.

You can only tell if you have a detail or topic sentence by comparing the sentences with each other.

Look at this sample paragraph:

> Fall is the best of the four seasons. The leaves change colors to create a beautiful display of golds, reds, and oranges. The air turns crisp and windy. The scents of pumpkin muffins and apple pies fill the air. Finally, Halloween marks the start of the holiday season. Fall is my favorite time of year!

Breakdown of sentences:

Fall is the best of the four seasons. (TOPIC SENTENCE)
The leaves change colors to create a beautiful display of golds, reds, and oranges. (DETAIL)
The air turns crisp and windy. (DETAIL)
The scents of pumpkin muffins and apple pies fill the air. (DETAIL)
Finally, Halloween marks the start of the holiday season. (DETAIL)
Fall is my favorite time of year! (CLOSING SENTENCE – Often a restatement of the topic sentence.)

The first sentence introduces the main idea, and the other sentences support and give the many uses for the product.

Tips for Finding the Topic Sentence

- The topic sentence is usually first one in a paragraph, but it could be in any position in the paragraph.

- A topic is usually more "general" than the other sentences; that is, it covers many things and looks at the big picture. Sometimes it refers to more that one thing. Plurals and the words "many," "numerous," or "several" often signal a topic sentence.

- Detail sentences are usually more "specific" than the topic; that is, they usually cover one single idea or a small part or side of an idea. The words "for example," "i.e.," "that is," "first," "second," "third," and "finally" often signal a detail.

- Most of the detail sentences support, give examples, prove, talk about, or point toward the topic in some way.

How can you be sure that you have a topic sentence? Try this trick: Switch the sentence you think is the topic sentence into a question. If the other sentences seem to "answer" the question, then that is probably the topic sentence.

For example:

Reword the topic sentence "Fall is the best of the four seasons" in one of the following ways:

"Why is fall the best of the four season?"
"Which season is the best season?"
"Is fall the best season of the year?"

Then, as you read the remaining sentences (the ones you didn't pick), you will find that they answer (support) your question.

If you attempt this with a sentence other than the topic sentence, it won't work

For example:

Suppose you select "Halloween marks the start of the holiday season," and you reword it in the following way:

"Which holiday is the start of the holiday season?"

You will find that the other sentences fail to help you answer (support) your question.

Supporting Details

The **supporting details** are sentences that give more information about the topic and the main idea.

The supporting details in the aforementioned paragraph about Henry Ford would be that he was an inventor and that before he created his Model-T, only rich people could afford cars because they were too expensive.

Inferences and Conclusions

In order to draw **inferences** and make **conclusions**, a reader must use prior knowledge and apply it to the current situation. A conclusion or inference is never stated. A reader must instead rely on common sense.

Read the following passage:

The Smith family waited patiently around carousel number seven for their luggage to arrive. They were exhausted after their five hour trip and were anxious to get to their hotel. After about an hour, they realized that they no longer recognized any of the other passengers' faces. Mrs. Smith asked the person who appeared to be in charge if they were at the right carousel. The man replied, "Yes, this is it, but we finished unloading that baggage almost half an hour ago."

From the man's response we can infer that:

        (A) The Smiths were ready to go to their hotel.
        (B) The Smith's luggage was lost.
        (C) The man had their luggage.
        (D) They were at the wrong carousel.

Since the Smiths were still waiting for their luggage, we know that they were not yet ready to go to their hotel. From the man's response, we know that they were not at the wrong carousel and that he did not have their luggage. Therefore, though not directly stated, it appears that their luggage was lost. Choice (B) is the correct answer.

Cause and Effect

Linking cause to effect seems to be ingrained in human thinking. We get chilled and then the next day come down with a cold; therefore, we think that getting chilled caused the cold even though medical experts tell us that the virus that causes colds must be communicated by another human being. Socrates and the other Greek orators broke down this kind of thinking and developed a whole system for analyzing the links between causes and their effects, as well as when they are valid—that is, when such and such a cause did, in fact, bring about a particular effect. These orators spelled out ways to determine whether reasoning is reliable or whether it is not reliable (in which case it is called a fallacy).

A common fallacy in reasoning is the *post hoc ergo propter hoc* ("after this, therefore because of this") or the false-cause fallacy. This occurs in cause/effect reasoning, which may either go from cause to effect or effect to cause. This happens when an inadequate cause is offered for a particular effect; when the possibility of more than one cause is ignored; and when a connection between a particular cause and a particular effect is not made.

An example of a *post hoc*:

Our sales shot up 35 percent after we ran that television campaign; therefore, the campaign caused the increase in sales.

It might have been a cause, of course, but more evidence is needed to prove it.

An example of an inadequate cause for a particular effect:

An Iraqi truck driver reported that Saddam Hussein had nuclear weapons; therefore, Saddam Hussein is a threat to world security.

More causes were needed to prove the conclusion.

An example of failing to make a connection between a particular cause and an effect assigned to it:

Anna fell into a putrid pond on Saturday; on Monday she came down with polio. Therefore, the polio was caused by the water in the pond.

This, of course, is not acceptable unless the polio virus is found in a sample of water from the pond. A connection must be proven.

Conclusions are drawn as a result of a line of reasoning. **Inductive reasoning** begins with particulars and reasons to a generality.

For example:

"When I was a child, I bit into a green apple from my grandfather's orchard, and it was sour." (specific fact #1)

"I once bought green apples from a roadside vendor, and when I bit into one, it was sour." (specific fact #2)

"My grocery store had a sale on green Granny Smith apples last week, and I bought several only to find that they were sour when I bit into them." (specific fact #3)

Conclusion: All green apples are sour. While this is an example of inductive reasoning, it is also an example of the weakness of such reasoning. The speaker has not tasted all the green apples in the world, and there very well may be some apples that are green that are not sour.

Deductive reasoning begins with the generalization: "Green apples are sour" and supports that generalization with the specifics.

An inference is drawn from an inductive line of reasoning. The most famous one is "all men are mortal," which is drawn from the observation that everyone a person knows has died or will die, and that everyone else concurs in that judgment. It is assumed to be true and for that reason can be used as proof of another conclusion: "Socrates is a man; therefore, he will die."

Sometimes the inference is assumed to be proven when it is not reliably true in all cases, such as "aging brings physical and mental infirmity." As a result of reasoning from that inference, many companies will not hire anyone above a certain age. However, in actuality, being old does not necessarily imply physical and/or mental impairment. There are many instances in which elderly people have made important contributions that require exceptional ability.

Fact and Opinion

Facts are statements that are verifiable. **Opinions** are statements that must be supported in order to be accepted. Facts are used to support opinions. For example, "Jane is a bad girl" is an opinion. However, "Jane hit her sister with a baseball bat" is a *fact* upon which the opinion is based.

Judgments are also opinions—decisions or declarations based on an observation or reasoning that express approval or disapproval. Facts report what has happened or exists; they come from observation, measurement, or calculation. Facts can be tested and verified, whereas opinions and judgments cannot.

Most statements cannot be so clearly distinguished. "I believe that Jane is a bad girl" is a fact. The speaker knows what he or she believes. However, it obviously includes a judgment that could be disputed by another person who might believe otherwise. Judgments are not usually so firm. They are, rather, plausible opinions that provoke thought or lead to factual development.

Author's Purpose

An author may have more than one purpose in writing. An **author's purpose** may be to entertain, to persuade, to inform, to describe, or to narrate.

There are no tricks or rules to follow in attempting to determine an author's purpose. It is up to the reader to use his or her own judgment.

Consider the following paragraph:

Charles Lindbergh had no intention of becoming a pilot. He was enrolled in the University of Wisconsin until a flying lesson changed the entire course of his life. He began his career as a pilot by performing daredevil stunts at fairs.

The author wrote this paragraph primarily to

      (A) describe
      (B) inform
      (C) entertain
      (D) narrate

Since the author is simply telling us (informing us) about the life of Charles Lindbergh, the correct answer here is (B).

Author's Tone and Point-of-View

The **author's tone** is his or her attitude as reflected in the statement or passage. His or her choice of words will help the reader to determine the overall tone of a statement or passage.

Consider the following paragraph.

> I was shocked by your article, which said that sitting down to breakfast was a thing of the past. Many families consider breakfast time to be family time. Children need to realize the importance of having a good breakfast. It is imperative that they be taught this at a young age. I cannot believe that a writer with your reputation has difficulty comprehending this.

The author's tone in this passage is one of

      (A) concern
      (B) anger
      (C) excitement
      (D) disbelief

Since the author directly states that he or she "cannot believe" that the writer feels this way, the answer is (D).

Valid and Invalid Arguments

An **argument** is a generalization that is proven or supported with facts. If the facts are not accurate, the generalization remains unproven. Using inaccurate "facts" to support an argument is called a **fallacy** in reasoning.

Some factors to consider in judging whether the facts used to support an argument are accurate are as follows:

1. Are the facts current or are they out of date? For example, if the proposition "birth defects in babies born to drug-using mothers are increasing," then the data must include the latest that is available.
2. Another important factor to consider in judging the accuracy of a fact is its source. Where was the data obtained, and is that source reliable?
3. The calculations on which the facts are based may be unreliable. It is a good idea to run one's own calculations before using a piece of derived information.

Even facts that are true and have a sharp impact on the argument may not be relevant to the case at hand.

1. Health statistics from an entire state may have no relevance, or little relevance, to a particular county or zip code. Statistics from an entire country cannot be used to prove very much about a particular state or county.
2. An analogy can be useful in making a point, but the comparison must match up in all characteristics or it will not be relevant. Analogy should be used very carefully. It is often just as likely to destroy an argument as it is to strengthen it.

The importance or significance of a fact may not be sufficient to strengthen an argument. For example, of the millions of immigrants in the United States, using a single family to support a solution to the immigration problem will not make much difference overall (even though those single-example arguments are often used to support one approach or another). These examples may achieve a positive reaction, but they will not prove that one solution is better than another. If enough cases were cited from a variety of geographical locations, the information might be significant.

In writing, how many facts or examples are enough? Generally speaking, three strong supporting facts are sufficient to establish the thesis of an argument, although this is not always the case. To use a previous example:

Conclusion: All green apples are sour.

- When I was a child, I bit into a green apple from my grandfather's orchard, and it was sour.
- I once bought green apples from a roadside vendor, and when I bit into one, it was sour.
- My grocery store had a sale on green Granny Smith apples last week, and I bought several only to find that they were sour when I bit into them.

The main fallacy in the above argument is that the sample was insufficient. A more exhaustive search of literature, etc., will probably turn up some green apples that are not sour.

Sometimes, more than three arguments are too many. On the other hand, it's not unusual to hear public speakers, particularly politicians, who will cite a long litany of facts to support their positions.

A very good example of the omission of facts in an argument is the resumé of an applicant for a job. The applicant is arguing that he or she should be chosen to be awarded a particular job. The application form will ask for information about past employment, and unfavorable dismissals from jobs in the past may simply be omitted. Employers are usually suspicious of periods of time when the applicant has not listed an employer.

A writer makes choices about which facts will be used and which will be discarded in developing an argument. Those choices may exclude anything that is not supportive of the point-of-view the arguer is taking. It is always a good idea for the reader to do some research to spot the omissions and to ask whether they have impact on the overall acceptance of the point-of-view presented in the argument.

No judgment is either black or white. If the argument seems too neat or too compelling, there are probably facts that might be relevant that have not been included.

Making Predictions

One theory or approach to the teaching of reading that gained currency in the late 1960s and the early 70s was the importance of asking inferential and critical thinking questions of the reader meant to challenge and engage the children in the text. This approach to reading went beyond the literal level of what was stated in the text to an inferential level of using text clues to make predictions and to a critical level of involving the child in evaluating the text.

While asking engaging and thought-provoking questions is still viewed as part of the teaching of reading, it is only viewed currently as a component of the teaching of reading.

Prior Knowledge

Prior knowledge can be defined as all of an individual's prior experiences, education, and development that precede his or her entrance into a specific learning situation or his or her attempts to comprehend a specific text. Sometimes, prior knowledge can be erroneous or incomplete. Obviously, if there are misconceptions in a child's prior knowledge, these must be corrected so that the child's overall comprehension skills can continue to progress. Even kindergarteners display prior knowledge, which typically includes their accumulated positive and negative experiences both in and out of school. Prior knowledge activities and opportunities might range from traveling with family, watching television, visiting museums, and visiting libraries to staying in hospitals, visiting prisons, and surviving poverty.

Whatever prior knowledge the child brings to the school setting, the independent reading and writing the child does in school will immeasurably expand his or her prior knowledge. This will further broaden his or her reading comprehension capabilities.

Literary response skills are dependent on prior knowledge, schemata, and background. **Schemata** (the plural of schema) are those structures that represent generic concepts stored in our memories. Effective comprehenders of text, whether they are adults or children, use both their schemata and prior knowledge *plus* the ideas from the printed text for reading comprehension, and graphic organizers help organize this information.

Graphic Organizers

Graphic organizers solidify, in a chart format, a visual relationship among various reading and writing ideas. The content of a graphic organizer may include sequence, timelines, character traits, fact and opinion, main idea and details, and differences and likenesses (generally done using a Venn diagram of interlocking circles, a KWL Chart, etc). These charts and formats are essential for providing scaffolding for instruction through activating pertinent prior knowledge.

KWL charts are exceptionally useful for reading comprehension, as they outline what children <u>K</u>NOW, what they <u>W</u>ANT to know, and what they've <u>L</u>EARNED after reading. Students are asked to activate prior knowledge about a topic and further develop their knowledge about a topic using this organizer. Teachers often opt to display and maintain KWL charts throughout a text to continually record pertinent information about students' reading.

What do I KNOW?	What do I WANT to know?	What did I LEARN?

When the teacher first introduces the KWL strategy, the children should be allowed sufficient time to brainstorm what they all actually <u>k</u>now about the topic. The children should have a three-columned KWL worksheet template for their journals, and there should be a chart to record the responses from class or group discussion. The children can write under each column in their own journal; they should also help the teacher with notations on the chart. This strategy involves the children in actually gaining experience in note taking and in having a concrete record of new data and information gleaned from the passage.

Depending on the grade level of the participating children, the teacher may also want to channel them into considering categories of information they hope to find out from the expository passage. For instance, they may be reading a book on animals to find out more about the animals' habitats during the winter or about the animals' mating habits.

When children are working on the middle (the what I w̲ant to know section of their KWL strategy sheet), the teacher may want to give them a chance to share what they would like to learn further about the topic and help them to express it in question format.

KWL can even be introduced as early as second grade with extensive teacher discussion support. It not only serves to support the child's comprehension of a particular expository text, but it also models for children a format for note taking. Additionally, when the teacher wants to introduce report writing, the KWL format provides excellent outlines and question introductions for at least three paragraphs of a report.

Cooper (2004) recommends this strategy for use with thematic units and with reading chapters in required science, social studies, or health text books. In addition to its usefulness with thematic unit study, KWL is wonderful for providing the teacher with a concrete format to assess how well children have absorbed pertinent new knowledge within the passage (by looking at the third L section). Ultimately it is hoped that students will learn to use this strategy, not only under explicit teacher direction with templates of KWL sheets, but also on their own by informally writing questions they want to find out about in their journals and then going back to their own questions and answering them after the reading.

Note Taking

Older children take notes in their reading journals, while younger children and those more in need of explicit teacher support contribute their ideas and responses as part of the discussion in class. Their responses can be recorded on an experiential chart.

Connecting Texts

The concept of readiness is generally regarded as a developmentally-based phenomenon. Various abilities, whether cognitive, affective, or psychomotor, are perceived to be dependent upon the mastery or development of certain prerequisite skills or abilities. Readiness, then, implies that the necessary prior knowledge, experience, and readiness prerequisites should be present before the child engages in the new task.

Readiness for subject area learning is dependent not only on prior knowledge, but also on affective factors such as interest, motivation, and attitude. These factors are often more influential on student learning than the pre-existing cognitive base.

When texts relate to a student's life, to other reading materials, or to additional areas of study, they become more meaningful and relevant to students' learning. Students enjoy seeing reading material that they can connect to on a deeper level.

Discussing the Text

Discussion is an activity in which the children (this activity works well from grades three through six and beyond) concentrate on a particular text. Among the prompts, the teacher-coach might suggest that the children focus on words of interest they encountered in the text. These can also be words that they heard if the text was read aloud. Children can be asked to share something funny or upsetting or unusual about the words they have read. Through this focus on children's responses to words as the center of the discussion circle, peers become more interested in word study.

Furthermore, in the current teaching of literacy, it is not uncommon for reading, writing, thinking, listening, viewing, and discussing to be developed and nurtured simultaneously and interactively.

COMPETENCY 4.0   LANGUAGE IN WRITING

Skill 4.1   Components of language in writing including the elements of grammar and usage

Conventions for language that appear in print have been developed over several centuries; they change somewhat from generation to generation but compared to the use of language in electronic media, they are fairly static. On the other hand, language use in radio and television has undergone rapid changes. Listening to a radio show from the thirties is a step back in time. The intonation had its own peculiar qualities. Even in its own time, it would not have been recognized as a conversation between two people. Listening to President Franklin Delano Roosevelt's "fireside chats" also takes us back in time, not only because of the content of the speeches, but also by the way they were delivered. "Declamation" is a good term for the radio presentation style of that day, and, to some extent, even the style of public speeches. Declamation was notable for rhetorical effect or display. The same is true of television. Listening to early television news shows—Edward R. Murrow, for example—reminds us instantly of an earlier time. It followed in the style of the radio shows. It was declamatory in nature and sounded more like an announcement than a conversation.

Radio and television speech nowadays is much more conversational in tone. In fact, on many of the news shows, there are two or more news people who will carry on a conversation before, after, and between the news stories. This would have seemed peculiar to earlier listeners.

Because so many aspects of language change while others stay the same, teachers must be cognizant of the proper rules and conventions of punctuation, capitalization, and spelling in the modern oral and written language. Competency exams are designed to ensure that this is true; they generally test the ability to apply advanced language skills.

To aid in meeting the expectations of the competency exams, a limited number of the more frustrating rules are presented here. Rules should be applied according to the American style of English (i.e., spelling *theater* instead of *theatre* and placing terminal marks of punctuation almost exclusively within other marks of punctuation). The most common conventions are discussed below.

Spelling

Concentration in this section will be on spelling plurals and possessives. The multiplicity and complexity of spelling rules based on phonics, letter doubling, and exceptions to rules that are not mastered by adulthood should be replaced by a good dictionary. As spelling mastery is also difficult for adolescents, the recommendation is the same; learning the use of a dictionary and thesaurus will be a more rewarding use of time.

Most plurals of nouns that end in hard consonant sounds followed by a silent *e* are made by adding *s*. Some words ending in vowels also only add an *s*.

fingers, numerals, banks, bugs, riots, homes, gates, radios, bananas

For nouns that end in the soft consonant sounds *s, j, x, z, ch,* and *sh*, add *es* to make them plural. Some nouns ending in *o* also add es.

dresses, waxes, churches, brushes, tomatoes, potatoes

Nouns ending in *y* preceded by a vowel are pluralized by just adding *s*.

boys, alleys

For nouns ending in *y* preceded by a consonant, change the *y* to *i* and add *es* to make them plural.

babies, corollaries, frugalities, poppies

Some noun plurals are formed irregularly or remain the same.

sheep, deer, children, leaves, oxen

Some nouns derived from foreign words, especially Latin, may make their plurals in two different ways. Sometimes, the meanings are the same; other times, the two plurals are used in slightly different contexts. It is always wise to consult the dictionary.

appendices, appendixes	criterion, criteria
indexes, indices	crisis, crises

Make the plurals of closed (solid) compound words in the usual way except for words ending in *ful*, which make their plurals on the root word.

timelines, hairpins, cupsful

Make the plurals of open or hyphenated compounds by adding the change in inflection to the word that changes in number.

fathers-in-law, courts-martial, masters of art, doctors of medicine

Make the plurals of letters, numbers, and abbreviations by adding *s*.

fives and tens, IBMs, 1990s, *p*s and *q*s (Note that letters are italicized.)

Sentence Completeness

Avoid fragments and run-on sentences. Recognizing sentence elements necessary to make a complete thought, properly using independent and dependent clauses, and using proper punctuation will correct such errors.

Capitalization

Capitalize all proper names of persons (including specific organizations or agencies of government); places (countries, states, cities, parks, and specific geographical areas); things (political parties, structures, historical and cultural terms, and calendar and time designations); and religious terms (any deity, revered person or group, sacred writings).

> Percy Bysshe Shelley, Argentina, Mount Rainier National Park, Grand Canyon, League of Nations, the Sears Tower, Birmingham, Lyric Theater, Americans, Midwesterners, Democrats, Renaissance, Boy Scouts of America, Easter, God, Bible, Dead Sea Scrolls, Koran

Capitalize proper adjectives and titles used with proper names.

California gold rush, President John Adams, French fries, Homeric epic, Romanesque architecture, Senator John Glenn

Note: Some words that represent titles and offices are not capitalized unless used with a proper name.

Capitalized	Not Capitalized
Congressman McKay	the congressman from Florida
Commander Alger	commander of the Pacific Fleet
Queen Elizabeth	the queen of England

Capitalize all main words in titles of works of literature, art, and music. (See "Using Italics" in the Punctuation section.)

Punctuation

In a quoted statement that is either declarative or imperative, place the period inside the closing quotation marks.

"The airplane crashed on the runway during takeoff."

If the quotation is followed by other words in the sentence, place a comma inside the closing quotations marks and a period at the end of the sentence.

"The airplane crashed on the runway during takeoff," said the announcer.

In most instances in which a quoted title or expression occurs at the end of a sentence, the period is placed before either the single or double quotation marks.

"The middle school readers were unprepared to understand Bryant's poem 'Thanatopsis.'"

Early book-length adventure stories like *Don Quixote* and *The Three Musketeers* were known as "picaresque novels."

There is an instance in which the final quotation mark would precede the period: if the content of the sentence were about a speech or quote, and the understanding of the meaning would be confused by the placement of the period.

The first thing out of his mouth was "Hi, I'm home."
but
The first line of his speech began "I arrived home to an empty house".

In sentences that are interrogatory or exclamatory, the question mark or exclamation point should be positioned outside the closing quotation marks if the quote itself is a statement or command or cited title.

Who decided to lead us in the recitation of the "Pledge of Allegiance"?

Why was Tillie shaking as she began her recitation, "Once upon a midnight dreary..."?

I was embarrassed when Mrs. White said, "Your slip is showing"!

In sentences that are declarative but the quotation is a question or an exclamation, place the question mark or exclamation point inside the quotation marks.

The hall monitor yelled, "Fire! Fire!"

"Fire! Fire!" yelled the hall monitor.

Cory shrieked, "Is there a mouse in the room?" (In this instance, the question supersedes the exclamation.)

Commas

Separate two or more coordinate adjectives that modify the same word and three or more nouns, phrases, or clauses in a list.

It was a dank, dark day.

Maggie's hair was dull, dirty, and lice-ridden.

Dickens portrayed the Artful Dodger as skillful pickpocket, loyal follower of Fagin, and defendant of Oliver Twist.

Ellen daydreamed about getting out of the rain, taking a shower, and eating a hot dinner.

In Elizabethan England, Ben Johnson wrote comedy, Christopher Marlowe wrote tragedies, and William Shakespeare composed both.

Use commas to separate antithetical or complimentary expressions from the rest of the sentence.

The veterinarian, not his assistant, would perform the delicate surgery.

The more he knew about her, the less he wished he had known.

Randy hopes to, and probably will, get an appointment to the Naval Academy.

His thorough, though esoteric, scientific research could not easily be understood by high school students.

Using Semicolons

Use semicolons to separate independent clauses when the second clause is introduced by a transitional adverb. (These clauses may also be written as separate sentences, preferably by placing the adverb within the second sentence.)

> The Elizabethans modified the rhyme scheme of the sonnet; thus, it was called the English sonnet.
>> *or*
> The Elizabethans modified the rhyme scheme of the sonnet. Thus, it was called the English sonnet.

Use semicolons to separate items in a series that are long and complex or have internal punctuation.

> The Italian Renaissance produced masters in the fine arts: Dante Alighieri, author of the *Divine Comedy;* Leonardo da Vinci, painter of *The Last Supper;* and Donatello, sculptor of the *Quattro Coronati*, the four saints.

> The leading scorers in the WNBA were Zheng Haixia, averaging 23.9 points per game; Lisa Leslie, 22; and Cynthia Cooper, 19.5.

Using Colons

Place a colon at the beginning of a list of items. (Note its use in the sentence about Renaissance Italians on the previous page.)

> The teacher directed us to compare Faulkner's three symbolic novels: *Absalom, Absalom; As I Lay Dying;* and *Light in August*.

Do **not** use a colon if the list is preceded by a verb.

> Three of Faulkner's symbolic novels are *Absalom, Absalom; As I Lay Dying;* and *Light in August*.

Subject-Verb Agreement

A verb should always agree in number with its subject. Making them agree relies on the ability to properly identify the subject.

One of the boys <u>was playing</u> too rough.

<u>No one</u> in the class, not the teacher nor the students, <u>was listening</u> to the message from the intercom.

The <u>candidates</u>, including a grandmother and a teenager, <u>are debating</u> some controversial issues.

If two singular subjects are connected by *and*, the verb must be plural.

A man *and* his dog <u>were jogging</u> on the beach.

If two singular subjects are connected by *or* or *nor,* a singular verb is required.

Neither Dot *nor* Joyce <u>has missed</u> a day of school this year.

Either Fran *or* Paul <u>is</u> missing.

If one singular subject and one plural subject are connected by *or* or *nor,* the verb agrees with the subject nearest to the verb.

Neither the coach *nor* the <u>players</u> <u>were able</u> to sleep on the bus.

If the subject is a collective noun, its sense of number in the sentence determines the verb: singular if the noun represents a group or unit, and plural if the noun represents individuals.

The <u>House of Representatives</u> <u>has adjourned</u> for the holidays.

The <u>House of Representatives</u> <u>have failed</u> to reach agreement on the subject of adjournment.

Use of Verbs (Tense)

Present tense is used to express that which is currently happening or is always true.

Randy is playing the piano.

Randy plays the piano like a pro.

Past tense is used to express action that occurred in a past time.

Randy learned to play the piano when he was six years old.

Future tense is used to express action or a condition of future time.

Randy will probably earn a music scholarship.

Present perfect tense is used to express action or a condition that started in the past and is continued to or completed in the present.

Randy has practiced piano every day for the last ten years.

Randy has never been bored with practice

Past perfect tense expresses action or a condition that occurred as a precedent to some other action or condition.

Randy had considered playing clarinet before he discovered the piano.

Future perfect tense expresses action that started in the past or the present and will conclude at some time in the future.

By the time he goes to college, Randy will have been an accomplished pianist for more than half of his life.

Use of Verbs (Mood)

Indicative mood is used to make unconditional statements; subjunctive mood is used for conditional clauses or wish statements that pose untrue conditions. Verbs in subjunctive mood are plural with both singular and plural subjects.

If I were a bird, I would fly.

I wish I were as rich as Donald Trump.

Verb Conjugation

The conjugation of verbs follows the patterns used in the discussion of tense above. However, the most frequent problems in verb use stem from the improper formation of past and past participial forms.

> Regular verb: believe, believed, (have) believed
> Irregular verbs: run, ran, run; sit, sat, sat; teach, taught, taught

Other problems stem from the use of verbs that are the same in some tenses but have different forms and different meanings in other tenses.

> I lie on the ground. I lay on the ground yesterday. I have lain down.
> I lay the blanket on the bed. I laid the blanket there yesterday. I have laid the blanket every night.

> The sun rises. The sun rose. The sun has risen. He raises the flag. He raised the flag. He had raised the flag.

> I sit on the porch. I sat on the porch. I have sat in the porch swing.
> I set the plate on the table. I set the plate there yesterday. I had set the table before dinner.

Two other common verb problems stem from misusing the preposition *of* for the verb auxiliary *have* and misusing the verb *ought* (now rare).

| Incorrect: | I should of gone to bed. |
| Correct: | I should have gone to bed. |

| Incorrect: | He hadn't ought to get so angry. |
| Correct: | He ought not to get so angry. |

Use of Pronouns

A pronoun used as a subject of predicate nominative is in nominative case.

> She was the drum majorette. The lead trombonists were Joe and he. The band director accepted whoever could march in step.

A pronoun used as a direct object, indirect object, or object of a preposition is in objective case.

> The teacher praised him. She gave him an A on the test. Her praise of him was appreciated. The students whom she did not praise will work harder next time.

Some common pronoun errors occur from the misuse of reflexive pronouns:

Singular: *myself, yourself, herself, himself, itself*
Plural: *ourselves, yourselves, themselves*

Incorrect:	Jack cut hisself shaving.
Correct:	Jack cut himself shaving.

Incorrect:	They backed theirselves into a corner.
Correct:	They backed themselves into a corner.

Use of Adjectives

An adjective should agree with its antecedent in number.

Those apples are rotten. This one is ripe. These peaches are hard.

Comparative adjectives end in -er and superlatives in -est, with some exceptions like *worse* and *worst*. Some adjectives that cannot easily make comparative inflections are preceded by *more* and *most*.

Mrs. Carmichael is the better of the two basketball coaches.

That is the hastiest excuse you have ever contrived.

Avoid double comparisons.

Incorrect:	This is the worstest headache I ever had.
Correct:	This is the worst headache I ever had.

When comparing one thing to others in a group, exclude the thing under comparison from the rest of the group.

Incorrect:	Joey is larger than any baby I have ever seen. (Since you have seen him, he cannot be larger than himself.)
Correct:	Joey is larger than <u>any other</u> baby I have ever seen.

Include all the words necessary to make a comparison clear in meaning.

I am as tall as my mother. I am as tall as she (is).

My cats are better behaved than those of my neighbor.

Skill 4.2   Syntax, sentence types

Syntax refers to the rules or patterned relationships that correctly create phrases and sentences from words. When readers develop an understanding of syntax, they begin to understand the structure of how sentences are built, and eventually the beginning of grammar.

> Example: "I am going to the movies"
> This statement is syntactically and grammatically correct.

> Example: "They am going to the movies."
> This statement is syntactically correct since all the words are in their correct place, but it is grammatically incorrect with the use of the word "They" rather than "I."

Types of Sentences

Sentences are made up of two parts: the subject and the predicate. The **subject** is the "do-er" of an action or the element that is being joined. Any adjectives describing this do-er or element are also part of the subject. The **predicate** is made up of the verb and any other adverbs, adjectives, pronouns, or clauses that describe the action of the sentence.

A **simple sentence** contains one independent clause (which contains one subject and one predicate).

In the following examples, the subject is underlined once and the predicate is underlined twice.

> The dancer bowed.

> Nathan skied down the hill.

A **compound sentence** is made up of two independent clauses that are joined by a conjunction, a correlative conjunction (e.g., either-or, neither-nor), or a semicolon. Both of these independent clauses are able to stand on their own, but for sentence variety, authors will often combine two independent clauses.

In the following examples, the subjects of each independent clause are underlined once, and the predicates of each independent clause are underlined twice. The conjunction is in bold.

Samantha ate the cookie, **and** she drank her milk.

Mark is excellent with computers; he has worked with them for years.

Either Terry runs the project **or** I will not participate.

A **complex sentence** is made up of one independent clause and at least one dependent clause. In the following examples, the subjects of each clause are underlined once, and the predicates are underlined twice. The independent clause is in plain text, and the dependent clause is in italics.

When Jody saw how clean the house was, she was happy.

Brian loves taking diving lessons, *which he has done* for years.

Skill 4.3   Orthography and morphology

The Structure of Language

Orthography is a method of representing a spoken language through the use of written symbols (commonly referred to as **spelling**). It involves the application of letters and their sequencing within words. Fundamentally, English orthography is made up of four basic word types:

1. Regular, for reading and spelling (e.g., cat, print)
2. Regular, for reading but not for spelling (e.g. float, brain - could be spelled "flote" or "brane," respectively)
3. Rule based (e.g., canning - doubling rule, faking - drop e rule)
4. Irregular (e.g., beauty).

Students must be taught to recognize all four types of words automatically in order to be effective readers. Repeated practice in pattern recognition is often necessary. Practice techniques for student development can include speed drills in which they read lists of isolated words with contrasting vowel sounds that are signaled by the syllable type.

The study of word structure is another important reading skill. When readers develop morphemic skills, they are developing an understanding of patterns they see in words. For example, English speakers realize that cat, cats, and caterpillar share some similarities in structure. This understanding helps readers to recognize words at a faster and easier rate, since each word doesn't need individual decoding.

Morphology is a branch of linguistics that uses applied rules of these word formation processes. The word formation processes are built on specific patterns (or regularities) in the way words are formed from smaller units, and they determine how those smaller units interact in speech. At the simplest level, they connect such words as "dog," "dogs," "dog-lover," and dog-catcher" according to relationships of spelling, meaning, use, and variation.

Unless rules are applied, ambiguity develops in defining a word. For example, "dog" and "dogs" are—in a sense—the same word. They are both nouns that refer to the same kind of animal, differing only in number. However, by application, they are different words. They are not interchangeable in a sentence without altering other words to support the change.

For example:

> That dog is one of the best hunters in this area
> *but*
> Those dogs are some of the best hunters in this area.

In the sense that "dog" and "dogs" are the same "word," the morphological term is a **lexeme**. In the second sense, when the two are different "words," the descriptive term is **word-form**. Thus, "dog" and "dogs" are different forms of the same lexeme. Dog, dog-catcher and dog-lover, on the other hand, are different lexemes; they refer to three different kinds of entities and are considered word-forms.

It is possible to distinguish two kinds of morphological rules. Some morphological rules relate different forms of the same lexeme, while other rules relate two different lexemes. Rules of the first kind are called **inflectional rules**, while those of the second kind are called **word-formation**. The English plural, as illustrated by "dog" and "dogs," is an inflectional rule; compounds like "dog-catcher" or "dog-lover" provide examples of a word-formation rule.

Furthermore, there are two distinctive types of word-formation: compounding and derivation. **Compounding** is the process of word-formation that involves combining complete word-forms into a single compound form. For example, dog-catcher is a compound because both dog and catcher were complete word-forms in their own right before the compounding process was applied. **Derivation** involves affixing bound (non-independent) forms to existing lexemes, whereby the addition of the affix derives a new lexeme. For example, the word "independent" is derived from the word "dependent" by prefixing it with the derivational prefix "in-," while "dependent" itself is derived from the verb "depend."

A **paradigm** is the complete set of related word-forms associated with a given lexeme. The conjugations of verbs and the declensions of nouns are examples of paradigms. Accordingly, the word-forms of a lexeme may be arranged conveniently into tables by classifying them according to shared inflectional categories such as tense, aspect, mood, number, gender, or case. For example, the personal pronouns in English can be organized into tables, using the categories of person, number, gender, and case.

An important difference between inflection and word-formation is that inflected word-forms of lexemes are organized into paradigms, which are defined by the requirements of syntactic rules, whereas the rules of word-formation are not restricted by any corresponding requirements of syntax. Inflection is therefore relevant to syntax, while word-formation is not. The part of morphology that covers the relationship between syntax and morphology is called **morphosyntax**; it concerns itself with inflection and paradigms, but not with word-formation or compounding.

Thus far, we have used morphological rules as analogies between word-forms: "dog" is to "dogs" as "cat" is to "cats" or as "dish" is to "dishes." In this instance, the analogy applies both to the form of the words and to their meanings: in each pair, the first word means "one of," while the second word means "two or more of." In these examples, the difference is always in having the plural form "-s" affixed to the second word, providing the distinction between singular and plural entities. In English, this one-to-one correspondence between meaning and form does not apply to every case. There are instances of word form pairs like ox/oxen, goose/geese, and sheep/sheep, where the difference between the singular and the plural is provided in a way that departs from the regular pattern. These cases, where the same distinction is effected by alternative changes to the form of a word, are called **allomorphy**.

Skill 4.4   Semantics

Semantics refers to the meaning expressed when words are arranged in a specific way. This is where connotation and denotation of words eventually will have a role with readers.

All of these skill sets are important to eventually developing effective word recognition skills, which help emerging readers develop fluency.

Skill 4.5   Vocabulary in context

The National Reading Panel has put forth the following conclusions about vocabulary instruction.

1. There is a need for direct instruction of vocabulary items required for a specific text.
2. Repetition and multiple exposure to vocabulary items are important. Students should be given items that will be likely to appear in many contexts.
3. Learning in rich contexts is valuable for vocabulary learning. Vocabulary words should be those that the learner will find useful in many contexts. When vocabulary items are derived from content learning materials, the learner will be better equipped to deal with specific reading matter in content areas.
4. Vocabulary tasks should be restructured as necessary. It is important to be certain that students fully understand what is asked of them in the context of reading rather than to focus only on the words to be learned.
5. Vocabulary learning is effective when it entails active engagement in learning tasks.
6. Computer technology can be used effectively to help teach vocabulary.
7. Vocabulary can be acquired through incidental learning. Much of a student's vocabulary will have to be learned in the course of doing things rather than through explicit vocabulary learning. Repetition, richness of context, and motivation may also add to the efficacy of incidental learning of vocabulary.
8. Dependence on a single vocabulary instruction method will not result in optimal learning. A variety of methods can be used effectively with emphasis on multimedia aspects of learning, richness of context in which words are to be learned, and the number of exposures to words that learners receive.

The National Reading Panel found that one critical feature of effective classrooms includes utilizing lessons and activities through which students apply their vocabulary knowledge and strategies to reading and writing. Included in the activities were discussions that allowed teachers and students to talk about words, their features, and strategies for understanding unfamiliar words.

There are many methods for directly and explicitly teaching words. In fact, the Panel found twenty-one methods that have been found effective in research projects. Many emphasize the underlying concept of a word and its connections to other words using graphics such as semantic mapping and diagrams. The keyword method uses words and illustrations that highlight salient features of meaning. Visualizing or drawing a picture either by the student or by the teacher was found to be effective. Many words cannot be learned in this way, so effective classrooms provide multiple ways for students to learn and interact with words. The Panel also found that computer-assisted activities can have a very positive role in the development of vocabulary.

Skill 4.6   Figurative language

Figurative language may also be called by its more familiar term: figures of speech. Most of us are aware of a number of figures of speech; in fact, if all of them that have ever been identified were listed, it would be a very long list! For the purpose of analyzing poetry or literature, the following list is fairly comprehensive and will allow for a suitable grasp.

Simile: A direct comparison between two things, often using the term "like" or "as" to foster the comparison. One very common example is "My love is like a red-red rose."

Metaphor: An indirect comparison between two things. It is the use of a word or phrase denoting one kind of object or action in place of another. While poets use them extensively, they are also integral to everyday speech. For example, chairs are said to have "legs" and "arms," even though they are typically unique to humans and other animals.

Parallelism: This is the arrangement of ideas into phrases, sentences, and paragraphs that balance one element with another of equal importance and similar wording. An example from Francis Bacon's *Of Studies* is "Reading maketh a full man, conference a ready man, and writing an exact man."

Personification: This occurs when human characteristics are attributed to an inanimate object, an abstract quality, or an animal. For example, John Bunyan wrote characters named Death, Knowledge, Giant Despair, Sloth, and Piety in his *Pilgrim's Progress.* The earlier metaphor of an "arm" of a chair is also a form of personification.

Euphemism: This is the substitution of an agreeable or inoffensive term for one that might offend or suggest something unpleasant. Many euphemisms are used to refer to death, including "passed away," "crossed over," or even simply "passed."

Hyperbole: A deliberate exaggeration for effect. This passage from Shakespeare's *The Merchant of Venice* is an example:

> Why, if two gods should play some heavenly match
> And on the wager lay two earthly women,
> And Portia one, there must be something else
> Pawned with the other, for the poor rude world
> Hath not her fellow.

Climax: A number of phrases or sentences arranged in ascending order of rhetorical forcefulness. This passage from Melville's *Moby Dick* is one example:

> All that most maddens and torments; all that stirs up the lees of things; all truth with malice in it; all that cracks the sinews and cakes the brain; all the subtle demonisms of life and thought; all evil, to crazy Ahab, were visibly personified and made practically assailable in Moby Dick.

Bathos: A ludicrous attempt to portray pathos—that is, to evoke pity, sympathy, or sorrow. It may result from inappropriately dignifying the commonplace, using elevated language to describe something trivial, or greatly exaggerating pathos.

Oxymoron: A contradiction in terms deliberately employed for effect. It is usually seen in a qualifying adjective whose meaning is contrary to that of the noun it modifies such as wise folly. For example, one fairly commonplace oxymoron is "jumbo shrimp."

Irony: The expression of something other than and particularly opposite to the literal meaning, such as words of praise when blame is intended. In poetry, it is often used as a sophisticated or resigned awareness of contrast between what is and what ought to be; it expresses a controlled pathos without sentimentality. It is a form of indirection that avoids overt praise or censure. An early example is the Greek comic character Eiron, a clever underdog who, by his wit, repeatedly triumphs over the boastful character Alazon.

Alliteration: This is the repetition of consonant sounds in two or more neighboring words or syllables. In its simplest form, it reinforces one or two consonant sounds. For example, notice the repetition in Shakespeare's Sonnet #12:

> When I do count the clock that tells the time.

Some poets have used more complex patterns of alliteration by creating similar consonant sounds both at the beginning of words and at the beginning of stressed syllables within words. For example, hear the sounds in Shelley's "Stanzas Written in Dejection Near Naples":

> The City's voice itself is soft like Solitude's

Onomatopoeia: The naming of a thing or action by a vocal imitation of the sound associated with it, such as "buzz" or "hiss." It is marked by the use of words whose sound suggests the sense. One good example is from "The Brook" by Tennyson:

> I chatter over stony ways,
> In little sharps and trebles,
> I bubble into eddying bays,
> I babble on the pebbles.

Malapropism: A verbal blunder in which one word is replaced by another that is similar in sound but different in meaning. The term itself comes from Sheridan's Mrs. Malaprop in *The Rivals* (1775). Thinking of the geography of contiguous countries, she spoke of the "geometry" of "contagious countries."

Poets and writers use figures of speech to sharpen the effect and meaning of their work and to help readers see things in ways they have never seen them before. Marianne Moore observed that a fir tree has "an emerald turkey-foot at the top." Her poem makes us aware of something we probably had never noticed before. The sudden recognition of the likeness yields pleasure in the reading.

Figurative language allows for the statement of truths that more literal language cannot. Skillfully used, a figure of speech will help the reader to see more clearly and to focus upon particulars. Figures of speech add many dimensions of richness to the reading and understanding of a poem; they also allow many opportunities for worthwhile analysis. The approach to take in analyzing a poem on the basis of its figures of speech is to ask pertinent questions: What does it do for the poem? Does it underscore meaning? Does it intensify understanding? Does it increase the intensity of our response?

Skill 4.7   Social, cultural, and historical influences of language

Social Influences

Social influences that impact language are mostly those imposed by family, peer groups, and mass media. For the most part, the economic and educational levels of families determine the properness of language use. Exposure to adults who encourage and assist children to speak well enhances readiness for other areas of learning; it also contributes to a child's ability to communicate his or her needs.

Historically, children learned language, speech patterns, and grammar from members of the extended family just as they learned the rules of conduct within their family unit and community. In modern times, the mother in a nuclear family became the dominant force in influencing the child's development. With increasing social changes, many children are not receiving the proper guidance in all areas of development, especially language.

Those who are fortunate to be in educational daycare programs like Head Start or in certified preschools develop better language skills than those whose care is entrusted to untrained care providers. Once a child enters elementary school, he or she is also greatly influenced by peer language. This peer influence becomes significant in adolescence, as the use of teen jargon gives teenagers a sense of identity within the chosen group(s) and independence from the influence of adults. In some lower socio-economic groups, children use Standard English in school and street language outside the school. Some children of immigrant families become bilingual by necessity if no English is spoken in the home.

Research has shown a strong correlation between socio-economic characteristics and all areas of intellectual development. Traditional paper measurement instruments rely on verbal ability to establish intelligence. Research findings and test scores reflect that children, reared in nuclear families who provide cultural experiences and individual attention, become more language proficient than those who are denied that security and stimulation.

Personal Influences

The rates of physical development and identifiable language disabilities also influence language development. Nutritional deficiencies, poor eyesight, and conditions such as stuttering or dyslexia can inhibit a child's ability to master language. Unless diagnosed early, these conditions can hamper communication into adulthood. These conditions also stymie the development of self-confidence and, therefore, the willingness to learn or to overcome the handicap. Children should receive proper diagnosis and positive corrective instruction.

In adolescence, children's choice of role models and their decisions about the future determine the growth of identity. Rapid physical and emotional changes and the stress of coping with the pressure of sexual awareness make concentration on any educational pursuits difficult. The easier the transition from childhood to adulthood, the better the competence will be in all learning areas.

Middle school and junior high school teachers are confronted by a student body ranging from fifth graders, who are still childish, to eighth or ninth graders who, if not in fact at least in their minds, are young adults. Teachers must approach language instruction as a social development tool with more emphasis on vocabulary acquisition, reading improvement, and speaking/writing skills. High school teachers can deal with the more formalized instruction of grammar, usage, and literature for older adolescents whose social development allows them to pay more attention to studies that will improve their chances for a better adult life.

As a tool, language must have relevance to the student's real environment. Many high schools have developed practical English classes for business/vocational students whose specific needs are determined by their desire to enter the workforce upon graduation. More emphasis is placed upon accuracy of mechanics and understanding verbal and written directions, as these are the skills desired most by employers. Writing résumés, completing forms, reading policy and operations manuals, and generating reports are some of the more specific skills necessary. Emphasis is placed on higher level thinking skills (including inferential thinking and literary interpretation) in literature classes for college-bound students.

COMPETENCY 5.0   COMMUNICATION SKILLS

Skill 5.1   Processes of communication as reflected in the stages of writing development

Discourse, whether in speaking or writing, falls naturally into four different forms: narrative, descriptive, expository, persuasive.

The first question to be asked when *reading* a written piece, *listening* to a presentation, or *writing* is "What is the point?" The answer to this question is usually called the thesis. When you have finished reading an essay, you want to be able to say, "The point of this piece is that the foster-care system in America is a disaster." If it's a play, you should also be able to say, "The point of that play is that good overcomes evil." The same is true of any written document or performance. If it doesn't make a point, the reader/listener/viewer is likely to be confused or feel that it was not worth the effort.

Knowing that writing should make a point is very helpful when you are sitting down to write your own document, be it essay, poem, or speech. What point do you want to make? We make these points in the forms that have been the structure of Western thinking since the Greek Rhetoricians.

Persuasion is a piece of writing, a poem, a play, or a speech whose purpose is to change the minds of the audience members or to get them to do something. This is achieved in many ways:

1) The credibility of the writer/speaker might lead the listeners/readers to a change of mind or a recommended action.

2) Reasoning is important in persuasive discourse. No one wants to believe that he or she accepts a new viewpoint or goes out and takes action just because he or she likes and trusts the person who recommended it. Logic comes into play in reasoning that is persuasive.

3) The third and most powerful force that leads to acceptance or action is emotional appeal. Even if audience members have been persuaded logically and reasonably that they should believe in a different way, they are unlikely to act on it unless moved emotionally. A person with resources might be convinced that people suffered in New Orleans after Katrina, but he or she will not be likely to do anything about it until he or she feels a deeper emotional connection to the disaster. Sermons are good examples of persuasive discourse.

Exposition is discourse whose only purpose is to inform. Expository writing is not interested in changing anyone's mind or getting anyone to take a certain action. It exists to give information. Some examples include directions to a particular place or the directions for putting together a toy that arrives unassembled. The writer doesn't care whether you do or don't follow the directions. He or she only wants to be sure you have the information in case you do decide to use it.

Narration is discourse that is arranged chronologically—something happened, and then something else happened, and then something else happened. It is also called a story. News reports are often narrative in nature, as are records of trips or experiences.

Description is discourse whose purpose is to make an experience available through one of the five senses—seeing, smelling, hearing, feeling (as with the fingers), and tasting. Descriptive words are used to make it possible for readers to "see" with their own mind's eye, hear through their own mind's ear, smell through their own mind's nose, taste with their own mind's tongue, and feel with their own mind's fingers. This is how language moves people. Only by experiencing an event can the emotions become involved. Poets are experts in descriptive language.

Types of Writing

Persuasive writing often uses all forms of discourse. The introduction may be a history or background of the idea being presented: **exposition**. Details supporting some of the points may be stories: **narrations**.

Descriptive writing is typically used to make sure the point is established emotionally.

A **paraphrase** is the rewording of a piece of writing. The result will not necessarily be shorter than the original, but it will use different vocabulary and possibly a different arrangement of details. Paraphrases are sometimes written to clarify a complex piece of writing. Sometimes, material is paraphrased because it cannot be borrowed due to copyright restraints.

A **summary** is a "distilling" of the elements of a piece of writing or speech. It will be much shorter than the original. To write a good summary, the writer must determine what the "bones" of the original piece are. What is its structure? What is the thesis and what are the sub-points? A summary does not make judgments about the original; it simply reports the original in condensed form.

Letters are often expository in nature—their purpose is to give information. However, letters are also often persuasive, as the writer may want to persuade or get the recipient to do something. They are also sometimes descriptive or narrative, such as when the writer shares an experience or tells about an event.

Research reports are a special kind of expository writing. A topic is researched—explored by some appropriate means such as searching literature, interviewing experts, or even conducting experiments—and the findings will be written up in such a way that a particular audience may know what was discovered. These reports can be very simple, such as delving into the history of an event, or very complex, such as a report on a scientific phenomenon that requires complicated testing and reasoning to explain. A research report often presents many possible conclusions but puts forth one as the best answer to the question that inspired the research in the first place. This typically becomes the thesis of the report.

Skill 5.2   Stages of the writing process

Students should always gather ideas before writing. **Prewriting** may include clustering, listing, brainstorming, mapping, free writing, and charting. Providing many ways for a student to develop ideas on a topic in these ways will increase his or her chances for success.

Remind students that as they prewrite, they need to consider their audience. Prewriting strategies assist students in a variety of ways. Listed below are the most common prewriting strategies students can use to explore, plan, and write on a topic. It is important to remember when teaching these strategies that not all prewriting must eventually produce a finished piece of writing. In fact, in the initial lesson of teaching prewriting strategies, it might be more effective to have students practice prewriting strategies without the pressure of having to write a finished product.

- Keep an idea book so that they can jot down ideas that come to mind.
- Write in a daily journal.
- Write down whatever comes to mind; this is called free writing. Students do not stop to make corrections or interrupt the flow of ideas.

A variation of this technique is focused free writing—writing on a specific topic—to prepare for an essay.

- Make a list of all ideas connected with their topic; this is called brainstorming.
- Make sure students know that this technique works best when they let their mind work freely. After completing the list, students should analyze the list to see if a pattern or way to group the ideas emerges.

- Ask the questions Who? What? When? Where? Why? and How? Help the writer to approach a topic from several perspectives.
- Create a visual map on paper to gather ideas. Cluster circles and lines to show connections between ideas. Students should try to identify the relationships that exist between their ideas. If they cannot see the relationships, have them pair up, exchange papers, and have their partners look for some related ideas.
- Observe details of sight, hearing, taste, touch, and taste.
- Visualize by making mental images of something and write down the details in a list.

After students have practiced with each of these prewriting strategies, ask them to pick out the ones they prefer and ask them to discuss how they might use the techniques to help them with future writing assignments. It is important to remember that they can use more than one prewriting strategy at a time. It is also important to reinforce that they may find that different writing situations may call for certain techniques.

When doing **research** in the library, note that most libraries will only allow the downloading and printing of seventy-five pages of information during any given month. The point is to provide the user with a hardcopy of specific information in a limited and environmentally friendly manner. Once the information is collected and categorized according to the research design and outline, the user can begin to take notes on the gathered information to create a cut and paste format for the final report.

Being an effective note taker requires consistent techniques, whether the mode of note taking is on 5x7 note cards, lined notebook paper, or on a computer. Organizing all collected information according to a research outline will allow the user to take notes on each section and begin the writing process. If the computer is used, then the actual format of the report can be word processed and information inputted to speed up the writing process of the final research report. Creating a title page and the bibliography page will allow each downloaded report to have its resources cited immediately in that section.

Note taking involves the identification of specific resources that include the author's or organization's name, year of publication, title, publisher location, and publisher. When taking notes—whether on the computer or using note cards—use the author's last name and page number on cited information. In citing information for major categories and subcategories on the computer, create a file for notes that includes summaries of information and direct quotes. When direct quotes are put into a word file, the cut and paste process for incorporation into the report is quick and easy.

In outline information, it is crucial to identify the headings and subheadings for the topic being researched. When researching information, it is easier to cut and paste information under the indicated headings in creating a visual flow of information for the report. In the actual drafting of the report, the writer is able to lift direct quotations and citations from the posted information to incorporate in the writing.

To revise comes from the Latin word *revidere*, meaning "to see again." **Revision** is probably the most important step for the writer in the writing process. Here, students examine their work and make changes in wording, details, and ideas. All too often, students write a draft and then feel that they are done; on the contrary, students must be encouraged to develop, change, and enhance their writing as they go, as well as once they've completed a draft.

Effective teachers realize that revision and editing go hand-in-hand and that students often move back and forth between these stages during the course of one written work. These stages must be practiced in small groups, pairs, and/or individually. Students must learn to analyze and improve their own work as well as the works of their peers. Teachers should encourage the following activities:

1. Students work in pairs to analyze sentences for variety.
2. Students work in pairs or groups to ask questions about unclear areas in the writing or to help add details, information, etc.
3. Students perform final edit.

Many teachers introduce a Writer's Workshop to their students to maximize learning about the writing process. Writer's Workshops vary across classrooms, but the main idea is for students to become comfortable with the writing process. A basic Writer's Workshop will include a block of classroom time committed to focusing on various projects (e.g., narratives, memoirs, book summaries, fiction, book reports, etc). Students use this time to write, meet with others to review/edit writing, make comments on writing, revise their own work, proofread, meet with the teacher, and publish their work.

Teachers who facilitate effective Writer's Workshops are able to meet with students one at a time and can guide that student in his or her individual writing needs. This approach allows the teacher to differentiate instruction for each student's writing level.

Students need to be trained to become effective at proofreading, revising, and editing strategies. Begin by training them using both desk-side and scheduled conferences. Listed below are some strategies to use to guide students through the final stages of the writing process (and these can easily be incorporated into Writer's Workshop):

- Provide some guide sheets or forms for students to use during peer responses.
- Allow students to work in pairs and limit the agenda.
- Model the use of the guide sheet or form for the entire class.
- Give students a time limit or number of written pieces to be completed in a specific amount of time.
- Have the students read their partners' papers and ask at least three who, what, when, why, how questions. The students answer the questions and use them as a place to begin discussing the piece.
- At this point in the writing process, a mini-lesson that focuses on some of the problems your students are having would be appropriate.

To help students revise, provide students with a series of questions that will assist them in revising their writing.

1. Do the details give a clear picture? Add details that appeal to more than just the sense of sight.
2. How effectively are the details organized? Reorder the details if needed.
3. Are the thoughts and feelings of the writer included? When relevant, add personal thoughts and feelings about the subject.

Writing Introductions

It is important to remember that in the writing process, the introduction should be written last. Until the body of the paper has been determined—the thesis as well as its development—it is difficult to make strategic decisions regarding the introduction. The Greek rhetoricians called this part of a discourse *exordium*, meaning "leading into." The basic purpose of the introduction, then, is to lead the audience into the discourse. It can let the reader know what the purpose of the discourse is and it can condition the audience to be receptive to what the writer wants to say. It can be very brief or it can take up a large percentage of the total word count. Aristotle said that the introduction could be compared to the flourishes that flute players make before their performance—an overture in which the musicians display what they can play best in order to gain the favor and attention of the audience for the main performance.

In order to do this, we must first of all know what we are going to say; who the readership is likely to be; what the social, political, economic, climate is; what preconceived notions the audience is likely to have regarding the subject; and how long the discourse is going to be.

There are many ways to introduce a topic in the introduction. The following list provides many options.

- Show that the subject is important.
- Show that although the points being presented may seem improbable, they are true.
- Show that the subject has been neglected, misunderstood, or misrepresented in the past.
- Explain an unusual mode of development.
- Forestall any misconception of the purpose.
- Apologize for a deficiency.
- Arouse interest in the subject with an anecdotal lead-in.
- Ingratiate oneself with the readership.
- Establish one's own credibility.

The introduction often ends with the **thesis**: the point or purpose of the paper. However, this is not set in stone; the thesis may open the body of the discussion, or it may conclude the discourse. The most important thing to remember is that the purpose and structure of the introduction should be deliberate if it is to serve the purpose of "leading the reader into the discussion."

Writing Conclusions

It is easier to write a conclusion after the decisions regarding the introduction have been made. Aristotle taught that the conclusion should strive to do five things:

1. Inspire the reader with a favorable opinion of the writer.
2. Amplify the force of the points made in the body of the paper.
3. Reinforce the points made in the body.
4. Arouse appropriate emotions in the reader.
5. Restate in a summary way what has been said in the paper.

The conclusion may be short or it may be long, depending on its purpose in the paper. **Recapitulation**, a brief restatement of the main points or certainly of the thesis, is the most common form of effective conclusions. A good example is the closing argument in a court trial.

Text Organization

In studies of professional writers and how they produce their successful works, it has been revealed that writing is a process that can be clearly defined (although in practice, it must have enough flexibility to allow for creativity). The teacher must be able to define the various stages that a successful writer goes through in order to make a statement that has value.

First of all, there must be a discovery stage when ideas, materials, supporting details, etc., are deliberately collected. These may come from many possible sources: the writer's own experience and observations, deliberate research of written sources, interviews of live persons, television presentations, or the Internet.

The next stage is the organization, during which the purpose, thesis, and supporting points are determined. Most writers will put forth more than one possible thesis; in the next stage, the writing of the paper, they will settle on one through the process trial and error.

Once the paper is written, the editing stage is necessary. This is probably the most important stage. This is not just about the polishing the paper; at this point, decisions must be made regarding whether the reasoning is cohesive: Does it hold together? Is the arrangement the best possible one or should the points be rearranged? Are there holes that need to be filled in? What form will the introduction take? Does the conclusion lead the reader out of the discourse, or is it inadequate or too abrupt?

Skill 5.3   Spelling development

o   *See Skill 3.3.*

Skill 5.4   Aspects of speaking and listening

Listening is a very specific skill for very specific circumstances. There are two aspects to listening that warrant attention: comprehension and purpose. **Comprehension** is simply understanding what someone says, the purposes behind the message, and the contexts in which it is said. **Purpose** comes in to play when considering that while someone may completely understand a message, they must also know what to do with it. Are they expected to just nod and smile? Go out and take action?

While listening comprehension is indeed a significant skill in itself—one that deserves a lot of focus in the classroom (much in the same way that reading comprehension does), we will focus on purpose here. Often, when we understand the purpose of listening in various contexts, comprehension will be much easier. Furthermore, when we know the purpose of listening, we can better adjust our comprehension strategies.

Purpose

When complex or new information is provided to us orally, we must analyze and interpret that information. What is the author's most important point? How do the figures of speech impact meaning? How can we arrive at conclusions? Often, making sense of this information can be difficult for oral presentations—first, because we have no way to go back and review material already stated; secondly, because oral language is so much less predictable than written language. However, when we focus on extracting the meaning, message, and speaker's purpose, rather than just "listening" and waiting for things to make sense for us—in other words, when we are more "active" in our listening—we have greater success in interpreting speech.

Listening is often done for the purpose of enjoyment. We like to listen to stories, we enjoy poetry, and we like radio dramas and theater. Listening to literature can also be a great pleasure. The problem today is that students have not learned how to extract great pleasure on a wide-spread scale from simply listening. Perhaps that is because we have not done a good enough job of showing students how listening to literature, for example, can indeed be more interesting than television or video games. In the classrooms of exceptional teachers, we will often find that students are captivated by the reading aloud of good literature. It is refreshing and enjoyable to just sit and soak in the language, story, and poetry of literature being read aloud. Therefore, we must teach students *how* to listen and enjoy such work. We do this by making it fun and giving many possibilities and alternatives to capture the wide array of interests in each classroom.

Let us consider listening in large and small group conversations. The difference here is that conversation requires more than just listening: it involves feedback and active involvement. This can be particularly challenging, as in our culture, we are trained to move conversations along, to discourage silence in a conversation, and to always get the last word in. This poses significant problems for the art of listening. In a discussion, for example, when we are instead preparing our next response—rather than listening to what others are saying—we do a large disservice to the entire discussion. Students need to learn how listening carefully to others in discussions actually promotes better responses on the part of subsequent speakers. One way teachers can encourage this in both large and small group discussions is to expect students to respond *directly* to the previous student's comments before moving ahead with their new comments. This will encourage them to pose their new comments in light of the comments that came just before them.

Making Sense of Oral Language

Oral speech can also be much less structured than written language. Yet, aside from re-reading, many of the skills and strategies that help us in reading comprehension can help us in listening comprehension. For example, as soon as we start listening to something new, we should tap into our prior knowledge in order to attach new information to what we already know. This will not only help us to understand the new information more quickly, but it will also assist us in remembering the material.

We can also look for transitions between ideas. Sometimes, in oral speech, this is pretty simple, such as when voice tone or body language changes; as listeners, we have access to the animation that comes along with live speech. Human beings have to try very hard to be completely non-expressive in their speech. Listeners should take advantage of this and notice how the speaker changes character and voice in order to signal a transition of ideas.

Listeners can also better comprehend the underlying intent of the author when they notice nonverbal cues. In oral speech, unlike written text, elements like irony are not indicated by the actual words, but rather by the tone and nonverbal cues. Simply looking to see expression on the face of a speaker can often do more to signal irony than trying to extract irony from actual words.

One good way to follow oral speech is to take notes and outline major points. Because oral speech can be more circular (as opposed to linear) than written text, it can be of great assistance to keep track of an author's message. Students can learn this strategy in many ways in the classroom: they can take notes during the teacher's oral messages as well as other students' presentations and speeches.

Other classroom methods can also be used to help students to learn good listening skills. For example, teachers can have students practice following complex directions. They can also have students orally retell stories—or retell (in writing or in oral speech) oral presentations of stories or other materials. These activities give students direct practice in the very important skills of listening. They provide students with outlets in which they can slowly improve their abilities to comprehend oral language and take decisive action based on oral speech.

Analyzing the speech of others is a very good technique for helping students to improve their own public speaking abilities. In most circumstances, students cannot view themselves as they give speeches and presentations; however, when they get the opportunity to critique, question, and analyze others' speeches, they begin to learn what works and what doesn't work in effective public speaking.

However, a very important word of warning: DO NOT have students critique each others' public speaking skills.

It could be very damaging to a student to have his or her peers point out what did not work in a speech. Instead, video is a great tool teachers can use. Any appropriate source of public speaking can be used in the classroom for students to analyze and critique.

Some of the things students can pay attention to include the following:

- Volume: A speaker should use an appropriate volume—not too loud to be annoying, but not too soft to be inaudible.
- Pace: The rate at which words are spoken should be appropriate—not too fast to make the speech incomprehensible, but not too slow so as to put listeners to sleep.
- Pronunciation: A speaker should make sure words are spoken clearly. Listeners do not have a text to go back and re-read things they didn't catch.
- Body language: While animated body language can help a speech, too much of it can be distracting. Body language should help convey the message, not detract from it.
- Word choice: The words speakers choose should be consistent with their intended purpose and the audience.
- Visual aids: Visual aids, like body language, should enhance a message. (However, remember that many visual aids can be distracting and can detract from the message.)

Overall, instead of telling students to keep these above factors in mind when presenting information orally, have them view speakers who do these things well and poorly. This will help them to remember what to do the next time they give a speech.

There are a number of factors that must be taken into consideration when giving or listening to a speech. Although some of these have been touched upon in the above passages, we have included a detailed list of tips to keep in mind:

Voice: Many people fall into one of two traps when speaking: using a monotone, or talking too fast. These are both typically caused by anxiety. A monotone restricts your natural inflection, but can be remedied by releasing tension in the upper and lower body muscles. Talking too fast on the other hand, is not necessarily a bad thing if the speaker is exceptionally articulate. However, if the speaker is not articulate, or if the speaker is talking about very technical things, it becomes far too easy for the audience to become lost.

If you talk too fast and begin tripping over your words, it is important to consciously pause after every sentence. Don't be afraid of brief silences. The audience needs time to absorb what you are saying.

Volume: Problems with volume, whether too soft or too loud, can usually be combated with practice. If you tend to speak too softly, have someone stand in the back of the room and give you a signal when your volume is strong enough. If possible, have someone in the front of the room as well to make sure you're not overcompensating with excessive volume. In this same vein, if you have a problem with speaking too loudly, have the person in the front of the room signal you when your voice is soft enough and check with the person in the back to make sure it is still loud enough to be heard. In both cases, note your volume level for future reference. Don't be shy about asking your audience, "Can you hear me in the back?" Suitable volume is beneficial for both you and the audience.

Pitch: Pitch refers to the length, tension, and thickness of a person's vocal bands. As your voice gets higher, the pitch gets higher. In an oral performance, pitch reflects upon the emotional arousal level. More variation in pitch typically corresponds to more emotional arousal, but can also be used to convey sarcasm or to highlight specific words.

Posture: Maintain a straight but not stiff posture. Instead of shifting weight from hip to hip, point your feet directly at the audience and distribute your weight evenly. Keep shoulders orientated towards the audience. If you have to turn your body to use a visual aid, turn 45 degrees and continue speaking towards the audience.

Movement: Instead of staying glued to one spot or pacing back and forth, stay within four to eight feet of the front row of your audience; take maybe a step or half-step to the side every once in a while. If you are using a lectern, feel free to move to the front or side of it to engage your audience more. Avoid distancing yourself from the audience. You want them to feel involved and connected.

Gestures: Gestures are a great way to keep a natural atmosphere when public speaking. Use them just as you would when speaking to a friend. They shouldn't be exaggerated, but they should be utilized for added emphasis. Avoid keeping your hands in your pockets or locked behind your back, wringing your hands, fidgeting nervously, or keeping your arms crossed.

Eye Contact: Many people are intimidated by using eye contact when speaking to large groups. Interestingly, eye contact usually *helps* the speaker to overcome speech anxiety by allowing him or her to connect with the attentive audience and by easing feelings of isolation. Instead of looking at a spot on the back wall or at your notes, scan the room and make eye contact for one to three seconds for each person.

Utilizing Appropriate Communication

In public speaking, not all speeches deserve the same type of speaking style. For example, when providing a humorous speech, it is important to utilize body language that accents the humorous moments. However, when giving instructions, it is extremely important to speak clearly and slowly, carefully noting the mood of the audience, so that if there is general confusion on peoples' faces, you can go back and review something. In group discussions, it is important to ensure that you are listening to others carefully and tailoring your messages so that what you say fits into the general mood and location of the discussion at hand. When giving an oral presentation, the mood should be both serious and friendly; you should focus on ensuring that the content is covered, while also relating to audience members as much as possible.

It used to be that we thought of speaking and communication only in terms of what is effective and what is not effective. Today, we realize that there is more to communication than just good and bad. We must take into consideration that we must adjust our communication styles for various audiences. While we should not stereotype audiences, we can still recognize that certain methods of communication are more appropriate with certain people than with others. Age is an easy one to consider: Adults know that when they talk to children, they should come across as pleasant and non-threatening, and they should use vocabulary that is simple for children to understand. On the other hand, teenagers realize that they should not speak to their grandmothers they way the speak with their peers. When dealing with communications between cultures and genders, people must be sensitive, considerate, and appropriate.

How do teachers help students to understand these "unspoken" rules of communication? Well, these rules are not easy to communicate in regular classroom lessons. Instead, teachers must model these behaviors, and they must have high expectations for students (clearly communicated, of course) inside and outside the classroom walls.

Teachers must also consider these aspects as they deal with colleagues, parents, community members, and even students. They must realize that all communication should be tailored so that it conveys appropriate messages and tones to listeners.

The differences between **informal** and **formal language** are distinctions made on the basis of the occasion as well as the audience. At a "formal" occasion (for example, a meeting of executives or of government officials), even conversational exchanges are likely to be formal. At a cocktail party or a golf game, the language is likely to be much more informal. Formal language uses fewer or no contractions, less slang, longer sentences, and more organization in longer segments. Speeches delivered to executives, college professors, government officials, etc., are likely to be formal. Speeches made to fellow employees are likely to be informal. Sermons tend to be formal; Bible lessons tend to be informal.

Combining Oral and Written Communication

The art of debating, discussion, and conversation is different from the basic writing forms of discourse. The ability to use language and logic to convince the audience to accept your reasoning and to side with you is an art. This form of writing/speaking is extremely confined and structured, logically sequenced, and contains supporting reasons and evidence. At its best, it is the highest form of propaganda. Position statements, evidence, reason, evaluation, and refutation are integral parts of this writing schema.

Interviewing provides opportunities for students to engage in expository and informative communication. It teaches them how to structure questions to evoke fact-filled responses. Compiling the information from an interview into a biographical essay or speech helps students to list, sort, and arrange details in an orderly fashion.

Speeches that encourage them to describe persons, places, or events in their own lives as well as oral interpretations of literature help students to sense the creativity and effort used by professional writers.

COMPETENCY 6.0   CRITICAL THINKING

Skill 6.1   Deductive reasoning

Deductive thinking is the process of arriving at a conclusion based on other statements that are all known to be true, such as theorems, axioms, or postulates. Conclusions found by deductive thinking based on true statements will *always* be true.

Skill 6.2   Inductive reasoning

Inductive thinking is the process of finding a pattern from a group of examples. The pattern is the conclusion that a set of examples seemed to indicate. It may be a correct conclusion or it may be an incorrect conclusion, as other examples may not follow the predicted pattern.

Example:

> Suppose:
> On Monday Mr.Peterson eats breakfast at McDonalds.
> On Tuesday Mr.Peterson eats breakfast at McDonalds.
> On Wednesday Mr.Peterson eats breakfast at McDonalds.
> On Thursday Mr.Peterson eats breakfast at McDonalds again.
>
> Conclusion: On Friday Mr. Peterson will eat breakfast at McDonalds again.

This is a conclusion based on inductive reasoning. Based on several days' observations, you conclude that Mr. Peterson will eat at McDonalds. This may or may not be true, but it is a valid inductive conclusion.

Skill 6.3   Adaptive reasoning

A **valid argument** is a statement made about a pattern or relationship between elements, thought to be true, which is subsequently justified through repeated examples and logical reasoning. Another term for a valid argument is a **proof**.

For example, the statement that the sum of two odd numbers is always even could be tested through actual examples.

Two Odd Numbers	Sum	Validity of Statement
1+1	2 (even)	Valid
1+3	4 (even)	Valid
61+29	90 (even)	Valid
135+47	182 (even)	Valid
253+17	270 (even)	Valid
1,945+2,007	3,952 (even)	Valid
6,321+7,851	14,172 (even)	Valid

Adding two odd numbers always results in a sum that is even. It is a valid argument based on the justifications in the table above.

Consider another example. The statement that a fraction of a fraction can be determined by multiplying the numerator by the numerator and the denominator by the denominator can be proven through logical reasoning. For example, one-half of one-quarter of a candy bar can be found by multiplying ½ x ¼. The answer would be one-eighth. The validity of this argument can be demonstrated as valid with a model.

The entire rectangle represents one whole candy bar. The top half section of the model is shaded in one direction to demonstrate how much of the candy bar remains from the whole candy bar. The left quarter, shaded in a different direction, demonstrates that one-quarter of the candy bar has been given to a friend. Since the whole candy bar is not available to give out, the area that is double-shaded is the fractional part of the ½ candy bar that has been actually given away. That fractional part is one-eighth of the whole candy bar, as shown in both the sketch and the algorithm.

Skill 6.4 Problem analysis

Conditional statements are frequently written in "**if-then**" form. The "if" clause of the conditional is known as the **hypothesis**, and the "then" clause is called the **conclusion**. In a proof, the hypothesis is the information that is assumed to be true, while the conclusion is what is to be proven true. A conditional is considered to be of the form:

> If p, then q
> p is the hypothesis and q is the conclusion.

Conditional statements can be diagrammed using a **Venn diagram**. This is done when a diagram is drawn with one circle inside another circle. The inner circle represents the hypothesis. The outer circle represents the conclusion. If the hypothesis is taken to be true, then you are located inside the inner circle. If you are located in the inner circle then you are also inside the outer circle, so that proves the conclusion is true.

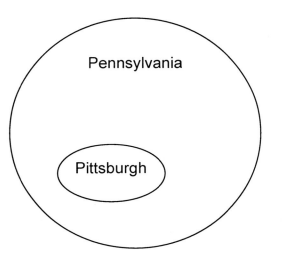

Example:
If you are in Pittsburgh, then you are in Pennsylvania.
In this statement "you are in Pittsburgh" is the hypothesis.
In this statement "you are in Pennsylvania" is the conclusion.

Example:
If an angle has a measure of 90 degrees, then it is a right angle.

In this statement "an angle has a measure of 90 degrees" is the hypothesis.
In this statement "it is a right angle" is the conclusion.

Conditional: If p, then q

p is the hypothesis and q is the conclusion.

Inverse: If ~p, then ~q.

Negate both the hypothesis (If not p) and the conclusion (then not q) from the original conditional.

Converse : If q, then p.

Reverse the two clauses. The original hypothesis (p) becomes the conclusion. The original conclusion (q) then becomes the new hypothesis.

Contrapositive: If ~q, then ~p.

Reverse the two clauses. The original hypothesis (p) becomes the conclusion. The original conclusion (q) then becomes the new hypothesis. THEN negate both the new hypothesis and the new conclusion.

Example:

Given the **conditional**:
If an angle measures 60°, then it is an acute angle.

Its **inverse**, in the form "If ~p, then ~q", would be:
If an angle doesn't measure 60°, then it is not an acute angle
NOTICE that the inverse is not true, even though the conditional statement was true.

Its **converse**, in the form "If q, then p", would be:
If an angle is an acute angle, then it has 60°.
NOTICE that the converse is not necessarily true, even though the conditional statement was true. It is a very common logical mistake to assume that the converse of a given statement is true. There are times (see below) where the converse is true, but in general it does not have to be true.

Its **contrapositive**, in the form "If q, then p", would be:
If an angle isn't an acute angle, then it doesn't have 60°.
NOTICE that the contrapositive is true, assuming the original conditional statement was true.

TIP: If you are asked to pick a statement that is logically equivalent to a given conditional, look for the contrapositive. The inverse and converse are not always logically equivalent to every conditional. The contrapositive is ALWAYS logically equivalent.

Example:

Find the inverse, converse, and contrapositive of the following conditional statement. Also determine if each of the four statements is true or false.

Conditional: If $x = 5$, then $x^2 - 25 = 0$. TRUE

Inverse: If $x \neq 5$, then $x^2 - 25 \neq 0$. FALSE, x could be $^-5$

Converse: If $x^2 - 25 = 0$, then $x = 5$. FALSE, x could be $^-5$

Contrapositive: If $x^2 - 25 \neq 0$, then $x \neq 5$. TRUE

Conditional: If $x = 5$, then $6x = 30$. TRUE

Inverse: If $x \neq 5$, then $6x \neq 30$. TRUE

Converse: If $6x = 30$, then $x = 5$. TRUE

Contrapositive: If $6x \neq 30$, then $x \neq 5$. TRUE

Sometimes, as in this example, all four statements can be logically equivalent; however, the only statement that will always be logically equivalent to the original conditional is the contrapositive.

Conditional statements can also be diagrammed using the Venn diagram.

Suppose that these statements are given to you, and you are asked to try to reach a conclusion. The statements are:

All swimmers are athletes.
All athletes are scholars.

In "if-then" form, these would be:

If you are a swimmer, then you are an athlete.
If you are an athlete, then you are a scholar.

Clearly, if you are a swimmer, then you are also an athlete. This includes you in the group of scholars.

Suppose that these statements are given to you, and you are asked to try to reach a conclusion. The statements are:

> All swimmers are athletes.
> All wrestlers are athletes.

In "if-then" form, these would be:

> If you are a swimmer, then you are an athlete.
> If you are a wrestler, then you are an athlete.

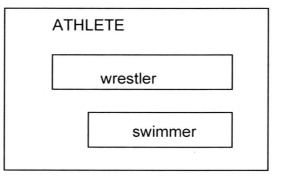

Clearly, if you are a swimmer or a wrestler, then you are also an athlete. This does NOT allow you to come to any other conclusions.

A swimmer may or may NOT also be a wrestler. Therefore, NO CONCLUSION IS POSSIBLE.

Suppose that these statements are given to you, and you are asked to try to reach a conclusion. The statements are:

> All rectangles are parallelograms.
> Quadrilateral ABCD is not a parallelogram.

In "if-then" form, the first statement would be:

> If a figure is a rectangle, then it is also a parallelogram.

The contrapositive of this statement, "if a figure is not a parallelogram, then it is not a rectangle" is also true. So we can conclude in the original question that Quadrilateral ABCD is not a rectangle. Looking at the Venn diagram below, if all rectangles are parallelograms, then rectangles are included as part of the parallelograms. Since quadrilateral ABCD is not a parallelogram, it is excluded from being placed anywhere inside the parallelogram box. This allows you to conclude that ABCD can not be a rectangle either.

```
┌─────────────────────────────┐
│ PARALLELOGRAMS              │    quadrilateral
│   ┌───────────────────┐     │    ABCD
│   │ rectangles        │     │
│   └───────────────────┘     │
└─────────────────────────────┘
```

Try These:

What conclusion, if any, can be reached? Assume each statement is true, regardless of any personal beliefs. (Hint: always create a contrapositive statement from the statement you are given, since you know that the contrapositive statement is always true.)

1. If the Red Sox win the World Series, I will die. I died.

2. If an angle's measure is between 0° and 90°, then the angle is acute. Angle B is not acute.

3. Students who do well in geometry will succeed in college. Annie is doing extremely well in geometry.

4. Left-handed people are witty and charming. You are left-handed.

COMPETENCY 7.0 NUMBER SENSE AND NUMERATION

Skill 7.1 Meaning and use of numbers

In order to effectively solve equations, it is important to acquaint yourself with the definitions of various mathematical terms.

Natural numbers- the counting numbers: 1,2,3...

Whole numbers- the counting numbers along with zero: 0,1,2...

Integers- the counting numbers, their opposites, and zero: ... -1,0,1...

Rationals- all of the fractions that can be formed from the whole numbers. *Zero cannot be the denominator*. In decimal form, these numbers will either be terminating or repeating decimals.

Irrationals- real numbers that cannot be written as a fraction. The decimal forms of these numbers are neither terminating nor repeating: $\pi, e, \sqrt{2}$, etc.

Real numbers- the set of numbers obtained by combining the rationals and irrationals. Complex numbers (i.e., numbers that involve i or $\sqrt{-1}$) are not real numbers.

Skill 7.2 The standard algorithms for the four basic operations

The **Order of Operations** are to be followed when evaluating algebraic expressions. Follow these steps in order:

1. Simplify inside grouping characters such as parentheses, brackets, square root, fraction bar, etc.
2. Multiply out expressions with exponents.
3. Do multiplication or division, from left to right.
4. Do addition or subtraction, from left to right.

Samples of simplifying expressions with exponents:

$$(-2)^3 = -8$$
$$(-2)^4 = 16$$
$$\left(\tfrac{2}{3}\right)^3 = \tfrac{8}{27}$$
$$5^0 = 1$$
$$4^{-1} = \tfrac{1}{4}$$
$$-2^3 = -8$$

Skill 7.3   Appropriate computation strategies and reasonableness of results

Estimation and approximation may be used to check the reasonableness of answers.

Example:
Estimate the answer.

$$\frac{58 \times 810}{1989}$$

58 becomes 60, 810 becomes 800 and 1989 becomes 2000.

$$\frac{60 \times 800}{2000} = 24$$

Word problems: An estimate may sometimes be all that is needed to solve a problem.

Example:
Janet goes into a store to purchase a CD on sale for $13.95. While shopping, she sees two pairs of shoes, prices $19.95 and $14.50. She only has $50. Can she purchase everything, assuming no sales tax?

Solve by rounding:
      $19.95→$20.00
      $14.50→$15.00
      $13.95→$14.00
            $49.00   Yes, she can purchase the CD and the
                          shoes.

Skill 7.4 Methods of mathematical investigation

The unit rate for purchasing an item is its price divided by the number of pounds (or ounces, etc.) in the item. The item with the lower unit rate is the lower price.

Example:
Find the item with the best unit price:

$1.79 for 10 ounces
$1.89 for 12 ounces
$5.49 for 32 ounces

$$\frac{1.79}{10} = .179 \text{ per ounce} \qquad \frac{1.89}{12} = .1575 \text{ per ounce} \qquad \frac{5.49}{32} = .172 \text{ per ounce}$$

$1.89 for 12 ounces is the best price.

A second way to find the better buy is to make a proportion with the price over the number of ounces, etc. Cross multiply the proportion, writing the products above the numerator that is used. The better price will have the smaller product.

Example:
Find the better buy:

$8.19 for 40 pounds or $4.89 for 22 pounds
Find the unit price.

$$\frac{40}{8.19} = \frac{1}{x} \qquad\qquad \frac{22}{4.89} = \frac{1}{x}$$
$$40x = 8.19 \qquad\qquad 22x = 4.89$$
$$x = .20475 \qquad\qquad x = .22\overline{27}$$

Since $.20475 < .22\overline{27}$, $8.19 is less and is a better buy.

To find the amount of sales tax on an item, change the percent of sales tax into an equivalent decimal number. Then multiply the decimal number times the price of the object to find the sales tax. The total cost of an item will be the price of the item plus the sales tax.

Example:
A guitar costs $120 plus 7% sales tax. How much are the sales tax and the total bill?

7% = .07 as a decimal
(.07)(120) = $8.40 sales tax
$120 + $8.40 = $128.40 ← total price

Example:
A suit costs $450 plus 6½% sales tax. How much are the sales tax and the total bill?

6½% = .065 as a decimal
(.065)(450) = $29.25 sales tax
$450 + $29.25 = $479.25 ← total price

Examining the change in area or volume of a given figure requires first to find the existing area given the original dimensions and then the new area given the increased dimensions.

Example:
Given the rectangle below, determine the change in area if the length is increased by 5 and the width is increased by 7.

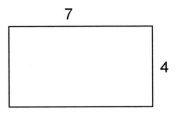

Draw and label a sketch of the new rectangle.

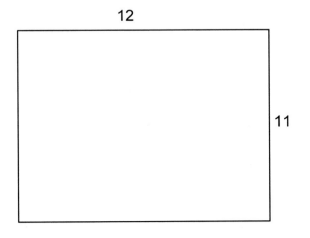

Find the areas.

Area of original = LW   Area of enlarged shape = LW
= (7)(4)   = (12)(11)
= 28 units^2 = 132 units^2

The change in area is 132 − 28 = 104 units^2

Skill 7.5   Number patterns

Arithmetic Sequences

When given a set of numbers where the common difference between the terms is constant, use the following formula:

$a_n = a_1 + (n-1)d$
where a_1 = the first term
n = the nth term (general term)
d = the common difference

<u>Example:</u>
Find the 8th term of the arithmetic sequence 5, 8, 11, 14, ...

$a_n = a_1 + (n-1)d$	
$a_n = 5$	identify the 1st term
$d = 8 - 5 = 3$	find d
$a_n = 5 + (8-1)3$	substitute
$a_n = 26$	

<u>Example:</u>
Given two terms of an arithmetic sequence, find a_1 and d.

$a_4 = 21$	$a_6 = 32$
$a_n = a + (n-1)d$	$a_4 = 21, n = 4$
$21 = a_1 + (4-1)d$	$a_6 = 32, n = 6$
$32 = a_1 + (6-1)d$	

$21 = a_1 + 3d$	solve the system of equations
$32 = a_1 + 5d$	

$21 = a_1 + 3d$	
$\underline{-32 = -a_1 - 5d}$	multiply by -1
$-11 = -2d$	add the equations
$5.5 = d$	

$21 = a_1 + 3(5.5)$	substitute d = 5.5, into one of the equations
$21 = a_1 + 16.5$	
$a_1 = 4.5$	

The sequence begins with 4.5 and has a common difference of 5.5 between numbers.

Geometric Sequences

When using geometric sequences, consecutive numbers are compared to find the common ratio.

$$r = \frac{a_{n+1}}{a_n}$$

where r = common ratio
a = the nth term

The ratio is then used in the geometric sequence formula:
$$a_n = a_1 r^{n-1}$$

Example:
Find the 8th term of the geometric sequence 2, 8, 32, 128 ...

$r = \frac{a_{n+1}}{a_n}$ use common ratio formula to find ratio

$r = 8/2$ substitute $a_n = 2$ $a_{n+1} = 8$
$r = 4$

$a_n = a_1 \times r^{n-1}$ use r = 4 to solve for the 8th term
$a_n = 2 \times 4^{8-1}$
$a_n = 32,768$

Skill 7.6   Place value

Decimals = deci = part of ten. To find the decimal equivalent of a fraction, use the denominator to divide the numerator as shown in the following example.

Example:

Find the decimal equivalent of $\frac{7}{10}$.

Since 10 cannot divide into 7 evenly,

$$\frac{7}{10} = 0.7$$

A number in standard form is represented by a number of digits separated by a decimal point. Each digit to the left of the decimal point increases progressively in powers of ten. Each digit to the right of the decimal point decreases progressively in powers of ten.

Example:
12345.6789 occupies the following powers of ten positions:

$$10^4 \quad 10^3 \quad 10^2 \quad 10^1 \quad 10^0 \quad . \quad 10^{-1} \quad 10^{-2} \quad 10^{-3} \quad 10^{-4}$$
$$1 \qquad 2 \qquad 3 \qquad 4 \qquad 5 \qquad . \qquad 6 \qquad 7 \qquad 8 \qquad 9$$

Names of power-of-ten positions:

10^0 = ones (note that any **non-zero** base raised to power zero is 1)

10^1 = tens   (number 1 and 1 zero or 10)

10^2 = hundred   (number 1 and 2 zeros or 100)

10^3 = thousand   (number 1 and 3 zeros or 1000)

10^4 = ten thousand   (number 1 and 4 zeros or 10000)

$10^{-1} = \dfrac{1}{10^1} = \dfrac{1}{10}$ = tenths   (1st digit after decimal point or 0.1)

$10^{-2} = \dfrac{1}{10^2} = \dfrac{1}{100}$ = hundredth   (2nd digit after decimal point or 0.01)

$10^{-3} = \dfrac{1}{10^3} = \dfrac{1}{1000}$ = thousandth   (3rd digit after decimal point or 0.001)

$10^{-4} = \dfrac{1}{10^4} = \dfrac{1}{10000}$ = ten thousandth   (4th digit after decimal point or 0.0001)

Example:
Write 73169.00537 in expanded form.

We start by listing all the powers of ten positions.

$$10^4 \quad 10^3 \quad 10^2 \quad 10^1 \quad 10^0 \quad . \quad 10^{-1} \quad 10^{-2} \quad 10^{-3} \quad 10^{-4} \quad 10^{-5}$$

Multiply each digit by its power of ten. Add all the results.

Thus $73169.00537 = (7 \times 10^4) + (3 \times 10^3) + (1 \times 10^2) + (6 \times 10^1)$
$$+ (9 \times 10^0) + (0 \times 10^{-1}) + (0 \times 10^{-2}) + (5 \times 10^{-3})$$
$$+ (3 \times 10^{-4}) + (7 \times 10^{-5})$$

Example:
Determine the place value associated with the underlined digit in 3.16$\underline{9}$5.

$$
\begin{array}{ccccc}
10^0 & . & 10^{-1} & 10^{-2} & 10^{-3} & 10^{-4} \\
3 & . & 1 & 6 & 9 & 5
\end{array}
$$

The place value for the digit 9 is 10^{-3} or $\dfrac{1}{1000}$.

Example:
Find the number that is represented by

$$(7 \times 10^3) + (5 \times 10^0) + (3 \times 10^{-3}).$$
$$= 7000 + 5 + 0.003$$
$$= 7005.003$$

Example:
Write 21×10^3 in standard form.

$$= 21 \times 1000 = 21{,}000$$

Example:
Write 739×10^{-4} in standard form.

$$= 739 \times \frac{1}{10000} = \frac{739}{10000} = 0.0739$$

Skill 7.7   Equivalence

COMMON EQUIVALENTS

$$
\begin{aligned}
&= 0.5 &&= 50\% \\
&= 0.33 &&= 33\% \\
&= 0.25 &&= 25\% \\
&= 0.2 &&= 20\% \\
&= 0.16 &&= 16\% \\
&= 0.12 &&= 12\% \\
&= 0.1 &&= 10\% \\
&= 0.66 &&= 66\% \\
&= 0.83 &&= 83\% \\
&= 0.37 &&= 37\% \\
&= 0.62 &&= 62\% \\
&= 0.87 &&= 87\% \\
1 &= 1.0 &&= 100\%
\end{aligned}
$$

Skill 7.8   Factors and multiples

GCF is the abbreviation for the **greatest common factor**. The GCF is the largest number that is a factor of all the numbers given in a problem. The GCF can be no larger than the smallest number given in the problem. If no other number is a common factor, then the GCF will be the number 1.

To find the GCF, list all possible factors of the smallest number given (include the number itself). Starting with the largest factor (which is the number itself), determine if it is also a factor of all the other given numbers. If so, that is the GCF. If that factor doesn't work, try the same method on the next smaller factor. Continue until a common factor is found. That is the GCF.

Note: There can be other common factors besides the GCF.

Example:
Find the GCF of 12, 20, and 36.

The smallest number in the problem is 12. The factors of 12 are 1,2,3,4,6, and 12. 12 is the largest factor, but it does not divide evenly into 20. Neither does 6, but 4 will divide into both 20 and 36 evenly. Therefore, 4 is the GCF.

Example:
Find the GCF of 14 and 15.

Factors of 14 are 1,2,7, and 14. 14 is the largest factor, but it does not divide evenly into 15. Neither does 7 or 2. Therefore, the only factor common to both 14 and 15 is the number 1, the GCF.

LCM is the abbreviation for **least common multiple**. The least common multiple of a group of numbers is the smallest number that all of the given numbers will divide into. The least common multiple will always be the largest of the given numbers or a multiple of the largest number.

Example:
Find the LCM of 20, 30, and 40.

The largest number given is 40, but 30 will not divide evenly into 40. The next multiple of 40 is 80 (2 x 40), but 30 will not divide evenly into 80 either. The next multiple of 40 is 120. 120 is divisible by both 20 and 30, so 120 is the LCM (least common multiple).

Example:
Find the LCM of 96, 16, and 24.

The largest number is 96. 96 is divisible by both 16 and 24, so 96 is the LCM.

Skill 7.9   Ratio, proportion, percent

Proportions can be used to solve word problems whenever relationships are compared. Some situations include scale drawings and maps, similar polygons, speed, time and distance, cost, and comparison shopping.

Example:
Which is the better buy, 6 items for $1.29 or 8 items for $1.69?

Find the unit price.

=	=
6x = 1.29	8x = 1.69
x = 0.215	x = 0.21125

Thus, 8 items for $1.69 is the better buy.

Example:
A car travels 125 miles in 2.5 hours. How far will it go in 6 hours?

Write a proportion comparing the distance and time.

Let x represent distance in miles. Then,

$$\frac{125}{2.5} = \frac{x}{6}$$ set up the proportion

$2.5x = 6 \cdot 125$ cross-multiply

$2.5x = 750$ simplify

$x = {}^{750}\!/_{2.5}$ divide both sides of the equation by 2.5

$x = 300 \text{ miles}$ simplify

Example:
The scale on a map is inch = 6 miles. What is the actual distance between two cities if they are 2 inches apart on the map?

Write a proportion comparing the scale to the actual distance.

	scale	actual
$x =$	1	× 6
$x =$		6
$2x =$		12

Thus, the actual distance between the cities is 12 miles.

Word problems involving percents can be solved by writing the problem as an equation, then solving the equation. Keep in mind that **"of" means "multiplication"** and **"is" means "equals."**

Example:
The Ski Club has 85 members. 80% of the members are able to attend the meeting. How many members attend the meeting?

Restate the problem.	What is 80% of 85?
Write an equation.	$n = 0.8 \times 85$
Solve.	$n = 68$

Sixty-eight members attend the meeting.

Example:
There are 64 dogs in the kennel. 48 are collies. What percent are collies?

Restate the problem.	48 is what percent of 64?
Write an equation.	$48 = n \times 64$
Solve.	$48 \div 64 = n$
	$n = 75\%$

75% of the dogs are collies.

Example:
The auditorium was filled to 90% capacity. There were 558 seats occupied. What is the capacity of the auditorium?

Restate the problem.	90% of what number is 558?
Write an equation.	$0.9n = 558$
Solve.	$n = {}^{558}/_{.09}$
	$n = 620$

The capacity of the auditorium is 620 people.

Example:
Shoes cost $42.00. Sales tax is 6%. What is the total cost of the shoes?

Restate the problem.	What is 6% of 42?
Write an equation.	$n = 0.06 \times 42$
Solve.	$n = 2.52$
Add the sales tax.	$42.00 + $2.52 = $44.52

The total cost of the shoes, including sales tax, is $44.52.

Skill 7.10   Representations

Mathematical operations include addition, subtraction, multiplication, and division.

Addition can be indicated by the expressions: sum, greater than, and, more than, increased by, added to.

Subtraction can be expressed by: difference, fewer than, minus, less than, decreased by.

Multiplication is shown by: product, times, multiplied by, twice.

Division is used for: quotient, divided by, ratio.

Examples:

7 added to a number	$n + 7$
a number decreased by 8	$n - 8$
12 times a number divided by 7	$12n \div 7$
28 less than a number	$n - 28$
4 times the sum of a number and 21	$4(n + 21)$

Mathematical operations can be shown using manipulatives, or drawings.

Multiplication can be shown using arrays.

3×4 □ □ □ □
         □ □ □ □
         □ □ □ □

Addition and subtractions can be demonstrated with symbols.

$\psi\ \psi\ \psi\ \xi\ \xi\ \xi\ \xi$
$3 + 4 = 7$
$7 - 3 = 4$

Fractions can be clarified using pattern blocks, fraction bars, or paper folding.

To read a bar graph or a pictograph, read the explanation of the scale that was used in the legend. Compare the length of each bar with the dimensions on the axes and calculate the value each bar represents. On a pictograph, count the number of pictures used in the chart and calculate the value of all the pictures.

To read a circle graph, find the total of the amounts represented on the entire circle graph. To determine the actual amount that each sector of the graph represents, multiply the percent in a sector times the total amount number.

To read a chart, read the row and column headings on the table. Use this information to evaluate the given information in the chart.

Skill 7.11   Calculator strategies

Calculators are important tools. They should be encouraged in the classroom and at home. They do not replace basic knowledge, but they can relieve the tedium of mathematical computations, assuming that the requisite basic knowledge is already present. This allows students to follow more challenging mathematical directions.

Students will be able to use calculators more intelligently if they are taught how. Students need to always check their work by estimating. The goal of mathematics is to prepare the child to survive in the real world, and technology is a reality in today's society.

Skill 7.12   Number lines

The absolute value of a number is the distance between that number and zero on a number line. Use the symbol $|\ |$ for absolute value.

Example:

$|3| = 3$

$|^-4| = 4$

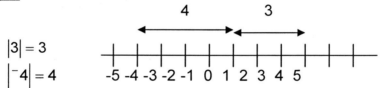

Compare 15 and 20 on the number line.

Since 20 is further away from the zero than 15 is, 20 is greater than 15, or $20 > 15$.

COMPETENCY 8.0   ALGEBRAIC CONCEPTS

Skill 8.1   Algebraic methods and representations

A relationship between two quantities can be shown using a table, graph or rule. In this example, the rule $y = 9x$ describes the relationship between the total amount earned, y, and the total amount of $9 sunglasses sold, x.

A table using this data would appear as:

number of sunglasses sold	1	5	10	15
total dollars earned	9	45	90	135

Each *(x,y)* relationship between a pair of values is called the **coordinate pair**, and can be plotted on a graph. The coordinate pairs *(1,9)*, *(5,45)*, *(10,90)*, and *(15,135)*, are plotted on the graph below.

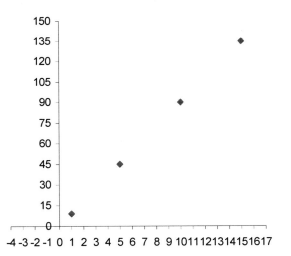

The graph above shows a linear relationship. A **linear relationship** is one in which two quantities are proportional to each other. Doubling *x* also doubles *y*. On a graph, a straight line depicts a linear relationship.

Another type of relationship is a **nonlinear relationship**. This is one in which change in one quantity does not affect the other quantity to the same extent. Nonlinear graphs have a curved line, such as the graph below.

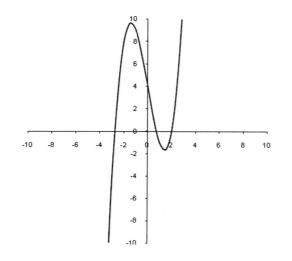

Skill 8.2   Associative, commutative, and distributive properties

Field Properties

Real numbers exhibit the following addition and multiplication properties, where *a, b*, and *c* are real numbers.

Note: Multiplication is implied when there is no symbol between two variables. Thus, *a* × *b* can be depicted as *ab*. Multiplication can also be indicated by a raised dot ·

Closure
a + *b* is a real number

Example:
Since 2 and 5 are both real numbers, 7 is also a real number.

ab is a real number

Example:
Since 3 and 4 are both real numbers, 12 is also a real number.

The sum or product of two real numbers is a real number.

Denseness
Between any pair of rational numbers, there is at least one rational number. The set of natural numbers is <u>not</u> dense because between two consecutive natural numbers, there may not exist another natural number.

Example:
Between 7.6 and 7.7, there is the rational number 7.65 in the set of real numbers.

Between 3 and 4 there exists no other natural number.

Commutative
$a + b = b + a$

Example:
5 + ¯8 = ¯8 + 5 = ¯3

$ab = ba$

Example:
¯2 × 6 = 6 × ¯2 = ¯12

The order of the addends or factors does not affect the sum or product.

Associative
$(a + b) + c = a + (b + c)$

Example:
(¯2 + 7) + 5 = ¯2 + (7 + 5)
5 + 5 = ¯2 + 12 = 10

$(ab) \, c = a \, (bc)$

Example:
(3 × ¯7) × 5 = 3 × (¯7 × 5)
¯21 ×5 = 3 × ¯35 = ¯105

The grouping of the addends or factors does not affect the sum or product.

Distributive

$a (b + c) = ab + ac$

Example:
$6 \times (\ ^-4 + 9) = (6 \times\ ^-4) + (6 \times 9)$
$6 \times 5 =\ ^-24 + 54 = 30$

To multiply a sum by a number, multiply each addend by the number, then add the products.

Skill 8.3   Additive and multiplicative inverses

Additive Identity (Property of Zero)
$a + 0 = a$

Example:
$17 + 0 = 17$

The sum of any number and zero is that number.

Multiplicative Identity (Property of One)
$a \cdot 1 = a$

Example:
$^-34 \times 1 =\ ^-34$

The product of any number and one is that number.

Additive Inverse (Property of Opposites)
$a +\ ^-a = 0$

Example:
$25 +\ ^-25 = 0$

The sum of any number and its opposite is zero.

Multiplicative Inverse (Property of Reciprocals)
$a \times \frac{1}{a} = 1$

Example:
$5 \times \frac{1}{5} = 1$

The product of any number and its reciprocal is one.

Skill 8.4   Function Machines

The function or relationship between two quantities may be analyzed to determine how one quantity depends on the other. For example, the function below shows a relationship between y and x:

$$y=2x+1$$

The relationship between two or more variables can be analyzed using a table, graph, written description, or symbolic rule. The function, $y=2x+1$, is written as a symbolic rule. The same relationship is also shown in the table below:

x	0	2	3	6	9
y	1	5	7	13	19

A relationship could be written in words by saying "the value of y is equal to two times the value of x, plus one." This relationship could be shown on a graph by plotting given points, such as the ones shown in the table above.

Another way to describe a function is as a process in which one or more numbers are input into an imaginary machine that produces another number as the output. If 5 is input, (x), into a machine with a process of x +1, the output, (y), will equal 6.

In real situations, relationships can be described mathematically. The function, $y=x+1$, can be used to describe the idea that people age one year on their birthdays. To describe the relationship in which a person's monthly medical costs are 6 times a person's age, we could write $y=6x$. The monthly cost of medical care could be predicted using this function. A 20 year-old person would spend $120 per month (120=20*6). An 80 year-old person would spend $480 per month (480=80*6). Therefore, one could analyze the relationship to say: as you get older, medical costs increase $6.00 each year.

Skill 8.5   Properties of zero

o   *See Skills 8.2 and 8.3*

Skill 8.6   Equalities and inequalities, patterns, and algebraic formulas

Word problems can sometimes be solved by using a system of two equations in two unknowns. This system can then be solved using substitution, the addition-subtraction method, or graphing.

Example:
Mrs. Winters bought 4 dresses and 6 pairs of shoes for $340. Mrs. Summers went to the same store and bought 3 dresses and 8 pairs of shoes for $360. If all the dresses were the same price and all the shoes were the same price, find the price charged for a dress and for a pair of shoes.

Let x = price of a dress
Let y = price of a pair of shoes

Mrs. Winters' equation would be: $4x + 6y = 340$
Mrs. Summers' equation would be: $3x + 8y = 360$

To solve by addition-subtraction:

Multiply the first equation by 4: $4(4x + 6y = 340)$
Multiply the other equation by $^-3$: $^-3(3x + 8y = 360)$

By doing this, the equations can be added to each other to eliminate one variable and to solve for the other variable.

$$16x + 24y = 1360$$
$$\underline{-9x - 24y = {}^-1080}$$
$$7x = 280$$
$$x = 40 \leftarrow \text{the price of a dress was \$40}$$

solving for y, $y = 30$ $\leftarrow$ the price of a pair of shoes, $30

Example:
Aardvark Taxi charges $4 initially plus $1 for every mile traveled. Baboon Taxi charges $6 initially plus $.75 for every mile traveled. Determine when it is cheaper to ride with Aardvark Taxi or to ride with Baboon Taxi.

Aardvark Taxi's equation:	$y = 1x + 4$
Baboon Taxi's equation :	$y = .75x + 6$
Using substitution:	$.75x + 6 = x + 4$
Multiplying by 4:	$3x + 24 = 4x + 16$
Solving for x :	$8 = x$

This tells you that at 8 miles, the total charge for the two companies is the same. If you compare the charge for 1 mile, Aardvark charges $5 and Baboon charges $6.75. Therefore, Aardvark is cheaper for distances up to 8 miles, but Baboon Taxi is cheaper for distances greater than 8 miles.

This problem can also be solved by graphing the 2 equations.

$$y = 1x + 4 \qquad\qquad y = .75x + 6$$

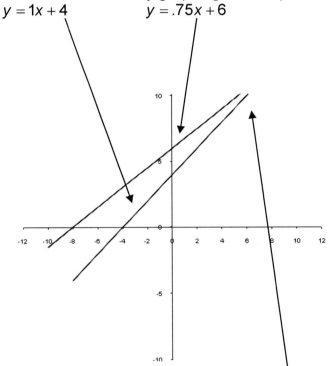

The lines intersect at (8, 12); therefore at 8 miles, both companies charge $12. At values of less than 8 miles, Aardvark Taxi charges less (the graph is below Baboon). Greater than 8 miles, Aardvark charges more (the graph is above Baboon).

Some word problems can be solved using a system of equations or inequalities. Watch for words like greater than, less than, at least, or no more than, as they indicate the need for inequalities.

Example:
The YMCA wants to sell raffle tickets to raise at least $32,000. If they must pay $7,250 in expenses and prizes out of the money collected from the tickets, how many tickets worth $25 each must they sell?

Since they want to raise **at least $32,000**, that means they would be happy to get 32,000 **or more**. This requires an inequality.

Let x = number of tickets sold
Then $25x$ = total money collected for x tickets

Total money minus expenses is greater than $32,000.

$$25x - 7250 \geq 32000$$
$$25x \geq 39250$$
$$x \geq 1570$$

If they sell **1,570 tickets or more**, they will raise AT LEAST $32,000.

Example:
The Simpsons went out for dinner. All 4 of them ordered the aardvark steak dinner. Bert paid for the 4 meals and included a tip of $12 for a total of $84.60. How much was an aardvark steak dinner?

Let x = the price of one aardvark dinner.
So $4x$ = the price of 4 aardvark dinners.
$$4x + 12 = 84.60$$
$$4x = 72.60$$
$$x = \$18.50 \text{ for each dinner.}$$

Example:
Sharon's Bike Shoppe can assemble a 3 speed bike in 30 minutes or a 10 speed bike in 60 minutes. The profit on each bike sold is $60 for a 3 speed or $75 for a 10 speed bike. How many of each type of bike should they assemble during an 8 hour day (480 minutes) to make the maximum profit? Total daily profit must be at least $300.

Let $x =$ number of 3 speed bikes.
$y =$ number of 10 speed bikes.

Since there are only 480 minutes to use each day,
$30x + 60y \leq 480$ is the first inequality.

Since the total daily profit must be at least $300,
$60x + 75y \geq 300$ is the second inequality.

$32x + 65y \leq 480$ solves to $y \leq 8 - 1/2\,x$
$60x + 75y \geq 300$ solves to $y \geq 4 - 4/5\,x$

Graph these two inequalities:

$y \leq 8 - 1/2\,x$
$y \geq 4 - 4/5\,x$

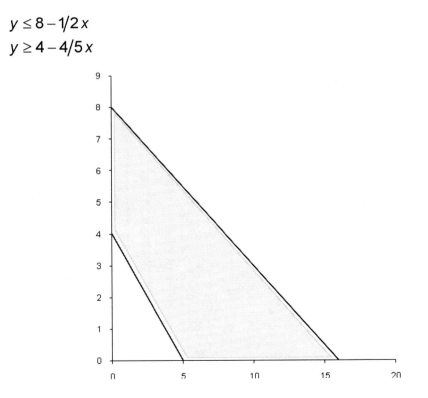

Realize that $x \geq 0$ and $y \geq 0$, since the number of bikes assembled can not be a negative number. Graph these as additional constraints on the problem.

The number of bikes assembled must always be an integer value, so points within the shaded area of the graph must have integer values. The maximum profit will occur at or near a corner of the shaded portion of this graph. Those points occur at (0,4), (0,8), (16,0), or (5,0).

Since profits are $60/3-speed or $75/10-speed, the profit would be :

$(0,4)$ $60(0) + 75(4) = 300$

$(0,8)$ $60(0) + 75(8) = 600$

$(16,0)$ $60(16) + 75(0) = 960 \leftarrow$ Maximum profit

$(5,0)$ $60(5) + 75(0) = 300$

The maximum profit would occur if 16 3-speed bikes are made daily.

COMPETENCY 9.0   INFORMAL GEOMETRY AND MEASUREMENT

Skill 9.1   Pure and real-world properties and relationships in figures and shapes in two and three dimensions

We refer to three-dimensional figures in geometry as **solids**. A solid is the union of all points on a simple closed surface and all points in its interior. A **polyhedron** is a simple closed surface formed from planar polygonal regions. Each polygonal region is called a **face** of the polyhedron. The vertices and edges of the polygonal regions are called the **vertices** and **edges** of the polyhedron.

We may form a cube from three congruent squares. However, if we tried to put four squares about a single vertex, their interior angle measures would add up to 360° (i.e., four edge-to-edge squares with a common vertex lie in a common plane and therefore cannot form a corner figure of a regular polyhedron).

There are five ways to form corner figures with congruent regular polygons:

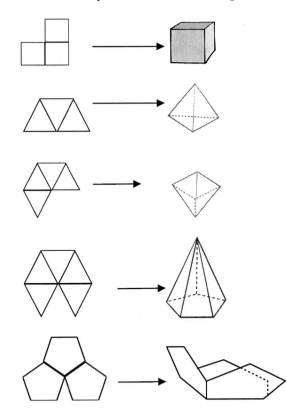

In order to represent three-dimensional figures, we need three coordinate axes (X, Y, and Z) that are all mutually perpendicular to each other. Since we cannot draw three mutually perpendicular axes on a two-dimensional surface, we use oblique representations.

Example:
Represent a cube with sides of 2.

We draw three sides along the three axes to make things easier.

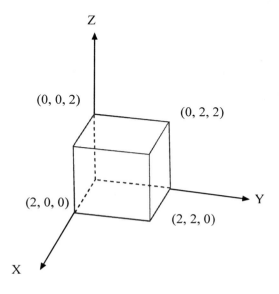

Each point has three coordinates (x, y, z).

Skill 9.2   Pythagorean theorem

The Pythagorean theorem states that *in a right triangle*, the square of the length of the hypotenuse is equal to the sum of the squares of the lengths of the legs. Symbolically, this is stated as:

$$c^2 = a^2 + b^2$$

Given the right triangle below, find the missing side.

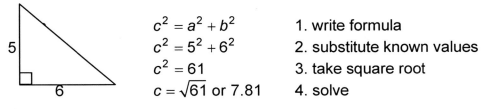

$c^2 = a^2 + b^2$	1. write formula
$c^2 = 5^2 + 6^2$	2. substitute known values
$c^2 = 61$	3. take square root
$c = \sqrt{61}$ or 7.81	4. solve

The converse of the Pythagorean theorem states that if the square of one side of a triangle is equal to the sum of the squares of the other two sides, then the triangle is a right triangle.

Example:
Given $\triangle XYZ$, with sides measuring 12, 16, and 20 cm, determine if this a right triangle.

$$c^2 = a^2 + b^2$$
$$20^2 \: ? \: 12^2 + 16^2$$
$$400 \: ? \: 144 + 256$$
$$400 = 400$$

Yes, the triangle is a right triangle.

This theorem can be expanded to determine if triangles are obtuse or acute.

If the square of the longest side of a triangle is greater than the sum of the squares of the other two sides, then the triangle is an obtuse triangle.
and
If the square of the longest side of a triangle is less than the sum of the squares of the other two sides, then the triangle is an acute triangle.

Example:

Given $\triangle LMN$ with sides measuring 7, 12, and 14 inches, is the triangle right, acute, or obtuse?

$$14^2 \ ? \ 7^2 + 12^2$$
$$196 \ ? \ 49 + 144$$
$$196 > 193$$

Therefore, the triangle is obtuse.

Real-World Example:

Find the area and perimeter of a rectangle if its length is 12 inches and its diagonal is 15 inches.

1. Draw and label sketch.
2. Since the height is still needed find the missing leg of the triangle

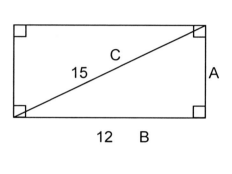

$$A^2 + B^2 = C^2$$
$$A^2 + 12^2 = 15^2$$
$$A^2 = 15^2 - 12^2$$
$$A^2 = 81$$
$$A = 9$$

Now use this information to find the area and perimeter.

$A = LW$	$P = 2(L + W)$	1. write formula
$A = (12)(9)$	$P = 2(12 + 9)$	2. substitute
$A = 108 \text{ in}^2$	$P = 42 \text{ inches}$	3. solve

<u>Real-World Example:</u>
Given the figure below, find the area by dividing the polygon into smaller shapes.

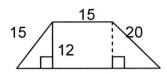

1. divide the figure into two triangles and a rectangle

2. find the missing lengths

3. find the area of each part

4. find the sum of all areas

Find base of both right triangles using Pythagorean formula:

$$a^2 + b^2 = c^2$$
$$a^2 + 12^2 = 15^2$$
$$a^2 = 225 - 144$$
$$a^2 = 81$$
$$a = 9$$

$$a^2 + b^2 = c^2$$
$$a^2 + 12^2 = 20^2$$
$$a^2 = 400 - 144$$
$$a^2 = 256$$
$$a = 16$$

Area of triangle 1   Area of triangle 2   Area of rectangle

$$A = \frac{1}{2}bh$$
$$A = \frac{1}{2}(9)(12)$$
$$A = 54 \text{ sq. units}$$

$$A = \frac{1}{2}bh$$
$$A = \frac{1}{2}(16)(12)$$
$$A = 96 \text{ sq. units}$$

$$A = LW$$
$$A = (15)(12)$$
$$A = 180 \text{ sq. units}$$

Find the sum of all three figures.

$$54 + 96 + 180 = 330 \text{ square units}$$

Given the special right triangles below, we can find the lengths of other special right triangles.

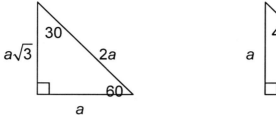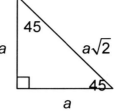

Sample problems:

1.

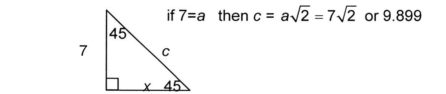

if $8 = a\sqrt{2}$ then $a = 8/\sqrt{2}$ or 5.657

2.

if $7 = a$ then $c = a\sqrt{2} = 7\sqrt{2}$ or 9.899

3.

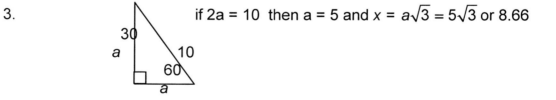

if $2a = 10$ then $a = 5$ and $x = a\sqrt{3} = 5\sqrt{3}$ or 8.66

Skill 9.3   Transformations

A **transformation** is a change in the position, shape, or size of a geometric figure. **Transformational geometry** is the study of manipulating objects by flipping, twisting, turning, and scaling them. **Symmetry** is exact similarity between two parts or halves, as if one were a mirror image of the other.

A **translation** is a transformation that "slides" an object a fixed distance in a given direction. The original object and its translation have the same shape, the same size, and they face in the same direction.

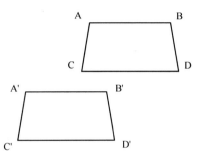

An example of a translation in architecture would be stadium seating. The seats are the same size, the same shape, and they face in the same direction.

A **rotation** is a transformation that turns a figure about a fixed point called the center of rotation. An object and its rotation are the same shape and size, but the figures may be turned in different directions. Rotations can occur in either a clockwise or a counterclockwise direction.

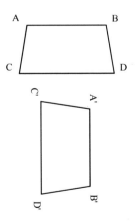

Rotations can often be seen in wallpaper and art. A Ferris wheel is an example of rotation.

An object and its **reflection** have the same shape and size, but the figures face in opposite directions.

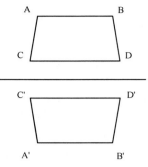

The line (where a mirror may be placed) is called the **line of reflection**. The distance from a point to the line of reflection is the same as the distance from the point's image to the line of reflection.

A **glide reflection** is a combination of a reflection and a translation.

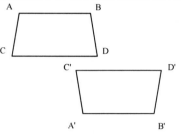

Another type of transformation is **dilation**. Dilation is a transformation that "shrinks" an object or makes it bigger.

<u>Example:</u>
Use dilation to transform a diagram.

Starting with a triangle whose center of dilation is point P,

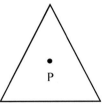

we dilate the lengths of the sides by the same factor to create a new triangle.

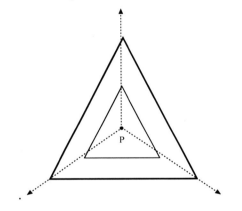

Skill 9.4   Geometric models

Tessellations

A **tessellation** is an arrangement of closed shapes that completely covers the plane without overlapping or leaving gaps. Unlike **tilings**, tessellations do not require the use of regular polygons. In art, the term is used to refer to pictures or tiles—mostly in the form of animals and other life forms—that cover the surface of a plane in a symmetrical way without overlapping or leaving gaps. M. C. Escher is known as the "father" of modern tessellations. Tessellations are used for tiling, mosaics, quilts, and art.

If you look at a completed tessellation, you will see that the original motif repeats in a pattern. There are seventeen possible ways that a pattern can be used to tile a flat surface or "wallpaper."

The tessellation below is a combination of the four types of transformational symmetry we have discussed:

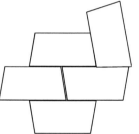

Three Dimensional Figures

When creating a three-dimensional figure, if we know any two values of the vertices, faces, and edges, we can find the remaining value by using **Euler's Formula**: $V + F = E + 2$.

For example:

We want to create a pentagonal pyramid, and we know it has six vertices and six faces. Using Euler's Formula, we compute:

$$V + F = E + 2$$
$$6 + 6 = E + 2$$
$$12 = E + 2$$
$$10 = E$$

Thus, we know that our figure should have 10 edges.

Skill 9.5   Nets

The union of all points on a simple closed surface and all points in its interior form a space figure called a **solid**. The five regular solids, or **polyhedra**, are the cube, tetrahedron, octahedron, icosahedron, and dodecahedron. A **net** is a two-dimensional figure that can be cut out and folded up to make a three-dimensional solid. Below are models of the five regular solids with their corresponding face polygons and nets.

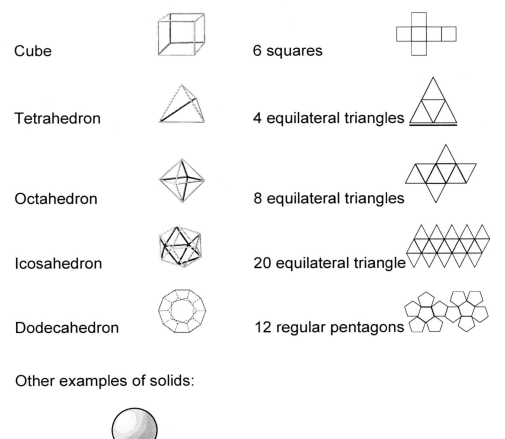

Cube   6 squares

Tetrahedron   4 equilateral triangles

Octahedron   8 equilateral triangles

Icosahedron   20 equilateral triangle

Dodecahedron   12 regular pentagons

Other examples of solids:

Sphere

Cone

Skill 9.6   Standard Units of Measurement

"When you can measure what you are speaking about and express it in numbers, you know something about it; but when you cannot measure it, when you cannot express it in numbers, your knowledge is of a meager and unsatisfactory kind." ----Lord Kelvin

Non-standard units of measurement are sometimes used when standard instruments might not be available. For example, students might measure the length of a room by their arm-spans. An inch originated as the length of three barley grains placed end to end. Seeds or stones might be used for measuring weight. In fact, our current "carat," used for measuring precious gems, was derived from carob seeds. In ancient times, baskets, jars, and bowls were used to measure capacity.

To estimate measurement of familiar objects, it is first necessary to determine the units to be used.

Examples:

Length
1. The coastline of Florida   miles or kilometers
2. The width of a ribbon   inches or millimeters
3. The thickness of a book   inches or centimeters
4. The length of a football field yards or meters
5. The depth of water in a pool   feet or meters

Weight or mass
1. A bag of sugar   pounds or grams
2. A school bus   tons or kilograms
3. A dime   ounces or grams

Capacity
1. Paint to paint a bedroom   gallons or liters
2. Glass of milk   cups or liters
3. Bottle of soda   quarts or liters
4. Medicine for child   ounces or milliliters

It is necessary to be familiar with the metric and customary system in order to estimate measurements.

Some common equivalents include:

ITEM	APPROXIMATELY EQUAL TO	
	METRIC	IMPERIAL
large paper clip	1 gram	0.1 ounce
	1 quart	1 liter
average sized man	75 kilograms	170 pounds
	1 yard	1 meter
math textbook	1 kilogram	2 pounds
	1 mile	1 kilometer
	1 foot	30 centimeters
thickness of a dime	1 millimeter	0.1 inches

Estimate the measurement of the following items:

the length of an adult cow = _____ meters
the thickness of a compact disc = _____ millimeters
your height = _____ meters
length of your nose = _____ centimeters
weight of your math textbook = _____ kilograms
weight of an automobile = _____ kilograms
weight of an aspirin = _____ grams

The units of **length** in the customary system are inches, feet, yards and miles.

> 12 inches (in.) = 1 foot (ft.)
> 36 in. = 1 yard (yd.)
> 3 ft. = 1 yd.
> 5280 ft. = 1 mile (mi.)
> 1760 yd. = 1 mi.

To change from a **larger unit to a smaller unit, multiply**.
To change from a **smaller unit to a larger unit, divide**.

Example:
    4 mi. = _____ yd.
    Since 1760 yd. = 1 mile, multiply 4 × 1760 = 7040 yd.

Example:
    21 in. = _____ ft.
    21 ÷ 12 = 1.75 ft. (or 1 foot and 9 inches)

The units of **weight** are ounces, pounds, and tons.

> 16 ounces (oz.) = 1 pound (lb.)
> 2,000 lb. = 1 ton (T.)

Example:

2 T. = _____ lb

2 × 2,000 = 4,000 lb.

The units of **capacity** are fluid ounces, cups, pints, quarts, and gallons.

> 8 fluid ounces (fl. oz.) = 1 cup (c.)
> 2 c. = 1 pint (pt.)
> 4 c. = 1 quart (qt.)
> 2 pt. = 1 qt.
> 4 qt. = 1 gallon (gal.)

Example:

3 gal. = _____ qt.

3 × 4 = 12 qt.

Example:

1 cups = _____ oz.

1 × 8 = 8 oz.

Example:

7 c. = _____ pt.

7 ÷ 2 = 3.5 pt.

Square units can be derived with knowledge of basic units of length by squaring the equivalent measurements.

> 1 square foot (sq. ft.) = 144 sq. in.
> 1 sq. yd. = 9 sq. ft.
> 1 sq. yd. = 1296 sq. in.

Example:

14 sq. yd. = _____ sq. ft.

14 × 9 = 126 sq. ft.

Metric Units

The metric system is based on multiples of <u>ten</u>. Conversions are made by simply moving the decimal point to the left or right.

kilo-   1000   thousands
hecto-   100   hundreds
deca-   10   tens
unit
deci-   .1   tenths
centi-   .01   hundredths
milli-   .001   thousandths

The basic unit for **length** is the meter.
The basic unit for **weight** or mass is the gram.
The basic unit for **volume** is the liter.

These are the most commonly used units.

1 m = 100 cm	1000 mL= 1 L	1000 mg = 1 g
1 m = 1000 mm	1 kL = 1000 L	1 kg = 1000 g
1 cm = 10 mm		
1000 m = 1 km		

The prefixes are commonly listed from left to right for ease in conversion.

k h da U d c m

<u>Example:</u>

63 km = _____ m

Since there are 3 steps from <u>K</u>ilo to <u>U</u>nit, move the decimal point 3 places to the right.

63 km = 63,000 m

<u>Example:</u>

14 mL = _____ L

Since there are 3 steps from <u>M</u>illi to <u>U</u>nit, move the decimal point 3 places to the left.

14 mL = 0.014 L

<u>Example:</u>

56.4 cm = _____ mm
56.4 cm = 564 mm

<u>Example:</u>

$$9.1 \text{ m} = \underline{\hspace{2cm}} \text{ km}$$
$$9.1 \text{ m} = 0.091 \text{ km}$$

<u>Example:</u>

$$75 \text{ kg} = \underline{\hspace{2cm}} \text{g}$$
$$75 \text{ kg} = 75{,}000 \text{g}$$

The distance around a circle is the **circumference**. The ratio of the circumference to the diameter is represented by the Greek letter pi. π ~ 3.14 ~.

The circumference of a circle is found by the formula C = 2Πr or C = Πd, where r is the radius of the circle and d is the diameter.

The **area** of a circle is found by the formula A = Πr².

<u>Example:</u>
Find the circumference and area of a circle whose radius is 7 meters.

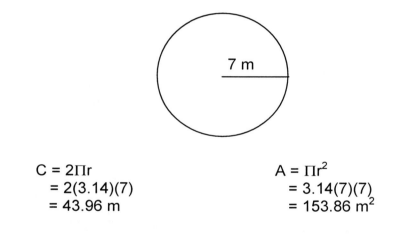

C = 2Πr
  = 2(3.14)(7)
  = 43.96 m

A = Πr²
  = 3.14(7)(7)
  = 153.86 m²

You can also compute the area remaining when sections are cut out of a given figure composed of triangles, squares, rectangles, parallelograms, trapezoids, or circles. The strategy for solving problems of this nature should be to identify the given shapes and choose the correct formulas. Subtract the smaller cut out shape from the larger shape.

<u>Example:</u>
Find the area of one side of the metal in the circular flat washer shown below:

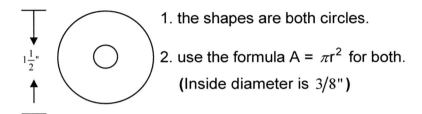

1. the shapes are both circles.

2. use the formula $A = \pi r^2$ for both.

(Inside diameter is $3/8"$)

Area of larger circle   Area of smaller circle

$A = \pi r^2$ $A = \pi r^2$
$A = \pi(.75^2)$ $A = \pi(.1875^2)$
$A = 1.76625$ in^2 $A = .1104466$ in^2

Area of metal washer = larger area − smaller area

$= 1.76625$ in$^2 - .1104466$ in^2
$= 1.6558034$ in^2

Skill 9.7   Coordinate graphing

We can represent any two-dimensional geometric figure in the **Cartesian** or **rectangular coordinate system**. The Cartesian or rectangular coordinate system is formed by two perpendicular axes (coordinate axes): the x-axis and the y-axis. If we know the dimensions of a two-dimensional, or planar, figure, we can use this coordinate system to visualize the shape of the figure.

Example:
Represent an isosceles triangle with two sides with a length of 4.

Draw the two sides along the x- and y- axes and connect the points (vertices).

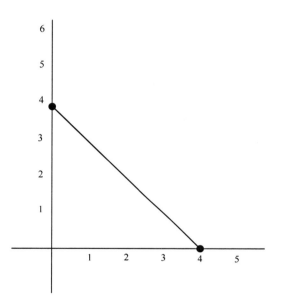

Skill 9.8 Perimeter, area, volume

The **perimeter** of any polygon is the sum of the lengths of the sides.

P = sum of sides

Since the opposite sides of a rectangle are congruent, the perimeter of a rectangle equals twice the sum of the length and width, or:

P_{rect} = 2l + 2w or
2(l + w)

Similarly, since all the sides of a square have the same measure, the perimeter of a square equals four times the length of one side or

P_{square} = 4s

The **area** of a polygon is the number of square units covered by the figure.

A_{rect} = l × w
A_{square} = s^2

Example:
Find the perimeter and the area of this rectangle.

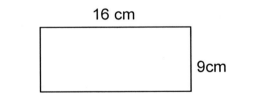

16 cm

9cm

P_{rect} = 2l + 2w A_{rect} = l × w
= 2(16) + 2(9)   = 16(9)
= 32 + 18 = 50 cm   = 144 cm^2

Example:
Find the perimeter and area of this square.

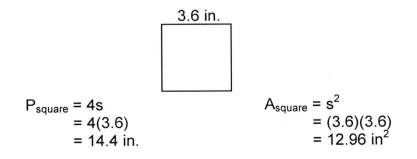

3.6 in.

P_{square} = 4s A_{square} = s^2
= 4(3.6)   = (3.6)(3.6)
= 14.4 in.   = 12.96 in^2

In the following formulas, b = the base and h = the height of an altitude drawn to the base.

$$A_{parallelogram} = bh$$
$$A_{triangle} = \frac{1}{2}bh$$
$$A_{trapezoid} = \frac{1}{2}h(b_1 + b_2)$$

<u>Example:</u>
Find the area of a parallelogram whose base is 6.5 cm and the height of the altitude to that base is 3.7 cm.

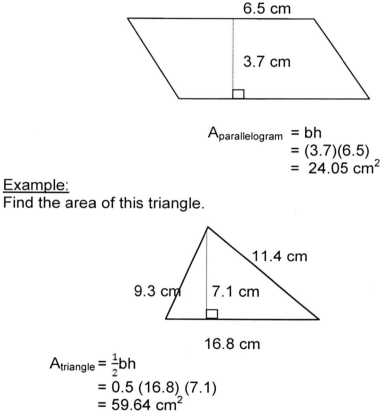

$$A_{parallelogram} = bh$$
$$= (3.7)(6.5)$$
$$= 24.05 \text{ cm}^2$$

<u>Example:</u>
Find the area of this triangle.

$$A_{triangle} = \frac{1}{2}bh$$
$$= 0.5\,(16.8)\,(7.1)$$
$$= 59.64 \text{ cm}^2$$

Note that the altitude is drawn to the base measuring 16.8 cm. The lengths of the other two sides are unnecessary.

Example:
Find the area of a right triangle whose sides measure 10 inches, 24 inches, and 26 inches.

Since the hypotenuse of a right triangle must be the longest side, then the two perpendicular sides must measure 10 and 24 inches.

$$A_{triangle} = \tfrac{1}{2}bh$$
$$= \tfrac{1}{2}(10)(24)$$
$$= 120 \text{ sq. in.}$$

Example:
Find the area of this trapezoid.

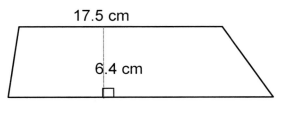

17.5 cm

6.4 cm

23.7 cm

The area of a trapezoid equals one-half the sum of the bases times the altitude.

$$A_{trapezoid} = \tfrac{1}{2}h(b_1 + b_2)$$
$$= 0.5(6.4)(17.5 + 23.7)$$
$$= 131.84 \text{ cm}^2$$

You can also compute the area remaining when sections are cut out of a given figure composed of triangles, squares, rectangles, parallelograms, trapezoids, or circles.

Example:

You have decided to fertilize your lawn. The shapes and dimensions of your lot, house, pool, and garden are given in the diagram below. The shaded area will not be fertilized. If each bag of fertilizer costs $7.95 and covers 4,500 square feet, find the total number of bags needed and the total cost of the fertilizer.

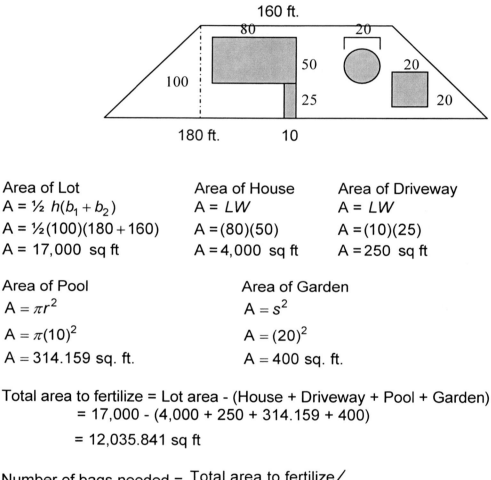

Area of Lot
$A = \frac{1}{2} h(b_1 + b_2)$
$A = \frac{1}{2}(100)(180 + 160)$
$A = 17,000$ sq ft

Area of House
$A = LW$
$A = (80)(50)$
$A = 4,000$ sq ft

Area of Driveway
$A = LW$
$A = (10)(25)$
$A = 250$ sq ft

Area of Pool
$A = \pi r^2$
$A = \pi(10)^2$
$A = 314.159$ sq. ft.

Area of Garden
$A = s^2$
$A = (20)^2$
$A = 400$ sq. ft.

Total area to fertilize = Lot area - (House + Driveway + Pool + Garden)
= 17,000 - (4,000 + 250 + 314.159 + 400)

= 12,035.841 sq ft

Number of bags needed = Total area to fertilize / 4,500 sq.ft. bag

= 12,035.841 / 4,500

= 2.67 bags

Since we cannot purchase 2.67 bags we must purchase 3 full bags.

Total cost = Number of bags * $7.95
    = 3 * $7.95
    = $23.85

The **lateral** area is the area of the faces excluding the bases.

The **surface area** is the total area of all the faces, including the bases.

The **volume** is the number of cubic units in a solid. This is the amount of space a figure holds.

Right prism

$V = Bh$ (where B = area of the base of the prism and h = the height of the prism)

Rectangular right prism

$S = 2(lw + hw + lh)$ (where l = length, w = width and h = height)
$V = lwh$

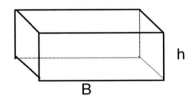

Example:
Find the height of a box where the volume is 120 cubic meters and the area of the base is 30 square meters.

        $V = Bh$
     $120 = 30h$
       $h = 4$ meters

Regular pyramid

$V = \frac{1}{3}Bh$

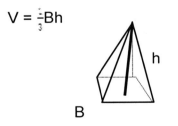

Right circular cylinder

$S = 2\Pi r(r + h)$ (where r is the radius of the base)
$V = \Pi r^2 h$

Right circular cone

$V = \frac{1}{3}Bh$

Skill 9.9   Rates

To solve word problems involving rates, first write the equation. To solve it, multiply each term by the LCD of all fractions. This will cancel out all of the denominators and give an equivalent algebraic equation that can be solved.

1. Elly Mae can feed the animals in 15 minutes. Jethro can feed them in 10 minutes. How long will it take them if they work together?

Solution: If Elly Mae can feed the animals in 15 minutes, then she could feed 1/15 of them in 1 minute, 2/15 of them in 2 minutes, $x/15$ of them in x minutes. In the same fashion, Jethro could feed $x/10$ of them in x minutes. Together they complete 1 job. The equation is:

$$\frac{x}{15} + \frac{x}{10} = 1$$

Multiply each term by the LCD of 30:

$$2x + 3x = 30$$
$$x = 6 \text{ minutes}$$

2. A salesman drove 480 miles from Pittsburgh to Hartford. The next day he returned the same distance to Pittsburgh in half an hour less time than his original trip took, because he increased his average speed by 4 mph. Find his original speed.

Since distance = rate x time   then   time = $\dfrac{\text{distance}}{\text{rate}}$

original time $- 1/2$ hour $=$ shorter return time

$$\frac{480}{x} - \frac{1}{2} = \frac{480}{x+4}$$

Multiplying by the LCD of $2x(x+4)$, the equation becomes:

$$480\left[2(x+4)\right] - 1\left[x(x+4)\right] = 480(2x)$$
$$960x + 3840 - x^2 - 4x = 960x$$
$$x^2 + 4x - 3840 = 0$$
$$(x+64)(x-60) = 0$$
$$x = 60 \qquad \text{60 mph is the original speed}$$
$$\qquad\qquad\qquad \text{64 mph is the faster return speed}$$

Try these:

1. Working together, Larry, Moe, and Curly can paint an elephant in 3 minutes. Working alone, it would take Larry 10 minutes or Moe 6 minutes to paint the elephant. How long would it take Curly to paint the elephant if he worked alone?

2. The denominator of a fraction is 5 more than twice the numerator. If the numerator is doubled, and the denominator is increased by 5, the new fraction is equal to 1/2. Find the original number.

3. A trip from Augusta, Maine to Galveston, Texas is 2108 miles. If one car drove 6 mph faster than a truck and got to Galveston 3 hours before the truck, find the speeds of the car and truck.

Skill 9.10   Angles

The classifying of angles refers to the angle measure. The naming of angles refers to the letters or numbers used to label the angle.

Sample Problem:

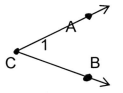

$\overrightarrow{CA}$ (read ray CA) and $\overrightarrow{CB}$ are the sides of the angle.
The angle can be called $\angle ACB$, $\angle BCA$, $\angle C$ or $\angle 1$.

Angles are classified according to their size as follows:

acute: greater than 0 and less than 90 degrees.
right: exactly 90 degrees.
obtuse: greater than 90 and less than 180 degrees.
straight: exactly 180 degrees

Angles can be classified in a number of ways. Some of those classifications are outlined here.

Adjacent angles have a common vertex and one common side but no interior points in common.

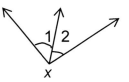

Complementary angles add up to 90 degrees.

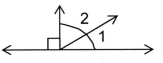

Supplementary angles add up to 180 degrees.

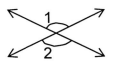

Vertical angles have sides that form two pairs of opposite rays.

Corresponding angles are in the same corresponding position on two parallel lines cut by a transversal.

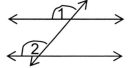

Alternate interior angles are diagonal angles on the inside of two parallel lines cut by a transversal.

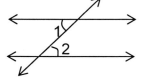

Alternate exterior angles are diagonal on the outside of two parallel lines cut by a transversal.

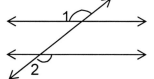

Skill 9.11 Money, temperature, time

Some problems can be solved using equations with rational expressions. First write the equation. To solve it, multiply each term by the LCD of all fractions. This will cancel out all of the denominators and give an equivalent algebraic equation that can be solved.

1. The denominator of a fraction is two less than three times the numerator. If 3 is added to both the numerator and denominator, the new fraction equals 1/2 .

original fraction: $\dfrac{x}{3x-2}$ revised fraction: $\dfrac{x+3}{3x+1}$

$$\dfrac{x+3}{3x+1}=\dfrac{1}{2} \qquad 2x+6=3x+1$$

$$x=5$$

original fraction: $\dfrac{5}{13}$

COMPETENCY 10.0   DATA ORGANIZATION AND INTERPRETATION

Skill 10.1   Visual displays of quantitative information

To make a **bar graph** or a **pictograph**, determine the scale to be used for the graph. Then determine the length of each bar on the graph, or determine the number of pictures needed to represent each item of information. Be sure to include an explanation of the scale in the legend.

Example:
A class had the following grades:

    4 As, 9 Bs, 8 Cs, 1 D, and 3 Fs.
    Graph these on a bar graph and a pictograph.

Pictograph

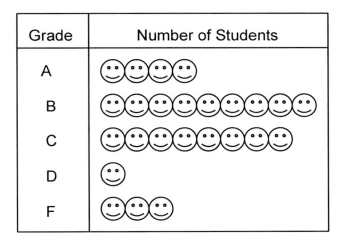

Bar graph

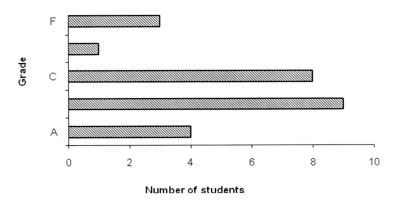

To read a bar graph or a pictograph, read the explanation of the scale that was used in the legend. Compare the length of each bar with the dimensions on the axes and calculate the value each bar represents. On a pictograph, count the number of pictures used in the chart and calculate the value of all the pictures.

To make a **line graph**, determine appropriate scales for both the vertical and horizontal axes (based on the information to be graphed). Describe what each axis represents and mark the scale periodically on each axis. Graph the individual points of the graph and connect the points on the graph from left to right.

Example:
Graph the following information using a line graph.

The number of National Merit finalists/school year

	90-'91	91-'92	92-'93	93-'94	94-'95	95-'96
Central	3	5	1	4	6	8
Wilson	4	2	3	2	3	2

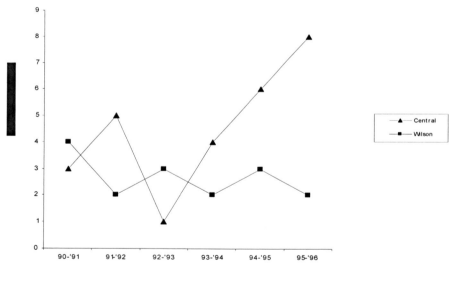

To make a **circle graph**, total all the information that is to be included on the graph. Determine the central angle to be used for each sector of the graph using the following formula:

$$\frac{\text{information}}{\text{total information}} \times 360° = \text{central angle}$$

Lay out the central angles to these sizes, label each section, and include each section's percent.

Example:
Graph this information on a circle graph:

Monthly expenses:

    Rent, $400
    Food, $150
    Utilities, $75
    Clothes, $75
    Church, $100
    Misc., $200

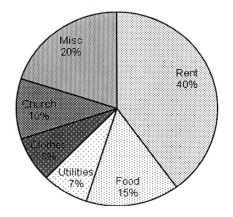

To read a circle graph, find the total of the amounts represented on the entire circle graph. To determine the actual amount that each sector of the graph represents, multiply the percent in a sector times the total amount number.

Histograms are used to summarize information from large sets of data that can be naturally grouped into intervals. The vertical axis indicates **frequency** (the number of times any particular data value occurs), and the horizontal axis indicates data values or ranges of data values. The number of data values in any interval is the **frequency of the interval**.

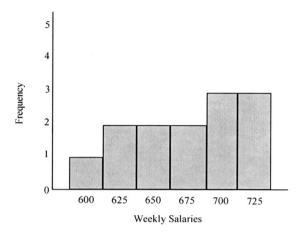

To read a chart, read the row and column headings on the table. Use this information to evaluate the given information in the chart.

Skill 10.2   Simple probability

o   *See Skill 10.4.*

Skill 10.3   Outcomes

o   *See Skill 10.4.*

Skill 10.4   Events

Dependent events occur when the probability of the second event depends on the outcome of the first event. For example, consider the two events: A) it is sunny on Saturday and B) you go to the beach. If you intend to go to the beach on Saturday, rain or shine, then A and B may be independent. If however, you plan to go to the beach only if it is sunny, then A and B may be dependent. In this situation, the probability of event B will change depending on the outcome of event A.

Suppose you have a pair of dice: one red and one green. If you roll a three on the red die and then roll a four on the green die, we can see that these events do not depend on the other. The total probability of the two independent events can be found by multiplying the separate probabilities.

$$P(A \text{ and } B) = P(A) \times P(B)$$
$$= 1/6 \times 1/6$$
$$= 1/36$$

Many times, however, events are not independent. Suppose a jar contains 12 red marbles and 8 blue marbles. If you randomly pick a red marble, replace it, and then randomly pick again, the probability of picking a red marble the second time remains the same. However, if you pick a red marble, and then pick again without replacing the first red marble, the second pick becomes dependent upon the first pick.

$$P(\text{Red and Red}) \text{ with replacement} = P(\text{Red}) \times P(\text{Red})$$
$$= 12/20 \times 12/20$$
$$= 9/25$$

$$P(\text{Red and Red}) \text{ without replacement} = P(\text{Red}) \times P(\text{Red})$$
$$= 12/20 \times 11/19$$
$$= 33/95$$

Odds are defined as the ratio of the number of favorable outcomes to the number of unfavorable outcomes. The sum of the favorable outcomes and the unfavorable outcomes should always equal the total possible outcomes.

For example, given a bag of 12 red and 7 green marbles, compute the odds of randomly selecting a red marble.

$$\text{Odds of red} = \frac{12}{19} : \frac{7}{19} \text{ or } 12:7.$$
$$\text{Odds of not getting red} = \frac{7}{19} : \frac{12}{19} \text{ or } 7:12.$$

In the case of flipping a coin, it is equally likely that a head or a tail will be tossed. The odds of tossing a head are 1:1. This is called even odds.

Skill 10.5 Sample spaces

In probability, the **sample space** is a list of all possible outcomes of an experiment. For example, the sample space of tossing two coins is the set {HH, HT, TT, TH}, the sample space of rolling a six-sided die is the set {1, 2, 3, 4, 5, 6}, and the sample space of measuring the height of students in a class is the set of all real numbers {R}.

When conducting experiments with a large number of possible outcomes, it is important to determine the size of the sample space. The size of the sample space can be determined by using the fundamental counting principle and the rules of combinations and permutations.

The **fundamental counting principle** states that if there are m possible outcomes for one task and n possible outcomes of another, there are (m x n) possible outcomes of the two tasks together.

A **permutation** is the number of possible arrangements of items, without repetition, where order of selection is important.

A **combination** is the number of possible arrangements, without repetition, where order of selection is not important.

Example:
Find the size of the sample space of rolling two six-sided die and flipping two coins.

List the possible outcomes of each event:
each dice: {1, 2, 3, 4, 5, 6}
each coin: {Heads, Tails}

Apply the fundamental counting principle:
size of sample space = 6 x 6 x 2 x 2 = 144

Skill 10.6 Counting techniques

The Addition Principle of Counting states:

If A and B are events, $n(AorB) = n(A) + n(B) - n(A \cap B)$.

Example:
In how many ways can you select a black card or a Jack from an ordinary deck of playing cards?

Let B denote the set of black cards and let J denote the set of Jacks. Then,
$n(B) = 26, n(J) = 4, n(B \cap J) = 2$ and

$$n(BorJ) = n(B) + n(J) - n(B \cap A)$$
$$= 26 + 4 - 2$$
$$= 28.$$

The Addition Principle of Counting for Mutually Exclusive Events states:

If A and B are mutually exclusive events, $n(AorB) = n(A) + n(B)$.

Example:
A travel agency offers 40 possible trips: 14 to Asia, 16 to Europe, and 10 to South America. In how many ways can you select a trip to Asia or Europe through this agency?

Let A denote trips to Asia and let E denote trips to Europe. Then, $A \cap E = \varnothing$ and

$$n(AorE) = 14 + 16 = 30.$$

Therefore, the number of ways you can select a trip to Asia or Europe is 30.

The Multiplication Principle of Counting for Dependent Events states:

Let A be a set of outcomes of Stage 1 and B a set of outcomes of Stage 2. Then the number of ways $n(AandB)$, that A and B can occur in a two-stage experiment is given by:

$$n(AandB) = n(A)n(B|A),$$

where $n(B|A)$ denotes the number of ways B can occur given that A has already occurred.

Example:
How many ways from an ordinary deck of 52 cards can two Jacks be drawn in succession if the first card is drawn but not replaced in the deck and then the second card is drawn?

This is a two-stage experiment for which we wish to compute $n(AandB)$, where A is the set of outcomes for which a Jack is obtained on the first draw and B is the set of outcomes for which a Jack is obtained on the second draw.

If the first card drawn is a Jack, then there are only three remaining Jacks left to choose from on the second draw. Thus, drawing two cards without replacement means the events A and B are dependent.

$$n(AandB) = n(A)n(B|A) = 4 \cdot 3 = 12$$

The Multiplication Principle of Counting for Independent Events states:

Let A be a set of outcomes of Stage 1 and B a set of outcomes of Stage 2. If A and B are independent events, then the number of ways $n(AandB)$, that A and B can occur in a two-stage experiment is given by:

$$n(AandB) = n(A)n(B).$$

Example:
How many six-letter code "words" can be formed if repetition of letters is not allowed?

Since these are code words, a word does not have to look like a word; for example, abcdef could be a code word. Since we must choose a first letter *and* a second letter *and* a third letter *and* a fourth letter *and* a fifth letter *and* a sixth letter, this experiment has six stages.

Since repetition is not allowed there are 26 choices for the first letter; 25 for the second; 24 for the third; 23 for the fourth; 22 for the fifth; and 21 for the sixth. Therefore, we have:

n(six-letter code words without repetition of letters)
$= 26 \cdot 25 \cdot 24 \cdot 23 \cdot 22 \cdot 21$
$= 165,765,600$

Skill 10.7   Tree diagrams

Suppose you want to look at the possible sequence of events for having two children in a family. Since a child will be either a boy or a girl, you would have the following tree diagram to illustrate the possible outcomes:

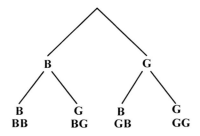

From the diagram, you see that there are 4 possible outcomes, 2 of which are the same.

Skill 10.8   Combinations

Combinations are a way to demonstrate the number of ways in which elements can be arranged. Combination in probability does not involve any specific order.

For example, if you want to know how many different 12-person juries can be chosen from a pool of 20 jurors, you would use the formula:

$$_nC_r = \frac{n!}{r!(n-r)!}$$

$$\frac{20!}{12!(20-12)!} = 125,970$$

The difference between permutations and combinations is that in permutations, all the possible ways of writing an arrangement of objects are given; in a combination, a given arrangement of objects is listed only once.

Skill 10.9   Permutations

A permutation is similar to a combination, but it has an ordered arrangement.

For example, suppose 7 numbers are chosen for the lottery winning number from a possible 10 (zero to 9). The possible number of permutations would be determined as follows:

$$_nP_r = \frac{n!}{(n-r)!} = \frac{10!}{(10-7)!} = 604,800$$

Many problems involve finding both the combination and the permutation for a given set. In this way, the two concepts are inexorably linked.

Example:
Given the set {1, 2, 3, 4}, list the arrangements of two numbers that can be written as a combination and as a permutation.

Combination	Permutation
12, 13, 14, 23, 24, 34	12, 21, 13, 31, 14, 41,
	23, 32, 24, 42, 34, 43,
six ways	twelve ways

Using the formulas given below, the same results can be found.

Permutation:

The notation $_nP_r$ is read "the number of permutations of n objects taken r at a time."

$$_nP_r = \frac{n!}{(n-r)!}$$

Substitute known values.

$$_4P_2 = \frac{4!}{(4-2)!}$$

Solve.

$$_4P_2 = 12$$

Combination:

The number of combinations when r objects are selected from n objects.

$$_nC_r = \frac{n!}{(n-r)!r!}$$

Substitute known values.

$$_4C_2 = \frac{4!}{(4-2)!2!}$$

Solve.

$$_4C_2 = 6$$

Skill 10.10   Mean, median, mode

Mean, median and mode are three measures of central tendency. The **mean** is the average of the data items. The **median** is found by putting the data items in order from smallest to largest and selecting the item in the middle (or the average of the two items in the middle). The **mode** is the most frequently occurring item.

Range is a measure of variability. It is found by subtracting the smallest value from the largest value.

Example:
Find the mean, median, mode, and range of the test score listed below:

85	77	65
92	90	54
88	85	70
75	80	69
85	88	60
72	74	95

Mean = sum of all scores ÷ number of scores
    = 78

Median = put numbers in order from smallest to largest. Pick middle number.
54, 60, 65, 69, 70, 72, 74, 75, 77, 80, 85, 85, 85, 88, 88, 90, 92, 95
                    -- --
                both in middle
Therefore, median is average of two numbers in the middle, or 78.5

Mode = most frequent number
    = 85

Range = largest number minus the smallest number
      = 95 – 54
      = 41

Different situations require different information. If we examine the circumstances under which an ice cream store owner may use statistics collected in the store, we find different uses for different information.

Over a 7-day period, the store owner collected data on the ice cream flavors sold. He found that the mean number of scoops sold was 174 per day. The most frequently sold flavor was vanilla. This information was useful in determining how much ice cream to order in all and in what amounts for each flavor.

In this case, the median and range had little business value for the owner.

Consider the set of test scores from a math class: 0, 16, 19, 65, 65, 65, 68, 69, 70, 72, 73, 73, 75, 78, 80, 85, 88, and 92. The mean is 64.06 and the median is 71. Since there are only three scores less than the mean out of the eighteen scores, the median (71) would be a more descriptive score.

Retail store owners may be most concerned with the most common dress size so they may order more of that size than any other.

Using Definitions in Statistical Data

An understanding of the definitions is important in determining the validity and uses of statistical data. All definitions and applications in this section apply to ungrouped data.

Data item: each piece of data is represented by the letter X.

Mean: the average of all data is represented by the symbol $\overline{X}$.

Sum of the Squares: sum of the squares of the differences between each item and the mean.
$$Sx^2 = (X - \overline{X})^2$$

Variance: the sum of the squares quantity divided by the number of items. (the lower case Greek letter sigma squared (σ^2)represents variance).
$$\frac{Sx^2}{N} = \sigma^2$$

The larger the value of the variance, the larger the spread

small variation   larger variation

Standard Deviation: the square root of the variance. The lower case Greek letter sigma (σ) is used to represent standard deviation.

$$\sigma = \sqrt{\sigma^2}$$

Most statistical calculators have standard deviation keys on them and should be used when asked to calculate statistical functions. It is important to become familiar with the calculator and the location of the keys needed.

<u>Example:</u>
Given the ungrouped data below, calculate the mean, range, standard deviation, and variance.

    15   22   28   25   34   38
    18   25   30   33   19   23

Mean ($\overline{X}$) = 25.8333333
Range: $38 - 15 = 23$
standard deviation (σ) = 6.6936952

Variance (σ^2) = 44.805556

COMPETENCY 11.0   GEOGRAPHY

Skill 11.0   The world in spatial terms

Spatial organization is a description of how things are grouped in a given space. In geographical terms, this can describe people, places, and environments anywhere and everywhere on earth.

The most basic form of spatial organization for people is where they live. The vast majority of people live near other people in villages, towns, cities, and settlements. These people live near others in order to take advantage of the goods and services that naturally arise from cooperation. These villages, towns, cities, and settlements are, to varying degrees, near bodies of water. Water is a staple of survival for every person on the planet; it is also a good source of energy for factories and other industries, as well as a form of transportation for people and goods.

Another way to describe where people live is by the **geography** and **topography** around them. The vast majority of people on the planet live in areas that are very hospitable. Yes, people live in the Himalayas and in the Sahara, but the populations in those areas are very small when compared to the plains of China, India, Europe, and the United States. People naturally want to live where they do not have to work really hard just to survive, and world population patterns reflect this.

We can examine the spatial organization of the places where people live. For example, in a city, where are the factories and heavy industry buildings? Are they near airports or train stations? Are they on the edge of town, near major roads? What about housing developments? Are they near these industries, or are they far away? Where are the other industry buildings? Where are the schools and hospitals and parks? What about the police and fire stations? How close are homes to each of these things?

Towns and especially cities are routinely organized into neighborhoods so that each house or home is near most things that its residents might need on a regular basis. This means that large cities have multiple schools, hospitals, grocery stores, fire stations, etc.

The distances between cities, towns, villages, or settlements are also related to settlement patterns. In certain parts of the United States and in many European countries, population settlement patterns achieve megalopolis standards, with no clear boundaries from one town to the next. Other, more sparsely populated areas have towns that are few and far between with relatively few people in them. Some exceptions to this exist, of course, like oases in the deserts; for the most part, however, population centers tend to be relatively near one another or at least near smaller towns.

Most populated places in the world also tend to be close to agricultural lands. Food makes the world go round. Although some cities are more agriculturally inclined than others, it is rare to find a city that grows absolutely no crops. The kind of food grown is almost entirely dependent on the kind of available land and the climate surrounding that land. Rice doesn't grow well in the desert, for instance, nor do bananas grow well in snowy lands. Certain crops are easier to transport than others, and the ones that aren't are usually grown near ports or other areas of export.

The five themes of geography are:

Location – This includes relative and absolute location. A **relative location** refers to the surrounding geography (e.g., on the banks of the Mississippi River). **Absolute location** refers to a specific point, such as 41 degrees North latitude, 90 degrees West longitude, or 123 Main Street.

Place – This is something that has both human and physical characteristics. Physical characteristics include features such as mountains, rivers, and deserts. Human characteristics are the features created by human interaction with the environment (such as canals and roads).

Human-Environmental Interaction – The theme of human-environmental interaction has three main concepts: humans adapt to the environment (wearing warm clothing in a cold climate), humans modify the environment (planting trees to block a prevailing wind), and humans depend on the environment (for food, water, and raw materials).

Movement – The theme of movement covers how humans interact with one another through trade, communications, emigration, and other forms of contact.

Regions – A region is an area that has some kind of unifying characteristic, such as a common language or a common government. There are three main types of regions. **Formal regions** are areas defined by actual political boundaries, such as a city, county, or state. **Functional regions** are defined by a common function, such as the area covered by a telephone service. **Vernacular regions** are less formally defined areas that are formed by people's perception (e.g., "the Middle East" or "the South").

Skill 11.2   Places and regions

Landforms

A **landform** comprises a geomorphological unit. Landforms are categorized by characteristics such as elevation, slope, orientation, stratification, rock exposure, and soil type. By name, they include such features as berms, mounds, hills, cliffs, valleys, and others. Oceans and continents exemplify highest-order landforms; however, landform elements can be further broken down. The generic landform elements are pits, peaks, channels, ridges, passes, pools, and planes; these can be often extracted from a digital elevation model using some automated or semi-automated techniques.

Elementary landforms (segments, facets, and relief units) are the smallest homogeneous divisions of the land surface at a given scale or resolution. A plateau or a hill can be observed at various scales, ranging from a few hundred meters to hundreds of kilometers. Hence, the spatial distribution of landforms is often fuzzy and scale-dependent. as is the case for soils and geological strata.

A number of factors, ranging from plate tectonics to erosion and deposition, can generate and affect landforms. Biological factors can also influence landforms—for example, consider the role of plants in the development of dune systems and salt marshes, and the work of corals and algae in the formation of coral reefs.

The earth's surface is made up of 70 percent water and 30 percent land. Physical features of the land surface include mountains, hills, plateaus, valleys, and plains. Other minor landforms include deserts, deltas, canyons, mesas, basins, foothills, marshes, and swamps. Earth's water features include oceans, seas, lakes, rivers, and canals.

Earth's Physical Features

Mountains are landforms with rather steep slopes at least 2,000 feet or more above sea level. Mountains are found in groups called mountain chains or mountain ranges. At least one range can be found on six of the earth's seven continents. North America has the Appalachian and Rocky Mountains; South America the Andes; Asia the Himalayas; Australia the Great Dividing Range; Europe the Alps; and Africa the Atlas, Ahaggar, and Drakensburg Mountains. Mountains are commonly formed by volcanic activity, or when land is thrust upward where two tectonic plates collide.

Hills are elevated landforms rising to an elevation of about 500 to 2000 feet. They are found everywhere on Earth—including Antarctica, where they are covered by ice.

Plateaus are elevated landforms that are usually level on top. Some plateaus are dry because they are surrounded by mountains that keep out any moisture. Some examples include the Kenya Plateau in East Africa, which is very cool. The plateau extending north from the Himalayas is extremely dry, while those in Antarctica and Greenland are covered with ice and snow. Plateaus can be formed by underground volcanic activity, erosion, or colliding tectonic plates.

Plains are described as areas of flat or slightly rolling land, usually lower than the landforms next to them. Sometimes called **lowlands** (and often located along **seacoasts),** they support the majority of the world's people. Many have been formed by large rivers, which provided extremely fertile soil for successful cultivation of crops and numerous large settlements of people. In North America, the vast plains areas extend from the Gulf of Mexico north to the Arctic Ocean and between the Appalachian and Rocky Mountains. In Europe, rich plains extend east from Great Britain into central Europe on into the Siberian region of Russia. Plains in river valleys are found in China (the Yangtze River valley), India (the Ganges River valley), and Southeast Asia (the Mekong River valley).

Valleys are land areas that are found between hills and mountains. Some have gentle slopes containing trees and plants; others have very steep walls and are referred to as canyons. One famous example is Arizona's Grand Canyon of the Colorado River, which was formed by erosion.

Deserts are large dry areas of land receiving ten inches or less of rainfall each year. Among the better known deserts are Africa's large Sahara Desert, the Arabian Desert on the Arabian Peninsula, and the desert Outback covering roughly one-third of Australia. Deserts are found mainly in the tropical latitudes and are formed when surrounding features such as mountain ranges extract most of the moisture from the prevailing winds

Deltas are areas of lowlands formed by soil and sediment deposited at the mouths of rivers. The soil is generally very fertile; most fertile river deltas are important crop-growing areas. One well-known example is the delta of Egypt's Nile River, known for its production of cotton.

Mesas are the flat tops of hills or mountains, usually with steep sides. Mesas are similar to plateaus, but smaller.

Basins are low areas drained by rivers or low spots in mountains.

Foothills are generally considered a low series of hills found between a plain and a mountain range.

Marshes and swamps are wet lowlands providing growth of such plants as rushes and reeds.

Oceans are the largest bodies of water on the planet. The four oceans of the earth are the **Atlantic Ocean**, one-half the size of the Pacific and separating North and South America from Africa and Europe; the **Pacific Ocean**, covering almost one-third of the entire surface of the earth and separating North and South America from Asia and Australia; the **Indian Ocean**, touching Africa, Asia, and Australia; and the ice-filled **Arctic Ocean,** extending from North America and Europe to the North Pole. The waters of the Atlantic, Pacific, and Indian Oceans also touch the shores of Antarctica.

Seas are smaller than oceans and are surrounded by land. Some examples include the Mediterranean Sea found between Europe, Asia, and Africa and the Caribbean Sea, touching the West Indies, South America, and Central America.

A **lake** is a body of water surrounded by land. The Great Lakes in North America are a good example.

Rivers, considered a nation's lifeblood, usually begin as very small streams, formed by melting snow and rainfall. They flow from higher to lower land, emptying into a larger body of water—usually a sea or an ocean. Examples of important rivers for the people and countries affected by and/or dependent on them include the Nile, Niger, and Zaire Rivers of Africa; the Rhine, Danube, and Thames Rivers of Europe; the Yangtze, Ganges, Mekong, Hwang He, and Irrawaddy Rivers of Asia; the Murray-Darling in Australia; and the Orinoco in South America. **River systems** are made up of large rivers as well as the numerous smaller rivers or tributaries flowing into them. Examples include the vast Amazon River system in South America and the Mississippi River system in the United States.

Canals are man-made water passages constructed to connect two larger bodies of water. Famous examples include the **Panama Canal** across Panama's isthmus, which connects the Atlantic and Pacific Oceans, and the **Suez Canal** in the Middle East between Africa and the Arabian peninsulas connecting the Red and Mediterranean Seas.

Weather and Climate

Weather is the condition of the air that affects the day-to-day atmospheric conditions. It includes factors such as temperature, air pressure, wind, and moisture or precipitation (which includes rain, snow, hail, or sleet).

Climate is the term used to describe the average weather or daily weather conditions for a specific region over a long period of time. Studying the climate of an area includes information gathered on the area's monthly and yearly temperatures as well as its monthly and yearly amounts of precipitation. In addition, one characteristic of an area's climate is the length of its growing season.

In northern and central United States, northern China, south central and southeastern Canada, and the western and southeastern parts of the former Soviet Union, there is a "climate of four seasons." This is also known as the **humid continental climate**, which includes spring, summer, fall, and winter. Cold winters, hot summers, and enough rainfall to grow a variety of crops are the major characteristics of this climate. In areas where the humid continental climate is found, there are some of the world's best farmlands as well as important activities such as trading and mining. Differences in temperatures throughout the year are typically determined by the distance a place is inland, away from the coasts.

The steppe or **prairie climate** is located in the interiors of the large continents like Asia and North America. These dry flatlands are far from ocean breezes and are called prairies (or the Great Plains in Canada and the United States and steppes in Asia). Although the summers are hot and the winters are cold, the big difference is rainfall. In the steppe climate, rainfall is light and uncertain at ten to twenty inches per year. Where rain is more plentiful, grass grows; in areas of less rainfall, the steppes or prairies gradually become deserts. These are found in the Gobi Desert of Asia, in central and western Australia, in southwestern United States, and in the smaller deserts found in Pakistan, Argentina, and Africa south of the Equator.

The two major climates found in the high latitudes are **tundra** and taiga. The word tundra, meaning marshy plain, is a Russian word; it aptly describes the climatic conditions in the northern areas of Russia, Europe, and Canada. Winters are extremely cold and very long. Most of the year the ground is frozen, but it becomes rather mushy during the very short summer months. Surprisingly less snow falls in the area of the tundra than in the eastern part of the United States. However, due to the harshness of the extreme cold, very few people live there and almost no crops can be raised. Despite having a small human population, many plants and animals are found there.

The **taiga** is the northern forest region located south of the tundra. The world's largest forestlands are found here, along with vast mineral wealth and fur-bearing animals. The climate is so extreme that very few people live here, as they are not able to raise crops due to the extremely short growing season. The winter temperatures are colder and the summer temperatures are hotter than those in the tundra because the taiga climate region is farther from the waters of the Arctic Ocean. The taiga is found in the northern parts of Russia, Sweden, Norway, Finland, Canada, and Alaska with most of their lands covered with marshes and swamps.

The humid **subtropical climate** is found north and south of the tropics. It is categorized by its high levels of moisture. The areas with this type of climate include the southeastern coasts of Japan, mainland China, Australia, Africa, South America, and the United States. One interesting feature of these locations is that warm ocean currents are found there. The winds that blow across these currents bring in warm moist air all year round. Long, warm summers; short, mild winters; and a long growing season allow for different crops to be grown several times a year. These conditions contribute to the productivity of this climate type, which supports more people than any of the other climates.

The **marine climate** is found in Western Europe, the British Isles, the U.S. Pacific Northwest, the western coast of Canada, southern Chile, southern New Zealand, and southeastern Australia. A common characteristic of these lands is that they are either near water or surrounded by it. The ocean winds are wet and warm, bringing a mild rainy climate to these areas. In the summer, the daily temperatures average at or below 70 degrees F. During the winter, because of the warming effect of the ocean waters, the temperatures rarely fall below freezing.

In certain areas of the earth, there exists a type of climate unique to areas with high mountains. This type of climate is called a **vertical climate** because the temperatures, crops, vegetation, and human activities change and become different as one ascends through the different levels of elevation. At the foot of the mountain, a hot and rainy climate is found with the cultivation of many lowland crops. As one climbs higher, the air becomes cooler, the climate changes sharply, and different economic activities change, such as grazing sheep and growing corn. At the top of many mountains, snow is found year round.

Skill 11.3   Physical and human systems

Social scientists use the term **culture** to describe the way of life of a group of people. This term includes not only art, music, and literature but also beliefs, customs, languages, traditions, and inventions—in short, any way of life, whether complex or simple. Although term **geography** is defined as the study of the earth's features, it also includes the study of living things as it pertains to their location, the relationships of these locations with each other, how they came to be there, and what impact these have on the world.

Physical geography is concerned with the locations of such features as climate, water, and land as well as how these relate to and affect each other. It includes how they affect human activities and what forces shaped and changed them.

All three of these earth features (climate, water, and land) affect the lives of all humans, ultimately having a direct influence on what is made and produced, where this production occurs, how it occurs, and what makes it possible. The combination of the different climatic conditions and types of landforms and other surface features work together all around the earth to give the many varied cultures their unique characteristics and distinctions.

Cultural geography studies the location, characteristics, and influence of the physical environment on different cultures around the earth. Also included in these studies are comparisons and influences of the many varied cultures.

Physical locations of the earth's surface features include the four major hemispheres and the parts of the earth's continents in them. **Political locations** are the political divisions, if any, within each continent. Both physical and political locations are precisely determined in two ways: 1) surveying is done to determine boundary lines and distance from other features, and 2) exact locations are precisely determined by imaginary lines of latitude (**parallels**) and longitude (**meridians**). The intersection of these lines at right angles forms a grid, making it possible to pinpoint an exact location of any place using any two grip coordinates.

The **Eastern Hemisphere** is located between the North and South Poles, between the Prime Meridian (0 degrees longitude) east to the International Date Line (180 degrees longitude). It consists of most of Europe, all of Australia, most of Africa, and all of Asia (except for a tiny piece of the easternmost part of Russia that extends east of 180 degrees longitude).

The **Western Hemisphere** is located between the North and South Poles, between the Prime Meridian (0 degrees longitude) west to the International Date Line (180 degrees longitude). It consists of all of North and South America, a tiny part of the easternmost part of Russia that extends east of 180 degrees longitude, and a part of Europe that extends west of the Prime Meridian.

The **Northern Hemisphere,** located between the North Pole and the Equator, contains all of the continents of Europe and North America and parts of South America, Africa, and most of Asia.

The **Southern Hemisphere,** located between the South Pole and the Equator, contains all of Australia, a small part of Asia, about one-third of Africa, most of South America, and all of Antarctica.

The Seven Continents

Of the seven continents, only one contains just one entire country. It is also the only island continent: **Australia**. Its political divisions consist of six states and one territory: Western Australia, South Australia, Tasmania, Victoria, New South Wales, Queensland, and Northern Territory.

Africa is made up of fifty-four separate countries, the major ones being Egypt, Nigeria, South Africa, Zaire, Kenya, Algeria, Morocco, and the large island of Madagascar.

Asia consists of forty-nine separate countries, some of which include China, Japan, India, Turkey, Israel, Iraq, Iran, Indonesia, Jordan, Vietnam, Thailand, and the Philippines.

Some of **Europe's** forty-three separate nations include France, Russia, Malta, Denmark, Hungary, Greece, and Bosnia.

North America consists of Canada, the United States of America, the island nations of the West Indies, and the "land bridge" of Middle America, including Cuba, Jamaica, Mexico, Panama, and others.

Thirteen separate nations together occupy the continent of **South America,** among them such nations as Brazil, Paraguay, Ecuador, and Suriname.

The continent of **Antarctica** has no political boundaries or divisions but has a number of science and research stations managed by nations such as Russia, Japan, France, Australia, and India.

Skill 11.4   Environment and society

Natural resources are naturally occurring substances that are considered valuable in their natural form. A **commodity** is generally considered a natural resource when the primary activities associated with it are extraction and purification, as opposed to creation. Thus, mining, petroleum extraction, fishing, and forestry are generally considered natural resource industries while agriculture is not.

Natural resources are often classified into renewable and nonrenewable resources. **Renewable resources** are generally living resources (fish, coffee, and forests, for example), which can restock (renew) themselves if they are not over harvested. Renewable resources can restock themselves and be used indefinitely if they are sustained. Once renewable resources are consumed at a rate that exceeds their natural rate of replacement, the standing stock will diminish and eventually run out.

The rate of sustainable use of a renewable resource is determined by the replacement rate and amount of standing stock of that particular resource. Non-living renewable natural resources include soil, as well as water, wind, tides, and solar radiation. **Nonrenewable resources** are natural resources that cannot be remade or regenerated in the same proportion that they are used. Examples of nonrenewable resources are fossil fuels such as coal, petroleum, and natural gas.

In recent years, the renewal of natural capital and attempts to move to sustainable development have been a major focus of development agencies. This is of particular concern in rainforest regions, which hold most of the earth's natural biodiversity—irreplaceable genetic natural capital. Conservation of natural resources is the major focus of Natural Capitalism, environmentalism, the ecology movement, and Green Parties. Some view this depletion as a major source of social unrest and conflicts in developing nations.

Environmental policy is concerned with the sustainability of the earth. The concern of environmental policy is the preservation of a region, habitat, or ecosystem. Because humans, both individually and within communities, rely upon the environment to sustain human life, social and environmental policies must be mutually supportable.

If modern societies have no understanding of the limitations of natural resources or how their actions affect the environment, and they act without regard for the sustainability of the earth, it will become impossible for the earth to sustain human existence. For centuries, social policies, economic policies, and political policies have ignored the impact of human existence and human civilization upon the environment. Human civilization has disrupted the ecological balance, contributed to the extinction of animal and plant species, and destroyed ecosystems through uncontrolled harvesting. In an age of global warming, unprecedented demand upon natural resources, and a shrinking planet, social and environmental policies must become increasingly interdependent if the planet is to continue to support life and human civilization.

Skill 11.5   Uses of geography

Studying the geographic features of the earth is essential to understand the history of the physical environment and the history of humanity. Only when a comprehensive worldview is obtained through extensive geographical research can we have a complete understanding of the earth, its lands, and its peoples throughout time. In this way, geography is useful as a historical and evaluative tool.

At the same time, geography is also useful for looking toward the future. To understand the world we live in today and the world we will inhabit in the future, we have to be aware of the geographic concepts that drive world events. This includes, but is not limited to, environmental concerns.
Geographical studies are divided into:

Regional - The elements and characteristics of a place or region.

Topical - One earth feature or one human activity occurring throughout the entire world.

Physical - Earth's physical features, what creates and changes them, their relationships to each other, and their relationships to human activities.

Human - Human activity patterns and how they relate to the environment including political, cultural, historical, urban, and social geographical fields of study.

Special research methods used by geographers include mapping, interviewing, field studies, mathematics, statistics, and scientific instruments.

COMPETENCY 12.0   WORLD HISTORY

Skill 12.1   Prehistory and early civilizations

The earliest known civilizations developed in the Tigris-Euphrates Valley of Mesopotamia (modern Iraq) and the Nile Valley of Egypt between 4000 BCE and 3000 BCE. Because these civilizations arose in river valleys, they are known as **fluvial civilizations**. Geography and the physical environment played a critical role in the rise and the survival of both of these civilizations.

The Fertile Crescent was bounded on the west by the Mediterranean Sea, on the south by the Arabian Desert, on the north by the Taurus Mountains, and on the east by the Zagros Mountains.

The rivers provided a source of water that sustained life, including animal life. The hunters of the society had ample access to a variety of animals, which were hunted to provide food, as well as hides, bones, and antlers from which clothing, tools, and art was made. The proximity to water provided a natural attraction to animals, which could be herded and husbanded to provide a stable supply of food and animal products. The rivers of these regions also overflowed their banks each year, leaving behind a deposit of very rich soil. As these early people began to experiment with growing crops rather than gathering food, they discovered that the soil was fertile and that water was readily available to produce sizeable harvests. In time, the people developed systems of irrigation that channeled water to the crops without significant human effort on a continuing basis.

The designation "Fertile Crescent" was applied by the famous historian and Egyptologist James Breasted to the part of the Near East that extended from the Persian Gulf to the Sinai Peninsula. It included Mesopotamia, Syria, and Palestine. In early years, this region was marked by almost constant invasions and migrations. These invaders and migrants seemed to have destroyed the culture and civilization that existed; however, upon taking a longer view, it is apparent that they actually absorbed and supplemented the civilization that existed before their arrival. This is one of the reasons the civilization developed so quickly and created such an advanced culture.

The culture of Mesopotamia was definitely autocratic in nature. The various civilizations spread throughout the Fertile Crescent were very much top-heavy, with a single ruler at the head of the government who, in many cases, also served as the head of the religion. The people followed his strict instructions or faced the consequences, which were usually dire and often life-threatening.

The civilizations of the Sumerians, Amorites, Hittites, Assyrians, Chaldeans, and Persians controlled various areas of the land we now call Mesopotamia. With few exceptions, tyrants and military leaders controlled the vast majority of aspects of society, including trade, religions, and laws. Each Sumerian city-state (of which there were many) had its own god, with the city-state's leader doubling as the high priest of worship of that local god. Subsequent cultures had a handful of gods as well, although they had more of a national worship structure, with high priests centered in the capital city as advisors to the leader.

Trade was vastly important to these civilizations, since they had access to some but not all of the things that they needed to survive. Some trading agreements led to occupation, as was the case with the Sumerians, who didn't bother to build walls to protect their wealth of knowledge. Egypt and the Phoenician cities were powerful and regular trading partners of the various Mesopotamian cultures.

Legacies handed down to us from these people include:
- The first use of writing, the wheel, and banking (Sumeria);
- The first written set of laws (Code of Hammurabi);
- The first epic story (*Gilgamesh*);
- The first library dedicated to preserving knowledge (instituted by the Assyrian leader Ashurbanipal);
- The Hanging Gardens of Babylon (built by the Chaldean Nebuchadnezzar)

The ancient civilization of the **Sumerians** invented the wheel; developed irrigation through the use of canals, dikes, and devices for raising water; devised the system of cuneiform writing; learned to divide time; and built large boats for trade. The Babylonians devised the famous **Code of Hammurabi**, a code of laws.

Egypt made numerous significant contributions, including construction of the great pyramids; development of hieroglyphic writing; preservation of bodies after death; creation of paper from papyrus; contributions to developments in arithmetic and geometry; invention of the method of counting in groups of 1-10 (the decimal system); completion of a solar calendar; and formation of the foundation for science and astronomy.

The earliest historical record of the **Kush** civilization is in Egyptian sources. They describe a region upstream from the first cataract of the Nile as "wretched." This civilization was characterized by a settled way of life in fortified mud-brick villages. They subsisted on hunting and fishing, herding cattle, and gathering grain. Skeletal remains suggest that the people were a blend of Negroid and Mediterranean peoples. This civilization appears to be the second-oldest in Africa (after Egypt).

During the period of Egypt's Old Kingdom (ca. 2700-2180 BCE), this civilization was essentially a diffused version of Egyptian culture and religion. When Egypt came under the domination of the Hyksos, Kush reached its greatest power and cultural energy (1700-1500 BCE). When the Hyksos were eventually expelled from Egypt, the New Kingdom brought Kush back under Egyptian colonial control.

The ancient **Assyrians** were warlike and aggressive due to a highly organized military; they also used horse-drawn chariots.

The **Hebrews**, also known as the ancient Israelites, instituted "monotheism," which is the worship of one God (as opposed to many). The Hebrew Scriptures became the Old Testament of the Christian Bible.

The **Minoans** had a system of writing using symbols to represent syllables in words. They built palaces with multiple levels containing many rooms, water and sewage systems with flush toilets, bathtubs, hot and cold running water, and bright paintings on the walls.

The **Mycenaeans** changed the Minoan writing system to aid their own language and used symbols to represent syllables.

The **Phoenicians** were sea traders well-known for their manufacturing skills in glass and metals as well as the development of their famous purple dye. They became so proficient in the skill of navigation that they were able to sail by the stars at night. Furthermore, they devised an alphabet using symbols to represent single sounds, which was an improved extension of the Egyptian principle and writing system.

China is considered by some historians to be the oldest, uninterrupted civilization in the world; it was in existence around the same time as the ancient civilizations founded in Egypt, Mesopotamia, and the Indus Valley. The Chinese studied nature and weather; stressed the importance of education, family, and a strong central government; followed the religions of Buddhism, Confucianism, and Taoism; and invented such things as gunpowder, paper, printing, and the magnetic compass. China began building the Great Wall; practiced crop rotation and terrace farming; increased the importance of the silk industry; and developed caravan routes across Central Asia for extensive trade. They also increased proficiency in rice cultivation and developed a written language based on drawings or pictographs.

The ancient **Persians** developed an alphabet; contributed the religions and philosophies of **Zoroastrianism**, **Mithraism**, and **Gnosticism**; and allowed conquered peoples to retain their own customs, laws, and religions.

The classical civilization of **Greece** reached the highest levels in human achievement based on the foundations already laid by such ancient groups as the Egyptians, Phoenicians, Minoans, and Mycenaeans.

Among the more important contributions of Greece was the Greek alphabet derived from the Phoenician letters, which formed the basis for the Roman alphabet and our present-day alphabet. Extensive trading and colonization resulted in the spread of Greek civilization. The love of sports, with emphasis on a physically sound body, led to the tradition of the Olympic games. Greece was responsible for the rise of independent, strong city-states. Other important areas that the Greeks are credited with influencing include drama, epic and lyric poetry, fables, myths centered on the many gods and goddesses, science, astronomy, medicine, mathematics, philosophy, art, architecture, and recording historical events.

The conquests of Alexander the Great spread Greek ideas to the areas he conquered and brought to the Greek world many ideas from Asia. Above all, the value of ideas, wisdom, curiosity, and the desire to learn as much about the world as possible were major objectives of the conquests.

The ancient civilization of **Rome** lasted approximately 1,000 years (including the periods of the Republic and the Empire), although its lasting influence on Europe and its history was for a much longer period. There was a very sharp contrast between the curious, imaginative, inquisitive Greeks and the practical, simple, down-to-earth Romans, who spread and preserved the ideas of ancient Greece and other cultural groups. The contributions and accomplishments of the Romans are numerous, but their greatest included language, engineering, building, law, government, roads, trade, and the "Pax Romana." Pax Romana was the long period of peace enabling free travel and trade, spreading people, cultures, goods, and ideas all over a vast area of the known world.

In **India**, Hinduism was a continuing influence along with the rise of Buddhism. Industry and commerce developed along with extensive trading with the Near East. Outstanding advances in the fields of science and medicine were made, and the civilization was one of the first to be active in navigation and maritime enterprises during this time. In India, the caste system was developed and the principle of zero in mathematics was discovered.

The civilization in **Japan** appeared during this time, having borrowed much of its culture from China. It was the last of the classical civilizations to develop. Although they used, accepted, and copied Chinese art, law, architecture, dress, and writing, the Japanese refined these into their own unique way of life, including incorporating the religion of Buddhism into their culture.

During this time, the civilizations in **Africa** south of the Sahara were developing the refining and use of iron, especially for farm implements and later for weapons. Trading happened over land by using camels and over sea at important seaports. The Arab influence was extremely important, as was the Arabs' later contact with Indians, Christian Nubians, and Persians. In fact, these trading activities were probably the most important factor in the spread and assimilation of different ideas as well as stimulation of cultural growth.

The people who lived in the Americas before Columbus arrived had a thriving, connected society. The civilizations in North America tended to be spread farther and were in occasional conflict; however, for the most part, they each maintained their sovereignty. On the contrary, the South American civilizations tended to migrate into empires, with the strongest city or tribe assuming control of the lives and resources of the rest of the nearby peoples.

Native Americans in North America had a spiritual and personal relationship with the various spirits of nature and a keen appreciation of the ways of woodworking and metalworking. Various tribes dotted the landscape of what is now the United States. They struggled against one another for control of resources such as food and water but had no concept of ownership of land, since they believed that they were living on the land with the permission of the spirits. The North Americans mastered the art of growing many crops and, to their credit, were willing to share that knowledge with the various Europeans who eventually immigrated to their land. Artwork made of hides, beads, and jewels were popular at this time within various Native American cultures.

The most well-known empires of South America were the **Aztec, Inca,** and **Maya** civilizations. Each of these empires had a central capital which housed the emperor. The emperor controlled all aspects of the lives of his subjects. The empires traded with other peoples; if the relations soured, the results were usually absorption of the trading partners into the empire. These empires, especially the Aztecs, had access to large numbers of metals and jewels, and they created weapons and artwork that continue to impress historians today. The Incan Empire stretched across a vast period of territory down the western coast of South America and was connected by a series of roads. A series of messengers ran along these roads, carrying news and instructions from the capital, Cusco. The Mayas are most well-known for their famous pyramids and calendars, as well as their language, which still stumps archaeologists.

Skill 12.2   Classical civilizations

Ancient Greece is often called the Cradle of Western Civilization because of the enormous influence it had not only on the time in which it flourished, but on western culture ever since.

Early Greek institutions have survived for thousands of years and have influenced the entire world. The Athenian form of democracy, with all citizens having an equal vote in their own government, is a philosophy upon which all modern democracies are based. In the United States, the Greek tradition of democracy was honored in the choice of Greek architectural styles for the nation's government buildings. The modern Olympic Games are a revival of an ancient Greek tradition, and many of the events are recreations of original contests.

The works of the Greek epic poet Homer, author of the Iliad and the Odyssey, are considered the earliest in western literature, and are still read and taught today. The tradition of the theater was born in Greece, with the plays of Aristophanes and others. In philosophy, Aristotle developed an approach to learning that emphasized observation and thought, and Socrates and Plato contemplated the nature of being and the origins and ideals of government and political relations. Greek mythology has been the source of inspiration for literature into the present day.

In the field of mathematics, Pythagoras and Euclid laid the foundation of geometry and Archimedes calculated the value of pi. Herodotus and Thucydides were the first to apply research and interpretation to written history.

In the arts, Greek sensibilities were held as perfect forms to which others might strive. In sculpture, the Greeks achieved an idealistic aesthetic that had not been perfected before that time.

The Greek civilization served as an inspiration to the Roman Republic, which followed in its tradition of democracy and was directly influenced by its achievements in art and science. Later, during the Renaissance, European scholars and artists would rediscover ancient Greece's love for dedicated inquiry and artistic expression, leading to a surge in scientific discoveries and advancements in the arts.

The ancient civilization of **Rome** owed much to the Greeks. Romans admired Greek architecture and arts, and built upon these traditions to create a distinct tradition of their own that would influence the western world for centuries.

In government, the Romans took the Athenian concept of democracy and built it into a complex system of a representative government that included executive, legislative, and judicial functions. In the arts, Romans created a realistic approach to portraiture, in contrast to the more idealized form of the Greeks. In architecture, Rome borrowed directly from the Greek tradition, but also developed the dome and the arch, allowing for larger and more dramatic forms. The Romans continued the Greek tradition of learning, often employing Greeks to educate their children.

The Roman Republic flourished in the centuries leading up to the advent of the Christian era. An organized bureaucracy and active political population provided elite Roman citizens with the means to ascend to positions of considerable authority. During the first century BCE, Gaius Julius Caesar ambitiously began to gather support among the ruling authorities of the Republic, eventually being named one of the two Consuls who were elected annually. Caesar was ultimately named dictator for life, and was the transitional leader between the Roman Republic and what would become the Roman Empire.

Like the Republic, the Roman Empire also looked to the east, to Greece, for inspiration. The Macedonian conqueror Alexander, who had unified Greece and introduced the culture throughout the eastern world, provided many Roman emperors with a role model.

The Roman Empire extended through much of Europe, and Roman culture extended with it. Everywhere the Romans went, they built roads, established cities, and left their mark on the local population. The Roman language, Latin, spread as well and was transformed into the Romance languages of French and Spanish. The Roman alphabet, which was based on the Greek transformation of Phoenician letters, was adopted throughout the empire and is still used today. The empire itself has served as a model for modern government, especially in federal systems such as that found in the United States. The eventual decline and fall of the empire has been a subject that has occupied historians for centuries.

Skill 12.3   The rise of non-European civilizations

Between the fourth and ninth centuries, Asia was a story of religions and empires, of kings and wars, and of increasing and decreasing contact with the West.

India began this period recovering from the invasion of Alexander the Great. One strong man who met the great Alexander was Chandragupta Maurya, who began one of his country's most successful dynasties. Chandragupta conquered most of what we now call India. His grandson, Asoka, was a more peaceful ruler, but powerful nonetheless. He was also a great believer in the practices and power of Buddhism, sending missionaries throughout Asia to preach the ways of the Buddha. Succeeding the Mauryas were the Guptas, who ruled India for a longer period of time and brought prosperity and international recognition to their people.

The Guptas were great believers in science and mathematics, especially as they pertained to the production of goods. They invented the decimal system and had a concept of zero, two things that put them ahead of the rest of the world on the mathematics timeline. They were the first to make cotton and calico, and their medical practices were much more advanced than those in Europe and elsewhere in Asia at the time. These inventions and innovations created high demand for Indian goods throughout Asia and Europe.

The idea of a united India continued after the Gupta Dynasty ended. It was especially favorable to the invading Muslims, who took over in the eleventh century, ruling the country for hundreds of years through a series of sultanates. The most famous Muslim leader of India was Tamerlane, who founded the Mogul Dynasty and began a series of conquests that expanded the borders of India. Tamerlane's grandson Akbar is considered the greatest Mogul. He believed in freedom of religion and is perhaps most well-known for the series of buildings that he had built, including mosques, palaces, forts, and tombs—some of which are still standing today. During the years that Muslims ruled India, Hinduism continued to be respected, although it was a minority religion; however, Buddhism died out almost entirely from the country that begot its founder.

The story of **China** during this time is one of dynasties controlling various parts of what is now China and Tibet. The Tang Dynasty was one of the most long-lasting and the most proficient, inventing the idea of civil service and the practice of block printing. The Sung Dynasty was also very influential, as it produced some of the world's greatest paintings and porcelain pottery. However, it failed to unify China in a meaningful way; this would prove instrumental in the takeover of China by the Mongols, led by Genghis Khan and his most famous grandson, Kublai.

Genghis Khan was known as a conqueror, and Kublai was known as a uniter. However, they both extended the borders of their empire; at its height, the Mongol Empire was the largest the world has ever seen, encompassing all of China, Russia, Persia, and central Asia. Following the Mongols were the Ming and Manchu Dynasties, both of which focused on isolation. As a result, China at the end of the eighteenth century knew very little of the outside world, and vice versa. Ming artists created beautiful porcelain pottery, but not much of it saw its way into the outside world until much later. The Manchus were known for their focus on farming and road-building, two practices that were instituted in greater numbers in order to try to keep up with expanding population. Confucianism, Taoism, and ancestor worship—the staples of Chinese society for hundreds of years—continued to flourish during all this time.

The other major power in Asia was **Japan**, which developed independently and tried to keep itself that way for hundreds of years. Early Japanese society focused on the emperor and the farm, in that order. Japan was often influenced early on by China, from which it borrowed many things, including religion (Buddhism), a system of writing, a calendar, and even fashion. The Sea of Japan protected Japan from outside invasion, including the famous campaign of the Mongols.

The power of the emperor declined as it was usurped by the era of the Daimyo and his loyal soldiers, the samurai. Japan flourished economically and culturally during many of these years, although the policy of isolation the country developed kept the rest of the world from knowing such things. Buddhism and local religions were joined by Christianity in the sixteenth century, but it wasn't until the mid-nineteenth century that Japan rejoined the world community.

African civilizations during these centuries were few and far between. Most of northern coastal Africa had been conquered by Moslem armies. The preponderance of deserts and other inhospitable lands restricted African settlements to a few select areas. The city of Zimbabwe became a trading center in south-central Africa in the fifth century, but it didn't last long. More successful was **Ghana**, a Muslim-influenced kingdom that arose in the ninth century and lasted for nearly 300 years. Ghanaians had large farming areas and also raised cattle and elephants. They traded with people from Europe and the Middle East. Eventually overrunning Ghana was Mali, whose trade center Timbuktu survived its own empire's demise and blossomed into one of the world's caravan destinations.

Iron, tin, and leather came out of **Mali** in abundance. The succeeding civilization of the Songhai had relative success in maintaining the accomplishments of their predecessors. Religion in all of these places was mostly Muslim. Even after extended contact with other cultures, technological advancements were few and far between.

The **North American** and **South American Native Americans** were vastly different cultures. Differences in geography, economic focus, and the preponderance of visitors from overseas produced differing patterns of occupation, survival, and success.

In North America, the landscape was much more hospitable to settlement and exploration. The North American continent, especially in what is now the United States, has few mountain ranges and a handful of wide rivers but nothing near the dense jungles and staggeringly high mountains that South America has. The area that is now Canada was cold but otherwise conducive to settlement. As a result, the Native Americans in the northern areas of the Americas were more spread out and their cultures more diverse than their South American counterparts.

One of the best known of the North American tribes were the Pueblo, who lived in what is now the American Southwest. They are perhaps best known for the challenging vista-based villages that they constructed from the sheer faces of cliffs and rocks as well as for their *adobes*, mud-brick buildings that housed their living and meeting quarters. The Pueblos chose their own chiefs. This was perhaps one of the oldest representative governments in the world. Known also for their organized government were the Iroquois, who lived in the American Northeast. The famous Five Nations of the Iroquois made treaties among themselves and shared leadership of their peoples.

Religion was a personal affair for nearly all of these tribes, with beliefs in higher powers extending to spirits in the sky and elsewhere in nature. Native Americans had none of the one-god-only mentality that developed in Europe and the Middle East, nor did they have the wars associated with the conflict that those monotheistic religions had with one another. Those people who lived in North America had large concentrations of people and houses, but they didn't have the kind of large civilization centers like cities elsewhere in the world. These people did not have an exact system of writing, either. These were two technological advances that were found in many other places in the world, including, to varying degrees, South America.

We know the most about the empires of South America: the Aztec, Inca, and Maya. However, people lived in South America before the advent of these empires; one of the earliest people of record was the Olmecs, who left behind little to prove their existence except a series of huge carved figures.

The **Aztecs** dominated Mexico and Central America. They weren't the only people living in these areas, just the most powerful ones. The Aztecs had many enemies, some of whom were only too happy to help Hernán Cortés precipitate the downfall of the Aztec society. The Aztecs had access to large numbers of metals and jewels; they used many of the metals to make weapons and the jewels to trade for items they didn't already possess. On the whole, however, the Aztecs didn't do a whole lot of trading; rather, they conquered neighboring tribes and demanded tribute from them. This was the source of so much of the Aztec riches.

They also believed in a handful of gods and that these gods demanded human sacrifice in order to continue to smile on the Aztecs. The center of Aztec society was the great city of Tenochtitlan, which was built on an island so as to be easier to defend. It boasted a population of 300,000 at the time of the arrival of the conquistadors. Tenochtitlan was known for its canals and its pyramids, none of which survive today.

The **Inca** Empire stretched across a vast period of territory down the western coast of South America and was connected by a series of roads. A series of messengers ran along these roads, carrying news and instructions from the capital, Cusco, another large city along the lines of but not as spectacular as Tenochtitlan. The Incas are known for inventing the *quipu*, a string-based device that provided them with a method of keeping records. The Inca Empire, like the Aztec Empire, was very much a centralized state, with all income going to the state coffers and all trade going through the emperor. The Incas worshiped the dead, their ancestors, and nature.

The most advanced Native American civilization were the **Maya**, who lived primarily in Central America. They were the only Native American civilization to develop writing, which consisted of a series of symbols that has still not been deciphered. The Mayas also built huge pyramids and other stone figures and sculptures, mostly of the gods they worshiped. The Mayas are most famous, however, for their calendars and mathematics. The Mayan calendars were the most accurate on the planet until the sixteenth century. The Mayas also invented the idea of zero, something that no other culture had thought of except for India. Maya worship resembled the practices of the Aztec and Inca, although human sacrifices were rare. The Mayas also traded heavily with their neighbors.

Skill 12.4   Cross-cultural comparisons

As the main civilizations grew and came into contact with each other, cultural exchanges took place at an increasing rate. Nevertheless, distinct religious, governments, and technological differences existed among the major civilizations during the first millennium CE.

Following the collapse of the Roman Empire and the division of the Christian Church in the fifth century, much of Europe became Christian, including the Visigoths who had taken control of Rome and much of the continent. The western Christian church became the Roman Catholic Church, and the Christian sect centered at Constantinople became the Eastern Orthodox Church. In Asia at this time, Confucianism was spreading from China as a religious and moral philosophy, and was adopted in China as the official core of the educational system. During the seventh century, the religion of Islam arose in the Middle East following the prophet Muhammad. In India, the already ancient religion of Hinduism was widely practiced.

Government among the various peoples during the first millennium was largely vested in a single leader: a king or emperor. Religion also played an important part in government and was often tightly connected to the figure of the king. In Europe, the concept of the divine right of kings emerged; it held that kings received authority to rule from God and held absolute power. Kings ruled through military power and by granting authority to other royal supporters. The system of feudalism arose as a method of ensuring military strength while providing a social order. In China, a vast bureaucracy was established to exercise control over the large area covered by the country. Confucianism was adopted as the basis for the exams given to those applying to enter the government service. In the Muslim areas of the Middle East, law was based on the Koran, the primary religious text of Islam. In the eighth century, the Pala Empire arose in India, a monarchical administration of Buddhist leaders who restored the Buddhist faith from near extinction in India.

In the area of science and technology, India was the first civilization to begin refining iron into steel around the third century CE. China developed printing and papermaking technologies that allowed information to be widely distributed. Muslim scholars made great strides in the fields of astronomy and mathematics, developing algebra and naming several stars. In Europe, Vikings were extending the range of boats and small ships, allowing for greater movement over the sea and setting the stage for the Age of Exploration that would follow in the next millennium.

Skill 12.5   The rise and expansion of Europe

As civilizations progressed through the Middle Ages and on into early modern times, the ways in which people communicated, explored, fought, and traded expanded. Methods of transportation were being updated all the time, with land-based vehicles growing ever larger and ships increasing in size and purpose. Ways to build, as in cities and towns, were increasing technologically as well.

At the same time that an emphasis was being put on connecting with the outside world, people were increasingly looking inward, both in their pursuit of "the next life," as most religions would style it, and in their desire to protect what they had earned. The same groups of people who worked together to build ships to sail the high seas also worked together to build tall castles to watch over their houses and towns. Advances in technology extended to warfare as well, with powerful new weapons like gunpowder making old ways of fighting obsolete. It was a turbulent time throughout the world.

Mountains and rivers still formed formidable boundaries for countries and civilizations as well. The ways that men killed other men had advanced, but the ways in which men crossed rivers and mountains hadn't kept pace. Mountains still had to be marched over, and rivers still had to be ferried or rafted across. If the defender was at the top of the mountain or on the other side of the river, it didn't matter how many advanced weapons the attackers had; the defender still had the edge. This was true in the high mountains of Asia and South America, in the delta-dotted plains of India and Central Asia, and in Europe, which boasted more than its fair share of high mountains (Alps and Pyrenees) and wide rivers (like the Rhine and the Rhone). This was the case everywhere around the world, except, of course, in the sands of sub-Saharan Africa, where struggles took the form of wars of attrition, the victors being those who weathered the sandstorms and lack of water the best.

As in the earliest days of civilization, people lived near waterways because they depended on those waterways for trade. The larger the boats, the more they could carry; this certainly increased the efficiency of trade. Foods and spices that previously were nonexistent in the markets of Europe because they would spoil before they ever reached their destination were increasingly for sale, since travel times had dramatically decreases due to improvements in travel technology. Following the stunningly successful example of the Roman Empire, more and more people built serviceable roads, making land-based trade less of a desperate adventure and more a viable alternative to water trading.

Especially in Europe during this period, the castle was a dominant feature on the landscape of towns, villages, and countries. Castles housed kings, soldiers, retinues, and peasants. They also served as watchtowers, guardhouses, and barracks. It was commonly known that if you wanted to take over a country, you had to take over the castles so your enemy couldn't stockpile soldiers and resources to make a counterstrike when you least expected it. Some conquerors made a habit of targeting castles, taking them over and then razing them, in order to eliminate the enemy's ability to fight back. Other conquerors felt compelled to build castles every few miles, as guard towers or, more likely, as symbols of their newfound authority. In a way, the castle was the new "high ground." In battles of old, the army that held the high ground had the advantage because its opponents would have to tire themselves out running uphill just to engage, while the high ground holders could pepper them with rocks, arrows, and other airborne weapons. Walled cities were certainly popular as defensible positions throughout history, but they weren't as easy to create as castles were and they couldn't be as easily defended. By building castles, the people of these periods changed their landscape in their favor, in effect creating a huge advantage where none had been before.

This was perhaps the way that the landscapes of the world changed the most—the way that people changed it. Where broad plains had been before, towns and villages, castles and fortifications, and ports and trade centers dotted the landscape. Despite such episodes as the devastating Black Plague and a seemingly endless series of wars, the populations of the world continued to expand, with people always seeking to expand their living spaces. More people meant not only more living space, but also more demand for basic and exotic goods. As civilization spread outward from its beginnings in the Fertile Crescent, ancient Africa, and along the rivers Indus and Yangtze, the needs and signatures of mankind spread with it.

Skill 12.6 Twentieth-century developments and transformations for world history

During the twentieth century, the world witnessed unprecedented strides in communications, a major expansion of international trade, and significant international diplomatic and military activity, including two world wars.

The rise of **nationalism** in Europe at the end of the nineteenth century led to a series of alliances and agreements among European nations. These agreements eventually led to the First World War, as nations called on their military allies to provide assistance and defense.

A new model of international relations was proposed following the devastation of WWI, one based on the mission to preserve peace. The **League of Nations** was formed to promote this peace, but it ultimately failed, having no way to enforce its resolutions. When Germany, led by Adolph Hitler, rebelled against the restrictions placed on it following WWI and began a campaign of military expansion through Europe, World War II ensued. Great Britain, the United States, and other allied nations combined forces to defeat Germany and the Axis powers.

Taking a lesson from the failure of the League of Nations, the world's nations organized the **United Nations**, an international assembly given the authority to arrange and enforce international resolutions.

World War II left Europe in ruins. As a result, the United States and the Soviet Union emerged as the two major world powers. Although allies in the war, tension arose between the two powers as the United States engaged in a policy of halting the spread of communism sponsored by the Soviets and China. The United States and the Soviet Union never engaged in direct military conflict during this "**Cold War**," but they were each involved in protracted conflicts in Korea and Vietnam. The threat of nuclear war increased as each power produced more and more weapons in an extended arms race. The threat of the spread of nuclear weapons largely diminished after the fall of the Soviet Union in the early 1990s, which ended the Cold War.

In Asia, new economies matured and the formerly tightly-controlled Chinese market became more open to foreign investment, increasing China's influence as a major economic power. In Europe, the **European Union** made a bold move to a common currency, the Euro, in a successful effort to consolidate the region's economic strength. In South America, countries such as Brazil and Venezuela showed growth despite political unrest, as Argentina suffered a near complete collapse of its economy. As the technology sector expanded, so did the economy of India, where hi-tech companies found a highly educated work force.

Conflict between the Muslim world and the United States increased during the last decade of the twentieth century, culminating in a terrorist attack on New York City and Washington, D.C., in 2001. These attacks, sponsored by the radical group Al-Qaeda, prompted a military invasion by the United States into Afghanistan, where the group is based. Shortly afterwards, the United States, England, and several smaller countries addressed further instability in the region by ousting Iraqi dictator Saddam Hussein in a military campaign. In the eastern Mediterranean, tension between Israelis and Palestinians continued to build, regularly erupting into violence.

COMPETENCY 13.0 UNITED STATES HISTORY

Skill 13.1 European exploration and colonization

Colonists from England, France, Holland, Sweden, and Spain all settled in North America on lands once frequented by Native Americans. Spanish colonies were mainly in the south, French colonies were mainly in the extreme north and in the middle of the continent, and the rest of the European colonies were in the northeast and along the Atlantic coast. These colonists got along with their new neighbors to varying degrees of success.

Of all of them, the French colonists seemed the most willing to work with the Native Americans. Even though their pursuit of animals to fill the growing demand for the fur trade was overpowering, they managed to find a way to maintain a relative peace with their new neighbors; the French and Native Americans even fought on the same side of the war against England. The Dutch and Swedish colonists were interested mostly in surviving in their new homes. However, they didn't last long in their struggles against England.

The English and Spanish colonists had the worst relations with the Native Americans, mainly because the Europeans made a habit of taking land, signing and then breaking treaties, massacring, and otherwise abusing their new neighbors. The Native Americans were only too happy to share their agriculture and jewel-making secrets with the Europeans; what they got in return was grief and deceit. The term "Manifest Destiny" meant nothing to the Native Americans, who believed that they lived on land loaned to them by the gods above.

The colonies were generally divided into three regions: New England, Middle Atlantic, and Southern. The culture of each was distinct and affected attitudes, ideas towards politics, religion, and economic activities. The geography of each region also contributed to their unique characteristics.

The **New England** colonies consisted of Massachusetts, Rhode Island, Connecticut, and New Hampshire. Life in these colonies was centered on the towns. Each family farmed its own plot of land, but a short summer growing season and limited amount of good soil gave rise to other economic activities such as manufacturing, fishing, shipbuilding, and trade. The vast majority of the settlers shared similar origins, mostly arriving from England and Scotland. Towns were carefully planned and laid out in similar fashions. The form of government was the town meeting where all adult males met to make the laws. The legislative body, the General Court, consisted of an upper and lower house.

The **Middle or Middle Atlantic** colonies included New York, New Jersey, Pennsylvania, Delaware, and Maryland. New York and New Jersey were at one time the Dutch colony of New Netherland, and Delaware was at one time New Sweden. These five colonies, from their beginnings, were considered "melting pots," with settlers from many different nations and backgrounds. The main economic activity was farming; the settlers were scattered over the countryside cultivating rather large farms. The Indians were not as much of a threat as they were in New England so the colonists did not have to settle in small farming villages. The soil was very fertile, the land was gently rolling, and a milder climate provided a longer growing season. These farms produced a large surplus of food, not only for the colonists themselves but also for sale. This colonial region became known as the "breadbasket" of the New World, and the New York and Philadelphia seaports were constantly filled with ships being loaded with meat, flour, and other foodstuffs for the West Indies and England.

There were other economic activities such as shipbuilding, iron mining, and producing paper, glass, and textiles in factories. The legislative body in Pennsylvania was unicameral or consisted of one house. In the other four colonies, the legislative body had two houses. Units of local government were found in counties and towns.

The **Southern** colonies were Virginia, North and South Carolina, and Georgia. Virginia was the first permanent successful English colony and Georgia was the last. The year 1619 was a very important year in the history of Virginia as well as the United States, with the occurrence of three very significant events. First, sixty women were sent to Virginia to marry and establish families; second, twenty Africans, the first of thousands, arrived; and third and most importantly, the Virginia colonists were granted the right to self-government. They began by electing their own representatives to the House of Burgesses—their own legislative body.

The major economic activity in this region was farming. Here too the soil was very fertile, and the climate was very mild with an even longer growing season than farther north. The large plantations, eventually requiring large numbers of slaves, were found in the coastal or tidewater areas. Although the wealthy slave-owning planters set the pattern of life in this region, most of the people lived inland away from coastal areas. They were small farmers and very few, if any, owned slaves.

The settlers in these four colonies came from diverse backgrounds and cultures. Virginia was colonized mostly by people from England, while Georgia was started as a haven for debtors from English prisons. Pioneers from Virginia settled in North Carolina, while South Carolina welcomed people from England and Scotland, French Protestants, Germans, and emigrants from islands in the West Indies.

Products from farms and plantations included rice, tobacco, indigo, cotton, some corn, and wheat. Other economic activities included lumber and naval stores (tar, pitch, rosin, and turpentine) from the pine forests and fur trade on the frontier. Cities such as Savannah and Charleston were important seaports and trading centers.

Skill 13.2 The American Revolution and the founding of the nation

Causes for the War for Independence

- With the end of the French and Indian War (The Seven Years' War), England decided to reassert control over the colonies in America. They particularly needed the revenue from the control of trade to pay for the recent war and to defend the new territory obtained as a result of the war.
- English leaders decided to impose a tax that would pay for the military defense of the American lands. The colonists rejected this idea for two reasons: 1) They were undergoing an economic recession, and 2) They believed it unjust to be taxed unless they had representation in the Parliament.
- England passed a series of laws that provoked fierce opposition:

  o The Proclamation Act prohibited English settlement beyond the Appalachian Mountains to appease the Native Americans.
  o The Sugar Act imposed a tax on foreign molasses, sugar, and other goods imported into the colonies.
  o The Currency Act prohibited colonial governments from issuing paper money.

Opposition melded in Massachusetts. Leaders denounced "taxation without representation" and a boycott was organized against imported English goods. The movement rapidly spread to other colonies.

The Stamp Act placed a tax on newspapers, legal documents, licenses, almanacs, and playing cards. This was the first instance of an "internal" tax on the colonies. In response, the colonists formed secret groups called "the Sons of Liberty" and staged riots against the agents who collected the taxes and marked items with a special stamp. In October of 1765, representatives of nine colonies met in the Stamp Act Congress. They drafted resolutions stating their reasons for opposing the Act and sent them to England. Merchants throughout the colonies applied pressure with a large boycott of imported English goods. The Stamp Act was repealed three months later.

England then had a dual concern: to generate revenue and to regain control of the colonists. They passed the Townshend Acts in 1767. These acts placed taxes on lead, glass, paint, paper, and tea.

This led to another very successful boycott of English goods. England responded by limiting the tax to tea. This ended the boycotts of everything except tea. The situation between colonists and British troops was becoming increasingly strained. Despite a skirmish in New York and the "Boston Massacre" in 1770, tensions abated over the next few years.

The Tea Act of 1773 gave the British East India Company a monopoly on sales of tea. The colonists responded with the "Boston Tea Party." England responded with the "Coercive Acts" (called the "Intolerable Acts" by the colonists) in 1774. This closed the port of Boston, changed the charter of the Massachusetts colony, and suppressed town meetings. Eleven colonies sent delegates to the first Continental Congress in 1774. The group issued the "Declaration of Rights and Grievances" which vowed allegiance to the king but protested the right of Parliament to tax the colonies. The boycotts resumed at the same time.

Massachusetts mobilized its colonial militia in anticipation of difficulties with England. The British troops attempted to seize their weapons and ammunition. The result was two clashes with "minute men" at Lexington and Concord. The Second Continental Congress met a month later. Many of the delegates recommended a declaration of independence from Britain. The group established an army and commissioned George Washington as its commander.

British forces attacked patriot strongholds at Breed's Hill and Bunker Hill. Although the colonists withdrew, the loss of life for the British was nearly fifty percent of the army. The next month King George III declared the American colonies to be in a state of rebellion. The war quickly began in earnest. On July 3, 1776, British General Howe arrived in New York Harbor with 10,000 troops to prepare for an attack on the city. The following day, the Second Continental Congress accepted the final draft of the Declaration of Independence by unanimous vote.

Although the colonial army was quite small in comparison to the British army, and although it was lacking in formal military training, the colonists had learned a new method of warfare from the Indians. To be sure, many battles were fought in the traditional style of two lines of soldiers facing off and firing weapons, but the advantage the patriots had was the understanding of guerilla warfare–fighting from behind trees and other defenses. When the war began, the colonies began to establish state governments. To a significant extent, the government that was defined for the new nation was intentionally weak. The colonies/states feared centralized government; however, the lack of continuity between the individual governments was confusing and economically damaging.

Skill 13.3   Growth and expansion of the Republic

The Constitutional Convention of 1787 devised an entirely new form of government and outlined it in the Constitution of the United States. The Constitution was ratified quickly and took effect in 1789. Concerns that had been raised in or by the states regarding civil liberties and states rights led to the immediate adoption of twelve amendments to the Constitution; the first ten are known as the Bill of Rights.

In regards to the current American political system, it is important to realize that political parties are never mentioned in the United States Constitution. In fact, George Washington himself warned against the creation of "factions" in American politics that cause "jealousies and false alarms" as well as the damage they could cause to the body politic. Thomas Jefferson echoed this warning, yet he would come to lead a party himself.

Americans had good reason to fear the emergence of political parties. They had witnessed how parties worked in Great Britain. Parties, called "factions" in Britain, were made up of a few people who schemed to win favors from the government. They were more interested in their own personal profits and advantages than in the public good. Thus, the new American leaders were very interested in keeping factions from forming. It was, ironically, disagreements between two of Washington's chief advisors, **Thomas Jefferson** and **Alexander Hamilton**, that spurred the formation of the first political parties in the newly formed United States of America.

The two parties that developed throughout the early 1790s were led by Jefferson as the Secretary of State and Alexander Hamilton as the Secretary of the Treasury. Jefferson and Hamilton were different in many ways, including their views on what should be the proper form of government of the United States. This difference helped to shape the parties that formed around them.

Hamilton wanted the federal government to be stronger than the state governments. Jefferson believed that the state governments should be stronger. Hamilton supported the creation of the first Bank of the United States; Jefferson opposed it because he felt that it gave too much power to wealthy investors who would help to run it. Jefferson interpreted the Constitution strictly; he argued that nowhere did the Constitution give the federal government the power to create a national bank.

Hamilton interpreted the Constitution much more loosely. He pointed out that the Constitution gave Congress the power to make all laws "necessary and proper" to carry out its duties. He reasoned that since Congress had the right to collect taxes, then Congress had the right to create the bank.

Hamilton also wanted the government to encourage economic growth. He favored the growth of trade, manufacturing, and the rise of cities as the necessary parts of economic growth. He favored the business leaders and mistrusted the common people. Jefferson believed that the common people, especially the farmers, were the backbone of the nation. He thought that the rise of big cities and manufacturing would corrupt American life.

Before long, leaders in other states began to organize support for either Jefferson or Hamilton. Jefferson's supporters called themselves **Democratic-Republicans** (often this was shortened just to Republicans, though in actuality it was the forerunner of today's Democratic Party). Hamilton and his supporters were known as **Federalists**, because they favored a strong federal government. The Federalists had the support of the merchants and ship owners in the Northeast and some planters in the South. Small farmers, craft workers, and some of the wealthier landowners supported Jefferson and the Democratic-Republicans.

By the time Washington retired from office in 1796, the new political parties would come to play an important role in choosing his successor. Each party would put up its own candidates for office. The election of 1796 was the first one in which political parties played a role. By the beginning of the 1800s, the Federalist Party, torn by internal divisions, began suffering a decline. This was exacerbated in 1800 when Thomas Jefferson was elected president. After the leader of the Federalist Party, Alexander Hamilton, was killed in 1804 in a duel with Aaron Burr, the Federalist Party began to collapse. By 1816, after losing a string of important elections (Jefferson was reelected in 1804, and James Madison, a Democratic-Republican was elected in 1808), the Federalist Party ceased to be an effective political force, and soon passed off the national stage.

By the late 1820s, new political parties had grown up. The **Democratic-Republican** Party, or simply the **Republican** Party, had been the major party for many years, but differences within it about the direction the country was headed caused a split after 1824. Those who favored strong national growth took the name **Whigs** after a similar party in Great Britain and united around then President John Quincy Adams. Many business people in the Northeast as well as some wealthy planters in the South supported it.

Those who favored slower growth and were more worker and small farmer oriented went on to form the new **Democratic Party**, with Andrew Jackson acting as its first leader (he also became its first President). It was the forerunner of today's present party of the same name.

In the mid-1850s, the slavery issue was beginning to heat up; in 1854, those opposed to slavery, the Whigs, along with some Northern Democrats, united to form the Republican Party. Before the Civil War, the Democratic Party was more heavily represented in the South and was thus primarily pro-slavery.

Therefore, by the time of the Civil War, the present configuration of the major political parties had been formed. Though there would sometimes be drastic changes in ideology and platforms over the years, no other political parties would manage to gain enough strength to seriously challenge the "Big Two" parties.

In fact, they have shown themselves adaptable to changing times. In many instances, they have managed to shut out other parties by simply adapting their platforms, such as in the 1930s during the Great Depression and in the years immediately preceding. The Democratic Party adapted much of the Socialist Party platform and, under Franklin Roosevelt, put much of it into effect, thus managing to eliminate the Socialist Party as any serious threat.

Since the Civil War, no other political party has managed to gain enough support to either elect substantial members to Congress or to elect a President. Some have come closer than others, but barring any unforeseen circumstances, the absolute monopoly on national political debate seems very secure in the hands of the Republican and Democratic Parties.

In the United States, territorial expansion occurred in the expansion westward under the banner of **Manifest Destiny**. In addition, the United States was involved in the War with Mexico, the Spanish-American War, and the support of the Latin American colonies of Spain in their revolt for independence. In Latin America, the Spanish colonies were successful in their fight for independence and self-government

After the United States purchased the Louisiana Territory, Jefferson appointed Captains Meriwether Lewis and William Clark to explore it, to find out exactly what had been bought. The expedition, called the Corps of Discovery, eventually included a slave named York, a dog, forty young men, a female Indian named Sacagawea and her infant son. They went all the way to the Pacific Ocean, returning two years later with maps, journals, and artifacts. This led the way for future explorers to make available more knowledge about the territory; it also resulted in the Westward Movement and the later belief in the doctrine of Manifest Destiny.

Initially, the United States and Britain shared the Oregon country. By the 1840s, with the increase in the free and slave populations and the demand of the settlers for control and government by the United States, the conflict had to be resolved. In a treaty signed in 1846 by both nations, a peaceful resolution occurred with Britain giving up its claims south of the 49th parallel.

In the American Southwest, the results were exactly the opposite. Spain had claimed this area since the 1540s, had spread northward from Mexico City, and, in the 1700s, had established missions, forts, villages, towns, and very large ranches. After the purchase of the Louisiana Territory in 1803, Americans began moving into Spanish territory. A few hundred American families in what is now Texas were allowed to live there but had to agree to become loyal subjects to Spain. In 1821, Mexico successfully revolted against Spanish rule, won independence, and chose to be more tolerant towards American settlers and traders. The Mexican government encouraged and allowed extensive trade and settlement, especially in Texas. Many of the new settlers were southerners who brought their slaves with them. Slavery was outlawed in Mexico and technically illegal in Texas, although the Mexican government often looked the other way.

Friction increased between land-hungry Americans swarming into western lands and the Mexican government that controlled these lands. The clash was not only political but also cultural and economic. The Spanish influence permeated all parts of southwestern life: law, language, architecture, and customs. By this time, the doctrine of Manifest Destiny was in the hearts and on the lips of those seeking new areas of settlement and a new life. Americans were demanding U.S. control of not only the Mexican Territory but also of Oregon. Although peaceful negotiations with Great Britain secured Oregon, it took two years of war to gain control of the southwestern United States.

To make the tensions worse, the Mexican government owed debts to U.S. citizens whose property was damaged or destroyed during its struggle for independence from Spain. By the time war broke out in 1845, Mexico had not paid its war debts. The government was weak, corrupt, irresponsible, torn by revolutions, and not in decent financial shape. Mexico was also bitter over American expansion into Texas and the 1836 revolution, which resulted in Texas' independence. In the 1844 presidential election, the Democrats pushed for the annexation of Texas and Oregon and after winning, they started the procedure to admit Texas to the Union.

When statehood occurred, diplomatic relations between the United States and Mexico were ended. President Polk wanted U.S. control of the entire southwest, from Texas to the Pacific Ocean. He sent a diplomatic mission with an offer to purchase New Mexico and Upper California, but the Mexican government refused to even receive the diplomats. Consequently, in 1846, each nation claimed aggression on the part of the other and war was declared. The treaty signed in 1848 and a subsequent one in 1853 completed the southwestern boundary of the United States, reaching to the Pacific Ocean, as President Polk wished.

The impact of the entire westward movement resulted in the completion of the borders of the present-day contiguous United States. Overall, the major contributing factors included the bloody war with Mexico; the ever-growing controversy over slave versus free states, which affected the balance of power in the U.S. Congress, especially the Senate; and the Civil War.

The Civil War began through a series of events that spanned decades. Tensions between the southern states and the northern states were increasing; in 1833, Congress lowered tariffs, this time at a level acceptable to South Carolina, which had been growing increasingly dissatisfied with the federal government. Although President Jackson believed in states' rights, he also firmly believed in and was determined to preserve the Union. Through Jackson's efforts, a constitutional crisis had been averted, but sectional divisions were getting deeper and more pronounced. The abolition movement was also growing rapidly, becoming an important issue in the North. The slavery issue was at the root of every problem, crisis, event, decision, and struggle from then on.

The next crisis involved the issue concerning Texas. By 1836, Texas was an independent republic with its own constitution. During its fight for independence, Americans were sympathetic to and supportive of the Texans, and some individuals recruited volunteers who crossed into Texas to help the struggle. Problems arose when the state petitioned Congress for statehood. Texas wanted to allow slavery, but Northerners in Congress opposed admission to the Union because it would disrupt the balance between free and slave states and give Southerners in Congress increased influence.

A few years later, Congress took up consideration of new territories between Missouri and present-day Idaho. Again, heated debate over permitting slavery in these areas flared up. Those opposed to slavery used the **Missouri Compromise** to prove their point showing that the land being considered for territories was part of the area the Compromise had been designated as banned to slavery. On May 25, 1854, Congress passed the infamous **Kansas-Nebraska Act** which nullified the provision creating the territories of Kansas and Nebraska. This allowed the people of these two territories to decide for themselves whether or not to permit slavery to exist there. Feelings were so deep and divided that any further attempts to compromise met with little, if any, success. Political and social turmoil swirled everywhere. Kansas was called "Bleeding Kansas" because of the extreme violence and bloodshed throughout the territory due to the two governments that existed there: one pro-slavery and the other anti-slavery.

In 1857, the Supreme Court handed down a decision guaranteed to cause explosions throughout the country. Dred Scott was a slave whose owner had taken him from slave state Missouri, then to free state Illinois, into Minnesota Territory (free under the provisions of the Missouri Compromise), and finally back to slave state Missouri. Abolitionists pursued the dilemma by presenting a court case, stating that since Scott had lived in a free state and free territory, he was in actuality a free man.

Two lower courts ruled before the Supreme Court became involved: one ruling in favor and one against. The Supreme Court decided that residing in a free state and free territory did not make Scott a free man because Scott (and all other slaves) was not a U.S. citizen or a state citizen of Missouri. Therefore, he did not have the right to sue in state or federal courts. The Court went a step further and ruled that the old Missouri Compromise was now unconstitutional because Congress did not have the power to prohibit slavery in the Territories.

In 1858, Abraham Lincoln and Stephen A. Douglas were running for the office of U.S. Senator from Illinois; they participated in a series of debates that directly affected the outcome of the 1860 presidential election. Douglas, a Democrat, was up for re-election and knew that if he won this race, he had a good chance of becoming president in 1860. Lincoln, a Republican, was not an abolitionist but he believed that slavery was morally wrong. He firmly believed in and supported the Republican Party principle that slavery must not be allowed to extend any further. The final straw came with the election of Lincoln to the Presidency the next year. Due to a split in the Democratic Party, there were four candidates from four political parties. With Lincoln receiving a minority of the popular vote and a majority of electoral votes, the Southern states, one by one, voted to secede from the Union, as they had promised they would do if Lincoln and the Republicans were victorious. The die was cast.

Both sides quickly prepared for war. The North had more in its favor: a larger population; superiority in finances and transportation facilities; and manufacturing, agricultural, and natural resources. The North possessed most of the nation's gold, had about 92 percent of all industries, and had almost all the known supplies of copper, coal, iron, and various other minerals. Most of the nation's railroads were in the North and mid-West; men and supplies could be moved wherever needed and food could be transported from the farms of the mid-West to workers in the East as well as to soldiers on the battlefields. Trade with nations overseas could go on as usual due to control of the navy and the merchant fleet.

The Northern states numbered twenty-four and included western (California and Oregon) and border (Maryland, Delaware, Kentucky, Missouri, and West Virginia) states. The Southern states numbered eleven and included South Carolina, Georgia, Florida, Alabama, Mississippi, Louisiana, Texas, Virginia, North Carolina, Tennessee, and Arkansas, making up the Confederacy.

Although outnumbered in population, the South was completely confident of victory. They knew that all they had to do was fight a defensive war and protect their own territory. The North had to invade and defeat an area almost the size of Western Europe. Another advantage of the South was that a number of its best officers had graduated from the U.S. Military Academy at West Point and had long years of army experience. Many had exercised varying degrees of command in the Indian Wars and the war with Mexico. Men from the South were conditioned to living outdoors and were more familiar with horses and firearms than men from northeastern cities. Since cotton was such an important crop, Southerners felt that British and French textile mills were so dependent on raw cotton that they would be forced to help the Confederacy in the war.

The South won decisively until the **Battle of Gettysburg**, July 1 - 3, 1863. Until Gettysburg, Lincoln's commanders, McDowell and McClellan, were less than desirable; Burnside and Hooker, not what was needed. Lee, on the other hand, had many able officers; Jackson and Stuart were depended on heavily by him. Jackson died at Chancellorsville and was replaced by Longstreet. Lee decided to invade the North and depended on J.E.B. Stuart and his cavalry to keep him informed of the location of Union troops and their strengths.

The day after Gettysburg, on July 4, Vicksburg, Mississippi surrendered to Union General Ulysses Grant, thus severing the western Confederacy from the eastern part. In September 1863, the Confederacy won its last important victory at Chickamauga. In November, the Union victory at Chattanooga made it possible for Union troops to go into Alabama and Georgia, splitting the eastern Confederacy in two. Lincoln gave Grant command of all Northern armies in March of 1864. Grant led his armies into battles in Virginia while Phil Sheridan and his cavalry did as much damage as possible. In a skirmish at a place called Yellow Tavern, Virginia, Sheridan's and Stuart's forces met, with Stuart being fatally wounded.

The Civil War took more American lives than any other American war in history, the South losing one-third of its soldiers in battle compared to about one-sixth for the North. More than half of the total deaths were caused by disease and the horrendous conditions of field hospitals. Destruction was pervasive in towns, farms, trade, and industry. The lives and homes of men, women, children were almost entirely destroyed and an entire Southern way of life lost. The South had no voice in the political, social, and cultural affairs of the nation, lessening to a great degree the influence of the more traditional Southern ideals. The Northern Yankee Protestant ideals of hard work, education, and economic freedom became the standard of the United States and helped influence the development of the nation into a modem, industrial power.

The effects of the Civil War were tremendous. It changed the methods of waging war and has been called the first modern war. It introduced weapons and tactics that, when improved later, were used extensively in wars of the late 1800s and 1900s. Civil War soldiers were the first to fight in trenches, the first to fight under a unified command, and the first to wage a defense called "major cordon defense" (a strategy of advance on all fronts). They were also the first to use repeating and breech loading weapons. Observation balloons were first used during the war along with submarines, ironclad ships, and mines. Telegraphy and railroads were also first put to use during this time.

By executive proclamation and constitutional amendment, slavery was officially ended, although there remained deep prejudice and racism (which is still apparent today). The Union was preserved and the states were finally truly united. Sectionalism, especially in the area of politics, remained strong for another 100 years but not to the degree and with the violence as existed before 1861.

It has been noted that the Civil War may have been American democracy's greatest failure, as calm reason, which is basic to democracy, fell victim to human passion. Yet democracy did survive. The victory of the North established that no state has the right to end or leave the Union. Because of this unity, the United States became a major global power. It is important to remember that Lincoln never proposed to punish the South. He was most concerned with restoring the South to the Union in a program that was flexible and practical rather than rigid and unbending. In fact, he never really felt that the states had succeeded in leaving the Union, but that they had left the 'family circle" for a short time.

The conclusion of the Civil War opened the floodgates for **westward migration** and the settlement of new land. The availability of cheap land and the expectation of great opportunities prompted thousands to travel across the Mississippi River and settle the Great Plains and California. The primary activities of the new western economy were farming, mining, and ranching. Both migration and the economy were facilitated by the expansion of the railroad and the completion of the transcontinental railroad in 1869.

Migration and settlement were not easy. As the settlers moved west, they encountered Native American tribes who believed they had a natural right to the lands upon which their ancestors had lived for generations. Resentment of the encroachment of new settlers was particularly strong among the tribes that had been ordered to relocate to "Indian Country" prior to 1860. Conflict was intense and frequent until 1867, when the government established two large tracts of land called "reservations" in Oklahoma and the Dakotas to which all tribes would be confined.

With the war over, troops were sent west to enforce the relocation and reservation containment policies. There were frequent wars, particularly as white settlers attempted to move onto Indian lands and as the tribes resisted this confinement.

Continuing conflict led to the passage of the Dawes Act of 1887. This was a recognition that confinement in reservations was not working. The law was intended to break up the Indian communities and bring about assimilation into white culture by deeding portions of the reservation lands to individual Indians who were expected to farm their land. The policy continued until 1934.

Armed resistance essentially came to an end by 1890. The surrender of Geronimo and the massacre at Wounded Knee led to a change of strategy by the Indians. Thereafter, the resistance strategy was to preserve their culture and traditions.

There was a marked degree of **industrialization** before and during the Civil War, but at war's end, industry in America was small. After the war, dramatic changes took place: machines replaced hand labor; extensive nationwide railroad service made possible the wider distribution of goods; new products were made available in large quantities; and large amounts of money from bankers and investors were available for the expansion of business operations. American life was definitely affected by this phenomenal industrial growth. Cities became the centers of this new business activity, resulting in mass population movements and tremendous growth. This new boom in business resulted in huge fortunes for some Americans and extreme poverty for many others. The discontent this caused resulted in a number of new reform movements from which came measures controlling the power and size of big business and helping the poor.

The use of machines in industry enabled workers to produce a large quantity of goods much faster than they could by hand. With the increase in business, hundreds of workers were hired and assigned to perform specific jobs in the production process. This was a method of organization called the "division of labor"; by its ability to increase the rate of production, businesses lowered prices for their products, making the products affordable for more people. As a result, sales and businesses were increasingly successful and profitable.

A great variety of new products and inventions became available, including the typewriter, the telephone, barbed wire, the electric light, the phonograph, and the gasoline automobile. From this list, the one that had the greatest effect on America's economy was the automobile.

The increase in business and industry was greatly affected by the many rich **natural resources** that were found throughout the nation. The industrial machines were powered by an abundant water supply. The construction industry as well as products made from wood depended heavily on lumber from the forests. Coal and iron ore in abundance were needed for the steel industry, which profited and increased from the use of steel in such things as skyscrapers, automobiles, bridges, railroad tracks, and machines. Other minerals such as silver, copper, and petroleum played a large role in industrial growth (especially petroleum, from which gasoline was refined as fuel for the increasingly popular automobile).

The developments in communication, such as the telephone and telegraph, increased the efficiency and prosperity of big business. Steam power generation, sophisticated manufacturing equipment, the ability to move about the country quickly by railroad, and the invention of the steam powered tractor resulted in a phenomenal growth in industrial output. The new steel and oil industries provided a significant impetus to industrial growth and added thousands of new jobs. The "inventive spirit" of the time was a major force propelling the industrial revolution forward. This spirit led to an improvement in products, the development of new production processes and equipment, and even to the creation of entirely new industries. During the last forty years of the nineteenth century, inventors registered almost 700,000 new patents.

One result of industrialization was the growth of the **Labor Movement**. There were numerous boycotts and strikes that often became violent when the police or the militia were called in. Labor and farmer organizations were created and became a political force. Industrialization also brought an influx of immigrants from Asia (particularly from China and Japan) and from Europe (particularly European Jews, the Irish, and Russians). High rates of immigration led to the creation of cultural communities within various cities, such as "little Russia" or "little Italy."

Industrialization also led to the overwhelming growth of cities as workers moved closer to their places of work. The economy was booming, but it was based on basic needs and luxury goods, for which there was to be only limited demand, especially during times of economic recession or depression.

Skill 13.4   Twentieth-century developments and transformations

The United States underwent significant social and economic changes during the twentieth century, and it became a dominant world power internationally. Economically, the United States saw periods of great prosperity, as well as severe depression, emerging as primary economic forces.

The **industrialization** that had started following the end of the Civil War in the mid-nineteenth century continued into the early decades of the twentieth century. A huge wave of immigration at the turn of the century provided industry with a large labor pool and established millions of immigrants and their families in the working class.

Populism is a philosophy concerned with the common sense needs of average people. Populism often finds expression as a reaction against perceived oppression of the average people by the wealthy elite in society. The prevalent claim of populist movements is that they will put the people first. Populist movements claim to represent the majority of the people and call them to stand up to institutions or practices that seem detrimental to their well-being.

Populism flourished in the late nineteenth and early twentieth centuries in the United States. Several political parties were formed out of this philosophy, including the Greenback Party, the Populist Party, the Farmer-Labor Party, the Single Tax movement of Henry George, the Share Our Wealth movement of Huey Long, the Progressive Party, and the Union Party.

The tremendous changes that resulted from the Industrial Revolution led to a demand for reform that would control the power wielded by big corporations. The gap between the industrial moguls and the working people was growing; this disparity resulted in a public outcry for reform at the same time that there was an outcry for governmental reform that would end the political corruption and elitism of the day.

The reforms initiated by leaders and the spirit of **Progressivism** were far-reaching. Politically, many states enacted initiatives and referendums for progressive movements. The adoption of the recall occurred in many states, and several states enacted legislation that would undermine the power of political machines. On a national level, the two most significant political changes were: 1) the ratification of the Seventeenth Amendment, which required that all U.S. Senators be chosen by popular election, and 2) the ratification of the Nineteenth Amendment, which granted women the right to vote.

Major economic reforms of the period included the aggressive enforcement of the Sherman Antitrust Act and the passage of the Elkins Act and the Hepburn Act, which gave the Interstate Commerce Commission greater power to regulate the railroads. The Pure Food and Drug Act prohibited the use of harmful chemicals in food; the Meat Inspection Act regulated the meat industry to protect the public against tainted meat; over two-thirds of the states passed laws prohibiting child labor; workmen's compensation was mandated; and the Department of Commerce and Labor was created.

Responding to concern over the environmental effects of the timber, ranching, and mining industries, Roosevelt set aside 238 million acres of federal lands to be protected from development. Wildlife preserves were established, the national park system was expanded, and the National Conservation Commission was created. The Newlands Reclamation Act also provided federal funding for the construction of irrigation projects and dams in semi-arid areas of the country.

The Wilson Administration carried out additional reforms. The Federal Reserve Act created a national banking system, providing a more stable money supply. The Sherman Act and the Clayton Antitrust Act defined unfair competition, made corporate officers liable for the illegal actions of employees, and exempted labor unions from antitrust lawsuits. The Federal Trade Commission was established to enforce these measures. Finally, the Sixteenth Amendment was ratified, establishing an income tax. This measure was designed to relieve the poor of a disproportionate burden in funding the federal government and to make the wealthy pay a greater share of the nation's tax burden.

Before 1800, most manufacturing activities were done in small shops or in homes. However, starting in the early 1800s, factories with modern machines were built, making it easier to produce goods faster. The eastern part of the country became a major industrial area, although some industry was developed in the west. At about the same time, improvements began to be made in building roads, railroads, canals, and steamboats. The increased ease of travel facilitated the westward movement as well as boosted the economy with faster and cheaper shipment of goods and products, covering larger and larger areas. Some of the innovations arising from these changes included the Erie Canal, which connects the interior and Great Lakes with the Hudson River and the coastal port of New York. Many other natural waterways were connected by canals during this time.

Robert Fulton's Clermont, the first commercially successful steamboat, led the pack as the fastest way to ship goods, making it the most important means to do so. Later, steam-powered railroads became the biggest rival of the steamboat as a means of shipping, eventually becoming the most important transportation method opening the west.

With expansion into the interior of the country, the United States became the leading agricultural nation in the world. The hardy pioneer farmers produced a vast surplus, and emphasis went to producing products with a high-sale value. Implements such as the cotton gin and the reaper aided in higher production. Travel and shipping were greatly assisted in areas not yet reached by railroad; they were also facilitated by improved and new roads, such as the National Road in the east and the Oregon and Santa Fe Trails in the west.

As travel and communication became faster, people became more exposed to works of literature, art, newspapers, drama, live entertainment, and political rallies. More information was desired about previously unknown areas of the country, especially the west, and the discovery of gold and other mineral wealth resulted in a literal surge of settlers.

Public schools were established in many of the states, and more and more children were able to get an education. With higher literacy and more participation in literature and the arts, the young nation was developing its own unique culture, becoming less and less influenced by and dependent on that of Europe.

At the same time, more industries and factories required more labor. Women, children, and, at times, entire families worked dangerously long hours until the 1830s. By that time, factories were getting even larger and employers began hiring immigrants who were coming to America in huge numbers. Before then, efforts were made to organize a labor movement to improve working conditions and increase wages. It never really caught on until after the Civil War.

The prosperity of industrial and economic changes was interrupted by America's entry into the **First World War** in 1917. While reluctant to enter the hostilities, the United States played a decisive role in ending the war and in the creation of the League of Nations that followed, establishing its central position in international relations that would increase in importance through the century.

The **World War I** effort required a massive production of weapons, ammunition, radios, and other equipment of war. During wartime, work hours were shortened, wages were increased, and working conditions improved. When the war ended, and business and industrial owners attempted to return to pre-war conditions, the workers revolted. These conditions contributed to the establishment of new labor laws.

The United States resumed its prosperous industrial growth in the years after WWI, but even as industrial profits and stock market investments skyrocketed, farm prices and wages fell, creating an unbalanced situation that caused an economic collapse in 1929, when the stock market crashed. The United States plummeted into economic depression with high unemployment. This period is known as the **Great Depression**.

President Franklin Roosevelt proposed that the federal government assist in rebuilding the economy, something his predecessor, President Hoover, thought the government should not do. Roosevelt's **New Deal** policies were adopted to wide success, and marked an important shift in the role that the U.S. government plays in economic matters and social welfare.

The nation's recovery was underway when, in late 1941, it entered the Second World War to fight against Japan and Germany and their allied Axis powers. Fifty-nine nations became embroiled in **World War II**, which began September 1, 1939 and ended September 2, 1945. These dates include both the European and Pacific Theaters of war. The horribly tragic results of this second global conflagration were more deaths and more destruction than those of any other armed conflict. It completely uprooted and displaced millions of people. The end of the war brought renewed power struggles, especially in Europe and China; many Eastern European nations as well as China came under the control and domination of the communists, supported and backed by the Soviet Union. $

With the development of and a two-time deployment of atomic bombs against two Japanese cities, the world found itself in the nuclear age. The peace settlement established by the United Nations Organization after the war still exists and operates today.

The years between WWI and WWII produced significant advancements in aircraft technology, and the pace of aircraft development and production was dramatically increased during WWII. Major developments included flight-based weapon delivery systems, the long-range bomber, the first jet fighter, the first cruise missile, and the first ballistic missile. Although they were invented, cruise and ballistic missiles were not widely used during the war. Glider planes were heavily used in WWII because they were silent upon approach. Another significant development was the broad use of paratrooper units. Hospital planes also came into use to extract the seriously wounded from the front and to transport them to hospitals for treatment.

Weapons and technology in other areas also improved rapidly during this time. These advances were critical in determining the outcome of the war. Radar, electronic computers, nuclear weapons, and new tank designs were used for the first time. More new inventions were registered for patents than ever before; most of these new ideas were aimed to either kill or prevent being killed.

The war began with essentially the same weaponry that had been used in WWI. However, as the war progressed, so did technology. The aircraft carrier joined the battleship; the Higgins boat, the primary landing craft, was invented; light tanks were developed to meet the needs of a changing battlefield; and other armored vehicles were developed. Submarines were also perfected during this period.

Numerous other weapons were also developed or invented to meet the needs of battle during WWII: the bazooka, the rocket propelled grenade, anti-tank weapons, assault rifles, the tank destroyer, mine-clearing Flail tanks, Flame tanks, submersible tanks, cruise missiles, rocket artillery and air launched rockets, guided weapons, torpedoes, self-guiding weapons, and napalm. The Atomic Bomb was also developed and used for the first time during WWII. The war industry fueled another period of economic prosperity that lasted through the post-war years. The 1950s saw the emergence of a large consumer culture in the United States, which has bolstered not only the American economy ever since, but has been an important development for other countries that produce goods for the U.S. market.

The United States first established itself as an important world military leader at the turn of the twentieth century during the Spanish American War; it cemented this position during the two World Wars. Following WWII, with Europe struggling to recover from the fighting, the United States and the Soviet Union emerged as the two dominant world powers. This remained the situation for three decades while the two super powers engaged in a Cold War between the ideals of communism and capitalism. In the 1980s, the Soviet Union underwent a series of reforms that resulted in the collapse of the country and the end of the Cold War, leaving the United States as the true world power. Thus, the United States changed from a reluctant participant in international affairs into a central leader.

Major technological developments in the post WWII era:
- Discovery of penicillin (1945)
- Detonation of the first atomic bombs (1945)
- Xerography process invented (1946)
- Exploration of the South Pole
- Studies of X-ray radiation
- U.S. airplane first flies at supersonic speed (1947)
- Invention of the transistor (1947)
- Long-playing record invented (1948)
- Studies begin in the science of chemo-genetics (1948)
- Mount Palomar reflecting telescope created (1948)
- Idlewild Airport (now known as JFK International Airport) opens in NY City
- Cortisone discovered (1949)
- USSR tests first atomic bomb (1949)
- U.S. guided missile launched and traveled 250 miles (1949)
- Plutonium separated (1950)
- Tranquilizer meprobamate comes to wide use (1950)
- Antihistamines become popular in treating colds and allergies (1950)
- Electric power produced from atomic energy (1951)
- First heart-lung machine devised (1951)
- First solo flight over the North Pole (1951)
- Yellow fever vaccine developed (1951)

- Isotopes used in medicine and industry (1952)
- Contraceptive pill produced (1952)
- First hydrogen bomb exploded (1952)
- Nobel Prize in medicine for discovery of streptomycin (1952)
- Cave Cougnac discovered with prehistoric paintings (1953)
- USSR explodes hydrogen bomb (1953)
- Hillary and Tenzing reach the summit of Mount Everest (1953)
- Lung cancer connected to cigarette smoking (1953)
- First U.S. submarine converted to nuclear power (1954)
- Polio vaccine invented (1954)
- Discovery of Vitamin B12 (1955)
- Discovery of the molecular structure of insulin (1955)
- First artificial manufacture of diamonds (1955)
- Beginning of development of "visual telephone" (1956)
- Beginning of Transatlantic cable telephone service (1956)
- USSR launches first earth satellites (Sputnik I and II) (1957)
- Mackinac Straits Bridge in Michigan opens as the longest suspension bridge (1957)
- Stereo recordings introduced (1958)
- NASA created (1958)
- USSR launches rocket with two monkeys aboard (1959)
- Nobel Prize for Medicine for synthesis of RNA and DNA (1959)

COMPETENCY 14.0 POLITICAL SCIENCE

Skill 14.1 The nature and purpose of government

Historically, the functions of government (or people's concepts of government and its purpose and function) have varied considerably. In the theory of political science, the function of government is to secure the common welfare of the members of the given society over which it exercises control. In different historical eras, governments have attempted to achieve the common welfare by means in accordance with the traditions and ideologies of the given society.

Among primitive peoples, systems of control were rudimentary at best. They arose directly from the ideas of right and wrong that had been established in the group and that were common in that particular society. Control was exercised most often by means of group pressure, typically in the forms of taboos and superstitions—and in many cases by ostracism, or banishment from the group. Thus, in most cases, because of the extreme tribal nature of society in those early times, this led to very unpleasant circumstances for the individual so treated. Without the protection of the group, a lone individual was most often in for a sad and very short fate. (No other group would accept such an individual into their midst, and survival alone was extremely difficult.)

Among civilized peoples, governments began to assume more institutional forms. They rested on a well-defined legal basis. They imposed penalties on violators of the social order. They used force, which was supported and sanctioned by their people. The government was charged to establish the social order and was supposed to do so in order to be able to discharge its functions.

Eventually, the ideas of government, such as who should govern and how, came to be considered by various thinkers and philosophers. The most influential of these were the ancient Greek philosophers Plato and Aristotle. Aristotle's conception of government was based on a simple idea. The function of government was to provide for the general welfare of its people. A good government, and one that should be supported, was one that did so in the best way possible, with the least pressure on the people. Bad governments were those that subordinated the general welfare to that of the individuals who ruled. At no time should any function of any government be that of personal interest of any one individual, no matter who that individual is. This does not mean that Aristotle had no sympathy for the individual or individual happiness (as at times Plato has been accused). Rather, Aristotle believed that a society is greater than the sum of its parts, or that "the good of the many outweighs the good of the few and also of the one."

Yet, a good government and one that carries out its functions well will always weigh the relative merits of what is good for a given individual in society and what is good for the society as a whole. This basic concept has continued to our own time and has found its fullest expression in the idea of representative democracy and political and personal freedom. In addition, the most ideal government is one that maintains good social order while allowing the greatest possible exercise of autonomy for individuals.

Skill 14.2   The forms of government

Anarchism – A political movement believing in the elimination of all government and its replacement by a cooperative community of individuals. It has sometimes involved political violence, such as assassinations of important political or governmental figures. The historical banner of this movement is a black flag.

Communism - A belief as well as a political system characterized by a classless, stateless social organization. It calls for the common ownership of national goods. This ideology is the same as Marxism. The historical banner of the movement is a red flag and variation of stars, hammer and sickles, representing the various types of workers.

Dictatorship - Also called an Oligarchy, it is the rule by an individual or small group of individuals; it centralizes all political control in itself and enforces its will with a strong police force.

Fascism - A belief as well as a political system opposed ideologically to Communism, though similar in basic structure, with a one-party state and centralized political control. Unlike Communism, it tolerates private ownership of the means of production, though it maintains tight overall control. Central to its belief is the idolization of the Leader, a "Cult of the Personality," and most often an expansionist ideology. Examples have been German Nazism and Italian Fascism.

Monarchy - The rule of a nation by a monarch (a non-elected usually hereditary leader), most often a king or queen. This form of government may or may not be accompanied by some measure of democratically open institutions and elections at various levels. A modern example is Great Britain, which is called a Constitutional Monarchy.

Parliamentary System - A system of government with a legislature, usually involving a multiplicity of political parties and often coalition politics. There is division between the head of state and head of government. The head of government is usually known as a prime minister, who is also usually the head of the largest party. The head of government and cabinet usually both sit and vote in the parliament. The head of state is most often an elected president, (though in the case of a constitutional monarchy, like Great Britain, the sovereign may take the place of a president as head of state). A government may fall when a majority in parliament votes "no confidence" in the government.

Presidential System - A system of government with a legislature, involving few or many political parties, with no division between head of state and head of government: the president serves in both capacities. The president is elected either by direct or indirect election. A president and cabinet usually do not sit or vote in the legislature, and the president may or may not be the head of the largest political party. A president can thus rule even without a majority in the legislature. He can only be removed from office for major infractions of the law.

Socialism – A political belief and system in which the state takes a guiding role in the national economy and provides extensive social services to its population. It may or may not own outright means of production, but even where it does not, it exercises tight control. It usually promotes democracy (Democratic-Socialism), though the heavy state involvement produces excessive bureaucracy and usually inefficiency. Taken to an extreme it may lead to Communism as government control increases and democratic practice decreases. Ideologically. the two movements are very similar in both belief and practice, as Socialists also preach the superiority of their system to all others and that it will become the eventual natural order. It is also considered for that reason a variant of Marxism. It also has used a red flag as a symbol.

U.S. Government System

The various governments of the United States and of Native American tribes have many similarities and a few notable differences. They are more similar than not; all in all, they reflect the tendency of their people to prefer a representative that has checks and balances and that looks out for the people as a whole.

The United States Government has three distinct branches: the Executive, the Legislative, and the Judicial. Each has its own function and its own "check" on the other two.

The Legislative Branch consists primarily of the House of Representatives and the Senate. Each house has a set number of members, the House with 435 apportioned according to national population trends and the Senate with 100 (two from each state). House members serve two-year terms; Senators serve six-year terms. Each house can initiate a bill, but that bill must be passed by a majority of both houses in order to become a law. The House is primarily responsible for initiating spending bills; the Senate is responsible for ratifying treaties that the president might sign with other countries.

The Executive Branch has the president and vice-president as its two main figures. The president is the commander-in-chief of the armed forces and the person who can approve or veto all bills from Congress. (Vetoed bills can become law anyway if two-thirds of each house of Congress vote to pass them over the president's objections.) The president is elected to a four-year term by the electoral college, which usually mirrors the popular will of the people. The president can serve a total of two terms. The Executive Branch also has several departments consisting of advisors to the president. These departments include State, Defense, Education, Treasury, and Commerce, among others. Members of these departments are appointed by the president and approved by Congress.

The Judicial Branch consists of a series of courts and related entities, with the top body being the Supreme Court. The Court decides whether laws of the land are constitutional; any law invalidated by the Supreme Court is no longer in effect. The Court also regulates the enforcement and constitutionality of the Amendments to the Constitution. The Supreme Court is the highest court in the land. Cases make their way to it from federal Appeals Courts, which hear appeals of decisions made by federal District Courts. These lower two levels of courts are found in regions around the country. Supreme Court justices are appointed by the president and confirmed by the Senate. They serve for life. Lower-court judges are elected in popular votes within their states.

Skill 14.3   The United States Constitution

The **United States Constitution** is the written document that describes and defines the system and structure of the United States government. Ratification of the Constitution by the required number of states (nine of the original thirteen), was completed on June 21, 1788, and thus the Constitution officially became the law of the land.

In 1786, an effort to regulate interstate commerce ended in what is known as the **Annapolis Convention**. Because only five states were represented, this Convention was not able to accomplish definitive results. The debates, however, made it clear that foreign and interstate commerce could not be regulated by a government with as little authority as the government established by the Confederation. Congress was therefore asked to call a convention to provide a constitution that would address the emerging needs of the new nation.

The convention met under the presidency of George Washington, with fifty-five of the sixty-five appointed members present. A constitution was written in four months. The **Constitution of the United States** is the fundamental law of the republic. It is a precise, formal, written document of the extraordinary, or supreme, type of constitution. The founders of the Union established it as the highest governmental authority. There is no national power superior to it. The foundations were so broadly laid as to provide for the expansion of national life and to make it an instrument that would last for all time. To maintain its stability, the framers created a difficult process for making any changes to it. No amendment can become valid until it is ratified by three fourths of all of the states.

The British system of government was part of the basis of the final document. However, significant changes were necessary to meet the needs of a partnership of states that were tied together as a single federation, yet sovereign in their own local affairs. This constitution established a system of government that was unique and advanced far beyond other systems of its day.

There were, to be sure, differences of opinion. The compromises that resolved these conflicts are reflected in the final document. The first point of disagreement and compromise was related to the presidency. Some wanted a strong, centralized, individual authority. Others feared autocracy or the growth of monarchy. The compromise was to give the president broad powers but to limit the amount of time, through term of office, that any individual could exercise that power. The power to make appointments and to conclude treaties was controlled by the requirement of the consent of the Senate.

The second conflict was between large and small states. The large states wanted power proportionate to their voting strength; the small states opposed this plan. The compromise was that all states should have equal voting power in the Senate, but to have membership of the House of Representatives be determined in proportion to population.

The third conflict was about slavery. The compromise was that a) fugitive slaves should be returned by states to which they might flee for refuge, and b) that no law would be passed for twenty years prohibiting the importation of slaves.

The fourth major area of conflict was how the president would be chosen. One side of the disagreement argued for election by direct vote of the people. The other side thought that the president should be chosen by Congress. One group feared the ignorance of the people; the other feared the power of a small group of people. The compromise was the Electoral College.

The Constitution binds the states in a governmental unity in everything that affects the welfare of all. At the same time, it recognizes the rights of the people of each state to independence of action in matters that relate only to them. Since the Federal Constitution is the law of the land, all other laws must conform to it. The debates conducted during the Constitutional Congress represent the issues and the arguments that led to the compromises in the final document. The debates also reflect the concerns of the Founding Fathers that the rights of the people be protected from abrogation by the government itself as well as the determination that no branch of government should have enough power to override the others. There is, therefore, a system of checks and balances.

The **Federalist Papers** were written to win popular support for the new proposed Constitution. In these publications, the debates of the Congress and the concerns of the founding fathers were made available to the people of the nation. In addition to providing an explanation of the underlying philosophies and concerns of the Constitution and the compromises that were made, the Federalist Papers conducted what has frequently been called the most effective marketing and public relations campaign in human history.

An **Amendment** is a change or addition to the United States Constitution. To date, there are only twenty-seven amendments to the Constitution that have passed. An amendment may be used to cancel out a previous one (such as the Eighteenth Amendment of 1919, known as Prohibition, and canceled by the Twenty-First Amendment in 1933). Amending the United States Constitution is an extremely difficult thing to do.

An Amendment must start in Congress. One or more lawmakers propose it, and then each house votes on it in turn. The Amendment must have the support of two-thirds of each house separately in order to progress on its path into law. (It should be noted here that this two-thirds need be only two-thirds of a quorum, which is just a simple majority. Thus, it is theoretically possible for an Amendment to be passed and be legal even though it has been approved by less than half of one or both houses.)

The final and most difficult step for an Amendment is the ratification of the state legislature. A total of three-fourths of those must approve the Amendment. Approvals there need be only a simple majority, but the number of states that must approve the Amendment is thirty-eight. Hundreds of Amendments have been proposed through the years.

A key element in some of those failures has been the time limit that Congress has the option to put on Amendment proposals. A famous example of an Amendment that got close but didn't reach the threshold before the deadline expired was the Equal Rights Amendment, which was proposed in 1972 but couldn't muster enough support for passage, even though its deadline was extended from seven to ten years.

The first ten Amendments are called the **Bill of Rights**; they were approved at the same time, shortly after the Constitution was ratified. The Eleventh and Twelfth Amendments were ratified around the turn of the nineteenth century and, respectively, voided foreign suits against states and revised the method of presidential election. The Thirteenth, Fourteenth, and Fifteenth Amendments were passed in succession after the end of the Civil War. Slavery was outlawed by the Thirteenth Amendment. The Fourteenth and Fifteenth Amendments provided for equal protection and for voting rights, respectively, without consideration of skin color.

The first Amendment of the twentieth century was the Sixteenth Amendment, which provided for a federal income tax. Providing for direct election to the Senate was the Seventeenth Amendment. (Before this, Senators were appointed by state leaders, not elected by the public at large.)

The Eighteenth Amendment prohibited the use or sale of alcohol across the country. The long battle for voting rights for women ended in success with the passage of the Nineteenth Amendment. The date for the beginning of terms for the President and the Congress was changed from March to January by the Twentieth Amendment. With the Twenty-first Amendment came the only instance in which an Amendment was repealed. In this case, it was the Eighteenth Amendment and its prohibition of alcohol consumption or sale.

The Twenty-second Amendment limited the number of terms that a President could serve to two. Presidents since George Washington had followed Washington's practice of not running for a third term; this changed when Franklin D. Roosevelt ran for re-election a second time, in 1940. He was re-elected that time and a third time, too, four years later. He didn't live out his fourth term, but he did convince Congress and most of the state legislature that some sort of term limit should be in place.

The little-known Twenty-third Amendment provided for representation of Washington, D.C., in the Electoral College. The Twenty-fourth Amendment prohibited poll taxes, which people had had to pay in order to vote.

Presidential succession is the focus of the Twenty-fifth Amendment, which provides a blueprint of what to do if the president is incapacitated or killed. The Twenty-sixth Amendment lowered the legal voting age for Americans from twenty-one to eighteen. The final Amendment, the Twenty-seventh, prohibits members of Congress from substantially raising their own salaries. This Amendment was one of twelve originally proposed in the late eighteenth century. Ten of those twelve became the Bill of Rights, and one has yet to become law.

A host of potential Amendments have made news headlines in recent years. A total of six Amendments have been proposed by Congress and passed muster in both houses but have not been ratified by enough state legislatures. The aforementioned Equal Rights Amendment is one. Another one, which would grant the District of Columbia full voting rights equivalent to states, has not passed; like the Equal Rights Amendment, its deadline has expired. A handful of others remain on the books without expiration dates, including an amendment to regulate child labor.

Skill 14.4 The rights and responsibilities of citizens

Bill Of Rights - The first ten amendments to the United States Constitution deal with civil liberties and civil rights. They were written mostly by James Madison. Here they are in brief:

1. Freedom of Religion
2. Right To Bear Arms
3. Security from the quartering of troops in homes
4. Right against unreasonable search and seizures
5. Right against self-incrimination
6. Right to trial by jury, right to legal council
7. Right to jury trial for civil actions
8. No cruel or unusual punishment allowed
9. These rights shall not deny other rights the people enjoy
10. Powers not mentioned in the Constitution shall be retained by the states or the people

It is presumed that all citizens of the United States will recognize their responsibilities to the country and that the surest way of protecting their rights is by exercising those rights, which also entail a responsibility. Some examples include the *right* to vote and the *responsibility* to be well-informed on various issues, the *right* to a trial by jury and the *responsibility* to ensure the proper working of the justice system by performing jury duty (rather than avoiding it). In the end, it is only by the mutual recognition of the fact that an individual has both rights and responsibilities in society that enables the society to function in order to protect those very rights.

Skill 14.5 State and local government

State governments are mirror images of the federal government, with a few important exceptions: Governors are not technically commanders in chief of armed forces; state supreme court decisions can be appealed to federal courts; terms of state representatives and senators vary; judges, even of the state supreme courts, are elected by popular vote; and governors and legislators have term limits that vary by state.

Local governments vary widely across the country, although none of them has a judicial branch per se. Some local governments consist of a city council, of which the mayor is a member and has limited powers; in other cities, the mayor is the head of the government and the city council members are the chief lawmakers. Local governments also have fewer strict requirements for people running for office than do the state and federal governments.

The format of the governments of the various Native American tribes varies as well. Most tribes have governments along the lines of the U.S. federal or state governments. An example is the Cherokee Nation, which has a fifteen-member Tribal Council as the head of the Legislative branch; a Principal Chief and Deputy Chief who head up the Executive branch and carry out the laws passed by the Tribal Council; and a Judicial branch made up of the Judicial Appeals Tribunal and the Cherokee Nation District Court. Members of the Tribunal are appointed by the Principal Chief. Members of the other two branches are elected by popular vote of the Cherokee Nation.

COMPETENCY 15.0   ANTHROPOLOGY, SOCIOLOGY, AND PSYCHOLOGY

Skill 15.1   Kinship patterns, social institutions, social stratification, and cultural changes

Anthropology is the scientific study of human culture and humanity: the relationship between humans and their cultures. Anthropologists study different groups, patterns of behavior, how they relate to one another, and their similarities and differences. Their research is two-fold: it is cross-cultural and comparative. The major method of study is referred to as "participant observation." In it, the anthropologist studies and learns about the culture's members by living among them and participating with them in their daily lives. Other methods may be used, but this is the most common. For example, in the 1920s, Margaret Mead lived among the Samoans, observing their ways of life. Her study resulted in the book *Coming of Age in Samoa*. The Leakey family, comprised of Louis, his wife Mary, and their son Richard, were anthropologists who did much field work to further the study of human origins.

Many aspects of anthropology and the study of human cultures interact with the study of geography. Because the earth's physical features contribute to the actions and livelihoods of all cultures around the globe, the two fields of study are inexorably linked. Therefore, it is not uncommon to find discussions of geography interspersed in cultural studies.

A **population** is a group of people living within a certain geographic area. Populations are usually measured on a regular basis by a census, which also measures age, economic, ethnic, and other data.

Populations change over time due to many factors, and these changes can have significant impact on cultures. When a population grows in size, it becomes necessary for it to either expand its geographic boundaries to make room for new people or to increase its density. **Population density** is simply the number of people in a population divided by the geographic area in which they live. Cultures with a high population density are likely to have different ways of interacting with one another than those with low density, as people in the former category live in closer proximity.

As a population grows, its economic needs change. More basic needs are required, and more workers are needed to produce them. If a population's production or purchasing power does not keep pace with its growth, its economy can be adversely affected. The age distribution of a population can also impact the economy if the number of young and old people who are not working is disproportionate to those who are.

Growth in some areas may spur **migration** to other parts of a population's geographic region that are less densely populated. This redistribution of population also places demands on the economy, as infrastructure is needed to connect these new areas to older population centers, and land is put to new use.

Populations can grow naturally (when the rate of birth is higher than the rate of death) or by adding new people from other populations through **immigration**. Immigration is often a source of societal change, as people from other cultures bring their institutions and language to a new area. Immigration also impacts a population's educational and economic institutions, as they enter the workforce and place their children in schools. Populations can also decline in number naturally (when the death rate exceeds the birth rate) or when people migrate to another area. War, famine, disease, and natural disasters can also dramatically reduce a population. The economic problems arising from population decline can be similar to those from overpopulation because economic demands may be higher than can be met. In extreme cases, a population may decline to the point where it can no longer perpetuate itself; its members and their culture either disappear or are absorbed into another population.

Cultural identity is the identification of individuals or groups as they are influenced by their particular group or culture. This term refers to the sense of who one is, what values are important, what racial or ethnic characteristics are important in one's self-understanding, and the manner of interacting with the world and with others. In the United States, a nation with a well-deserved reputation as a "melting pot," the attachment to cultural identities can become a divisive factor in communities and societies. **Cosmopolitanism**, its alternative, tends to blur those cultural differences in the creation of a shared new culture.

Throughout the history of the nation, groups have defined themselves and/or assimilated into the larger population to varying degrees. In order for a society to function as a cohesive and unifying force, there must be some degree of enculturation of all groups. The alternative is a competing, and often conflicting, collection of sub-groups that are not able to cohere into a society. This failure to assimilate will often result in culture wars, as values and lifestyles come into conflict. Cross-cultural exchanges, however, can enrich every involved group of persons with the discovery of shared values and needs, as well as an appreciation for unique cultural characteristics of each. For the most part, the history of this nation has been a story of successful enculturation and cultural enrichment. The notable failures often resulted from prejudice or intolerance. For example, **cultural biases** led to the oppression of the Irish or the Chinese immigrants in various parts of the country. **Racial biases** have led to various kinds of suppressive and oppressive activities. For example, the bias of the European settlers against the civilization and culture of the Native peoples of North America caused mass extermination, relocation, and isolation.

Skill 15.2 Socialization and acculturation, ethnic groups and societal change, and stereotypes and biases

Socialization is the process by which humans learn the expectations their society has for their behavior, in order that they might successfully function within that society. Socialization takes place primarily in children as they learn and are taught the rules and norms of their culture. For example, children grow up eating the common foods of a culture and develop a "taste" for these foods. By observing adults and older children, they learn about gender roles and appropriate ways to interact. Socialization also takes place among adults who change their environment and are expected to adopt new behaviors. Joining the military, for example, requires a different type of dress and behavior than civilian culture. Taking a new job or going to a new school are other examples of situations where adults must re-socialize.

Two primary ways that socialization takes place are through positive and negative **sanctions**. Positive sanctions are rewards for appropriate or desirable behavior, and negative sanctions are punishments for inappropriate behavior. Recognition from peers and praise from a parent are examples of positive sanctions that reinforce expected social behaviors. Negative sanctions might include teasing by peers for unusual behavior or punishment by a parent. Sanctions can be either formal or informal. Public awards and prizes are ways a society formally reinforces positive behaviors. Laws that provide for punishment of specific infractions are formal negative sanctions.

Innovation is the introduction of new ways of performing work or organizing societies; they can spur drastic changes in a culture. Prior to the innovation of agriculture, for instance, human cultures were largely nomadic and survived by hunting and gathering their food. Agriculture led directly to the development of permanent settlements and instigated a radical change in social organization. Likewise, technological innovations in the Industrial Revolution of the nineteenth century changed the way work was performed and transformed the economic institutions of Western cultures. Recent innovations in communications are changing the way cultures interact today.

Cultural diffusion is the movement of cultural ideas or materials between populations independent of the movement of those populations. Cultural diffusion can take place when two populations are close to one another through direct interaction, or across great distances through mass media and other routes. For example, American movies are popular all over the world. Within the United States, hockey, traditionally a Canadian pastime, has become a popular sport. These are both examples of cultural diffusion.

Adaptation is the process through which individuals and societies change their behaviors and organization to cope with social, economic, and environmental pressures.

Acculturation is the exchange or adoption of cultural features when two cultures come into regular direct contact. An example of acculturation is the adoption of Christianity and Western dress by many Native Americans in the United States.

Assimilation is the process of a minority ethnic group adopting the culture of the larger group it exists within. These groups are typically immigrants moving to a new country, as with the European immigrants who traveled to the United States at the beginning of the twentieth century.

Extinction is the complete disappearance of a culture. Extinction can occur suddenly (from disease, famine, or war) when the people of a culture are completely destroyed, or slowly over time as a culture adapts, acculturates, or assimilates to the point where its original features are lost.

Skill 15.3   Human development and growth, human behavior, and gender roles and differences

The developmental stages of children are described as intellectual, moral, physical, and social. The latter of these, social development, is evident as children develop self concepts, attitudes, and interpersonal skills. The term **psychosocial** describes the relationship between culture and the social environment on the emotional needs of the child. Erik Erikson based his study of personality by hypothesizing that humans pass through eight psychosocial stages of development. At each stage there are crises or critical issues that need to be resolved in a positive way so that the child can move to the next stage and develop a healthy personality. These stages occur in a) the preschool years, b) the elementary and middle school years, c) adolescence, and d) adulthood.

Physical development is influenced by hereditary and environment factors. The biological processes, including genetic make-up and hormonal influences, are vital to the development of the child, particularly as it pertains to motor skill development. Simultaneously, the effects of the many influences by the caregivers and the child's personal experiences stimulate the growth of the child from an immature infant to a competent child and adolescent. In many ways the pattern of the child's physical growth and motor skill development is determined by the setting, resources, and beliefs of the society in which he or she lives. Physical growth, including brain development and the maturation of motor skills, manifest themselves in growth spurts usually during infancy and adolescence.

Research studies have indicated that there are no significant differences in intelligence or aptitudes between males and females. Any noted differences seem to be caused by environmental influences. From birth, males and females are treated differently. Parents' expectations, whether consciously or unconsciously, are different for daughters and sons. These different social patterns continue in school, where teachers have different expectations for their male and female students. These differences stand out particularly in the teaching of mathematics and science. In science classes, the boys are more apt to be allowed to use the science equipment and are asked to complete lab demonstrations. In mathematics, the difference is attributed to higher expectations for males by the teachers. This greatly influences career choices, and there is a continued decline in females entering professions requiring a major in science or mathematics.

COMPETENCY 16.0   ECONOMICS

Skill 16.1   Key terms and major concepts of the economic market

Please refer to the following material for key terms and concepts of the economic market.

Skill 16.2   The individual and the market

A **market** is defined as the mechanism that brings buyers and sellers in contact with each other so that they can buy and sell. Buyers and sellers do not have to meet face to face; for example, when the consumer buys a good from a catalog or through the Internet, the buyer never comes face to face with the seller, yet both buyer and seller are part of a bona fide market.

Markets exist in both the input and output sides of the economy. The **input market** is the market in which factors of production, or resources, are bought and sold. Factors of production, or inputs, fall into four broad categories: land, labor, capital, and entrepreneurship. Each of these four inputs is used in the production of every good and service. **Output markets** refer to the market in which goods and services are sold. When the consumer goes to the local shoe store to buy a pair of shoes, the shoes are the output, and the consumer is taking part in the output market. However, the shoe store is a participant in both the input and output market. The sales clerk and workers are hiring out their resource of labor in return for a wage rate. Therefore they are participating in the input market.

In a **market oriented economy**, all of these markets function on the basis of supply and demand. The **equilibrium price** is determined as the overlap of the buying decisions of buyers with the selling decision of sellers. This is true whether the market is an input market, with a market rate of wage, or an output market, with a market price of the output. A market oriented economy results in the most efficient allocation of resources.

The best place to see **supply and demand** and markets in action is at a stock exchange or at a commodity futures exchange. Buyers and sellers come face to face in the trading pit and accomplish trades by open outcry. Sellers who want to sell stocks or futures contracts call out the prices at which they will sell. Buyers who want to buy stocks or futures contracts call out the prices at which they will buy. When the two sides agree on price, a trade is made. This process goes on throughout trading hours. It is easiest to see how markets and supply and demand function in this kind of setting because it is open and very obvious.

The same kinds of forces are at work at your local shopping mall or grocery store, even though the price appears as a given to you the consumer. The price you see was arrived at through the operation of supply and demand. In this way, the **equilibrium price** is the price that clears the markets. The term "clears the market" means that there are no shortages or surpluses. If the price is too high, consumers won't buy the product and the store will have a surplus of the good. The stores then have to lower prices to eliminate the surplus merchandise. If the price is too low, consumers will buy so much that there will be a shortage. The shortage is then alleviated as the price goes up, rationing the good to those that are willing and able to pay the higher price for the good.

In cases where government imposes legally mandated prices, the results can either be a shortage, with a price imposed below the market price, or a surplus, with a price imposed below the market price. The existence of price supports in agriculture is the reason for the surplus in agricultural products.

Skill 16.3   Economics' effect on population and resources

The scarcity of resources is the basis for the existence of economics. Economics is defined as a study of how scarce resources are allocated to satisfy unlimited wants. In this sense, "resources" refer to the four factors of production mentioned above: **labor, capital, land,** and **entrepreneurship**.

- *Labor* refers to anyone who sells his or her ability to produce goods and services.
- *Capital* is anything that is manufactured to be used in the production process.
- *Land* refers to the land itself and everything occurring naturally on it (such as oil, minerals, and lumber).
- *Entrepreneurship* is the ability of an individual to combine the three inputs with his or her own talents to produce a viable good or service. The entrepreneur takes the risk and experiences the losses or profits.

The fact that the supply of these resources is finite means that society cannot have as much of everything that it wants. There is a constraint on production and consumption as well as on the kinds of goods and services that can be produced and consumed. Scarcity means that choices have to be made. If society decides to produce more of one good, this means that there are fewer resources available for the production of other goods. For example, assume that a society can produce two goods: good X and good Y. The society uses resources in the production of each good. If producing one unit of good X requires the same amount of resources used to produce three units of good Y, then producing one more unit of good X results in a decrease in three units of good Y. In effect, one unit of good X "costs" three units of good Y. This cost is referred to as **opportunity cost**.

Opportunity cost is essentially the value of the sacrificed alternative: the value of what had to be given up in order to have the output of good X. Opportunity cost does not just refer to production. Your opportunity cost of studying with this guide is the value of what you are not doing because you are studying, whether it is watching TV, spending time with family, or working. Every choice has an opportunity cost.

If wants were limited and/or if resources were unlimited, the concepts of choice and opportunity cost would not exist, and neither would the field of economics. There would be enough resources to satisfy the wants of consumers, businesses, and governments. The allocation of resources wouldn't be a problem. Society could have more of both good X and good Y without having to give up anything. There would be no opportunity cost. However, this isn't the situation that societies are faced with.

Because resources are scarce, society doesn't want to waste them. Society wants to obtain the most satisfaction it can from the consumption of the goods and services produced with its scarce resources. The members of the society don't want their scarce resources wasted through inefficiency. This means that producers must choose an efficient production process, which is the lowest cost means of production. High costs mean wasted resources.

Consumers also don't want society's resources to be wasted by producing goods that they don't want. Producers reduce this kind of inefficiency by determining which goods their consumers want. They do this by watching how consumers spend their money, essentially "voting" with their dollar spending. A desirable good, one that consumers want, earns profits. A good that incurs losses is a good that society doesn't want its resources wasted on. This signals the producer that society, as a whole, wants its resources used in another way.

Skill 16.4 The role of government in economics and the impact of economics on government

Even in a capitalist economy, there is a role for government. Government is required to provide the framework for the functioning of the economy. This requires a legal system, a monetary system, and a "watch dog" authority to protect consumers from bad or dangerous products and practices. Society needs a government to correct for the misallocation of resources when the market doesn't function properly, as in the case of externalities, like pollution. Another function of the government is to correct for the unequal distribution of income that results from a market oriented system. Government functions to provide public goods, like national defense, and to correct for macro-instability like inflation and unemployment through the use of monetary and fiscal policies. Although there are countless more ways in which the government acts on the economy, these are the more important roles.

In the same way, economics impacts government. First, the government has to respond to economic situations. Inflation and unemployment call on the government to implement various economic policies. The business cycle and the policies implemented to counter the business cycle affect the level of tax revenues that the government receives. This affects the budget and the amount of dollars that government has to spend on various programs. A government that has lower tax revenues due to economic conditions has to postpone certain discretionary spending programs until the economy improves. Unlike individuals, government can spend more tax dollars than it receives and operate in a debt condition financed by selling bonds. These are dollars that have to be repaid at some future date. Different economic conditions and situations call on the government to respond with different policies; the government has to figure out what to do and how much to do in each situation.

Skill 16.5   Economic systems

Economic systems refer to the arrangements a society has devised to answer what are known as the "three questions": 1) what goods to produce, 2) how to produce the goods, and 3) for whom the goods are being produced (or how the allocation of the output is determined). Different economic systems answer these questions in different ways. These are the different "isms" that exist to define the method of resource and output allocation.

A **market economy** answers these questions in terms of demand and supply and the use of markets. Consumers vote for the products they want with their dollar spending. Goods acquiring enough dollar votes are profitable, signaling to the producers that society wants its scarce resources used in this way. This is how the what question is answered. The producer then hires inputs in accordance with the goods consumers want, looking for the most efficient or lowest cost method of production. The lower the firm's costs for any given level of revenue, the higher the firm's profits. This is the way in which the how question is answered in a market economy. The for whom question is answered in the marketplace by the determination of the equilibrium price. Price serves to ration the goods to those who can and will transact at the market price or better. Those who can't or won't are excluded from the market. The United States has a market economy.

The opposite of the market economy is called the **centrally planned economy**. This used to be called Communism, even though the term is not correct in a strict Marxian sense. In a planned economy, the means of production are publicly owned, with little, if any private ownership. Instead of the "three questions" being solved by markets, there is a planning authority who makes the decisions. The planning authority decides what will be produced and how. Since most planned economies direct resources into the production of capital and military goods, there is little remaining for consumer goods; the result is often chronic shortages. Price functions as an accounting measure and does not reflect scarcity. The former Soviet Union and most of the Eastern Bloc countries were planned economies of this sort.

In between the two extremes is **market socialism**. This is a mixed economic system that uses both markets and planning. Planning is usually used to direct resources at the upper levels of the economy, with markets used to determine the prices of consumer goods and wages. This kind of economic system answers the "three questions" with planning and markets. The former Yugoslavia was a market socialist economy.

You can put each nation of the world on a continuum in terms of these characteristics and rank them from most capitalistic to the most planned. The United States would probably rank as the most capitalistic and North Korea would probably rank as the most planned, but this doesn't mean that the United States doesn't engage in planning or that economies like mainland China don't use markets.

Skill 16.6   Impact of technological developments on the economy

The **supply curve** represents the selling and production decisions of the seller and is based on the costs of production. The costs of production of a product are based on the costs of the resources used in its production. The costs of resources are based on the scarcity of the resource. The scarcer a resource is, relatively speaking, the higher its price. A diamond costs more than paper because diamonds are scarcer than paper is. All of these concepts are embodied in the seller's supply curve.

The same thing is true on the buying side of the market. The buyer's preferences, taste, and income—all of his or her buying decisions—are embodied in the **demand curve**. Where the demand and supply curves intersect is where the buying decisions of buyers are equal to the selling decisions of sellers. The quantity that buyers want to buy at a particular price is equal to the quantity that sellers want to sell at that particular price. This is where the market is in equilibrium, which is evident in the chart below.

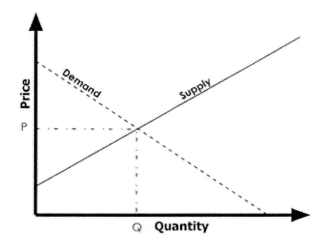

What happens when there is a change? Technological developments result in newer and more efficient ways of doing things. Technology means more efficient production techniques that allow for larger output at lower costs. Suppose a new big oil field is found. Also, suppose there is a technology that allows its recovery and refining at a fraction of the present costs. The result is a big increase in the supply of oil at lower costs, as reflected by a rightward shifting oil supply curve. Oil is used as an input into almost all production. Firms now have lower costs. This means that the firm can produce the same amount of output at a lower cost or can produce a larger amount of output at the same cost. The result is a rightward shift of the firm's, and therefore, the industry supply curve. This means that sellers are willing and able to offer for sale larger quantities of output at each price. Assuming buyers' buying decisions stay the same, there is a new market equilibrium, or new point of intersection of the shifted supply curve with the buyers' demand curve. The result is a lower price with a larger quantity of output. The market has achieved a new equilibrium based on the increase in the quantity of a resource.

Technological progress and innovation allow for the production of more output at lower prices. This leads to increased consumption for consumers. Technology can also result in unemployment by displacing workers. This is referred to as **structural unemployment**. The displaced workers must be retrained to find jobs in other industries.

Skill 16.7   International economics

The theory of **comparative advantage** states that trade should be based on the comparative opportunity costs between two nations. The nation that can produce a good more cheaply should specialize in the production of that good and trade for the good in which it has the comparative disadvantage. In this way both nations will experience gains from trade.

A basis for trade exists if there are differing comparative costs in each country. Suppose country A can produce 10 units of good X or 10 units of good Y with its resources. Country B can produce 30 units of X or 10 units of Y with its resources. What are the relative costs in each country? In country A, 1 X costs 1 unit of Y. In country B, 1 X costs 3 units of Y. Good Y is cheaper in country B than it is in country A (1/3X = 1Y in country B versus 1Y = 1X in country A). Country B has the comparative advantage in the production of Y, and country A has the comparative advantage in the production of good X. According to trade theory, each country should specialize in the production of the good in which it has the comparative advantage. Country B will devote all of its resources to the production of good Y and country A will devote all of its resources to the production of good X. Each country will then trade for the good in which it has the comparative disadvantage.

To determine the gains from trade, we must first consider the pre-trade production and consumption positions of both countries. In A, the pre-trade position was where they could have either 10 units of X or 10 units of Y or any combination in between. Let's assume country A chose a combination of 7Y and 3X. In country B, their resources allowed either 30 units of Y or 10 units of X or any combination in between. Let's assume country B chose the combination of 18Y and 4 X. Now let's consider the production and consumption situation before and after trade. Before trade, the total production of good Y was 18 from country B and 7 from country A for a total of 25Y. After trade, total world production is 30Y, with country B specializing in the production of Y. For good X, the pre-trade situation was 3 units of X from country A and 4 units of X from country B, for a total of 7 units of X. After trade, with country A specializing in the production of X, total world production of X is 10 units. Specialization and trade according to comparative advantage results in the world having 30Y rather than 25Y and 10X instead of 7X. This increase is referred to as the gains from trade. Both countries have higher consumption levels of both good due to specialization. This example refers to free unrestricted trade. Trade barriers introduce distortions.

When nations trade, the traded goods and services must be paid for. This involves the use of **foreign exchange**. The exchange rates of most currencies today are determined in a floating exchange rate system. In a clean float, supply and demand factors for each currency in terms of another are what determine the equilibrium price or the exchange rate. A clean float is a market functioning without any government interference, purely on the basis of demand and supply. Sometimes nations will intervene in the market to affect the value of their currency vis-à-vis the other currency. This situation is referred to as a managed or dirty float. A government is not required to intervene to maintain a currency value, as they were under a system of fixed exchange rates. A government that intervenes in the currency market now does so because it wants to, not because it is required to.

For example, if the U.S. government thinks the dollar is depreciating too much against the Canadian dollar, the U.S. government will buy U.S. dollars in the open market and pay for them with Canadian dollars. This increases the demand for U.S. dollars and increases the supply of Canadian dollars. The U.S. dollar appreciates, or increases in value, and the Canadian dollar depreciates, or decreases in value, in response to the government intervention. A stronger U.S. dollar means Canadian goods are cheaper for Americans, and American goods are more expensive for Canadians.

All nations have records of their international transactions. A nation's international transactions are recorded in the Balance of Payments. The Balance of Payment consists of two major accounts: the Current Account, which gives the figures for the exchange of goods, services, and unilateral transfers; and the Capital Account, which provides the figures for capital flows resulting from the exchange of real and financial assets. The Current Account contains the Balance of Trade, which are a nation's merchandise imports minus its merchandise exports. If the nation's exports are greater than its imports, it has a **trade surplus**. If its imports are greater than its exports, it has a **trade deficit**. Adding in the category of exports and imports of services gives the Balance on Goods and Services. Adding unilateral transfers, military expenditures, and other miscellaneous items yields the Balance on Current Account. The Capital Account consists of strictly financial items in various categories. There is also a category of Statistical Discrepancies, which is a balancing entry that allows the overall Balance of Payments to always balance. This has to do with floating exchange rate systems. It is the trade account that is watched closely today.

COMPETENCY 17.0   EARTH SCIENCE

Skill 17.1   The structure of the earth system

Earth's Plates

Data obtained from many sources led scientists to develop the theory of **plate tectonics**. This theory is the most current model that explains not only the movement of the continents, but also the changes in the earth's crust caused by internal forces.

Plates are rigid blocks of the earth's crust and upper mantle. These rigid solid blocks make up the lithosphere. The earth's lithosphere is broken into nine large sections and several small ones. These moving slabs are called plates. The major plates are named after the continents they are "transporting." The plates float on and move with a layer of hot, plastic-like rock in the upper mantle. Geologists believe that the heat currents circulating within the mantle cause this plastic zone of rock to slowly flow, carrying along the overlying crustal plates.

Movement of these crustal plates creates areas where the plates diverge as well as areas where the plates converge. A major area of **divergence** is located in the Mid-Atlantic. Currents of hot mantle rock rise and separate at this point of divergence, creating new oceanic crust at the rate of 2 to 10 centimeters per year. **Convergence** is when the oceanic crust collides with either another oceanic plate or a continental plate. The oceanic crust sinks, forming an enormous trench and generating volcanic activity. Convergence also includes continent to continent plate collisions. When two plates slide past one another, a transform fault is created.

These movements produce many major features of the earth's surface, such as mountain ranges, volcanoes, and earthquake zones. Most of these features are located at plate boundaries, where the plates interact by spreading apart, pressing together, or sliding past each other. These movements are very slow, averaging only a few centimeters a year.

Boundaries form between spreading plates where the crust is forced apart in a process called **rifting**. Rifting generally occurs at mid-ocean ridges. Rifting can also take place within a continent, splitting the continent into smaller landmasses that drift away from each other, thereby forming an ocean basin between them. The Red Sea is a product of rifting. As the seafloor spreading takes place, new material is added to the inner edges of the separating plates. In this way the plates grow larger, and the ocean basin widens. This is the process that broke up the super continent Pangaea and created the Atlantic Ocean.

Boundaries between plates that are colliding are zones of intense crustal activity. When a plate of ocean crust collides with a plate of continental crust, the more dense oceanic plate slides under the lighter continental plate and plunges into the mantle. This process is called **subduction**, and the site where it takes place is called a subduction zone. A subduction zone is usually seen on the sea floor as a deep depression called a trench.

The crustal movement identified by plates sliding sideways past each other produces a plate boundary characterized by major faults that are capable of unleashing powerful earthquakes. The San Andreas Fault forms such a boundary between the Pacific Plate and the North American Plate.

Atmosphere

Dry air is composed of three basic components: dry gas, water vapor, and solid particles (dust from soil, etc.).

The most abundant dry gases in the atmosphere are:

(N_2)	Nitrogen	78.09 %
(O_2)	Oxygen	20.95 %
(AR)	Argon	0.93 %
(CO_2)	Carbon Dioxide	0.03 %

The atmosphere is divided into four main layers based on temperature. These layers are labeled troposphere, stratosphere, mesosphere, and thermosphere.

Troposphere - this layer is the closest to the earth's surface. All weather phenomena occur here because it is the layer with the most water vapor and dust. Air temperature decreases with increasing altitude. The average thickness of the troposphere is 7 miles (11 km).

Stratosphere - this layer contains very little water. Clouds within this layer are extremely rare. The ozone layer is located in the upper portions of the stratosphere. Air temperature is fairly constant but does increase somewhat with height due to the absorption of solar energy and ultraviolet rays from the ozone layer.

Mesosphere - air temperature again decreases with height in this layer. It is the coldest layer, with temperatures in the range of -100^0 C at the top.

Thermosphere - this layer extends upward into space. Oxygen molecules in this layer absorb energy from the sun, causing temperatures to increase with height. The lower part of the thermosphere is called the ionosphere. Here, charged particles (ions) and free electrons can be found. When gases in the ionosphere are excited by solar radiation, the gases give off light and glow in the sky. These glowing lights are called the Aurora Borealis in the Northern Hemisphere and Aurora Australis in Southern Hemisphere. The upper portion of the thermosphere is called the exosphere. Gas molecules are very far apart in this layer. Layers of exosphere are also known as the Van Allen Belts and are held together by earth's magnetic field.

Skill 17.2   Processes of the earth system

Mountains

Orogeny is the term given to natural mountain building. A mountain is terrain that has been raised high above the surrounding landscape by volcanic action, or some form of tectonic plate collisions. The plate collisions could either be intercontinental collisions or ocean floor collisions with a continental crust (subduction).

The physical composition of mountains includes igneous, metamorphic, and sedimentary rocks; some may have rock layers that are tilted or distorted by plate collision forces.

There are many different types of mountains. The physical attributes of a mountain range depend upon the angle at which plate movement thrusts layers of rock to the surface. Many mountains (Adirondacks, Southern Rockies) were formed along high angle faults.

Folded mountains (Alps, Himalayas) are produced by the folding of rock layers during their formation. The Himalayas are the highest mountains in the world; they contain Mount Everest, which rises almost 9 km above sea level. The Himalayas were formed when India collided with Asia. The movement that created this collision is still in process at the rate of a few centimeters per year.

Fault-block mountains (Utah, Arizona, and New Mexico) are created when plate movement produces tension forces instead of compression forces. The area under tension produces normal faults, and rock along these faults is displaced upward.

Dome mountains are formed as magma tries to push up through the crust but fails to break the surface. Dome mountains resemble a huge blister on the earth's surface.

Upwarped mountains (the Black Hills of South Dakota) are created in association with a broad arching of the crust. They can also be formed by rock thrust upward along high angle faults.

Mechanisms of Producing Mountains

Mountains are produced by different types of mountain-building processes. Most major mountain ranges are formed by the processes of **folding** and **faulting.**

In **folding**, mountains are produced by the folding of rock layers. Crustal movements may press horizontal layers of sedimentary rock together from the sides, squeezing them into wavelike folds. Up-folded sections of rock are called anticlines; down-folded sections of rock are called synclines. The Appalachian Mountains are an example of folded mountains, with long ridges and valleys in a series of anticlines, and synclines formed by folded rock layers.

Faults are fractures in the earth's crust that have been created by either tension or compression forces transmitted through the crust. These forces are produced by the movement of separate blocks of crust. Faultings are categorized on the basis of the relative movement between the blocks on both sides of the fault plane. The movement can be horizontal, vertical, or oblique.

A **dip-slip fault** occurs when the movement of the plates is vertical and opposite. The displacement is in the direction of the inclination, or dip, of the fault. Dip-slip faults are classified as normal faults when the rock above the fault plane moves down relative to the rock below.

Reverse faults are created when the rock above the fault plane moves up relative to the rock below. Reverse faults with a very low angle to the horizontal are also referred to as thrust faults.

Faults in which the dominant displacement is horizontal movement along the trend or strike (length) of the fault are called **strike-slip faults**. When a large strike-slip fault is associated with plate boundaries it is called a **transform fault**. The San Andreas Fault in California is a well-known transform fault.

Faults that have both vertical and horizontal movement are called **oblique-slip faults**.

Volcanoes

Volcanism is the term given to the movement of magma through the crust and its emergence as lava onto the earth's surface. Volcanic mountains are built up by successive deposits of volcanic materials.

An **active volcano** is one that is presently erupting or building to an eruption. A **dormant volcano** is one that is between eruptions but still shows signs of internal activity that might lead to an eruption in the future. An **extinct volcano** is said to be no longer capable of erupting. Most of the world's active volcanoes are found along the rim of the Pacific Ocean, which is also a major earthquake zone. This curving belt of active faults and volcanoes is often called the Ring of Fire. The world's best known volcanic mountains include Mount Etna in Italy and Mount Kilimanjaro in Africa. The Hawaiian Islands are actually the tops of a chain of volcanic mountains that rise from the ocean floor.

There are three types of volcanic mountains: shield volcanoes, cinder cones and composite volcanoes.

Shield Volcanoes are associated with quiet eruptions. Lava emerges from the vent or opening in the crater and flows freely out over the earth's surface until it cools and hardens into a layer of igneous rock. A repeated lava flow builds this type of volcano into the largest volcanic mountain. Mauna Loa in Hawaii is the largest shield volcano on earth.

Cinder Cone Volcanoes are associated with explosive eruptions as lava is hurled high into the air in a spray of droplets of various sizes. These droplets cool and harden into cinders and particles of ash before falling to the ground. The ash and cinder pile up around the vent to form a steep, cone-shaped hill called the cinder cone. Cinder cone volcanoes are relatively small but may form quite rapidly.

Composite Volcanoes are those built by both lava flows and layers of ash and cinders. Mount Fuji in Japan, Mount St. Helens in Washington, USA, and Mount Vesuvius in Italy are all famous composite volcanoes.

When lava cools, igneous rock is formed. This formation can occur either above ground or below ground.

Intrusive rock includes any igneous rock that was formed below the earth's surface. Batholiths are the largest structures of intrusive type rock and are composed of near granite materials; they are the core of the Sierra Nevada Mountains. **Extrusive rock** includes any igneous rock that was formed at the earth's surface.

Dikes are old lava tubes formed when magma entered a vertical fracture and hardened. Sometimes magma squeezes between two rock layers and hardens into a thin horizontal sheet called a **sill**. A **laccolith** is formed in much the same way as a sill, but the magma that creates a laccolith is very thick and does not flow easily. It pools and forces the overlying strata creating an obvious surface dome.

A **caldera** is normally formed by the collapse of the top of a volcano. This collapse can be caused by a massive explosion that destroys the cone and empties most, if not all, of the magma chamber below the volcano. The cone collapses into the empty magma chamber, forming a caldera.

An inactive volcano may have magma solidified in its pipe. This structure, called a volcanic neck, is resistant to erosion and today may be the only visible evidence of the past presence of an active volcano.

Rocks

The three major subdivisions of rocks are sedimentary, metamorphic and igneous.

Sedimentary rocks are created through a process known as lithification. It occurs when fluid sediments are transformed into solid rocks. One very common process affecting sediments is compaction, where the weights of overlying materials compress and compact the deeper sediments. The compaction process leads to cementation. Cementation is when sediments are converted to sedimentary rock.

Igneous rocks can be classified according to their texture, their composition, and the way they formed. They are made from molten rock. Molten rock is called magma. As magma cools, the elements and compounds begin to form crystals. The slower the magma cools, the larger the crystals grow. Rocks with large crystals are said to have a coarse-grained texture. Granite is an example of a coarse-grained igneous rock. Rocks that cool rapidly before any crystals can form have a glassy texture such as obsidian, also commonly known as volcanic glass.

Metamorphic rocks are formed by high temperatures and great pressures. The process by which the rocks undergo these changes is called metamorphism. The outcome of metamorphic changes include deformation by extreme heat and pressure, compaction, destruction of the original characteristics of the parent rock, bending and folding while in a plastic stage, and the emergence of completely new and different minerals due to chemical reactions with heated water and dissolved minerals.

Metamorphic rocks are classified into two groups: foliated (leaflike) rocks and unfoliated rocks. Foliated rocks consist of compressed, parallel bands of minerals, which give the rocks a striped appearance. Examples of such rocks include slate, schist, and gneiss. Unfoliated rocks are not banded and examples of such include quartzite, marble, and anthracite rocks.

Minerals are natural, non-living solids with a definite chemical composition and a crystalline structure. **Ores** are minerals or rock deposits that can be mined for a profit. **Rocks** are earth materials made of one or more minerals. A **rock facies** is a rock group that differs from comparable rocks (as in composition, age, or fossil content).

Glaciation

About 12,000 years ago, a vast sheet of ice covered a large part of the northern United States. This huge, frozen mass moved southward from the northern regions of Canada as several large bodies of slow-moving ice. These bodies of ice, called **glaciers**, are large masses of ice that move or flow over the land in response to gravity. Glaciers form among high mountains and in other cold regions. A time period in which glaciers advance over a large portion of a continent is called an **ice age**.

Evidence of glacial coverage remains as abrasive grooves, large boulders from northern environments dropped in southerly locations, glacial troughs created by the rounding out of steep valleys through glacial scouring, and the remains of glacial sources called **cirques** that were created by frost wedging the rock at the bottom of the glacier. Remains of plants and animals typically found in warm climates that have been discovered in the moraines and out wash plains help to support the theory of periods of warmth during the past ice ages.

The major Ice Age began about 2 -3 million years ago. This age saw the advancement and retreat of glacial ice over millions of years. Theories relating to the origin of glacial activity include plate tectonics, through which it can be demonstrated that some continental masses, now in temperate climates, were at one time blanketed by ice and snow. Another theory involves changes in the earth's orbit around the sun, changes in the angle of the earth's axis, and the wobbling of the earth's axis. Support for the validity of this theory has come from deep ocean research that indicates a correlation between climatic sensitive microorganisms and the changes in the earth's orbital status.

There are two main types of glaciers: valley glaciers and continental glaciers. Erosion by valley glaciers is characteristic of U-shaped erosion. They produce sharp-peaked mountains such as the Matterhorn in Switzerland. Erosion by continental glaciers is characteristic of the movement of glaciers over mountains, leaving smoothed, rounded mountains and ridges in their paths.

Fossilization

A **fossil** is the remains or trace of an ancient organism that has been preserved naturally in the earth's crust. Sedimentary rocks usually are rich sources of fossil remains. Those fossils found in layers of sediment were embedded in the slowly forming sedimentary rock strata. The oldest fossils known are the traces of 3.5 billion-year-old bacteria found in sedimentary rocks. Few fossils are found in metamorphic rock, and virtually none are found in igneous rocks. The magma is so hot that any organism trapped in the magma is destroyed.

Although the fairly well-preserved remains of a woolly mammoth embedded in ice were found in Russia in May of 2007, the best-preserved animal remains are typically discovered in natural tar pits. When an animal accidentally falls into the tar, it becomes trapped, sinking to the bottom. Preserved bones of the saber-toothed cat have been found in tar pits.

Prehistoric insects have been found trapped in ancient amber or fossil resin that was excreted by some extinct species of pine trees. Fossil molds are the hollow spaces in a rock previously occupied by bones or shells. A fossil cast is a fossil mold that fills with sediments or minerals and later hardens, forming a cast.

Fossil tracks are the imprints in hardened mud left behind by birds or animals.

Types of Weathering

Erosion is the inclusion and transportation of surface materials by another moveable material—usually water, wind, or ice. The most important cause of erosion is running water. Streams, rivers, and tides are constantly at work removing weathered fragments of bedrock and carrying them away from their original location.

A stream erodes bedrock by the grinding action of the sand, pebbles, and other rock fragments. This grinding against each other is called abrasion. Streams also erode rocks by dissolving or absorbing their minerals. Limestone and marble are readily dissolved by streams.

Deposition, also known as sedimentation, is the term for the process by which material from one area is slowly deposited into another area. This is usually due to the movement of wind, water, or ice containing particles of matter. When the rate of movement slows down, particles filter out and remain behind, causing a build-up of matter. Note that this is a result of matter being eroded and removed from another site.

The breaking down of rocks at or near to the earth's surface is known as **weathering**. Weathering breaks down these rocks into smaller and smaller pieces. There are two types of weathering: physical weathering and chemical weathering.

Physical weathering is the process by which rocks are broken down into smaller fragments without undergoing any change in chemical composition. Physical weathering is mainly caused by the freezing of water, the expansion of rock, and the activities of plants and animals.

One example of physical weathering occurs through frost wedging, which is the cycle of daytime thawing and refreezing at night. This cycle causes large rock masses, especially the rocks exposed on mountain tops, to be broken into smaller pieces. Another example would be the peeling away of the outer layers from a rock, which is called exfoliation. Rounded mountain tops are called exfoliation domes; they have been formed in this way.

Chemical weathering is the breaking down of rocks through changes in their chemical composition. Water, oxygen, and carbon dioxide are the main agents of chemical weathering. When water and carbon dioxide combine chemically, they produce a weak acid that breaks down rocks. An example would be the change of feldspar in granite to clay.

Skill 17.3   Earth history

Earth's history extends over more than four billion years and is reckoned in terms of a scale. Paleontologists who study the history of the earth have divided this huge period of time into four large time units called eons. Eons are divided into smaller units of time called eras. An era refers to a time interval in which particular plants and animals were dominant or present in great abundance. The end of an era is most often characterized by 1) a general uplifting of the crust, 2) the extinction of the dominant plants or animals, and 3) the appearance of new life-forms.

Each era is divided into several smaller divisions of time called periods. Some periods are divided into smaller time units called epochs. The following chart outlines these eras and periods by their major characteristics.

Era	Period	Time	Characteristics
Cenozoic	Quaternary	1.6 million years ago to the present	The Ice Age occurred, and human beings evolved.
	Tertiary	65-1.64 million years ago	Mammals and birds evolved to replace the great reptiles and dinosaurs that had just become extinct. Forests gave way to grasslands, and the climate become cooler.
Mesozoic	Cretaceous	135-65 million years ago	Reptiles and dinosaurs roamed the earth. Most of the modern continents had split away from the large landmass, Pangaea, and many were flooded by shallow chalk seas.
	Jurassic	350-135 million years ago	Reptiles were beginning to evolve. Pangaea started to break up. Deserts gave way to forests and swamps.
	Triassic		
Paleozoic	Permian	355-250 million years ago	Continents came together to form one big landmass, Pangaea. Forests (that formed today's coal) grew on deltas around the new mountains, and deserts formed.
	Carboniferous		
	Devonian	410-355 million years ago	Continents started moving toward each other. The first land animals, such as insects and amphibians, existed. Many fish swam in the seas.
	Silurian	510-410 million years ago	Sea life flourished, and the first fish evolved. The earliest land plants began to grow around shorelines and estuaries.
	Ordovician		
	Cambrian	570-510 million years ago	No life on land, but all kinds of sea animals existed.
Precambrian	Proterozoic	Beginning of the Earth to 570 million years ago (seven-eighths of the Earth's history)	Some sort of life existed.
	Archaean		No life.

Using Geologic Evidence to Understand the Past

The determination of the age of rocks by cataloging their composition has been outmoded since the middle 1800s. Today, a sequential history can be determined by the fossil content (principle of fossil succession) of a rock system as well as its superposition within a range of systems. This classification process was termed **stratigraphy** and permitted the construction of a Geologic Column in which rock systems are arranged in their correct chronological order.

Uniformitarianism is a fundamental concept in modern geology. It simply states that the physical, chemical, and biological laws that operated in the geologic past operate in the same way today. The forces and processes that we observe presently shaping our planet have been at work for a very long time. This idea is commonly stated as "the present is the key to the past." **Catastrophism** is the concept that the earth was shaped by catastrophic events of a short term nature.

Estimates of the earth's age have been made possible with the discovery of radioactivity and the invention of instruments that can measure the amount of radioactivity in rocks. The use of radioactivity to make accurate determinations of earth's age is called **absolute dating**. This process depends upon comparing the amount of radioactive material in a rock with the amount that has decayed in another element. Studying the radiation given off by atoms of radioactive elements is the most accurate method of measuring the earth's age.

Radioactive atoms are unstable and are continuously breaking down or undergoing decay. The radioactive element that decays is called the **parent element**. The new element that results from the radioactive decay of the parent element is called the **daughter element**. The time required for one half of a given amount of a radioactive element to decay is called the half-life of that element or compound.

Geologists also commonly use **carbon dating** to calculate the age of a fossil substance.

Skill 17.4   Earth and universe

Earth is the third planet away from the sun in our solar system. Earth's numerous types of motion and states of orientation greatly affect global conditions, such as seasons, tides, and lunar phases. The earth orbits the sun within a period of 365 days. During this orbit, the average distance between the earth and the sun is 93 million miles.

The shape of the earth's orbit around the sun deviates from the shape of a circle only slightly. This deviation, known as the earth's eccentricity, has a very small effect on the earth's climate. The earth is closest to the sun at perihelion, occurring around January 2 of each year, and farthest from the sun at aphelion, occurring around July 2. Because the earth is closest to the sun in January, the northern winter is slightly warmer than the southern winter.

Seasons

The rotation axis of the earth is not perpendicular to the orbital (ecliptic) plane. The axis of the earth is tilted $23.45°$ from the perpendicular; the tilt of this axis is known as the obliquity of the ecliptic, and is mainly responsible for the four seasons of the year by influencing the intensity of solar rays received by the northern and southern hemispheres.

The four seasons—spring, summer, fall, and winter—are extended periods of characteristic average temperature, rainfall, storm frequency, and vegetation growth or dormancy. The effect of the earth's tilt on climate is best demonstrated at the solstices, the two days of the year when the sun is farthest from the earth's equatorial plane. At the **summer solstice** (June), the earth's tilt on its axis causes the northern hemisphere to the lean toward the sun, while the southern hemisphere leans away. Consequently, the northern hemisphere receives more intense rays from the sun and experiences summer during this time, while the southern hemisphere experiences winter. At the **winter solstice** (December), it is the southern hemisphere that leans toward the sun and thus experiences summer. Spring and fall are produced by varying degrees of the same leaning toward or away from the sun.

Tides

The orientation of and gravitational interaction between the earth and the moon are responsible for the ocean tides that occur on earth. The term **tide** refers to the cyclic rise and fall of large bodies of water. Gravitational attraction is defined as the force of attraction between all bodies in the universe. At the location on earth closest to the moon, the gravitational attraction of the moon draws seawater toward the moon in the form of a tidal bulge. On the opposite side of the earth, another tidal bulge forms in the direction away from the moon because at this point, the moon's gravitational pull is the weakest.

Spring tides are the especially strong tides that occur when the earth, sun, and moon are in line, allowing both the sun and the moon to exert gravitational force on the earth, thereby increasing tidal bulge height. These tides occur during the full moon and the new moon. **Neap tides** are especially weak tides occurring when the gravitational forces of the moon and the sun are perpendicular to one another. These tides occur during quarter moons.

Lunar Phases

The earth's orientation in respect to the solar system is also responsible for our perception of the phases of the moon. While the earth orbits the sun within a period of 365 days, the moon orbits the earth every twenty-seven days. As the moon circles the earth, its shape in the night sky appears to change. The changes in the appearance of the moon from earth are known as **lunar phases**.

These phases vary cyclically according to the relative positions of the moon, the earth, and the sun. At all times, half of the moon is facing the sun; thus, it is illuminated by reflecting the sun's light. As the moon orbits the earth and the earth orbits the sun, the half of the moon that faces the sun changes. However, the moon is in synchronous rotation around the earth, meaning that nearly the same side of the moon faces the earth at all times. This side is referred to as the near side of the moon. Lunar phases occur as the earth and moon orbit the sun and the fractional illumination of the moon's near side changes.

When the sun and moon are on opposite sides of the earth, observers on Earth perceive a **full moon**, meaning the moon appears circular because the entire illuminated half of the moon is visible. As the moon orbits the earth, the moon "wanes" as the amount of the illuminated half of the moon that is visible from Earth decreases. A **gibbous** moon is between a full moon and a half moon, or between a half moon and a full moon. When the sun and the moon are on the same side of Earth, the illuminated half of the moon is facing away from Earth, and the moon appears invisible. This lunar phase is known as the **new moon**. The time between each full moon is approximately 29.53 days.

A list of all lunar phases includes:
- New Moon: the moon is invisible or the first signs of a crescent appear
- Waxing Crescent: the right crescent of the moon is visible
- First Quarter: the right quarter of the moon is visible
- Waxing Gibbous: only the left crescent is not illuminated
- Full Moon: the entire illuminated half of the moon is visible
- Waning Gibbous: only the right crescent of the moon is not illuminated
- Last Quarter: the left quarter of the moon is illuminated
- Waning Crescent: only the left crescent of the moon is illuminated

Viewing the moon from the southern hemisphere causes these phases to occur in the opposite order.

Planets

There are eight established planets in our solar system: Mercury, Venus, Earth, Mars, Jupiter, Saturn, Uranus, and Neptune. Pluto was an established planet in our solar system, but as of Summer 2006, its status is being reconsidered.

The planets are divided into two groups based on distance from the sun. The inner planets include Mercury, Venus, Earth, and Mars. The outer planets include Jupiter, Saturn, Uranus, and Neptune.

Mercury: the closest planet to the sun. Its surface has craters and rocks. The atmosphere is composed of hydrogen, helium, and sodium. Mercury was named after the Roman messenger god.

Venus: has a slow rotation when compared to Earth. Venus and Uranus rotate in opposite directions from the other planets. This opposite rotation is called **retrograde rotation**. The surface of Venus is not visible due to the extensive cloud cover. The atmosphere is composed mostly of carbon dioxide, while sulfuric acid droplets in the dense cloud cover give Venus a yellow appearance. Venus has a greater greenhouse effect than observed on Earth, and the dense clouds combined with carbon dioxide trap heat. Venus was named after the Roman goddess of love.

Earth: considered a water planet, with 70 percent of its surface covered by water. Gravity holds the masses of water in place. The different temperatures observed on Earth allow for the different states of water (solid, liquid, gas) to exist. The atmosphere is composed mainly of oxygen and nitrogen. Earth is the only planet that is known to support life.

Mars: the surface contains numerous craters, active and extinct volcanoes, ridges, and valleys with extremely deep fractures. Iron oxide found in the dusty soil makes the surface seem rust-colored and the skies seem pink in color. The atmosphere is composed of carbon dioxide, nitrogen, argon, oxygen, and water vapor. Mars has polar regions with ice caps composed of water as well as two satellites (moons). Mars was named after the Roman war god.

Jupiter: the largest planet in the solar system. Jupiter has sixteen moons. The atmosphere is composed of hydrogen, helium, methane, and ammonia. There are white-colored bands of clouds indicating rising gas and dark-colored bands of clouds indicating descending gases. The gas movement is caused by heat resulting from the energy of Jupiter's core. Jupiter has a Great Red Spot that is thought to be a hurricane-like cloud. Jupiter has a strong magnetic field.

Saturn: the second largest planet in the solar system. Saturn has rings of ice, rock, and dust particles circling it. Saturn's atmosphere is composed of hydrogen, helium, methane, and ammonia. Saturn has twenty plus satellites. Saturn was named after the Roman god of agriculture.

Uranus: the second largest planet in the solar system with retrograde revolution. Uranus is a gaseous planet. It has ten dark rings and fifteen satellites. Its atmosphere is composed of hydrogen, helium, and methane. Uranus was named after the Greek god of the heavens.

Neptune: another gaseous planet with an atmosphere consisting of hydrogen, helium, and methane. Neptune has three rings and two satellites. Neptune was named after the Roman sea god because its atmosphere is the same color as the seas.

Pluto: once considered the smallest planet in the solar system, its status as a planet is now being reconsidered . Pluto's atmosphere probably contains methane, ammonia, and frozen water. Pluto has one satellite. Pluto revolves around the sun every 250 years. Pluto was named after the Roman god of the underworld.

The Sun and Stars

The sun is considered the nearest star to Earth that produces solar energy. By the process of nuclear fusion, hydrogen gas is converted to helium gas. Energy flows out of the core to the surface; radiation then escapes into space.

Parts of the sun include:

1) **Core:** the inner portion of the sun where fusion takes place
2) **Photosphere:** considered the surface of the sun, it also produces **sunspots** (cool, dark areas that can be seen on its surface)
3) **Chromosphere:** hydrogen gas causes this portion to be red in color (also found here are solar flares [sudden brightness of the chromosphere] and solar prominences [gases that shoot outward from the chromosphere])
4) **Corona**, the transparent area of sun visible only during a total eclipse

Solar radiation is energy traveling from the sun that radiates into space. Solar flares produce excited protons and electrons that shoot outward from the chromosphere at great speeds reaching Earth. These particles disturb radio reception and also affect the magnetic field on Earth.

A star is a ball of hot, glowing gas that is hot enough and dense enough to trigger nuclear reactions, which fuel the star. In comparing the mass, light production, and size of the sun to other stars, astronomers find that the sun is a perfectly ordinary star. It behaves exactly the way they would expect a star of its size to behave. The main difference between the sun and other stars is that the sun is much closer to Earth.

Most stars have masses similar to that of the sun. The majority of stars' masses are between 0.3 to 3.0 times the mass of the sun. Theoretical calculations indicate that in order to trigger nuclear reactions and to create its own energy—that is, to become a star—a body must have a mass greater than 7 percent of the mass of the sun. Astronomical bodies that are less massive than this become planets or objects called brown dwarfs. The largest accurately determined stellar mass is of a star called V382 Cygni; it is twenty-seven times the mass of the sun.

The range of brightness among stars is much larger than the range of mass. Astronomers measure the brightness of a star by measuring its magnitude and luminosity. **Magnitude** allows astronomers to rank how bright different stars appear to humans. Because of the way our eyes detect light, a lamp ten times more luminous than a second lamp will appear less than ten times brighter to human eyes. This discrepancy affects the magnitude scale, as does the tradition of giving brighter stars lower magnitudes. The lower a star's magnitude, the brighter it is. Stars with negative magnitudes are the brightest of all.

Magnitude is given in terms of absolute and apparent values. Absolute magnitude is a measurement of how bright a star would appear if viewed from a set distance away. Astronomers also measure a star's brightness in terms of its **luminosity**. A star's absolute luminosity, or intrinsic brightness, is the total amount of energy radiated by the star per second. Luminosity is often expressed in units of watts.

Magnitude stars are twenty-one of the brightest stars that can be seen from Earth. These are the first stars noticed at night. In the northern hemisphere, there are fifteen commonly observed first magnitude stars.

Astronomers use groups or patterns of stars called **constellations** as reference points to locate other stars in the sky. Familiar constellations include Ursa Major (also known as the big bear) and Ursa Minor (known as the little bear). Within the Ursa Major, the smaller constellation The Big Dipper is found. Within the Ursa Minor, the smaller constellation The Little Dipper is found. Different constellations appear as the earth continues its revolution around the sun with the seasonal changes.

A vast collection of stars are defined as **galaxies**. Galaxies are classified as irregular, elliptical, and spiral. An irregular galaxy has no real structured appearance; most are in their early stages of life. An elliptical galaxy consists of smooth ellipses, containing little dust and gas, but composed of millions or trillions of stars. Spiral galaxies are disk-shaped and have extending arms that rotate around its dense center. Earth's galaxy is found in the Milky Way. It is a spiral galaxy.

A **pulsar** is defined as a variable radio source that emits signals in very short, regular bursts; it is believed to be a rotating neutron star. A **quasar** is defined as an object that photographs like a star but has an extremely large redshift and a variable energy output; it is believed to be the active core of a very distant galaxy.

Black holes are defined as objects that have collapsed to such a degree that light can not escape from the surface; light is trapped by the intense gravitational field.

The forces of gravity acting on particles of gas and dust in a cloud in an area of space produce stars. This cloud is called a **nebula**. Particles in this cloud attract each other; as the star grows, its temperature increases. With the increased temperature, the star begins to glow. Fusion occurs in the core of the star, releasing radiant energy at the star's surface.

When hydrogen becomes exhausted in a small, or even an average star, its core will collapse and cause its temperature to rise. This released heat causes nearby gases to heat, contract, carry out fusion, and produce helium. Stars at this stage are nearing the end of their life. These stars are called **red giants** or **supergiants**. A **white dwarf** is the dying core of a giant star. A **nova** is an ordinary star that experiences a sudden increase in brightness and then fades back to its original brightness. A **supernova** radiates even greater light energy. A **neutron star** is the result of mass left behind after a supernova. A **black hole** is a star with condensed matter and gravity so intense that light can not escape.

Comets, Asteroids, and Meteors

Astronomers believe that rocky fragments may have been the remains of the birth of the solar system that never formed into a planet. These **asteroids** are found in the region between Mars and Jupiter.

Comets are masses of frozen gases, cosmic dust, and small rocky particles. Astronomers think that most comets originate in a dense comet cloud beyond Pluto. A comet consists of a nucleus, a coma, and a tail. A comet's tail always points away from the sun. The most famous comet, **Halley's Comet,** is named after the person who first discovered it in 240 BCE. It returns to the skies near Earth every seventy-five to seventy-six years.

Meteoroids are composed of particles of rock and metal of various sizes. When a meteoroid travels through the earth's atmosphere, friction causes its surface to heat up and it begins to burn. The burning meteoroid falling through the earth's atmosphere is called a **meteor** (also known as a "shooting star").

Meteorites are meteors that strike the earth's surface. A physical example of a meteorite's impact on the earth's surface can be seen in Arizona; its **Barringer Crater** is a huge meteor crater. There are many other meteor craters throughout the world.

Oort Cloud and Kuiper Belt

The **Oort Cloud** is a hypothetical spherical cloud surrounding our solar system. It extends approximately three light years or 30 trillion kilometers from the sun. The cloud is believed to be made up of materials that were ejected out of the inner solar system because of interaction with Uranus and Neptune, but are gravitationally bound to the sun. It is named the Oort Cloud after Jan Oort, who suggested its existence in 1950. Comets from the Oort Cloud exhibit a wide range of sizes, inclinations, and eccentricities; they are often referred to as Long-Period Comets because they have a period of greater than 200 years.

The **Kuiper Belt** is the name given to a vast population of small bodies orbiting the sun beyond Neptune. There are more than 70,000 of these small bodies, some with diameters larger than 100 km extending outwards from the orbit of Neptune to 50AU. They exist mostly within a ring or belt surrounding the sun. It is believed that the objects in the Kuiper Belt are primitive remnants of the earliest phases of the solar system. It is also believed that the Kuiper Belt is the source of many Short-Period Comets (periods of less then 200 years). It is a reservoir for the comets in the same way that the Oort Cloud is a reservoir for Long-Period Comets.

Occasionally, the orbit of a Kuiper Belt object will be disturbed by the interactions of the giant planets in such a way as to cause the object to cross the orbit of Neptune. It will then very likely have a close encounter with Neptune, sending it out of the solar system or into an orbit crossing those of the other giant planets or even into the inner solar system. Prevailing theory states that scattered disk objects began as Kuiper Belt objects, which were scattered through gravitational interactions with the giant planets.

It seems that the Oort Cloud objects were formed closer to the sun than the Kuiper Belt objects. Small objects formed near the giant planets would have been ejected from the solar system by gravitational encounters. Those that didn't escape entirely formed the distant Oort Cloud. Small objects formed farther out had no such interactions and remained as the Kuiper Belt objects.

Origins of the Solar System and Universe

There are two main hypotheses of the origin of the solar system: 1) **the tidal hypothesis** and 2) **the condensation hypothesis**.

The tidal hypothesis proposes that the solar system began with a near collision of the sun and a large star. Some astronomers believe that as these two stars passed each other, the great gravitational pull of the large star extracted hot gases out of the sun. The mass from the hot gases started to orbit the sun, which began to cool, then condensing into the nine planets. (Few astronomers support this example.)

The condensation hypothesis proposes that the solar system began with rotating clouds of dust and gas. Condensation occurred in the center, forming the sun and the smaller parts of the cloud formed the nine planets. (This example is accepted by many astronomers.)

The two main theories to explain the origins of the universe include: 1) **the Big Bang theory** and 2) **the Steady-State theory.**

The Big Bang theory has been widely accepted by many astronomers. It states that the universe originated from a magnificent explosion spreading mass, matter, and energy into space. Galaxies formed from this material as it cooled during the next half-billion years.

The Steady-State theory is the least accepted theory. It states that the universe is continuously being renewed. Galaxies move outward and new galaxies replace the older galaxies. Astronomers have not found any evidence to prove this theory.

The future of the universe is hypothesized by the Oscillating Universe Hypothesis. It states that the universe will oscillate, or expand and contract. Galaxies will move away from one another and will in time slow down and stop. Then a gradual moving toward each other will again activate an explosion (another Big Bang).

COMPETENCY 18.0 LIFE SCIENCE

Skill 18.1 The structure and function of living systems

The organization of living systems builds by levels from small to increasingly more large and complex. All aspects of living beings, whether a cell or an ecosystem, have the same requirements to sustain life. Life is organized from simple to complex in the following way:

Organelles make up **cells**. Cells make up **tissues**, and tissues make up **organs**. Groups of organs make up **organ systems**. Organ systems work together to provide life for an **organism.**

Several characteristics identify living versus non-living substances.

1. **Living things are made of cells**: they grow, are capable of reproduction, and respond to stimuli.

2. **Living things must adapt to environmental changes or perish**.

3. **Living things carry on metabolic processes**: they use and make energy.

All organic life has a common element: carbon. Carbon is recycled through the ecosystem through both biotic and abiotic means. It is the link between biological processes and the chemical make-up of life.

The cell is the basic unit of all living things. The two types of cells are prokaryotic and eukaryotic. **Prokaryotic** cells consist only of bacteria and blue-green algae. Bacteria were most likely the first cells; they date back in the fossil record 3.5 billion years. These cells are grouped together because of the following:

1. They have no defined nucleus or nuclear membrane. The DNA and ribosomes float freely within the cell.
2. They have a thick cell wall. This is for protection, to give shape, and to keep the cell from bursting.
3. The cell walls contain amino sugars (glycoproteins). Penicillin works by disrupting the cell wall, which is bad for the bacteria but will not harm the host.
4. Some have a capsule made of polysaccharides that make them sticky.
5. Some have pili, which is a protein strand. This also allows for attachment of the bacteria and may be used for sexual reproduction (conjugation).
6. Some have flagella for movement.

Eukaryotic cells are found in protists, fungi, plants, and animals. Some features of eukaryotic cells include the following:

1. They are usually larger than prokaryotic cells.
2. They contain many organelles, which are membrane-bound areas for specific cell functions.
3. They contain a cytoskeleton that provides a protein framework for the cell.
4. They contain cytoplasm, which supports the organelles and contains the ions and molecules necessary for cell function.

Parts of Eukaryotic Cells

1. Nucleus - the brain of the cell. The nucleus contains:

- **chromosomes**: DNA, RNA, and proteins tightly coiled to conserve space while providing a large surface area.
- **chromatin**: the loose structure of chromosomes. Chromosomes are called chromatin when the cell is not dividing.
- **nucleoli**: where ribosomes are made. These are seen as dark spots in the nucleus.
- **nuclear membrane**: contains pores that let RNA out of the nucleus. The nuclear membrane is continuous with the endoplasmic reticulum, which allows the membrane to expand or shrink if needed.

2. Ribosomes - the site of protein synthesis. Ribosomes may be free floating in the cytoplasm or attached to the endoplasmic reticulum. There may be up to a half million ribosomes in a cell, depending on how much protein is made by the cell.

3. Endoplasmic Reticulum - these are folded and provide a large surface area. They are the "roadway" of the cell and allow for transport of materials. The lumen of the endoplasmic reticulum helps to keep materials out of the cytoplasm and headed in the right direction. The endoplasmic reticulum is capable of building new membrane material. There are two types:

- **smooth endoplasmic reticulum**: contain no ribosomes on their surface.
- **rough endoplasmic reticulum** - contain ribosomes on their surface. This form of ER is abundant in cells that make many proteins, such as in the pancreas, which produces many digestive enzymes.

4. Golgi Complex or Golgi Apparatus - this structure is stacked to increase surface area. The Golgi complex functions to sort, modify, and package molecules that are made in other parts of the cell. These molecules are either sent out of the cell or to other organelles within the cell.

5. Lysosomes - found mainly in animal cells. These contain digestive enzymes that break down food, substances not needed, viruses, damaged cell components, and eventually the cell itself. It is believed that lysosomes are responsible for the aging process.

6. Mitochondria - large organelles that make ATP to supply energy to the cell. Muscle cells have many mitochondria because they use a great deal of energy. The folds inside the mitochondria are called cristae. They provide a large surface where the reactions of cellular respiration occur. Mitochondria have their own DNA and are capable of reproducing themselves if a greater demand is made for additional energy. Mitochondria are found only in animal cells.

7. Plastids - found in photosynthetic organisms only. They are similar to the mitochondria due to their double membrane structure. They also have their own DNA and can reproduce if increased capture of sunlight becomes necessary. There are several types of plastids:

- **chloroplasts**: green in color, they function in photosynthesis. They are capable of trapping sunlight.
- **chromoplasts**: make and store yellow and orange pigments; they provide color to leaves, flowers, and fruits.
- **amyloplasts**: store starch and are used as a food reserve. They are abundant in roots like potatoes.

8. Cell Wall - found in plant cells only, it is composed of cellulose and fibers. It is thick enough for support and protection, yet porous enough to allow water and dissolved substances to enter. Cell walls are cemented to each other.

9. Vacuoles - hold stored food and pigments. Vacuoles are very large in plants. This allows them to fill with water in order to provide turgor pressure. Lack of turgor pressure causes a plant to wilt.

10. Cytoskeleton - composed of protein filaments attached to the plasma membrane and organelles. They provide a framework for the cell and aid in cell movement. They constantly change shape and move about. Three types of fibers make up the cytoskeleton:

- **microtubules**: largest of the three, they are made up of cilia and flagella for locomotion. Flagella grow from a basal body. Some examples are sperm cells and tracheal cilia. Centrioles are also composed of microtubules. They form the spindle fibers that pull the cell apart into two cells during cell division. Centrioles are not found in the cells of higher plants.
- **intermediate filaments**: they are smaller than microtubules but larger than microfilaments. They help the cell to keep its shape.
- **microfilaments**: smallest of the three, they are made of actin and small amounts of myosin (as in muscle cells). They function in cell movement such as cytoplasmic streaming, endocytosis, and ameboid movement. This structure pinches the two cells apart after cell division, forming two cells.

Taxomony

Carolus Linnaeus is termed the father of taxonomy. **Taxonomy** is the science of classification. Linnaeus based his system on morphology (study of structure). Later on, evolutionary relationships (phylogeny) were also used to sort and group species. The modern classification system uses binomial nomenclature. This consists of a two-word name for every species. The genus is the first part of the name and the species is the second part. Notice, in the levels explained below, that Homo sapiens is the scientific name for humans. Starting with the kingdom, the groups get smaller and more alike as one moves down the levels in the classification of humans:

Kingdom: Animalia
Phylum: Chordata
Subphylum: Vertebrata
Class: Mammalia
Order: Primate
Family: Hominidae
Genus: Homo
Species: sapiens

Species are defined by the ability to successfully reproduce with members of their own kind.

Five Kingdoms

Living organisms are divided into five major kingdoms: Monera, Protista, Fungi, Plantae, and Animalia.

Kingdom Monera - bacteria and blue-green algae, prokaryotic, have no true nucleus, unicellular.

Bacteria are classified according to their morphology (shape). **Bacilli** are rod shaped, **cocci** are round, and **spirillia** are spiral shaped. The **gram stain** is a staining procedure used to identify bacteria. Gram positive bacteria pick up the stain and turn purple. Gram negative bacteria do not pick up the stain and are pink in color.

Methods of locomotion - flagellates have a flagellum, ciliates have cilia, and ameboids move through use of pseudopodia.

Methods of reproduction - binary fission is simply dividing in half and is asexual. All new organisms are exact clones of the parent. Sexual modes provide more diversity. Bacteria can reproduce sexually through conjugation, where genetic material is exchanged.

Methods of obtaining nutrition - photosynthetic organisms or producers convert sunlight to chemical energy, while consumers or heterotrophs eat other living things. Saprophytes are consumers that live off dead or decaying material.

Kingdom Protista - eukaryotic, unicellular, some are photosynthetic, some are consumers. Microbiologists use methods of locomotion, reproduction, and how the organism obtains its food to classify protista.

Kingdom Fungi - eukaryotic, multicellular, absorptive consumers, contain a chitin cell wall.

Kingdom Plantae

Nonvascular Plants - small in size, they do not require vascular tissue (xylem and phloem) because individual cells are close to their environment. The nonvascular plants have no true leaves, stems, or roots.

- **Division Bryophyta** - mosses and liverworts; these plants have a dominant gametophyte generation. They possess rhizoids, which are root-like structures. Moisture in their environment is required for reproduction and absorption.

Vascular Plants - the development of vascular tissue enables these plants to grow in size. Xylem and phloem allow for the transport of water and minerals up to the top of the plant, as well as for the transport of food manufactured in the leaves to the bottom of the plant. All vascular plants have a dominant sporophyte generation.

- **Division Lycophyta** - club mosses; these plants reproduce with spores and require water for reproduction.
- **Division Sphenophyta** - horsetails; also reproduce with spores. These plants have small, needle-like leaves and rhizoids. They require moisture for reproduction.
- **Division Pterophyta** - ferns; they reproduce with spores and flagellated sperm. These plants have a true stem and need moisture for reproduction.
- **Gymnosperms** - the word means "naked seed." These were the first plants to evolve with seeds, which made them less dependent on water to assist in reproduction. Their seeds can travel by wind; pollen from the male is also easily carried by the wind. Gymnosperms have cones that protect the seeds.
- **Division Cycadophyta** - cycads; these plants look like palms with cones.
- **Divison Ghetophyta** - desert dwellers.
- **Division Coniferophyta** - pines; these plants have needles and cones.
- **Divison Ginkgophyta** - the Ginkgo is the only member of this division.

Angiosperms (Division Anthophyta) - the largest group in the plant kingdom. They are the flowering plants that produce true seeds for reproduction.

Kingdom Animalia

Annelida - the segmented worms. The Annelida have specialized tissue. The circulatory system is more advanced in these worms; it is a closed system with blood vessels. The nephridia are their excretory organs. They are hermaphrodidic, and each worm fertilizes the other upon mating. They support themselves with a hydrostatic skeleton and have circular and longitudinal muscles for movement.

Mollusca - clams, octopi, and soft-bodied animals. These animals have a muscular foot for movement. They breathe through gills, and most are able to make a shell for protection from predators. They have an open circulatory system, with sinuses bathing the body regions.

Arthropoda - insects, crustaceans, and spiders; this is the largest group of the animal kingdom. Phylum Arthropoda accounts for about 85 percent of all the animal species. Animals in the Phylum Arthropoda possess an exoskeleton made of chitin. They must molt to grow. Insects, for example, go through four stages of development. They begin as an egg, hatch into a larva, form a pupa, then emerge as an adult. Arthropods breathe through gills, trachea, or book lungs. Movement varies, with members being able to swim, fly, and crawl. There is a division of labor among the appendages (legs, antennae, etc). This is an extremely successful phylum, with members occupying diverse habitats.

Echinodermata - sea urchins and starfish; these animals have spiny skin. Their habitat is marine. They have tube feet for locomotion and feeding.

Chordata - all animals with a notocord or a backbone. The classes in this phylum include Agnatha (jawless fish), Chondrichthyes (cartilage fish), Osteichthyes (bony fish), Amphibia (frogs and toads; gills that are replaced by lungs during development), Reptilia (snakes, lizards; the first to lay eggs with a protective covering), Aves (birds; warm-blooded with wings consisting of a particular shape and composition designed for flight), and Mammalia (warm blooded animals with body hair who bear their young alive and possess mammary glands for milk production).

Skill 18.2   Reproduction and heredity

Reproductive System

Sexual reproduction greatly increases diversity due to the many combinations possible through meiosis and fertilization. **Gametogenesis** is the production of the sperm and egg cells. **Spermatogenesis** begins at puberty in the male. One spermatozoa produces four sperm. The sperm mature in the seminiferous tubules located in the testes. **Oogenesis**, the production of egg cells, is usually complete by the birth of a female. Egg cells are not released until menstruation begins at puberty. Meiosis forms one ovum with all the cytoplasm and three polar bodies, which are reabsorbed by the body. The ovum are stored in the ovaries and released each month from puberty to menopause.

Path of the sperm - sperm are stored in the seminiferous tubules in the testes where they mature. Mature sperm are found in the epididymis, located on top of the testes. After ejaculation, the sperm travels up the vas deferens where they mix with semen made in the prostate and seminal vesicles; they then travel out the urethra.

Path of the egg - eggs are stored in the ovaries. Ovulation releases the egg into the fallopian tubes, which are ciliated to move the egg along. Fertilization normally occurs in the fallopian tube. If pregnancy does not occur, the egg passes through the uterus and is expelled through the vagina during menstruation. Levels of progesterone and estrogen stimulate menstruation. In the event of pregnancy, hormonal levels are affected by the implantation of a fertilized egg, so menstruation does not occur.

Pregnancy - if fertilization occurs, the zygote implants in about two to three days in the uterus. Implantation promotes secretion of human chorionic gonadotropin (HCG). This is what is detected in pregnancy tests. The HCG keeps the level of progesterone elevated to maintain the uterine lining in order to feed the developing embryo until the umbilical cord forms. Labor is initiated by oxytocin, which causes labor contractions and dilation of the cervix. Prolactin and oxytocin cause the production of milk.

Cellular Reproduction

The purpose of cell division is to provide growth and repair in body (somatic) cells and to replenish or create sex cells for reproduction. There are two forms of cell division. **Mitosis** is the division of somatic cells and **meiosis** is the division of sex cells (eggs and sperm). The table below summarizes the major differences between the two processes.

Mitosis	**Meiosis**
1. Division of somatic cell	1. Division of sex cells
2. Two cells result from each division	2. Four cells or polar bodies result from each division
3. Chromosome number is identical to parent cells	3. Chromosome number is half the number of parent cells
4. For cell growth and repair	4. Recombinations provide genetic diversity

Some terms to know:

gamete - sex cell or germ cell; eggs and sperm
chromatin - loose chromosomes; this state is found when the cell is not dividing
chromosome - tightly coiled, visible chromatin; this state is found when the cell is dividing
homologues - chromosomes that contain the same information—they are of the same length and contain the same genes
diploid - two in number; diploid chromosomes are a pair of chromosomes (somatic cells)
haploid - one in number; haploid chromosomes are a half of a pair (sex cells)

Mitosis

The cell cycle is the life cycle of the cell. It is divided into two stages: **interphase** and **mitotic division** (where the cell is actively dividing). Interphase is divided into three steps:

1.   G1 (growth) period, where the cell is growing and metabolizing.
2.   S period (synthesis), where new DNA and enzymes are being made.
3.   G2 phase (growth), where new proteins and organelles are being made to prepare for cell division.

The mitotic stage consists of the stages of mitosis and the division of the cytoplasm. The stages of mitosis and their events are as follows. Be sure to know the correct order of steps. (IPMAT)

1. Interphase - chromatin is loose, chromosomes are replicated, and cell metabolism is occurring. Interphase is technically <u>not</u> a stage of mitosis.

2. Prophase - once the cell enters prophase, it proceeds through the following steps continuously, without stopping. The chromatin condenses to become visible chromosomes. The nucleolus disappears and the nuclear membrane breaks apart. Mitotic spindles form, which will eventually pull the chromosomes apart. They are composed of microtubules. The cytoskeleton breaks down and the spindles are pushed to the poles or opposite ends of the cell by the action of centrioles.

3. Metaphase - kinetechore fibers attach to the chromosomes, which causes the chromosomes to line up in the center of the cell (think **m**iddle for **m**etaphase)

4. Anaphase - centromeres split in half and homologous chromosomes separate. The chromosomes are pulled to the poles of the cell, with identical sets at either end.

5. Telophase – there are two nuclei with a full set of DNA identical to the parent cell. The nucleoli become visible and the nuclear membrane reassembles. A cell plate is visible in plant cells, whereas a cleavage furrow is formed in animal cells. The cell is pinched into two cells. Cytokinesis, or division, of the cytoplasm and organelles occurs.

Meiosis

Meiosis contains the same five stages as mitosis, but is repeated in order to reduce the chromosome number by one half. This way, when the sperm and egg join during fertilization, the haploid number is reached. The steps of meiosis are as follows:

Meiosis I
The major function is to replicate chromosomes; cells remain diploid.

Prophase I - replicated chromosomes condense and pair with homologues. This forms a tetrad. Crossing over (the exchange of genetic material between homologues to further increase diversity) occurs during Prophase I.

Metaphase I - homologous sets attach to spindle fibers after lining up in the middle of the cell.

Anaphase I - sister chromatids remain joined and move to the poles of the cell.

Telophase I - two new cells are formed and the chromosome number is still diploid.

Meiosis II
The major function is to reduce the chromosome number in half.

Prophase II - chromosomes condense.

Metaphase II - spindle fibers form again, sister chromatids line up in center of cell, centromeres divide, and sister chromatids separate.

Anaphase II - separated chromosomes move to opposite ends of cell.

Telophase II - four haploid cells form for each original sperm germ cell. One viable egg cell gets all the genetic information and three polar bodies form with no DNA. The nuclear membrane reforms and cytokinesis occurs.

Mutations

During these very intricate steps, mistakes do happen. Inheritable changes in DNA are called **mutations**. Mutations may be errors in replication or a spontaneous rearrangement of one or more segments by factors like radioactivity, drugs, or chemicals. The amount of the change is not as critical as where the change is. Mutations may occur on somatic or sex cells. Usually the ones on sex cells are more dangerous since they contain the basis of all information for the developing offspring. Mutations are not always bad. They are the basis of evolution, and if they make a more favorable variation that enhances the organism's survival, then they are beneficial. However, mutations may also lead to abnormalities, birth defects, and even death. There are several types of mutations:

Suppose a normal sequence was as follows:

Normal -   A B C D E F

Then:

Duplication - one gene is repeated   A B C C D E F

Inversion - a segment of the sequence is flipped around   A E D C B F

Deletion - a gene is left out   A B C E F

Insertion or Translocation - a segment from another place on the DNA is inserted in the wrong place   A B C R S D E F

Breakage - a piece is lost   A B C (DEF is lost)

Nondisjunction occurs during meiosis when chromosomes fail to separate properly. One sex cell may get both genes and another may get none. Depending on the chromosomes involved, this may or may not be serious. Offspring end up with either an extra chromosome or are missing one. An example of nondisjunction is Down Syndrome, where three of chromosome #21 are present.

Genetics

Gregor Mendel is recognized as the father of genetics. His work in the late 1800s is the basis of our knowledge of genetics. Although unaware of the presence of DNA or genes, Mendel realized there were factors (now known as **genes**) that were transferred from parents to their offspring. Mendel worked with pea plants; he fertilized the plants himself, keeping track of subsequent generations. His findings led to the Mendelian laws of genetics. Mendel found that two "factors" governed each trait, one from each parent. Traits or characteristics came in several forms, known as **alleles**. For example, the trait of flower color had white alleles and purple alleles.

Mendel formed three laws:

Law of dominance - in a pair of alleles, one trait may cover up the allele of the other trait. Example: brown eyes are dominant to blue eyes.

Law of segregation - only one of the two possible alleles from each parent is passed on to the offspring. (During meiosis, the haploid number insures that half the sex cells get one allele and half get the other.)

Law of independent assortment - alleles sort independently of each other. (Many combinations are possible, depending on which sperm ends up with which egg. Compare this to the many combinations of hands possible when dealing a deck of cards.)

Punnet squares are used to show the possible ways that genes combine and indicate probability of the occurrence of a certain genotype or phenotype. One parent's genes are put at the top of the box and the other parent at the side of the box. Genes combine on the square just like numbers that are added in addition tables we learned in elementary school. Below is an example of a **monohybrid cross**, which is a cross using only one trait—in this case, a trait labeled "g."

	G	g
G	GG	Gg
g	Gg	gg

In a **dihybrid cross**, sixteen gene combinations are possible, as each cross has two traits.

<u>Some definitions to know:</u>

Dominant - the stronger of two traits. If a dominant gene is present, it will be expressed. It is shown by a capital letter.

Recessive - the weaker of two traits. In order for the recessive gene to be expressed, there must be two recessive genes present. It is shown by a lower case letter.

Homozygous - (purebred) having two of the same genes present; an organism may be homozygous dominant with two dominant genes or homozygous recessive with two recessive genes.

Heterozygous - (hybrid) having one dominant gene and one recessive gene. Due to the Law of Dominance, the dominant gene will be expressed.

Genotype - the genes the organism has. Genes are represented with letters. AA, Bb, and tt are examples of genotypes.

Phenotype - how the trait is expressed in an organism. Blue eyes, brown hair, and red flowers are examples of phenotypes.

Incomplete dominance - neither gene masks the other; a new phenotype is formed. For example, red flowers and white flowers may have equal strength. A heterozygote (Rr) would have pink flowers. If a problem occurs with a third phenotype, incomplete dominance is occurring.

Codominance - genes may form new phenotypes. The ABO blood grouping is an example of codominance. A and B are of equal strength and O is recessive. Therefore, type A blood may have the genotypes of AA or AO, type B blood may have the genotypes of BB or BO, type AB blood has the genotype A and B, and type O blood has two recessive O genes.

Linkage - genes that are found on the same chromosome usually appear together unless crossing over has occurred in meiosis (for example blue eyes and blonde hair commonly occur together).

Lethal alleles - these are usually recessive due to the early death of the offspring. If a 2:1 ratio of alleles is found in offspring, a lethal gene combination may be the reason. Some examples of lethal alleles include sickle cell anemia, tay-sachs disease, and cystic fibrosis. In most cases, the coding for an important protein is affected.

Inborn errors of metabolism - these occur when the protein affected is an enzyme. Examples include PKU (phenylketonuria) and albinism.

Polygenic characters - many alleles code for a phenotype. There may be as many as twenty genes that code for skin color. This is why there is such a variety of skin tones. Another example is height. A couple of medium height may have very tall offspring.

Sex linked traits - the Y chromosome found only in males (XY) carries very little genetic information, whereas the X chromosome found in females (XX) carries very important information. Since men have no second X chromosome to cover up a recessive gene, the recessive trait is expressed more often in men. Women need the recessive gene on both X chromosomes to show the trait. Examples of sex linked traits include hemophilia and color-blindness.

Sex influenced traits - traits are influenced by the sex hormones. Male pattern baldness is an example of a sex influenced trait. Testosterone influences the expression of the gene. Most men lose their hair due to this trait.

Skill 18.3   Regulation and behavior

Animal communication is defined as any behavior by one animal that affects the behavior of another animal. Animals use body language, sound, and smell to communicate. Perhaps the most common type of animal communication is the presentation or movement of distinctive body parts. Many species of animals reveal or conceal body parts to communicate with potential mates, predators, and prey. In addition, many species of animals communicate with sound. Examples of vocal communication include the mating "songs" of birds and frogs and warning cries of monkeys. Many animals also release scented chemicals called pheromones and secrete distinctive odors from specialized glands to communicate with other animals. Pheromones are important in reproduction and mating, and glandular secretions of long-lasting smell alert animals to the presence of others.

Ecological and behavioral factors affect the interrelationships among organisms in many ways. Two important ecological factors are environmental conditions and resource availability. Important types of organismal behaviors are described as competitive, instinctive, territorial, and mating.

Competitive – In any system, organisms compete with other species for scarce resources. Organisms also compete with members of their own species for mates and territory. Many competitive behaviors involve rituals and dominance hierarchies. **Rituals** are symbolic activities that often settle disputes without undue harm. For example, dogs bare their teeth, erect their ears, and growl to intimidate competitors. A dominance hierarchy, or "pecking order," organizes groups of animals, simplifying interrelationships, conserving energy, and minimizing the potential for harm in a community.

Instinctive – Instinctive, or innate, behavior is common to all members of a given species; it is genetically preprogrammed. Environmental differences do not affect instinctive behaviors. For example, baby birds of many types and species beg for food by raising their heads and opening their beaks.

Territorial – Many animals act aggressively to protect their territory from other animals. Animals protect territories for use in feeding, mating, and rearing of young.

Mating – Mating behaviors are very important interspecies interactions. The search for a mate with which to reproduce is an instinctive behavior. Mating interrelationships often involve ritualistic and territorial behaviors that are competitive.

Environmental conditions such as climate influence organismal interrelationships by changing the dynamic of the ecosystem. Changes in climate (such as moisture levels and temperature) can alter the environment, changing the characteristics that are advantageous. For example, an increase in temperature will favor those organisms that can tolerate the temperature change. Thus, those organisms gain a competitive advantage. In addition, the availability of necessary resources influences interrelationships. For example, when necessary resources are scarce, interrelationships are more competitive than when resources are abundant.

Behavior may be innate or learned. **Innate behaviors** are defined as those that that are inborn or instinctual. An environmental stimulus (such as the length of day or temperature) results in a behavior. Hibernation among some animals is an innate behavior. **Learned behavior** is any behavior that is modified due to past experience.

Skill 18.4   Biological evolution

Charles Darwin defined the theory of Natural Selection in the mid-1800s. Through the study of finches on the Galapagos Islands, Darwin theorized that nature selects the traits that are advantageous to the organism. Those organisms that do not possess the desirable trait die and do not pass on their genes. Those more fit to survive get the opportunity to reproduce, thus increasing that gene in the population. Darwin listed four principles to define natural selection:

1. The individuals in a certain species vary from generation to generation.

2. Some of the variations are determined by the genetic makeup of the species.

3. More individuals are produced than will survive.

4. Some genes allow for better survival of an animal.

Causes of evolution - Certain factors increase the chances of variability in a population, thus leading to evolution. Items that increase variability include mutations, sexual reproduction, immigration, and large population. Items that decrease variation include natural selection, emigration, small population, and random mating.

Sexual selection - Genes that happen to come together determine the makeup of the gene pool. Animals that use mating behaviors may be successful or unsuccessful. An animal that lacks attractive plumage or has a weak mating call will not attract the female, thereby eventually limiting that gene in the gene pool. Mechanical isolation, where sex organs do not fit the female, has an obvious disadvantage.

Skill 18.5   Interdependence of organisms

Ecology is the study of organisms: where they live and their interactions with the environment. A **population** is a group of the same species in a specific area. A **community** is a group of populations residing in the same area. Communities that are ecologically similar in regards to temperature, rainfall, and the species that live there are called **biomes**. Specific biomes include:

- **Marine** - covers 75 percent of the earth. This biome is organized by the depth of the water. The intertidal zone is located from the tide line to the edge of the water. The littoral zone is from the water's edge to the open sea. It includes coral reef habitats and is the most densely populated area of the marine biome. The open sea zone is divided into the epipelagic zone and the pelagic zone. The epipelagic zone receives more sunlight and has a larger number of species. The ocean floor is called the benthic zone and is populated with bottom feeders.

- **Tropical Rain Forest** - temperature is constant (25 degrees C), and rainfall exceeds 200 cm per year. Located around the area of the equator, the rain forest has abundant, diverse species of plants and animals.

- **Savanna** - temperatures range from 0-25 degrees C depending on the location. Rainfall is from 90 to 150 cm per year. Plants include shrubs and grasses. The savanna is a transitional biome between the rain forest and the desert.

- **Desert** - temperatures range from 10-38 degrees C. Rainfall is under 25 cm per year. Plant species include xerophytes and succulents. Lizards, snakes, and small mammals are common animals.

- **Temperate Deciduous Forest** - temperatures range from -24 to 38 degrees C. Rainfall is between 65 to 150 cm per year. Deciduous trees are common, as are deer, bear, and squirrels.

- **Taiga** - temperatures range from -24 to 22 degrees C. Rainfall is between 35 to 40 cm per year. Taiga is located very north and very south of the equator, getting close to the poles. Plant life includes conifers and plants that can withstand harsh winters. Animals include weasels, mink, and moose.

- **Tundra** - temperatures range from -28 to 15 degrees C. Rainfall is limited, ranging from 10 to 15 cm per year. The tundra is located even further north and south than the taiga. Common plants include lichens and mosses. Animals include polar bears and musk ox.

- **Polar or Permafrost** - temperature ranges from -40 to 0 degrees C. It rarely gets above freezing. Rainfall is below 10 cm per year. Most water is bound up as ice. Life is limited.

Succession is defined as an orderly process of replacing a community that has been damaged or has begun where no life previously existed. **Primary succession** occurs after a community has been totally wiped out by a natural disaster or where life never existed before, as in a flooded area. **Secondary succession** takes place in communities that were once flourishing but were disturbed by some force, either human or natural, but not totally stripped. A **climax community** is a community that is established and flourishing.

Definitions of Feeding Relationships:

- **Parasitism** occurs when two species occupy a similar place, but the parasite benefits from the relationship while the host is harmed.

- **Commensalism** is when two species occupy a similar place, and neither species is harmed or benefits from the relationship.

- **Mutualism (symbiosis)** occurs when two species occupy a similar place and both species benefit from the relationship.

- **Competition** is when two species occupy the same habitat or eat the same food.

- **Predation** is when animals eat other animals. The animals they feed on are called the prey. Population growth depends upon competition for food, water, shelter, and space. The amount of predators determines the amount of prey, which in turn affects the number of predators.

- **Carrying Capacity** is the total amount of life a habitat can support. Once the habitat runs out of food, water, shelter, or space, the carrying capacity decreases and then re-stabilizes.

Ecological Problems

Nonrenewable resources are fragile and must be conserved for use in the future. Humankind's impact and knowledge of conservation will control our future. The following are just some of the ways in which the earth's ecology is altered by human interaction.

Biological magnification - chemicals and pesticides accumulate along the food chain. Tertiary consumers have more accumulated toxins than animals at the bottom of the food chain.

Simplification of the food web - three major crops feed the world (rice, corn, and wheat). Planting these foods in abundance wipes out habitats and pushes animals residing there into other habitats, causing overpopulation or extinction.

Fuel sources - strip mining and the overuse of oil reserves have depleted these resources. At the current rate of consumption, the only way to guarantee our future fuel sources is conservation or alternate fuel sources.

Pollution - although technology gives us many advances, pollution is a side effect of production. Waste disposal and the burning of fossil fuels have polluted our land, water, and air. Global warming and acid rain are two results of the burning of hydrocarbons and sulfur.

Global warming - rainforest depletion and the use of fossil fuels and aerosols have caused an increase in carbon dioxide production. This leads to a decrease in the amount of oxygen, which is directly proportional to the amount of ozone. As the ozone layer depletes, more heat enters our atmosphere and is trapped. This causes an overall warming effect, which may eventually melt polar ice caps and cause a rise in water levels or changes in climate that will affect weather systems world-wide.

Endangered species - construction of homes to house people has caused the destruction of habitats for other animals, leading to their extinction.

Overpopulation - the human race is still growing at an exponential rate. Carrying capacity has not been met due to our ability to use technology to produce more food and housing. However, space and water cannot be manufactured; eventually, our nonrenewable resources will reach a crisis state. Our overuse affects every living thing on this planet.

COMPETENCY 19.0   PHYSICAL SCIENCE

Skill 19.1   The structure and properties of matter

Matter

Everything in our world is made up of **matter**, whether it is a rock, a building, an animal, or a person. Matter is defined by its characteristics: it takes up space and it has mass.

Mass is a measure of the amount of matter in an object. Two objects of equal mass will balance each other on a simple balance scale no matter where the scale is located. For instance, two rocks with the same amount of mass that are in balance on Earth will also be in balance on the moon. They will feel heavier on the earth than on the moon because of the gravitational pull of the earth. Therefore, although the two rocks have the same mass, they will have different weight.

Weight is the measure of the earth's pull of gravity on an object. It can also be defined as the pull of gravity between other bodies. The units of weight measurement commonly used are the pound (English measure) and the kilogram (metric measure).

In addition to mass, matter also has the property of volume. **Volume** is the amount of cubic space that an object occupies. Volume and mass together give a more exact description of the object. Two objects may have the same volume, but different mass, or the same mass but different volumes. For instance, consider two cubes that are each one cubic centimeter, one made from plastic and one from lead. They have the same volume, but the lead cube has more mass. The measure that we use to describe the cubes takes into consideration both the mass and the volume. **Density** is the mass of a substance contained per unit of volume. If the density of an object is less than the density of a liquid, the object will float in the liquid. If the object is denser than the liquid, then the object will sink.

Density is stated in grams per cubic centimeter (g/cm^3), where the gram is the standard unit of mass. To find an object's density, you must measure its mass and its volume. Then divide the mass by the volume ($D = m/V$).
To discover an object's density, first use a balance to find its mass. Then calculate its volume. If the object is a regular shape, you can find the volume by multiplying the length, width, and height together. However, if it is an irregular shape, you can find the volume by seeing how much water it displaces. Measure the water in the container before and after the object is submerged. The difference will be the volume of the object.

Specific gravity is the ratio of the density of a substance to the density of water. For instance, the specific density of one liter of alcohol is calculated by comparing its mass (0.81 kg) to the mass of one liter of water (1 kg):

$$\frac{\text{mass of 1 L alcohol}}{\text{mass of 1 L water}} = \frac{0.81\ \text{kg}}{1.00\ \text{kg}} = 0.81$$

Physical and Chemical Properties of Matter

Physical properties and chemical properties of matter describe the appearance or behavior of a substance. A **physical property** can be observed without changing the identity of a substance. For instance, you can describe the color, mass, shape, and volume of a book. **Chemical properties** describe the ability of a substance to be changed into new substances. Baking powder goes through a chemical change as it changes into carbon dioxide gas during the baking process.

Matter constantly changes. A **physical change** is a change that does not produce a new substance. The freezing and melting of water is an example of physical change. A **chemical change** (or chemical reaction) is any change of a substance into one or more other substances. Burning materials turn into smoke; a seltzer tablet fizzes into gas bubbles. The **phase of matter** (solid, liquid, or gas) is identified by its shape and volume.

A **solid** has a definite shape and volume. A **liquid** has a definite volume, but no shape. A **gas** has no shape or volume because it will spread out to occupy the entire space of whatever container it is in. While **plasma** is really a type of gas, its properties are so unique that it is considered a unique phase of matter.

Plasma is a gas that has been ionized, meaning that at least one electron has been removed from some of its atoms. Plasma shares some characteristics with gas, specifically, the high kinetic energy of its molecules. Thus, plasma exists as a diffuse "cloud," though it sometimes includes tiny grains (this is termed **dusty plasma**). What most distinguishes plasma from gas is that it is electrically conductive and exhibits a strong response to electromagnetic fields. This property is a consequence of the charged particles that result from the removal of electrons from the molecules in the plasma.

Energy is the ability to cause changes in matter. Applying heat to a frozen liquid changes it from solid back to liquid. Continue heating it and it will boil and give off steam, a gas. **Evaporation** is the change in phase from liquid to gas. **Condensation** is the change in phase from gas to liquid.

Composition of Matter

An **element** is a substance that cannot be broken down into other substances. To date, scientists have identified 109 elements: 89 are found in nature and 20 are synthetic.

An **atom** is the smallest particle of an element that retains the properties of that element. All of the atoms of a particular element are the same. The atoms of each element are different from the atoms of other elements. Elements are assigned an identifying symbol of one or two letters. The symbol for oxygen is O; it stands for one atom of oxygen. However, because oxygen atoms in nature are joined together is pairs, the symbol O_2 represents oxygen.

This pair of oxygen atoms is a molecule. A **molecule** is the smallest particle of a substance that can exist independently and still have all of the properties of that substance. A molecule of most elements is made up of one atom. However, oxygen, hydrogen, nitrogen, and chlorine molecules are made of two atoms each.

A **compound** is made of two or more elements that have been chemically combined. Atoms join together when elements are chemically combined. The result is that the elements lose their individual identities; the compound that they become has different properties.

We use a formula to show the elements of a chemical compound. A **chemical formula** is a shorthand way of showing what is in a compound through symbols and subscripts. The letter symbols let us know what elements are involved and the number subscript tells how many atoms of each element are involved. No subscript is used if there is only one atom involved. For example, carbon dioxide is made up of one atom of carbon (C) and two atoms of oxygen (O_2), so the formula would be represented as CO_2.

Substances can combine without a chemical change. A **mixture** is any combination of two or more substances in which the substances keep their own properties. A fruit salad is a mixture (so is an ice cream sundae, although you might not recognize each part if it is stirred together). Colognes and perfumes are other examples. You may not readily recognize the individual elements; however, they can be separated.

Compounds and mixtures are similar in that they are made up of two or more substances. However, they have the following opposite characteristics:

Compounds:
- Made up of one kind of particle
- Formed during a chemical change
- Broken down only by chemical changes
- Properties are different from their parts
- Has a specific amount of each ingredient.

Mixtures:
- Made up of two or more particles
- Not formed by a chemical change
- Can be separated by physical changes
- Properties are the same as their parts.
- Does not have a definite amount of each ingredient.

Common compounds are **acids, bases, salts**, and **oxides**. These are classified according to their characteristics.

Atoms

The **nucleus** is the center of the atom. The positive particles inside the nucleus are called **protons.** The mass of a proton is about 2,000 times that of the mass of an electron. The number of protons in the nucleus of an atom is called the **atomic number.** All atoms of the same element have the same atomic number.

Neutrons are another type of particle in the nucleus. Neutrons and protons have about the same mass, but neutrons have no charge. Neutrons were discovered because scientists observed that not all atoms in neon gas have the same mass. They had identified isotopes. **Isotopes** of an element have the same number of protons in the nucleus, but have different masses. Neutrons explain the difference in mass.

The mass of matter is measured against a standard mass such as the gram. Scientists measure the mass of an atom by comparing it to that of a standard atom. The result is relative mass. The **relative mass** of an atom is its mass expressed in terms of the mass of the standard atom. The isotope of the element carbon is the standard atom. It has six (6) neutrons and is called carbon-12. It is assigned a mass of 12 atomic mass units (amu). Therefore, the **atomic mass unit (amu)** is the standard unit for measuring the mass of an atom. It is equal to the mass of a carbon atom.

The **mass number** of an atom is the sum of its protons and neutrons. In any element, there is a mixture of isotopes, some having slightly more or slightly fewer protons and neutrons. The **atomic mass** of an element is an average of the mass numbers of its atoms.

The following table summarizes the terms used to describe atomic nuclei:

Term	Example	Meaning	Characteristic
Atomic Number	# protons (p)	same for all atoms of a given element	Carbon (C) atomic number = 6 (6p)
Mass number	# protons + # neutrons (p + n)	changes for different isotopes of an element	C-12 (6p + 6n) C-13 (6p + 7n)
Atomic mass	average mass of the atoms of the element	usually not a whole number	atomic mass of carbon equals 12.011

Each atom has an equal number of electrons (negative) and protons (positive). Therefore, atoms are neutral. Electrons orbiting the nucleus occupy energy levels that are arranged in order and the electrons tend to occupy the lowest energy level available. A **stable electron arrangement** is an atom that has all of its electrons in the lowest possible energy levels.

Each energy level holds a maximum number of electrons. However, an atom with more than one level does not hold more than eight electrons in its outermost shell.

Level	Name	Max. # of Electrons
First	K shell	2
Second	L shell	8
Third	M shell	18
Fourth	N shell	32

This can help to explain why chemical reactions occur. Atoms react with each other when their outer levels are unfilled. When atoms either exchange or share electrons with each other, these energy levels become filled and the atom becomes more stable.

As an electron gains energy, it moves from one energy level to a higher energy level. The electron cannot leave one level until it has enough energy to reach the next level. **Excited electrons** are electrons that have absorbed energy and have moved farther from the nucleus.

Electrons can also lose energy. When they do, they fall to a lower level. However, they can only fall to the lowest level that has room for them. This explains why atoms do not collapse.

Skill 19.2   Energy

The kinetic theory states that matter consists of molecules that possess kinetic energies in continual random motion. The state of matter (solid, liquid, or gas) depends on the speed of the molecules and the amount of kinetic energy the molecules possess. The molecules of solid matter merely vibrate, allowing strong intermolecular forces to hold the molecules in place. The molecules of liquid matter move freely and quickly throughout the body, and the molecules of gaseous matter move randomly and at high speeds.

Matter changes state when energy is added or taken away. The addition of energy, usually in the form of heat, increases the speed and kinetic energy of the component molecules. Faster moving molecules more readily overcome the intermolecular attractions that maintain the form of solids and liquids. In conclusion, as the speed of molecules increases, matter changes state from solid to liquid to gas (melting and evaporation).

As matter loses heat energy to the environment, the speed of the component molecules decrease. Intermolecular forces have greater impact on slower moving molecules. Thus, as the speed of molecules decrease, matter changes from gas to liquid to solid (condensation and freezing).

Heat and temperature are different physical quantities. **Heat** is a measure of energy. **Temperature** is the measure of how hot (or cold) a body is with respect to a standard object.

Two concepts are important in the discussion of temperature changes. Objects are in thermal contact if they can affect each other's temperatures. Set a hot cup of coffee on a desk top. The two objects are in thermal contact with each other and will begin affecting each other's temperatures. The coffee will become cooler and the desktop warmer. Eventually, they will have the same temperature. When this happens, they are in **thermal equilibrium.**

We cannot rely on our sense of touch to determine temperature because the heat from a hand may be conducted more efficiently by certain objects, making them feel colder. **Thermometers** are used to measure temperature. In thermometers, a small amount of mercury in a capillary tube will expand when heated. The thermometer and the object whose temperature it is measuring are put in contact long enough for them to reach thermal equilibrium. The temperature can then be read from the thermometer scale.

Three temperature scales are used:

Celsius: The freezing point of water is set at 0 and the steam (boiling) point is 100. The interval between the two is divided into 100 equal parts called degrees Celsius.

Fahrenheit: The freezing point of water is 32 degrees and the boiling point is 212. The interval between is divided into 180 equal parts called degrees Fahrenheit.

Temperature readings can be converted from one to the other as follows.

Fahrenheit to Celsius	**Celsius to Fahrenheit**
C = 5/9 (F - 32)	F = (9/5) C + 32

The **Kelvin Scale** has degrees the same size as the Celsius scale, but the zero point is moved to the triple point of water. Water inside a closed vessel is in thermal equilibrium in all three states (ice, water, and vapor) at 273.15 degrees Kelvin. This temperature is equivalent to .01 degrees Celsius. Because the degrees are the same in the two scales, temperature changes are the same in Celsius and Kelvin.

Temperature readings can be converted from Celsius to Kelvin:

Celsius to Kelvin	**Kelvin to Celsius**
K = C + 273.15	C = K - 273.15

The **heat capacity** of an object is the amount of heat energy it takes to raise the temperature of the object by one degree.

Heat capacity (C) per unit mass (m) is called **specific heat** (c):

$$c = \frac{C}{m} = \frac{Q}{m}$$

There are a number of ways that heat is measured. In each case, the measurement is dependent upon raising the temperature of a specific amount of water by a specific amount. These conversions of heat energy and work are called the **mechanical equivalent of heat**.

A **calorie** is the amount of energy that it takes to raise one gram of water one degree Celsius.

A **kilocalorie** is the amount of energy that it takes to raise one kilogram of water by one degree Celsius. Food calories are kilocalories.

In the International System of Units **(SI),** the calorie is equal to 4.184 **joules**.

A **British thermal unit (BTU)** = 252 calories = 1.054 kJ

Heat energy that is transferred into or out of a system is **heat transfer.** The temperature change is positive for a gain in heat energy and negative when heat is removed from the object or system.

The formula for heat transfer is $Q = mc\Delta T$ where Q is the amount of heat energy transferred, m is the amount of substance (in kilograms), c is the specific heat of the substance, and ΔT is the change in temperature of the substance. It is important to assume that the objects in thermal contact are isolated and insulated from their surroundings.

If a substance in a closed container loses heat, then another substance in the container must gain heat.

A **calorimeter** uses the transfer of heat from one substance to another to determine the specific heat of the substance. When an object undergoes a change of phase it goes from one physical state (solid, liquid, or gas) to another. For instance, water can go from liquid to solid (freezing) or from liquid to gas (boiling). The heat that is required to change from one state to the other is called **latent heat.**

The **heat of fusion** is the amount of heat that it takes to change from a solid to a liquid or the amount of heat released during the change from liquid to solid.

The **heat of vaporization** is the amount of heat that it takes to change from a liquid to a gaseous state.

Heat is transferred in three ways: conduction, convection, and radiation.

Conduction occurs when heat travels through the heated solid. The transfer rate is the ratio of the amount of heat per amount of time it takes to transfer heat from area of an object to another. For example, if you place an iron pan on a flame, the handle will eventually become hot. How fast the handle gets too hot to handle is a function of the amount of heat and how long it is applied. Because the change in time is in the denominator of the function, the shorter the amount of time it takes to heat the handle, the greater the transfer rate.

Convection is heat transported by the movement of a heated substance. Warmed air rising from a heat source such as a fire or electric heater is a common example of convection. Convection ovens make use of circulating air to more efficiently cook food.

Radiation is heat transfer as the result of electromagnetic waves. The sun warms the earth by emitting radiant energy.

An example of all three methods of heat transfer occurs in a thermos bottle or Dewar flask. The bottle is constructed of double walls of Pyrex glass that have a space in between. Air is evacuated from the space between the walls and the inner wall is silvered. The lack of air between the walls lessens heat loss by convection and conduction. The heat inside is reflected by the silver, cutting down heat transfer by radiation. Hot liquids remain hotter and cold liquids remain colder for longer periods of time.

The relationship between heat, forms of energy, and work (mechanical, electrical, etc.) are the **Laws of Thermodynamics.** These laws deal strictly with systems in thermal equilibrium and not those within the process of rapid change or in a state of transition. Systems that are nearly always in a state of equilibrium are called **reversible systems.**

The first law of thermodynamics is a restatement of conservation of energy. The change in heat energy supplied to a system (Q) is equal to the sum of the change in the internal energy (U) and the change in the work done by the system against internal forces.

$$\Delta Q = \Delta U + \Delta W$$

The second law of thermodynamics is stated in two parts:

1. No machine is 100 percent efficient. It is impossible to construct a machine that only absorbs heat from a heat source and performs an equal amount of work because some heat will always be lost to the environment.

2. Heat cannot spontaneously pass from a colder to a hotter object. An ice cube sitting on a hot sidewalk will melt into a little puddle, but it will never spontaneously cool and form the same ice cube. Certain events have a preferred direction called the **arrow of time.**

Entropy is the measure of how much energy or heat is available for work. Work occurs only when heat is transferred from hot to cooler objects. Once this is done, no more work can be extracted. The energy is still being conserved, but it is not available for work as long as the objects are the same temperature. Theory has it that, eventually, all things in the universe will reach the same temperature. If this happens, energy will no longer be usable.

Skill 19.3   Interactions of energy and matter

The law of conservation of energy states that energy is neither created nor destroyed. Thus, energy changes form when energy transactions occur in nature. Because the total energy in the universe is constant, energy continually transitions between forms. For example, an engine burns gasoline, converting the chemical energy of the gasoline into mechanical energy; a plant converts radiant energy of the sun into chemical energy found in glucose; and a battery converts chemical energy into electrical energy.

Chemical reactions are the interactions of substances that result in chemical changes and changes in energy. Chemical reactions involve changes in electron motion as well as the breaking and forming of chemical bonds. **Reactants** are the original substances that interact to form distinct products. **Endothermic** chemical reactions consume energy while **exothermic** chemical reactions release energy with product formation. Chemical reactions occur continually in nature and are also induced by man for many purposes.

Nuclear reactions, or **atomic reactions**, are reactions that change the composition, energy, or structure of atomic nuclei. Nuclear reactions change the number of protons and neutrons in the nucleus. The two main types of nuclear reactions are **fission** (splitting of nuclei) and **fusion** (joining of nuclei). Fusion reactions are exothermic, releasing heat energy. Fission reactions are endothermic, absorbing heat energy. Fission of large nuclei (e.g., uranium) releases energy because the products of fission undergo further fusion reactions. Fission and fusion reactions can occur naturally, but are most recognized as manmade events. Particle acceleration and bombardment with neutrons are two methods of inducing nuclear reactions.

The law of conservation can also be applied to physical and biological processes. For example, when a rock is weathered, it does not just lose pieces. Instead it is broken down into its composite minerals, many of which enter the soil. Biology takes advantage of decomposers to recycle decaying material. Since energy is neither created nor destroyed, we know it must change form. An animal may die, but its body will be consumed by other animals or decay into the ecosystem. Either way, it enters another form and the matter still exists—it was not destroyed.

Dynamics is the study of the relationship between motion and the forces affecting motion. **Force** causes motion.
Surfaces that touch each other have a certain resistance to motion. This resistance is **friction.**

1. The materials that make up the surfaces will determine the magnitude of the frictional force.
2. The frictional force is independent of the area of contact between the two surfaces.
3. The direction of the frictional force is opposite to the direction of motion.
4. The frictional force is proportional to the normal force between the two surfaces in contact.

Static friction describes the force of friction of two surfaces that are in contact but do not have any motion relative to each other, such as a block sitting on an inclined plane. **Kinetic friction** describes the force of friction of two surfaces in contact with each other when there is relative motion between the surfaces. When an object moves in a circular path, a force must be directed toward the center of the circle in order to keep the motion going. This constraining force is called **centripetal force**. Gravity is the centripetal force that keeps a satellite circling the earth.

Electrical force is the influential power that results from electricity as an attractive or repulsive interaction between two charged objects. The electric force is determined using Coulomb's law. As shown below, the appropriate unit on charge is the Coulomb (C) and the appropriate unit on distance is meters (m). Use of these units will result in a force expressed in units of Newtons. The demand for these units emerges from the units on Coulomb's constant.

$$F_{elect} = k \cdot Q_1 \cdot Q_2 / d^2$$

There is something of a mystery as to how objects affect each other when they are not in mechanical contact. Newton wrestled with the concept of "action-at-a-distance" (as Electrical Force is now classified) and eventually concluded that it was necessary for there to be some form of ether, or intermediate medium, which made it possible for one object to transfer force to another. We now know that no ether exists. It is possible for objects to exert forces on one another without any medium to transfer the force. From our fluid notion of electrical forces, however, we still associate forces as being due to the exchange of something between the two objects. The electrical field force acts between two charges, in the same way that the gravitational field force acts between two masses.

Magnetic Force occurs when magnetized items interact with other items in very specific ways. If a magnet is brought close enough to a ferromagnetic material (that is not magnetized itself) the magnet will strongly attract the ferromagnetic material regardless of orientation. Both the north and south pole of the magnet will attract the other item with equal strength. In opposition, diamagnetic materials weakly repel a magnetic field. This occurs regardless of the north/south orientation of the field. Paramagnetic materials are weakly attracted to a magnetic field. This occurs regardless of the north/south orientation of the field. Calculating the attractive or repulsive magnetic force between two magnets is, in the general case, an extremely complex operation, as it depends on the shape, magnetization, orientation, and separation of the magnets.

In the **Nuclear Force**, the protons in the nucleus of an atom are positively charged. If protons interact, they are usually pushed apart by the electromagnetic force. However, when two or more nuclei come VERY close together, the nuclear force comes into play. The nuclear force is a hundred times stronger than the electromagnetic force, so the nuclear force may be able to "glue" the nuclei together to allow fusion to happen. The nuclear force is also known as the **strong force**. The nuclear force keeps together the most basic of elementary particles, the **quarks**. Quarks combine together to form the protons and neutrons in the atomic nucleus.

The **force of gravity** is the force at which the earth, moon, or other massively large object attracts another object towards itself. By definition, this is the weight of the object. All objects upon earth experience a force of gravity that is directed "downward" towards the center of the earth. The force of gravity on earth is always equal to the weight of the object as found by the equation:

$$\text{Fgrav} = m * g$$

where g = 9.8 m/s^2 (on Earth)
and m = mass (in kg)

Newton's Laws of Motion:

Newton's first law of motion is also called the law of inertia. It states that an object at rest will remain at rest and an object in motion will remain in motion at a constant velocity unless acted upon by an external force.

Newton's second law of motion states that if a net force acts on an object, it will cause the acceleration of the object. The relationship between force and motion is Force equals mass times acceleration.   (F = ma)

Newton's third law states that for every action there is an equal and opposite reaction. Therefore, if an object exerts a force on another object, that second object exerts an equal and opposite force on the first.

COMPETENCY 20.0 SCIENCE AS INQUIRY

Skill 20.1 Appropriate questioning techniques

Science may be defined as a body of knowledge that is systematically derived from study, observations, and experimentation. Its goal is to identify and establish principles and theories that may be applied to solve problems. Pseudoscience, on the other hand, is a belief that is not warranted. There is no scientific methodology or application. Some of the more classic examples of pseudoscience include witchcraft, alien encounters, or any topics that are explained by hearsay.

Scientific inquiry starts with observation. Observation is a very important skill by itself, as it leads to experimentation and communicating the experimental findings to the public. After observing, a question is formed, which starts with "why" or "how." To answer these questions, experimentation is necessary. Between observation and experimentation there are three more important steps. These are gathering information (or researching about the problem), forming a hypothesis, and designing the experiment.

Designing an experiment is very important since it involves identifying control, constants, independent variables, and dependent variables. A **control** is something we compare our results with at the end of the experiment. It is like a reference. **Constants** are the factors that are kept the same in an experiment to get reliable results. **Independent variables** are factors we change in an experiment. **Dependent variables** are the changes that arise from the experiment. It is very important to bear in mind that there should be more constants than variables to obtain reproducible results in an experiment.

After the experiment is done, it is repeated and results are graphically presented. The results are then analyzed and conclusions drawn. After the conclusion is drawn, the final step is communication. It is the responsibility of scientists to share the knowledge they obtain through their research. In this age, much emphasis is put on the way and the method of communication. The conclusions must be communicated by clearly describing the information using accurate data and visual presentations like graphs (bar/line/pie), tables/charts, diagrams, artwork, and other appropriate media. Modern technology should be used whenever it is necessary. The method of communication must be suitable to the audience.

Written communication is as important as oral communication. This is essential for submitting research papers to scientific journals, newspapers, and other magazines.

Skill 20.2 Planning and conducting simple investigations

The scientific method is the basic process behind science. It involves several steps, beginning with hypothesis formulation and working through to the conclusion.

Posing a question: Although many discoveries happen by chance, the standard thought process of a scientist begins with forming a question to research. The more limited the question, the easier it is to set up an experiment to answer it.

Form a hypothesis: Once the question is formulated, researchers should take an educated guess about the answer to the problem or question. This "best guess" is the hypothesis.

Do the test: To make a test fair, data from an experiment must have a variable or any condition that can be changed, such as temperature or mass. A good test will try to manipulate as few variables as possible to see which variable is responsible for the result. This requires a second example of a control. A control is an extra setup in which all the conditions are the same except for the variable being tested.

Observe and record the data: Reporting the data should include the specifics of how measurements were calculated. For example, a graduated cylinder needs to be read with proper procedures. As beginning students, technique must be part of the instructional process so as to give validity to the data.

Drawing a conclusion: After recording data, compare your data with that of other groups. A conclusion is the judgment derived from the data results.

Graphing data: Graphing utilizes numbers to demonstrate patterns. The patterns offer a visual representation, making it easier to draw conclusions.

Apply knowledge of designing and performing investigations: Normally, knowledge is integrated in the form of a lab report. A report has many sections. It should include a specific **title** that tells exactly what is being studied. The **abstract** is a summary of the report written at the beginning of the paper. The **purpose** should always be defined to state the problem. The purpose should include the **hypothesis** (educated guess) of what is expected from the outcome of the experiment. The entire experiment should relate to this problem.

It is important to describe exactly what was done to prove or disprove a hypothesis. A **control** is necessary to prove that the results occurred from the changed conditions and would not have happened normally. Only one variable should be manipulated at a time. **Observations** and **results** of the experiment, including all results from data, should be recorded. Drawings, graphs, and illustrations should be included to support information. Observations are objective, whereas analysis and interpretation are subjective. A **conclusion** should explain why the results of the experiment either proved or disproved the hypothesis.

A **scientific theory** is an explanation of a set of related observations based on a proven hypothesis. A **scientific law** usually lasts longer than a scientific theory and has more experimental data to support it.

Skill 20.3 Gathering data with the tools of science to organize and using data to draw reasonable conclusions

Whenever scientists begin an experiment or project, they must decide what pieces of data they are going to collect. This data could be qualitative or quantitative. Scientists use a variety of methods to gather and analyze this data. Some possibilities include storing the data in a table or analyzing the data using a graph. Scientists also make notes of their observations, what they see, hear, smell, etc., throughout the experiment. Scientists are then able to use the data and observations to make inferences and draw conclusions about a question or problem.

Several steps should be followed in the interpretation and evaluation of data.

First the scientist should **apply critical analysis and thinking strategies** asking questions about the accuracy of the data and the procedures of the experiment and procurement of the data.

Second is to **determine the important of information and its relevance to the essential question**. Any experiment may produce a plethora of data, not all of which is necessary to consider when analyzing the hypothesis. The useful information must then be **separated into component parts**.

At this point, the scientist may then **make inferences, identify trends, and interpret data**. The final step is to determine the most appropriate method of communicating these inferences and conclusions to the intended audience.

COMPETENCY 21.0 SCIENCE IN PERSONAL AND SOCIAL PERSPECTIVES

Skill 21.1 Personal health

The human population has been growing exponentially for centuries. People are living longer and healthier lives than ever before. Better health care and nutrition practices have helped in the survival of the population.

Human activity affects parts of the nutrient cycles by removing nutrients from one part of the biosphere and adding them to another. This results in nutrient depletion in one area and nutrient excess in another. This affects water systems, crops, wildlife, and humans.

Science and technology are often referred to as a "double-edged sword." Although advances in medicine have greatly improved the quality and length of life, certain moral and ethical controversies have arisen. Unforeseen environmental problems may result from technological advances. Advances in science have led to an improved economy through biotechnology as applied to agriculture, yet it has put our health care system at risk and has caused the cost of medical care to skyrocket. Society depends on science, yet is necessary that the public be scientifically literate and informed in order that potentially unethical procedures do not occur. Especially vulnerable are the areas of genetic research and fertility. It is important for science teachers to stay abreast of current research and to involve students in critical thinking and ethics whenever possible.

Skill 20.2 Science, technology, and society

Society as a whole influences biological research. For example, the pressure from the majority of society has led to bans and restrictions on human cloning research. Human cloning has been restricted in the United States and many other countries. The U.S. legislature has banned the use of federal funds for the development of human cloning techniques. Some individual states have banned human cloning regardless of where the funds originate.

The demand for genetically modified crops by society and industry has steadily increased over the years. Genetic engineering in the agricultural field has led to improved crops for human use and consumption. Crops are genetically modified for increased growth and insect resistance because of the demand for larger and greater quantities of produce.

With advances in biotechnology come those in society who oppose it. Ethical questions come into play when discussing animal and human research. Does it need to be done? What are the effects on humans and animals? There are no right or wrong answers to these questions. There are governmental agencies in place to regulate the use of humans and animals for research.

COMPETENCY 22.0   HISTORY AND THE NATURE OF SCIENCE

Skill 22.1   Science as a human endeavor

o   See Skill 22.3

Skill 22.2   Historical perspectives in science

The history of biology follows man's understanding of the living world from the earliest recorded history to modern times. Though the concept of biology as a field of science arose only in the nineteenth century, its origins could be traced back to the ancient Greeks (Galen and Aristotle). During the Renaissance and Age of Discovery, renewed interest in the rapidly increasing number of known organisms generated much interest in biology.

Andreas Vesalius (1514-1564) was a Belgian anatomist and physician whose dissections of the human body and written findings helped to correct the misconceptions of science. The books Vesalius wrote on anatomy were the most accurate and comprehensive anatomical texts of time.

Anton van Leeuwenhoek is known as the father of microscopy. In the 1650s, Leeuwenhoek began making tiny lenses that gave magnifications up to 300x. He was the first to see and describe bacteria, yeast plants, and the microscopic life found in water. Over the years, light microscopes have advanced to produce greater clarity and magnification. The scanning electron microscope (SEM) was developed in the 1950s. Instead of light, a beam of electrons passes through the specimen. Scanning electron microscopes have a resolution about one thousand times greater than light microscopes. The disadvantage of the SEM is that the chemical and physical methods used to prepare the sample result in the death of the specimen.

Carl Von Linnaeus (1707-1778), a Swedish botanist, physician, and zoologist, is well-known for his contributions in ecology and taxonomy. Linnaeus is famous for his binomial system of nomenclature in which each living organism has two names: a genus and a species name. He is considered the father of modern ecology and taxonomy.

In the late 1800s, Louis Pasteur discovered the role of microorganisms in the cause of disease; he also discovered pasteurization and the rabies vaccine. Robert Koch took his observations one step further by postulating that specific diseases were caused by specific pathogens. **Koch's postulates** are still used as guidelines in the field of microbiology. They state that the same pathogen must be found in every diseased person, the pathogen must be isolated and grown in culture, the disease must be induced in experimental animals from the culture, and the same pathogen must be isolated from the experimental animal.

In the eighteenth century, many fields of science like botany, zoology, and geology began to evolve as scientific disciplines in the modern sense.

In the twentieth century, the rediscovery of Mendel's work led to the rapid development of genetics by Thomas Hunt Morgan and his students.

DNA structure was another key event in biological study. In the 1950s, James Watson and Francis Crick discovered the structure of a DNA molecule as that of a double helix. This structure made it possible to explain DNA's ability to replicate and to control the synthesis of proteins.

Following the cracking of the genetic code, biology has largely split between organismal biology (consisting of ecology, ethology, systematics, paleontology, evolutionary biology, developmental biology, and other disciplines that deal with whole organisms or group of organisms) and the disciplines related to molecular biology (which include cell biology, biophysics, biochemistry, neuroscience, and immunology).

The use of animals in biological research has expedited many scientific discoveries. Animal research has allowed scientists to learn more about animal biological systems, including the circulatory and reproductive systems. One significant use of animals is for the testing of drugs, vaccines, and other products (such as perfumes and shampoos) before use or consumption by humans. There are both significant pros and cons of animal research. The debate about the ethical treatment of animals has been ongoing since the introduction of animals to research. Many people believe the use of animals in research is cruel and unnecessary. Animal use is federally and locally regulated. The purpose of the Institutional Animal Care and Use Committee (IACUC) is to oversee and evaluate all aspects of an institution's animal care and use program.

Skill 22.3   Science as a process

The combination of science, mathematics, and technology forms the scientific endeavor and makes science a success. It is impossible to study science on its own without the support of other disciplines like mathematics, technology, geology, physics, and other disciplines.

Science is tentative. By definition it is searching for information by making educated guesses. It must be replicable. Another scientist must be able to achieve the same results under the same conditions at a later time. The term **empirical** means a phenomenon must be assessed through tests and observations. Science changes over time. Science is limited by the available technology. An example of this would be the relationship of the discovery of the cell and the invention of the microscope. As our technology improves, more hypotheses will become theories and possibly laws.

Science is also limited by the data that is able to be collected. Data may be interpreted differently on different occasions. Science limitations cause explanations to be changeable as new technologies emerge. New technologies gather previously unavailable data and enable us to build upon current theories with new information.

The nature of science mainly consists of three important things:

1. **The scientific world view**
   It is possible to understand this highly organized world and its complexities with the help of the latest technology. Scientific ideas are subject to change. After repeated experiments, a theory is established, but this theory can be changed or supported in future. Only laws that occur naturally do not change. Scientific knowledge may not be discarded but can be modified (e.g., Albert Einstein didn't discard Newtonian principles but modified them in his theory of relativity). Also, science can't answer all of our questions. We can't find answers to questions related to our beliefs, moral values, and our norms.

2. **Scientific inquiry**
   Scientific inquiry starts with a simple question. This simple question leads to information gathering and an educated guess otherwise known as hypothesis. To prove the hypothesis, an experiment has to be conducted, which yields data and the conclusion. All experiments must be repeated at least twice to get reliable results. Thus, scientific inquiry leads to new knowledge or the verification of established theories. Science requires proof or evidence. Science is dependent on accuracy, not bias or prejudice. In science, there is no place for preconceived ideas or premeditated results. By using their senses and modern technology, scientists will be able to get reliable information. Science is a combination of logic and imagination. A scientist needs to think and imagine and be able to reason.

3. **Scientific enterprise**
   Science is a complex activity involving various people and places. A scientist may work alone or in a laboratory, in a classroom or pretty much anywhere. Most of the time, it is a group activity requiring the social skills of cooperation, communication of results or findings, consultations, and discussions. Science demands a high degree of communication to the governments, funding authorities, and to the public.

Science explains, reasons, and predicts. These three are interwoven and are inseparable. While reasoning is absolutely important for science, there should be no bias or prejudice. Science is not authoritarian because it has been shown that scientific authority can be wrong. No one can determine or make decisions for others on any issue.

Science is a process of checks and balances. It is expected that scientific findings will be challenged, and in many cases retested. Oftentimes, one experiment will be the beginning point for another. While bias does exist, the use of controlled experiments and an awareness on the part of the scientist can go far in ensuring a sound experiment. Even if the science is well done, it may still be questioned. It is through this continual search that hypotheses are made into theories, and sometimes become laws. It is also through this search that new information is discovered.

Scientific investigation is a very important part of science. Science investigation consists of a number of steps designed to solve a problem. Scientists start with a problem and solve it in an orderly fashion called the scientific method. This is made up of a series of steps, which, when applied properly, solve scientific problems. The key to the success of this method lies in minimizing human prejudice. As human beings, we tend to have biases.

The first step in a science investigation is identifying the problem. As we observe, we notice interesting things that arouse our curiosity. We ask ourselves the basic questions of enquiry: how, why, what, when, which and where. The two most important questions are how and why. We can classify observations into two types. The first is qualitative, which we describe in words. No mention of numbers or quantities is made–the water is very hot, or the solution is sour. The second type is quantitative, where numbers and quantities are used. This more precise–for mass, the format is 125 kg., for distance, it is 500 km.

The second step is gathering information. As much information as possible is collected from various sources such as the Internet, books, journals, knowledgeable people, and newspapers. This lays a solid foundation for formulating a hypothesis.

The third step is hypothesizing. This is making statement about the problem with the knowledge acquired and using the two important words: "if" and "when."

The next step is designing an experiment. Before this is done, scientists need to identify the control, the constants, the independent variables and the dependent variable.

For beginners, the simplest investigation is one that manipulates only one variable at a time. In this way, the experiment doesn't get too complicated and is easier to handle.

In order to draw conclusions, scientists need to study the data on hand. The data tell us whether or not the hypothesis is correct. If the hypothesis is not correct, another hypothesis has to be formulated and another experiment has to be done. If the hypothesis is tested and the results are repeated in further experimentation, a theory may be formulated. A **theory** is a hypothesis that is tested repeatedly by different scientists and has yielded the same results. A theory has more validity because it could be used to predict future events.

Scientific inquiries should end in formulating an explanation or model. Models should be physical, conceptual, and mathematical. While drawing conclusions, a lot of discussions and arguments may be generated. There may be several possible explanations for any given sets of results, and not all of them are reasonable. Carefully evaluating and analyzing the data will create a reasonable conclusion. The conclusion needs to be supported by scientific criteria.

Skill 22.4   Science as a career

Society is not the same as it used to be even twenty-five years ago. The use of technology has changed our patterns of lifestyle, our behavior, our ethical and moral thinking, our economy, and our career opportunities.

Science is an interesting, innovative, and thoroughly enjoyable subject. Science careers are challenging and stimulating, and the possibilities for scientific careers are endless.

Why do people choose careers in science? This is a very important question. The reasons are manifold and may include:

- A passion for science
- A desire to experiment and gain knowledge
- A desire to contribute to society's betterment
- An inquiring mind
- Wanting to work in a team

There are a number of opportunities in science. For the sake of ease and convenience, they are grouped under various categories:

1. Biological science
2. Physical science
3. Earth science
4. Space science
5. Forensic science
6. Medical science
7. Agricultural science

Let's take each category and examine the opportunities available.

1. Biological sciences: The study of living organisms and their life cycles, medicinal properties, and the like.

* Botanist
* Microbiologist

2. Physical Science: The study of matter and energy.

* Analytical Chemist
* Biochemist
* Chemist
* Physicist

3. Earth Science: Studying the earth, its changes over the years, and natural disasters such as earthquakes and hurricanes.

* Geologist
* Meteorologist
* Oceanographer
* Seismologist
* Volcanologist

4. Space science: Studying space, the universe, and planets.

* Astrophysicist
* Space Scientist

5. Forensic science: Solving crimes using various techniques.

* Forensic Pathologist

6. Medical science: Science with practical applications to the care and cure of diseases.

* Biomedical science
* Clinical Scientist

7. Agricultural science: Using science to grow and improve upon crops.

* Agriculturist
* Agricultural Service Industry
* Agronomist
* Veterinary science

There are so many career opportunities available in the field of science, but it is up to them to choose the right career. Students need to be made aware of the connection between today's learning and their future life. It is especially important to impress upon them how science is everywhere and how it has truly useful applications. When this is made clear to them, they may more seriously consider science as a career.

COMPETENCY 23.0   UNIFYING PROCESSES

Skill 23.1   Systems, order, and organization

The following are the concepts and processes generally recognized as common to all scientific disciplines:

1. Systems, order, and organization

Because the natural world is so complex, the study of science involves the **organization** of items into smaller groups based on interaction or interdependence. These groups are called **systems**. Examples of organization are the periodic table of elements and the five-kingdom classification scheme for living organisms. Examples of systems are the solar system, the cardiovascular system, Newton's laws of force and motion, and the laws of conservation.

Order refers to the behavior and measurability of organisms and events in nature. The arrangement of planets in the solar system and the life cycle of bacterial cells are examples of order.

2. Evidence, models, and explanation

Scientists use **evidence** and **models** to form **explanations** of natural events. Models are miniaturized representations of a larger event or system. Evidence is anything that furnishes proof.

3. Constancy, change, and measurement

Constancy and **change** describe the observable properties of natural organisms and events. Scientists use different systems of **measurement** to observe change and constancy. For example, the freezing and melting points of given substances and the speed of sound are the same under constant conditions. Growth, decay, and erosion are all examples of natural changes.

4. Evolution and equilibrium

Evolution is the process of change over a long period of time. While biological evolution is the most common example, one can also classify technological advancement, changes in the universe, and changes in the environment as evolution.

Equilibrium is the state of balance between opposing forces of change. Homeostasis and ecological balance are examples of equilibrium.

5. Form and function

Form and **function** are properties of organisms and systems that are closely related. The function of an object usually dictates its form and the form of an object usually facilitates its function. For example, the form of the heart (e.g., muscle and valves) allows it to perform its function of circulating blood through the body.

Skill 23.2   Structure and function models

The function of different systems in organisms from bacteria to humans dictates system structure. The basic principle that "form follows function" applies to all organismal systems. We will discuss a few examples to illustrate this principle. Keep in mind that we can relate the structure and function of all organismal systems.

- Mitochondria, subcellular organelles present in eukaryotic cells, provide energy for cell functions. Much of the energy-generating activity takes place in the mitochondrial membrane. To maximize this activity, the mitochondrial membrane has many folds to pack a relatively large amount of membrane into a small space.

- Bacterial cells maintain a high surface area to volume ratio to maximize contact with the environment and to allow for the exchange of nutrients and waste products. Bacterial cells achieve this high ratio by maintaining a small internal volume by cell division.

- The cardiovascular system of animals has many specialized structures that help to achieve the function of delivering blood to all parts of the body. The heart has four chambers for the delivery and reception of blood. The blood vessels vary in size to accommodate the necessary volume of blood. For example, vessels near the heart are large to accommodate large amounts of blood, and vessels in the extremities are very small to limit the amount of blood delivered.

- The structure of the skeletal systems of different animals varies based on the animal's method of movement. For example, the honeycombed structure of bird bones provides a lightweight skeleton of great strength to accommodate flight. The bones of the human skeletal system are dense, strong, and aligned in such a way as to allow walking on two legs in an upright position.

Skill 23.3 Changes over time

Math, science, and technology have common themes in how they are applied and understood. All three use models, diagrams, and graphs to simplify a concept for analysis and interpretation. Patterns observed in these systems lead to predictions based on these observations. Another common theme among these three systems is equilibrium. **Equilibrium** is a state in which forces are balanced, resulting in stability. **Static equilibrium** is stability due to a lack of changes and **dynamic equilibrium** is stability due to a balance between opposite forces.

The fundamental relationship between the natural and social sciences is the use of the scientific method and the rigorous standards of proof that both disciplines require. This emphasis on organization and evidence separates the sciences from the arts and humanities. Natural science, particularly biology, is closely related to social science, the study of human behavior. Biological and environmental factors often dictate human behavior; an accurate assessment of behavior requires a sound understanding of biological factors.

Science changes over time and is limited by the available technology. An example of this is the relationship of the discovery of the cell and the invention of the microscope. As our technology improves, more hypotheses will become theories and possibly laws.

However, science is also limited by the data that is able to be collected. Data may be interpreted differently on different occasions. Science limitations cause explanations to be changeable as new technologies emerge. New technologies gather previously unavailable data and enable us to build upon current theories with new information.

Skill 23.4 Cycles

Members of the five different kingdoms of the classification system of living organisms often differ in their basic life functions. Here we compare and analyze how members of the five kingdoms obtain nutrients, excrete waste, and reproduce.

Bacteria are prokaryotic, single-celled organisms that lack cell nuclei. The different types of bacteria obtain nutrients in a variety of ways. Most bacteria absorb nutrients from the environment through small channels in their cell walls and membranes (chemotrophs) while some perform photosynthesis (phototrophs). Chemoorganotrophs use organic compounds as energy sources while chemolithotrophs can use inorganic chemicals. Depending on the type of metabolism and energy source, bacteria release a variety of waste products (e.g., alcohols, acids, carbon dioxide) to the environment through diffusion.

All bacteria reproduce through binary fission (asexual reproduction), producing two identical cells. Bacteria reproduce very rapidly, dividing or doubling every twenty minutes in optimal conditions. Asexual reproduction does not allow for genetic variation, but bacteria achieve genetic variety by absorbing DNA from ruptured cells and conjugating or swapping chromosomal or plasmid DNA with other cells.

Animals are multicellular, eukaryotic organisms. All animals obtain nutrients by eating food (ingestion). Different types of animals derive nutrients from eating plants, other animals, or both. Animal cells perform digestion that converts food molecules, mainly carbohydrates and fats, into energy. The excretory systems of animals, like animals themselves, vary in complexity. Simple invertebrates eliminate waste through a single tube, while complex vertebrates have a specialized system of organs that process and excrete waste.

Most animals, unlike bacteria, exist in two distinct sexes. Members of the female sex give birth or lay eggs. Some less developed animals can reproduce asexually. For example, flatworms can divide in two, and some unfertilized insect eggs can develop into viable organisms. Most animals reproduce sexually through various mechanisms. For example, many aquatic animals reproduce by external fertilization of eggs, while mammals reproduce by internal fertilization. More developed animals possess specialized reproductive systems and cycles that facilitate reproduction and promote genetic variation.

Plants, like animals, are multi-cellular, eukaryotic organisms. Plants obtain nutrients from the soil through their root systems and convert sunlight into energy through photosynthesis. Many plants store waste products in vacuoles or organs (e.g., leaves, bark) that are discarded. Some plants also excrete waste through their roots.

More than half of the plant species reproduce by producing seeds from which new plants grow. Depending on the type of plant, flowers or cones produce seeds. Other plants reproduce by spores, tubers, bulbs, buds, and grafts. The flowers of flowering plants contain their reproductive organs. Pollination is the joining of male and female gametes that is often facilitated by movement of wind or animals.

Fungi are eukaryotic, mostly multi-cellular organisms. All fungi are heterotrophs, obtaining nutrients from other organisms. More specifically, most fungi obtain nutrients by digesting and absorbing nutrients from dead organisms. Fungi secrete enzymes outside of their body to digest organic material and then absorb the nutrients through their cell walls.

Most fungi can reproduce asexually and sexually. Different types of fungi reproduce asexually by mitosis, budding, sporification, or fragmentation. Sexual reproduction of fungi is different from sexual reproduction of animals. The two mating types of fungi are plus and minus, not male and female. The fusion of hyphae, the specialized reproductive structure in fungi, between plus and minus types produces and scatters diverse spores.

Protists are eukaryotic, single-celled organisms. Most protists are heterotrophic, obtaining nutrients by ingesting small molecules and cells and digesting them in vacuoles. All protists reproduce asexually by either binary or multiple fission. Like bacteria, protists achieve genetic variation by exchange of DNA through conjugation.

Skill 23.5   Equilibrium

Equilibrium is the state of balance between opposing forces of change. Homeostasis and ecological balance are examples of equilibrium.

- **See also** Skill 19.2 and 23.3

Pre-test

Subarea I. Child Development and Learning

1. What developmental patterns should a professional teacher assess to meet the needs of each student?

    A. Academic, regional, and family background

    B. Social, physical, and academic

    C. Academic, physical, and family background

    D. Physical, family, and ethnic background

2. The various domains of development are best described as:

    A. Integrated

    B. Independent

    C. Simultaneous

    D. Parallel

3. Which of the following best describes how different areas of development impact each other?

    A. Development in other areas cannot occur until cognitive development is complete.

    B. Areas of development are inter-related and impact each other.

    C. Development in each area is independent of development in other areas.

    D. Development in one area leads to a decline in other areas.

4. A student has developed and improved in vocabulary. However, the student is not confident enough to use the improved vocabulary, and the teacher is not aware of the improvement. What is this an example of?

    A. Latent development

    B. Dormant development

    C. Random development

    D. Delayed development

5. Which of the following has been shown to have the greatest impact on a student's academic performance?

   A. The teacher's expectations

   B. Strict discipline

   C. The student's social skills

   D. Measurable objectives

6. According to Piaget, when does the development of symbolic functioning and language first take place?

   A. Concrete operations stage

   B. Formal operations stage

   C. Sensory-motor stage

   D. Pre-operational stage

7. Playing team sports at young ages should be done for the following purpose:

   A. To develop the child's motor skills

   B. To prepare children for competition in high school

   C. To develop the child's interests

   D. Both A and C

8. The stages of play development from infancy stages to early childhood includes a move from:

   A. Cooperative to solitary

   B. Solitary to cooperative

   C. Competitive to collaborative

   D. Collaborative to competitive

9. Which of the following is NOT an economic factor that may influence the health of a child?

   A. Pollution

   B. Malnutrition

   C. Neglect

   D. Poor medical care

10. Which of the following is the main source of energy in the diet?

   A. Vitamins

   B. Minerals

   C. Water

   D. Carbohydrates

11. **Which of the following would be likely to influence a student's learning and academic progress?**

    A. Relocation

    B. Emotional abuse

    C. Bullying

    D. All of the above

12. **Which of the following best explains why emotional upset and emotional abuse can reduce a child's classroom performance?**

    A. They reduce the energy that students put towards schoolwork.

    B. They lead to a reduction in cognitive ability.

    C. They contribute to learning disorders such as dyslexia.

    D. They result in the development of behavioral problems.

13. **A teacher has a class with several students from low income families in it. What would it be most important for a teacher to consider when planning homework assignments to ensure that all students have equal opportunity for academic success?**

    A. Access to technology

    B. Ethnicity

    C. Language difficulties

    D. Gender

14. **Family members with high levels of education often have high expectations for student success. This shows how students are influenced by their family's:**

    A. Attitude

    B. Resources

    C. Income

    D. Culture

15. **Why is it most important for teachers to ensure that students from different economic backgrounds have access to the resources they need to acquire the academic skills being taught?**

   A. All students must work together on set tasks.

   B. All students must achieve the same results in performance tasks.

   C. All students must have equal opportunity for academic success.

   D. All students must be fully included in classroom activities.

16. **A teacher attempting to create a differentiated classroom should focus on incorporating activities that:**

   A. Favor academically advanced students

   B. Challenge special education students to achieve more

   C. Are suitable for whichever group of students is the majority

   D. Meet the needs of all the students in the class

17. **When developing lessons, it is important that teachers provide equity in pedagogy so that:**

   A. Unfair labeling of students will not occur

   B. Student experiences will be positive

   C. Students will achieve academic success

   D. All of the above

18. **Which of the following is NOT a communication issue related to diversity within the classroom?**

   A. Learning disorders

   B. Sensitive terminology

   C. Body language

   D. Discussing differing viewpoints and opinions

19. **One common factor for students with all types of disabilities is that they are also likely to demonstrate difficulty with:**

   A. Social skills

   B. Cognitive skills

   C. Problem-solving skills

   D. Decision-making skills

20. A student does not respond to any signs of affection and responds to other children by repeating back what they have said. What condition is the student most likely to have?

    A.   Mental retardation

    B.   Autism

    C.   Giftedness

    D.   Hyperactivity

21. Which of the following conditions is more common for girls than boys?

    A.   Attention deficit disorder

    B.   Aggression

    C.   Phobias

    D.   Autism

22. In successful inclusion of students with disabilities:

    A.   A variety of instructional arrangements are available

    B.   School personnel shift the responsibility for learning outcomes to the student

    C.   The physical facilities are used as they are

    D.   Regular classroom teachers have sole responsibility for evaluating student progress

23. Mr. Gorman has taught a concept to his class. All of the students have grasped the concept except for Sam. Mr. Gorman should:

    A.   Reteach the concept to the whole class in exactly the same way

    B.   Reteach the concept to Sam in exactly the same way

    C.   Reteach the concept to Sam in a different way

    D.   Reteach the concept to the whole class in a different way

24. Mrs. Gomez has a fully integrated early childhood curriculum. This is beneficial to students because it:

   A. Is easier to plan for and maintain

   B. Allows students to apply their unique skills

   C. Helps the students see the relationships between subjects and concepts

   D. Provides opportunities for social interaction

Subarea II. Communication, Language and Literacy Development

25. The relationship between oral language and reading skills is best described as:

   A. Reciprocal

   B. Inverse

   C. Opposite

   D. There is no relationship.

26. A teacher is showing students how to construct grammatically correct sentences. What is the teacher focusing on?

   A. Morphology

   B. Syntax

   C. Semantics

   D. Pragmatics

27. A teacher writes the following words on the board: cot, cotton, and cottage. What is the teacher most likely teaching the students about?

   A. Morphology

   B. Syntax

   C. Semantics

   D. Pragmatics

28. While standing in line at the grocery store, three-year-old Megan says to her mother in a regular tone of voice, "Mom, why is that woman so fat?" What does this indicate a lack of understanding of?

    A. Syntax

    B. Semantics

    C. Morphology

    D. Pragmatics

29. Which of the following is the first component of the constructivist model?

    A. There are at least seven different types of learning.

    B. Learning depends on the social environment.

    C. Learner creates knowledge

    D. Learning progresses through set stages.

30. Students are about to read a text that contains words that will need to be understood for the students to understand the text. When should the vocabulary be introduced to students?

    A. Before reading

    B. During reading

    C. After reading

    D. It should not be introduced.

31. Which of the following are examples of temporal words?

    A. Beside and behind

    B. Hotter and colder

    C. In and on

    D. Before and after

32. Which principle of Stephen Krashen's research suggests that the learning of grammatical structures is predictable?

    A. The affective filter hypothesis

    B. The input hypothesis

    C. The natural order hypothesis

    D. The monitor hypothesis

33. **Above what age does learning a language become increasingly difficult?**

    A. 3

    B. 5

    C. 7

    D. 10

34. **Ms. Chomski is presenting a new story to her class of first graders. In the story, a family visits their grandparents where they all gather around a record player and listen to music. Many students do not understand what a record player is, especially some children for whom English is not their first language. Which of the following would Ms. Chomski be best to do?**

    A. Discuss what a record player is with her students

    B. Compare a record player with a CD player

    C. Have students look up record player in a dictionary

    D. Show the students a picture of a record player

35. **Jose moved to the United States last month. He speaks little to no English at this time. His teacher is teaching the class about habitats in science and has chosen to read a story about various habitats to the class. The vocabulary is difficult. What should Jose's teacher do with Jose? (Skill 5.3; Average rigor)**

    A. Provide Jose with additional opportunities to learn about habitats

    B. Read the story to Jose multiple times

    C. Show Jose pictures of habitats from his native country

    D. Excuse Jose from the assignment

36. In the early childhood classroom, it is important to limit teacher talk. What is the main problem with teacher talk?

    A. It is often one sided and limited.

    B. The vocabulary is too difficult for children.

    C. It promotes misbehavior.

    D. It only creates gains in receptive language.

37. Which of the following is a convention of print that children learn during reading activities?

    A. The meaning of words

    B. The left to right motion

    C. The purpose of print

    D. The identification of letters

38. In her kindergarten class, Mrs. Thomas has been watching the students in the drama center. She has watched the children pretend to complete a variety of magic tricks. Mrs. Thomas decides to use stories about magic to share with her class. Her decision to incorporate their interests into the reading shows that Mrs. Thomas understands that:

    A. Including student interests is important at all times

    B. Teaching by themes is crucial for young children

    C. Young children respond to literature that reflects their lives

    D. Science fiction and fantasy are the most popular genres

39. Which of the following is NOT a characteristic of a fable?

    A. Have animal characters that act like humans

    B. Considered to be true

    C. Teaches a moral

    D. Reveals human foibles

40. Alphabet books are classified as:

    A.   Concept books

    B.   Easy-to-read books

    C.   Board books

    D.   Pictures books

41. The works of Paul Bunyan, John Henry, and Pecos Bill are all exaggerated accounts of individuals with superhuman strength. What type of literature are these works?

    A.   Fables

    B.   Fairytales

    C.   Tall tales

    D.   Myths

42. Which of the following is NOT a motivation behind providing reading activities, including reading aloud, to young children?

    A.   Developing word consciousness skills

    B.   Developing functions of print skills

    C.   Developing phonics skills

    D.   Developing language skills

43. Which of the following is an appropriate way for students to respond to literature?

    A.   Art

    B.   Drama

    C.   Writing

    D.   All of the above

44. John is having difficulty reading the word reach. In isolation, he pronounces each sound as /r/ /ee/ /sh/. Which of the following is a possible instructional technique which could help solve John's reading difficulty?

    A.   Additional phonemic awareness instruction

    B.   Additional phonics instruction

    C.   Additional skill and drill practice

    D.   Additional minimal pair practice

45. **According to Marilyn Jager Adams, which skill would a student demonstrate by identifying that cat does not belong in the group of words containing dog, deer, and dress?**

    A.   Recognize the odd member in a group

    B.   Replace sounds in words

    C.   Count the sounds in a word

    D.   Count syllables in a word

46. **Which of the following is NOT true about phonological awareness?**

    A.   It may involve print.

    B.   It is a prerequisite for spelling and phonics.

    C.   Activities can be done by the children with their eyes closed.

    D.   It starts before letter recognition is taught.

47. **Which of the following explains a significant difference between phonics and phonemic awareness?**

    A.   Phonics involves print, while phonemic awareness involves language.

    B.   Phonics is harder than phonemic awareness.

    C.   Phonics involves sounds, while phonemic awareness involves letters.

    D.   Phonics is the application of sounds to print, while phonemic awareness is oral.

48. **To decode is to:**

    A.   Construct meaning

    B.   Sound out a printed sequence of letters

    C.   Use a special code to decipher a message

    D.   Revise for errors in grammar

49. **Ms. Walker's lesson objective is to teach her first graders the concept of morphology in order to improve their reading skills. Which group of words would be most appropriate for her to use in this lesson?**

    A. Far, farm, farmer

    B. Far, feather, fever

    C. Far, fear, fare

    D. Far, fare, farce

50. **Which stage of reading skill development occurs first?**

    A. Schema stage

    B. Early semantic stage

    C. Orthographic stage

    D. Simultaneous stage

51. **Which of the following is an important feature of vocabulary instruction according to the National Reading Panel?**

    A. Repetition of vocabulary items

    B. Keeping a consistent task structure at all times

    C. Teaching vocabulary in more than one language

    D. Isolation vocabulary instruction from other subjects

52. **The attitude an author takes toward his or her subject is the:**

    A. Style

    B. Tone

    C. Point of view

    D. Theme

53. George has read his second graders three formats of the story "The Three Little Pigs." One is the traditional version, one is written from the wolf's point of view, and the third is written from the first pig's point of view. As George leads a discussion on the three texts with his students, he is trying to help his students develop their ability to:

A. Compare and contrast texts

B. Understand point of view

C. Recognize metaphors

D. Rewrite fictional stories

54. What is the first step in developing writing skills?

A. Early writing

B. Experimental writing

C Role play writing

D. Conventional writing

55. Which of the following is NOT a prewriting strategy?

A. Analyzing sentences for variety

B. Keeping an idea book

C. Writing in a daily journal

D. Writing down whatever comes to mind

56. Which of the following is probably the most important step for the writer in the writing process?

A. Revision

B. Discovery

C. Conclusion

D. Organization

57. **The students in Tina's classroom are working together in pairs. Each student is reading another student's paper and asking who, what, when, where, why, and who questions. What is this activity helping the students to do?**

   A. Draft their writing

   B. Paraphrase their writing

   C. Revise their writing

   D. Outline their writing

58. **Young children learning to write commonly grip the pencil:**

   A. Too far from the point

   B. With the wrong hand

   C. With too many fingers

   D. Too tightly

59. **Which of the following approaches to student writing assignments is most likely to lead to students becoming disinterested?**

   A. Designing assignments where students write for a variety of audiences.

   B. Designing assignments where the teacher is the audience.

   C. Designing assignments where students write to friends and family.

   D. Designing assignments where students write to real people such as mayors, the principle, or companies.

60. **As a part of prewriting, students should identify their audience. Which of the following questions will help students to identify their audience?**

   A. Why is the audience reading my writing?

   B. What does my audience already know about my topic?

   C. Both A and B

   D. None of the above

61. **Which of these describes the best way to teach spelling?**

   A. At the same time that grammar and sentence structure is taught.

   B. Within the context of meaningful language experiences.

   C. Independently so that students can concentrate on spelling.

   D. In short lessons as students pick up spelling almost immediately.

62. **When editing, teachers should direct students to:**

   A. Edit for general understanding, while ignoring grammar and spelling.

   B. Edit for one specific purpose at a time.

   C. Identify all spelling, capitalization, and punctuation errors.

   D. Be critical of their work and that of others.

Subarea III. Learning in the Content Areas

63. **Kindergarten students are participating in a calendar time activity. One student adds a straw to the "ones can" to represent that day of school. What math principle is being reinforced?**

   A. Properties of a base ten number system

   B. Sorting

   C. Counting by twos

   D. Even and odd numbers

64. **First grade students are arranging four small squares of identical size to form a larger square. Each small square represents what part of the larger square?**

   A. One half

   B. One whole

   C. One fourth

   D. One fifth

65. What is the answer to this problem?

    25 ÷ 5 =

    A.   5

    B.   30

    C.   125

    D.   20

66. Third grade students are studying percents. When looking at a circle graph divided into three sections, they see that one section is worth 80% and one section is worth 5%. What will the remaining section be worth?

    A.   100%

    B.   85%

    C.   75%

    D.   15%

67. Which of the following letters does NOT have a line of symmetry?

    A.   O

    B.   D

    C.   M

    D.   J

68. Kindergarten students are doing a butterfly art project. They fold paper in half. On one half, they paint a design. Then they fold the paper closed and reopen. The resulting picture is a butterfly with matching sides. What math principle does this demonstrate?

    A.   Slide

    B.   Rotate

    C.   Symmetry

    D.   Transformation

69. What number comes next in this pattern?

    3, 8, 13, 18, _____

    A.   21

    B.   26

    C.   23

    D.   5

70. **What is the main purpose of having kindergarten students count by twos?**

   A.   To hear a rhythm

   B.   To recognize patterns in numbers

   C.   To practice addition

   D.   To become familiar with equations

71. **The term *millimeters* indicates which kind of measurement?**

   A.   Volume

   B.   Weight

   C.   Length

   D.   Temperature

72. **What type of graph would be best to use to show changes in the height of a plant over the course of a month?**

   A.   Circle graph

   B.   Bar graph

   C.   Line graph

   D.   Pictograph

73. **A teacher completes a survey of student eye color. The teacher then creates a graph so students can compare how many students have each eye color. What type of graph should be used?**

   A.   Bar graph

   B.   Pictograph

   C.   Circle graph

   D.   Line graph

74. **Which of the following skills would a student develop first?**

   A.   Understanding place value

   B.   Recognizing number patterns

   C.   Counting objects

   D.   Solving number problems

75. Maddie is a first grade teacher who understands the importance of including the family when providing instruction. She wants to take several steps to provide families with a connection to what the students are doing in her math class. Which of the following is NOT a strategy she could incorporate?

A. Including a math portion in her regular newsletter

B. Incorporating manipulatives into her math lessons

C. Translating math homework into the native language of the students in her classroom

D. Having a family math night at school

76. George has successfully mastered his basic addition facts. However, as his teacher presents more complex addition problems, it is obvious to him that George is lacking a basic understanding of the concept of addition. What would George's teacher be best to do to increase his basic understanding?

A. Provide additional instruction with hands on materials

B. Have George practice his addition facts more frequently

C. Have George complete more challenging addition problems

D. Provide George with remediation

77. Carrie approaches her teacher after class and expresses her personal frustration with math and her feeling that she will never get it. Which of the following is NOT a suitable method Carrie's teacher can utilize to improve Carrie's feelings about math?

A. Incorporating some of Carrie's specific interests into math lessons

B. Holding Carrie to high expectations

C. Sharing with Carrie her own struggles and dislike for math

D. Providing Carrie with extra positive reinforcement and encouragement

78. The principal walks into your classroom during math class. He sees your students making cake mixtures. Later, the principal questions your lesson. What would be the best explanation for your lesson?

A. The students earned a reward time and it was free choice.

B. You were teaching the students how math is used in real-life situations.

C. You had paperwork to complete and needed the time to complete it.

D. It kept the students interested in math and prevented boredom.

79. What is a large, rotating, low-pressure system accompanied by heavy precipitation and strong winds known as?

A. A hurricane

B. A tornado

C. A thunderstorm

D. A tsunami

80. **What does a primary consumer most commonly refer to?**

    A.   Herbivore

    B.   Autotroph

    C.   Carnivore

    D.   Decomposer

81. **Airplanes generate pressure and remain balanced by:**

    A.   Fast air movement over wings and slow movement under wings

    B.   Slow air movement over wings and fast movement under wings

    C.   Air movement that is equal above and below wings

    D.   Air movement that only occurs over the wings

82. **The breakdown of rock due to acid rain is an example of:**

    A.   Physical weathering

    B.   Frost wedging

    C.   Chemical weathering

    D.   Deposition

83. **What is the last step in the scientific method?**

    A.   Pose a question

    B.   Draw a conclusion

    C.   Conduct a test

    D.   Record data

84. **Which term best describes Newton's universal gravitation?**

    A.   Theory

    B.   Hypothesis

    C.   Inference

    D.   Law

85. **When teaching science, which of the following is a method of focusing on students' intrinsic motivation?**

    A. Adapting the lessons to students' interests

    B. Providing regular feedback

    C. Supplying rewards for the highest achievers

    D. Having regular science tests

86. **What does geography include the study of?**

    A. Location

    B. Distribution of living things

    C. Distribution of the earth's features

    D. All of the above

87. **Economics is the study of how a society allocates its scarce resources to satisfy:**

    A. Unlimited and competing wants

    B. Limited and competing wants

    C. Unlimited and cooperative wants

    D. Limited and cooperative wants

88. **The two elements of a market economy are:**

    A. Inflation and deflation

    B. Supply and demand

    C. Cost and price

    D. Wants and needs

89. **Who has the power to veto a bill that has passed the House of Representatives and the Senate?**

    A. The President

    B. The Vice President

    C. The Speaker of the House

    D. Any member of Congress

90. **Which part of a map shows the relationship between a unit of measurement on the map versus the real world measure on the Earth?**

    A. Scale

    B. Title

    C. Legend

    D. Grid

91. **What is the most important focus in developing social studies skills during the early years?**

    A. Recalling facts

    B. Understanding statistics

    C. Discussing ideas

    D. Memorizing rights and responsibilities

92. **What is one of the ten essential themes identified by the National Council for Social Studies?**

    A. Culture

    B. Lifestyle

    C. Population

    D. Democracy

93. **Which subject would a color wheel most likely be used for?**

    A. Visual arts

    B. Music

    C. Movement

    D. Drama

94. **A student art sample book would include cotton balls and sand paper to represent:**

    A. Color

    B. Lines

    C. Texture

    D. Shape

95. **Which terms refers to the arrangement of one or more items so that they appear symmetrical or asymmetrical?**

    A. Balance

    B. Contrast

    C. Emphasis

    D. Unity

96. The four principles of modern dance are substance, form, metakinesis, and:

A. Dynamism

B. Function

C. Space

D. Performance

97. What should the arts curriculum for early childhood avoid?

A. Judgment

B. Open expression

C. Experimentation

D. Discovery

98. What would the viewing of a dance company performance be most likely to promote?

A. Critical-thinking skills

B. Appreciation of the arts

C. Improvisation skills

D. Music vocabulary

99. In which subject is it most important for students to work with costumes and props?

A. Visual arts

B. Music

C. Movement

D. Drama

100. According to Charles Fowler, why is it important for arts to be incorporated into the teaching of other subject areas?

A. It reduces loss of interest in the subject.

B. It enhances the likelihood that students will retain the information.

C. It provides a three dimensional view of the subject.

D. It encourages the development of personal connections with the subject.

Answer Key: Pre-test

1.	B	45.	A	89.	A
2.	A	46.	A	90.	A
3.	B	47.	D	91.	C
4.	A	48.	B	92.	A
5.	A	49.	A	93.	A
6.	D	50.	A	94.	C
7.	D	51.	A	95.	A
8.	B	52.	B	96.	A
9.	A	53.	A	97.	A
10.	D	54.	C	98.	B
11.	D	55.	A	99.	D
12.	A	56.	A	100.	C
13.	A	57.	C		
14.	A	58.	D		
15.	C	59.	B		
16.	D	60.	C		
17.	D	61.	B		
18.	A	62.	B		
19.	A	63.	A		
20.	B	64.	C		
21.	C	65.	A		
22.	A	66.	D		
23.	C	67.	D		
24.	C	68.	C		
25.	A	69.	C		
26.	B	70.	B		
27.	A	71.	C		
28.	D	72.	C		
29.	C	73.	A		
30.	A	74.	C		
31.	D	75.	B		
32.	C	76.	A		
33.	C	77.	C		
34.	D	78.	B		
35.	A	79.	A		
36.	A	80.	A		
37.	B	81.	A		
38.	C	82.	C		
39.	B	83.	B		
40.	A	84.	D		
41.	C	85.	A		
42.	C	86.	D		
43.	D	87.	A		
44.	A	88.	B		

Rationales with Sample Questions: Pre-test

Subarea I. Child Development and Learning

1. **What developmental patterns should a professional teacher assess to meet the needs of each student?**

    A. Academic, regional, and family background
    B. Social, physical, and academic
    C. Academic, physical, and family background
    D. Physical, family, and ethnic background

Answer B: Social, physical, and academic

The effective teacher applies knowledge of physical, social, and academic developmental patterns and of individual differences, to meet the instructional needs of all students in the classroom.

2. **The various domains of development are best described as:**

    A. Integrated
    B. Independent
    C. Simultaneous
    D. Parallel

Answer A: Integrated

The most important premise of child development is that all domains of development (physical, social, and academic) are integrated.

3. **Which of the following best describes how different areas of development impact each other?**

    A. Development in other areas cannot occur until cognitive development is complete.
    B. Areas of development are inter-related and impact each other.
    C. Development in each area is independent of development in other areas.
    D. Development in one area leads to a decline in other areas.

Answer B: Areas of development are inter-related and impact each other.

Child development does not occur in a vacuum. Each element of development impacts other elements of development. For example, as cognitive development progresses, social development often follows. The reason for this is that all areas of development are fairly inter-related.

4. **A student has developed and improved in vocabulary. However, the student is not confident enough to use the improved vocabulary, and the teacher is not aware of the improvement. What is this an example of?**

    A. Latent development
    B. Dormant development
    C. Random development
    D. Delayed development

Answer A: Latent development

Latent development refers to the way that development in students may not always be observable. A student that has developed and improved in the area of vocabulary, but lacks the confidence to use the vocabulary would not show any outward signs of the development, and so the change may remain hidden. Teachers should be aware of this in order to identify a child's future or near-future capabilities.

5. **Which of the following has been shown to have the greatest impact on a student's academic performance?**

   A. The teacher's expectations
   B. Strict discipline
   C. The student's social skills
   D. Measurable objectives

Answer A: The teacher's expectations

Considerable research has been done, over several decades, regarding student performance. Time and again, a direct correlation has been demonstrated between the teacher's expectations for a particular student and that student's academic performance. This may be unintended and subtle, but the effects are manifest and measurable.

6. **According to Piaget, when does the development of symbolic functioning and language first take place?**

   A. Concrete operations stage
   B. Formal operations stage
   C. Sensory-motor stage
   D. Pre-operational stage

Answer D: Pre-operational stage

The pre-operational stage is where children begin to understand symbols. For example, as they learn language, they begin to realize that words are symbols of thoughts, actions, items, and other elements in the world. This stage lasts into early elementary school.

7. **Playing team sports at young ages should be done for the following purpose:**

   A. To develop the child's motor skills
   B. To prepare children for competition in high school
   C. To develop the child's interests
   D. Both A and C

Answer D: Both A and C

Sports, for both boys and girls, can be very valuable. Parents and teachers, though, need to remember that sports at young ages should only be for the purpose of development of interests and motor skills—not competition. Many children will learn that they do not enjoy sports, and parents and teachers should be respectful of these decisions.

8. **The stages of play development from infancy stages to early childhood includes a move from:**

   A. Cooperative to solitary
   B. Solitary to cooperative
   C. Competitive to collaborative
   D. Collaborative to competitive

Answer B: Solitary to cooperative

The stages of play development move from mainly solitary in the infancy stages to cooperative in early childhood. However, even in early childhood, children should be able to play on their own and entertain themselves from time to time.

9. **Which of the following is NOT an economic factor that may influence the health of a child?**

   A. Pollution
   B. Malnutrition
   C. Neglect
   D. Poor medical care

Answer A: Pollution

Malnutrition, neglect, and poor medical care are economic factors that may influence the health of a child. Pollution could influence the health of a child, but it is not an economic factor.

10. **Which of the following is the main source of energy in the diet?**

   A. Vitamins
   B. Minerals
   C. Water
   D. Carbohydrates

Answer D: Carbohydrates

The components of nutrition are carbohydrates, proteins, fats, vitamins, minerals, and water. Carbohydrates are the main source of energy (glucose) in the human diet. Common sources of carbohydrates are fruits, vegetables, grains, dairy products, and legumes.

11. **Which of the following would be likely to influence a student's learning and academic progress?**

    A.   Relocation
    B.   Emotional abuse
    C.   Bullying
    D.   All of the above

Answer D: All of the above

Children can be influenced by social and emotional factors. Relocation, emotional, abuse, and bullying can all have a negative impact on a student's learning and academic progress.

12. **Which of the following best explains why emotional upset and emotional abuse can reduce a child's classroom performance?**

    A.   They reduce the energy that students put towards schoolwork.
    B.   They lead to a reduction in cognitive ability.
    C.   They contribute to learning disorders such as dyslexia.
    D.   They result in the development of behavioral problems.

Answer A: They reduce the energy that students put towards schoolwork.

Although cognitive ability is not lost due to abuse, neglect, emotional upset, or lack of verbal interaction, the child will most likely not be able to provide as much intellectual energy as the child would if none of these things were present. This explains why classroom performance is often negatively impacted.

13. **A teacher has a class containing several students from low income families. What would be the most important factor for a teacher to consider when planning homework assignments to ensure that all students have equal opportunity for academic success?**

    A.   Access to technology
    B.   Ethnicity
    C.   Language difficulties
    D.   Gender

Answer A: Access to technology

Families with higher incomes are able to provide increased opportunities for students. Students from lower income families will need to depend on the resources available from the school system and the community. To ensure that all students have equal opportunity for academic success, teachers should plan assessments so that not having access to technology does not disadvantage students from low income families.

14. **Family members with high levels of education often have high expectations for student success. This shows how students are influenced by their family's:**

    A.   Attitude
    B.   Resources
    C.   Income
    D.   Culture

Answer A: Attitude

Parental/family influences on students include the influence of attitude. Family members with high levels of education often have high expectations for student success and this can have a positive impact on the student. The opposite can occur for some students from families with low levels of education. However, some families have high expectations for student success based on aspirations for their children regardless of their own status.

15. **Why is it most important for teachers to ensure that students from different economic backgrounds have access to the resources they need to acquire the academic skills being taught?**

    A. All students must work together on set tasks.
    B. All students must achieve the same results in performance tasks.
    C. All students must have equal opportunity for academic success.
    D. All students must be fully included in classroom activities.

Answer C: All students must have equal opportunity for academic success.

The economic backgrounds of students can impact the resources they have. Regardless of the positive or negative impacts on the students' education from outside sources, it is the teacher's responsibility to ensure that all students in the classroom have an equal opportunity for academic success. This includes ensuring that all students have equal access to the resources needed to acquire the skills being taught.

16. **A teacher attempting to create a differentiated classroom should focus on incorporating activities that:**

    A. Favor academically advanced students
    B. Challenge special education students to achieve more
    C. Are suitable for whichever group of students is the majority
    D. Meet the needs of all the students in the class

Answer D: Meet the needs of all the students in the class

A differentiated classroom is one that meets the needs of special education students, the regular mainstream students, and those that are academically advanced. The purpose of the differentiated classroom is to provide appropriate activities for students at all levels.

17. **When developing lessons, it is important that teachers provide equity in pedagogy so that:**

    A. Unfair labeling of students will not occur
    B. Student experiences will be positive
    C. Students will achieve academic success
    D. All of the above

Answer D: All of the above

When there is equity pedagogy, teachers can use a variety of instructional styles to facilitate diversity in cooperative learning and individualized instruction that will provide more opportunities for positive student experiences and academic success. Empowering the school culture and climate by establishing an anti-bias learning environment and promoting multicultural learning inclusion will also discourage unfair labeling of certain students.

18. **Which of the following is NOT a communication issue related to diversity within the classroom?**

    A. Learning disorders
    B. Sensitive terminology
    C. Body language
    D. Discussing differing viewpoints and opinions

Answer A: Learning disorders

There are several communication issues that the teacher in a diverse classroom should be aware of. These include being sensitive to terminology, being aware of body language, and emphasizing the discussion of differing viewpoints and opinions.

19. **One common factor for students with all types of disabilities is that they are also likely to demonstrate difficulty with:**

   A. Social skills
   B. Cognitive skills
   C. Problem-solving skills
   D. Decision-making skills

Answer A: Social skills

Students with disabilities (in all areas) may demonstrate difficulty in social skills. For a student with a hearing impairment, social skills may be difficult because of not hearing social language. However, the emotionally disturbed student may have difficulty because of a special type of psychological disturbance. An autistic student, as a third example, would be unaware of the social cues given with voice, facial expression, and body language. Each of these students would need social skill instruction but in a different way.

20. **A student does not respond to any signs of affection and responds to other children by repeating back what they have said. What condition is the student most likely to have?**

   A. Mental retardation
   B. Autism
   C. Giftedness
   D. Hyperactivity

Answer B: Autism

There are six common features of autism. They are:

Apparent sensory deficit – lack of reaction to or overreaction to a stimulus.

Severe affect isolation – lack of response to affection, such as smiles and hugs.

Self-stimulation – repeated or ritualistic actions that make no sense to others.

Tantrums and self-injurious behavior (SIB) – throwing tantrums, injuring oneself, or aggression.

Echolalia (also known as "parrot talk") – repetition of sounds or responding to others by repeating what was said to him.

Severe deficits in behavior and self-care skills – behaving like children much younger than themselves.

21. **Which of the following conditions is more common for girls than boys?**

   A. Attention deficit disorder
   B. Aggression
   C. Phobias
   D. Autism

Answer C: Phobias

Many more boys than girls are identified as having emotional and behavioral problems, especially hyperactivity and attention deficit disorder, autism, childhood psychosis, and problems with undercontrol such as aggression and socialized aggression. Girls have more problems with overcontrol, such as withdrawal and phobias.

22. **In successful inclusion of students with disabilities:**

   A. A variety of instructional arrangements are available
   B. School personnel shift the responsibility for learning outcomes to the student
   C. The physical facilities are used as they are
   D. Regular classroom teachers have sole responsibility for evaluating student progress

Answer A: A variety of instructional arrangements are available

All students have the right to an education, but there cannot be a singular path to that education. A teacher must acknowledge the variety of learning styles and abilities among students within a class apply multiple instructional and assessment processes to ensure that every child has appropriate opportunities to master the subject matter, demonstrate such mastery, and improve and enhance learning skills with each lesson.

23. **Mr. Gorman has taught a concept to his class. All of the students have grasped the concept except for Sam. Mr. Gorman should:**

    A. Reteach the concept to the whole class in exactly the same way
    B. Reteach the concept to Sam in exactly the same way
    C. Reteach the concept to Sam in a different way
    D. Reteach the concept to the whole class in a different way

Answer C: Reteach the concept to Sam in a different way

There is always more than one way to approach a problem, an example, a process, fact or event, or any learning situation. Varying approaches for instruction helps to maintain the students' interest in the material and enables the teacher to address the diverse needs of individuals to comprehend the material.

24. **Mrs. Gomez has a fully integrated early childhood curriculum. This is beneficial to students because it:**

    A. Is easier to plan for and maintain
    B. Allows students to apply their unique skills
    C. Helps the students see the relationships between subjects and concepts
    D. Provides opportunities for social interaction

Answer C: Helps the students see the relationships between subjects and concepts

An integrated curriculum is a curriculum in which lessons are taught in several different subject areas according to the outcomes that deal with the same concepts. It may also be known as thematic teaching or interdisciplinary teaching.

Subarea II. Communication, Language and Literacy Development

25. **The relationship between oral language and reading skills is best described as:**

   A. Reciprocal
   B. Inverse
   C. Opposite
   D. There is no relationship.

Answer A: Reciprocal

A highly developed oral language vocabulary helps to build reading skills comprehension. The inverse is true as well, with highly developed reading and comprehension skills helping to develop oral language skills.

26. **A teacher is showing students how to construct grammatically correct sentences. What is the teacher focusing on?**

   A. Morphology
   B. Syntax
   C. Semantics
   D. Pragmatics

Answer B: Syntax

Syntax refers to the rules or patterned relationships that correctly create phrases and sentences from words. When readers develop an understanding of syntax, they begin to understand the structure of how sentences are built, and eventually the beginning of grammar.

27. **A teacher writes the following words on the board: cot, cotton, and cottage. What is the teacher most likely teaching the students about?**

    A. Morphology
    B. Syntax
    C. Semantics
    D. Pragmatics

Answer A: Morphology

Morphology is the study of word structure. When readers develop morphemic skills, they are developing an understanding of patterns they see in words. For example, English speakers realize that cat, cats, and caterpillar share some similarities in structure. This understanding helps readers to recognize words at a faster and easier rate, since each word doesn't need individual decoding.

28. **While standing in line at the grocery store, three-year-old Megan says to her mother in a regular tone of voice, "Mom, why is that woman so fat?" What does this indicate a lack of understanding of?**

    A. Syntax
    B. Semantics
    C. Morphology
    D. Pragmatics

Answer D: Pragmatics

Pragmatics is the development and understanding of social relevance to conversations and topics. It develops as children age. In this situation, Megan simply does not understand to the same level of an adult how that question could be viewed as offensive to certain members of society.

29. **Which of the following is the first component of the constructivist model?**

    A. There are at least seven different types of learning.
    B. Learning depends on the social environment.
    C. Learner creates knowledge
    D. Learning progresses through set stages.

Answer C: Learner creates knowledge

Researchers have shown that the constructivist model is comprised of the four components:

1. Learner creates knowledge

2. Learner constructs and makes meaningful new knowledge from existing knowledge

3. Learner shapes and constructs knowledge by life experiences and social interactions

4. In constructivist learning communities, the student, teacher and classmates establish knowledge cooperatively on a daily basis.

30. **Students are about to read a text that contains words that will need to be understood for the students to understand the text. When should the vocabulary be introduced to students?**

    A. Before reading
    B. During reading
    C. After reading
    D. It should not be introduced.

Answer A: Before reading

Vocabulary should be introduced before reading if there are words within the text that are definitely keys necessary for reading comprehension.

31. **Which of the following are examples of temporal words?**

    A.   Beside and behind
    B.   Hotter and colder
    C.   In and on
    D.   Before and after

Answer D: Before and after

Temporal words are words that indicate time. Before and after are two examples of temporal words.

32. **Which principle of Stephen Krashen's research suggests that the learning of grammatical structures is predictable?**

    A.   The affective filter hypothesis
    B.   The input hypothesis
    C.   The natural order hypothesis
    D.   The monitor hypothesis

Answer C: The natural order hypothesis

Stephen Krashen's natural order hypothesis suggests that the learning of grammatical structures is predictable and follows a natural order.

33. **Above what age does learning a language become increasingly difficult?**

    A.   3
    B.   5
    C.   7
    D.   10

Answer C: 7

The most important concept to remember regarding the difference between learning a first language and a second one is that if the learner is approximately age seven or older, learning a second language will occur very differently in the learner's brain than it would had the learner been younger. The reason for this is that there is a language-learning function that exists in young children that appears to go away as they mature. Learning a language prior to age seven is almost guaranteed, with relatively little effort.

34. **Ms. Chomski is presenting a new story to her class of first graders. In the story, a family visits their grandparents where they all gather around a record player and listen to music. Many students do not understand what a record player is, especially some children for whom English is not their first language. Which of the following would Ms. Chomski be best to do?**

    A.   Discuss what a record player is with her students
    B.   Compare a record player with a CD player
    C.   Have students look up record player in a dictionary
    D.   Show the students a picture of a record player

Answer D: Show the students a picture of a record player

The most effective method for ensuring adequate comprehension is through direct experience. Sometimes this cannot be completed and therefore it is necessary to utilize pictures or other visual aids to provide the students with experience in another mode besides oral language.

35. **Jose moved to the United States last month. He speaks little or no English at this time. His teacher is teaching the class about habitats in science and has chosen to read a story about various habitats to the class. The vocabulary is difficult. What should Jose's teacher do with Jose?**

    A.   Provide Jose with additional opportunities to learn about habitats
    B.   Read the story to Jose multiple times
    C.   Show Jose pictures of habitats from his native country
    D.   Excuse Jose from the assignment

Answer A: Provide Jose with additional opportunities to learn about habitats

Students who are learning English should be exposed to a variety of opportunities to learn the same concepts as native speakers. Content should not be changed, but the manner in which it is presented and reinforced should be changed.

36. **In the early childhood classroom, it is important to limit teacher talk. What is the main problem with teacher talk?**

    A. It is often one sided and limited.
    B. The vocabulary is too difficult for children.
    C. It promotes misbehavior.
    D. It only creates gains in receptive language.

Answer A: It is often one sided and limited.

While it is important to expose children to numerous opportunities throughout the day to read and interact with print, it is equally important for students to have the opportunity to express themselves and communicate with each other. Teacher-talk, is often one sided and limited. Instead, teachers should provide opportunities for students to develop and expand their vocabularies.

37. **Which of the following is a convention of print that children learn during reading activities?**

    A. The meaning of words
    B. The left to right motion
    C. The purpose of print
    D. The identification of letters

Answer B: The left to right motion

During reading activities, children learn conventions of print. Children learn the way to hold a book, where to begin to read, the left to right motion, and how to continue from one line to another.

38. In her kindergarten class, Mrs. Thomas has been watching the students in the drama center. She has watched the children pretend to complete a variety of magic tricks. Mrs. Thomas decides to use stories about magic to share with her class. Her decision to incorporate their interests into the reading shows that Mrs. Thomas understands that:

    A.   Including student interests is important at all times
    B.   Teaching by themes is crucial for young children
    C.   Young children respond to literature that reflects their lives
    D.   Science fiction and fantasy are the most popular genres

Answer C: Young children respond to literature that reflects their lives

Children's literature is intended to instruct students through entertaining stories, while also promoting an interest in the very act of reading, itself. Young readers respond best to themes that reflect their lives.

39. **Which of the following is NOT a characteristic of a fable?**

    A.   Have animal characters that act like humans
    B.   Considered to be true
    C.   Teaches a moral
    D.   Reveals human foibles

Answer B: Considered to be true

The common characteristics of fables are animals that act like humans, a focus on revealing human foibles, and teaching a moral or lesson. Fables are not considered to be true.

40. **Alphabet books are classified as:**

    A.   Concept books
    B.   Easy-to-read books
    C.   Board books
    D.   Pictures books

Answer A: Concept books

Concept books are books that combine language and pictures to show concrete examples of concepts. One category of concept books is alphabet books, which are popular with children from preschool through to grade 2.

41. The stories of Paul Bunyan, John Henry, and Pecos Bill are all exaggerated accounts of individuals with superhuman strength. What type of literature are these works?

    A. Fables
    B. Fairytales
    C. Tall tales
    D. Myths

Answer C: Tall tales

Tall tales are purposely exaggerated accounts of individuals with superhuman strength. The stories of Paul Bunyan, John Henry, and Pecos Bill are all examples of tall tales. Fables are usually stories about animals with human features that often teach a lesson. Fairytales usually focus on good versus evil, reward and punishment. Myths are stories about events from the earliest times.

42. Which of the following is NOT a motivation behind providing reading activities, including reading aloud, to young children?

    A. Developing word consciousness skills
    B. Developing functions of print skills
    C. Developing phonics skills
    D. Developing language skills

Answer C: Developing phonics skills

There are almost unlimited positive reasons for encouraging adults to provide reading activities for young children. While it can be true that reading aloud may improve the phonics skills for some students, it is not a motivation for providing such activities to students.

43. **Which of the following is an appropriate way for students to respond to literature?**

    A. Art
    B. Drama
    C. Writing
    D. All of the above

Answer D: All of the above

Responding to literature through art, writing, and drama helps children to reflect on the books they have read and make them a part of their lives.

44. **John is having difficulty reading the word reach. In isolation, he pronounces each sound as /r/ /ee/ /sh/. Which of the following is a possible instructional technique which could help solve John's reading difficulty?**

    A. Additional phonemic awareness instruction
    B. Additional phonics instruction
    C. Additional skill and drill practice
    D. Additional minimal pair practice

Answer A: Additional phonemic awareness instruction

John is having difficulty with the sound symbol relationship between the /ch/ and /sh/. While it may appear at first that this is a phonics problem, in fact, it is important to begin with the earlier skill of phonemic awareness to ensure the student has a solid foundational understanding of the oral portions before moving totally into the sound symbol arena. If John is able to distinguish between the two sounds orally, it is obvious more phonics instruction is needed. However, proceeding directly to phonics instruction may be pointless and frustrating for John if he is unable to hear the distinctions.

45. **According to Marilyn Jager Adams, which skill would a student demonstrate by identifying that cat does not belong in the group of words containing dog, deer, and dress?**

    A. Recognize the odd member in a group
    B. Replace sounds in words
    C. Count the sounds in a word
    D. Count syllables in a word

Answer A: Recognize the odd member in a group

One of Marilyn Jager Adams' basic types of phonemic awareness tasks involves the ability to do oddity tasks, which involves recognizing the member of a set that is different among the group. In this example, the word cat is the odd member because it starts with a different sound.

46. **Which of the following is NOT true about phonological awareness? (Skill 7.2; Average rigor)**

    A. It may involve print.
    B. It is a prerequisite for spelling and phonics.
    C. Activities can be done by the children with their eyes closed.
    D. It starts before letter recognition is taught.

Answer A: It may involve print.

All of the options are correct aspects of phonological awareness except the first one, because phonological awareness does not involve print.

47. **Which of the following explains a significant difference between phonics and phonemic awareness?**

    A. Phonics involves print, while phonemic awareness involves language.
    B. Phonics is harder than phonemic awareness.
    C. Phonics involves sounds, while phonemic awareness involves letters.
    D. Phonics is the application of sounds to print, while phonemic awareness is oral.

Answer D: Phonics is the application of sounds to print, while phonemic awareness is oral.

Both phonics and phonemic awareness activities involve sounds, but it is with phonics that the application of these sounds is applied to print. Phonemic awareness is an oral activity.

48. **To decode is to:**

   A. Construct meaning
   B. Sound out a printed sequence of letters
   C. Use a special code to decipher a message
   D. Revise for errors in grammar

Answer B: Sound out a printed sequence of letters

Decoding is the process students use to figure out unknown words when reading.

49. **Ms. Walker's lesson objective is to teach her first graders the concept of morphology in order to improve their reading skills. Which group of words would be most appropriate for her to use in this lesson?**

   A. Far, farm, farmer
   B. Far, feather, fever
   C. Far, fear, fare
   D. Far, fare, farce

Answer A: Far, farm, farmer

The concept of morphology is to understand how words relate to each other and can be built upon to increase reading skills. In the correct answer, the student can utilize the information they learned from learning to read far to help them decode the other words.

50. **Which stage of reading skill development occurs first?**

   A. Schema stage
   B. Early semantic stage
   C. Orthographic stage
   D. Simultaneous stage

Answer A: Schema stage

Reading develops in sequential skills levels. The first stage is the schema stage. This stage is a pre-reading level involving page turning and telling story from memory.

51. **Which of the following is an important feature of vocabulary instruction according to the National Reading Panel?**

    A. Repetition of vocabulary items
    B. Keeping a consistent task structure at all times
    C. Teaching vocabulary in more than one language
    D. Isolation vocabulary instruction from other subjects

Answer A: Repetition of vocabulary items

According to the National Reading Panel, repetition and multiple exposures to vocabulary items are important. Students should be given items that will be likely to appear in many contexts.

52. **The attitude an author takes toward his or her subject is the:**

    A. Style
    B. Tone
    C. Point of view
    D. Theme

Answer B: Tone

Tone is the attitude an author takes toward his or her subject. That tone is exemplified in the language of the text.

53. **George has read his second graders three formats of the story "The Three Little Pigs." One is the traditional version, one is written from the wolf's point of view, and the third is written from the first pig's point of view. As George leads a discussion on the three texts with his students, he is trying to help his students develop their ability to:**

    A. Compare and contrast texts
    B. Understand point of view
    C. Recognize metaphors
    D. Rewrite fictional stories

Answer A: Compare and contrast texts

George understands the importance of developing critical thinking skills in young children. He has read three different formats of the same story in order to help his students develop their ability to compare texts.

54.   What is the first step in developing writing skills?

      A.   Early writing
      B.   Experimental writing
      C   Role play writing
      D.   Conventional writing

Answer C: Role play writing

Children develop writing skills through a series of steps. These steps are: role play writing, experimental writing, early writing, and then conventional writing. In the role play writing stage, the child writes in scribbles and assigns a message to the symbols. Even though an adult would not be able to read the writing, the child can read what is written although it may not be the same each time the child reads it. S/he will be able to read back the writing because of prior knowledge that print carries a meaning.

55.   Which of the following is NOT a prewriting strategy?

      A.   Analyzing sentences for variety
      B.   Keeping an idea book
      C.   Writing in a daily journal
      D.   Writing down whatever comes to mind

Answer A: Analyzing sentences for variety

Prewriting strategies assist students in a variety of ways. Common prewriting strategies include keeping an idea book for jotting down ideas, writing in a daily journal, and writing down whatever comes to mind, which is also called "free writing." Analyzing sentences for variety is a revising strategy.

56. **Which of the following is probably the most important step for the writer in the writing process?**

    A. Revision
    B. Discovery
    C. Conclusion
    D. Organization

Answer A: Revision

Revision is probably the most important step for the writer in the writing process. Here, students examine their work and make changes in wording, details, and ideas. So many times, students write a draft and then feel they're done. Students must be encouraged to develop, change, and enhance their writing as they go, as well as once they've completed a draft.

57. **The students in Tina's classroom are working together in pairs. Each student is reading another student's paper and asking who, what, when, where, why, and who questions. What is this activity helping the students to do?**

    A. Draft their writing
    B. Paraphrase their writing
    C. Revise their writing
    D. Outline their writing

Answer C: Revise their writing

Students need to be trained to become effective at proofreading, revising and editing strategies. One way to do this is to have the students read their partners' papers and ask at least three who, what, when, why, how questions. The students answer the questions and use them as a place to begin discussing the piece.

58. **Young children learning to write commonly grip the pencil:**

  A. Too far from the point
  B. With the wrong hand
  C. With too many fingers
  D. Too tightly

Answer D: Too tightly

A common problem for all young children learning to write is gripping the pencil too tightly, which makes writing tiresome. Usually the student learns to relax their grip as writing skill develops, but teachers can remind students to hold the instrument gently.

59. **Which of the following approaches to student writing assignments is most likely to lead to students becoming disinterested?**

  A. Designing assignments where students write for a variety of audiences.
  B. Designing assignments where the teacher is the audience.
  C. Designing assignments where students write to friends and family.
  D. Designing assignments where students write to real people such as mayors, the principle, or companies.

Answer B: Designing assignments where the teacher is the audience

In the past, teachers have assigned reports, paragraphs and essays that focused on the teacher as the audience with the purpose of explaining information. However, for students to be meaningfully engaged in their writing, they must write for a variety of reasons. Writing for different audiences and aims allows students to be more involved in their writing. If they write for the same audience and purpose, they will continue to see writing as just another assignment

60. **As a part of prewriting, students should identify their audience. Which of the following questions will help students to identify their audience?**

    A.   Why is the audience reading my writing?
    B.   What does my audience already know about my topic?
    C.   Both A and B
    D.   None of the above

Answer C: Both A and B

As part of prewriting, students should identify the audience. Make sure students consider the following when analyzing the needs of their audience: why the audience is reading the writing; what the audience already knows about the topic; what the audience needs or wants to know; what will interest the reader; and what type of language will suit the reader.

61. **Which of these describes the best way to teach spelling?**

    A.   At the same time that grammar and sentence structure is taught.
    B.   Within the context of meaningful language experiences.
    C.   Independently so that students can concentrate on spelling.
    D.   In short lessons as students pick up spelling almost immediately.

Answer B: Within the context of meaningful language experiences.

Spelling should be taught within the context of meaningful language experiences. Giving a child a list of words to learn to spell and then testing the child on the words every Friday will not aid in the development of spelling. The child must be able to use the words in context and they must have some meaning for the child. The assessment of how well a child can spell or where there are problems also has to be done within a meaningful environment.

62. **When editing, teachers should direct students to:**

    A. Edit for general understanding, while ignoring grammar and spelling.
    B. Edit for one specific purpose at a time.
    C. Identify all spelling, capitalization, and punctuation errors.
    D. Be critical of their work and that of others.

Answer B: Edit for one specific purpose at a time.

Editing is a time-consuming task and it would be unreasonable to expect students to pick up on all the mistakes in a piece of writing. Therefore, teachers should ask students to edit for specific purposes at one time, such as correct spelling, capitalization or punctuation.

Subarea III. Learning in the Content Areas

63. **Kindergarten students are participating in a calendar time activity. One student adds a straw to the "ones can" to represent that day of school. What math principle is being reinforced?**

    A. Properties of a base ten number system
    B. Sorting
    C. Counting by twos
    D. Even and odd numbers

Answer A: Properties of a base ten number system

As the students group craft sticks into groups of tens to represent the days of school, they are learning the properties of our base ten number system.

64. **First grade students are arranging four small squares of identical size to form a larger square. Each small square represents what part of the larger square?**

    A. One half
    B. One whole
    C. One fourth
    D. One fifth

Answer C: One fourth

Four of the small squares make up the area of the large square. Each small square is one fourth of the larger square.

65. What is the answer to this problem?

$25 \div 5 =$

A. 5
B. 30
C. 125
D. 20

Answer A: 5

Twenty-five can be divided into five equal groups of five.

66. Third grade students are studying percents. When looking at a circle graph divided into three sections, they see that one section is worth 80% and one section is worth 5%. What will the remaining section be worth?

A. 100%
B. 85%
C. 75%
D. 15%

Answer D: 15%

Percentages use the base ten number system. Percentages of a total amount will always add up to 100%. Since the two sections add to 85%, the third section must be 15%.

67. Which of the following letters does NOT have a line of symmetry?

A. O
B. D
C. M
D. J

Answer D: J

For an object to show symmetry, it must be able to be divided into identical halves. The letter O has an unlimited number of lines of symmetry. The letter D has a horizontal line of symmetry. The letter M has a vertical line of symmetry. The letter J does not have a line of symmetry.

68. **Kindergarten students are doing a butterfly art project. They fold paper in half. On one half, they paint a design. Then they fold the paper closed and reopen. The resulting picture is a butterfly with matching sides. What math principle does this demonstrate?**

   A. Slide
   B. Rotate
   C. Symmetry
   D. Transformation

Answer C: Symmetry

By folding the painted paper in half, the design is mirrored on the other side, creating symmetry and reflection. The butterfly design is symmetrical about the center.

69. **What number comes next in this pattern?**

   3, 8, 13, 18, _____

   A. 21
   B. 26
   C. 23
   D. 5

Answer C: 23

This pattern is made by adding five to the preceding number. The next number is found by adding 5 to 18, which gives the answer 23.

70. **What is the main purpose of having kindergarten students count by twos?**

   A. To hear a rhythm
   B. To recognize patterns in numbers
   C. To practice addition
   D. To become familiar with equations

Answer B: To recognize patterns in numbers

Recognizing patterns in numbers is an early skill for multiplication. It will also help children recognize patterns in word families such as *bit, hit, fit.*

71. **The term *millimeters* indicates which kind of measurement?**

    A. Volume
    B. Weight
    C. Length
    D. Temperature

Answer C: Length

The term *millimeters* is a reference to length in the metric system.

72. **What type of graph would be best to use to show changes in the height of a plant over the course of a month?**

    A. Circle graph
    B. Bar graph
    C. Line graph
    D. Pictograph

Answer C: Line graph

A line graph shows trends over time. A line graph would show how the plant's height changed over time.

73. **A teacher completes a survey of student eye color. The teacher then creates a graph so students can compare how many students have each eye color. What type of graph should be used?**

    A. Bar graph
    B. Pictograph
    C. Circle graph
    D. Line Graph

Answer A: Bar graph

Bar graphs are used to compare various quantities. In this case, the bar graph would show the number of students with each eye color. By looking at the graph, students would be able to compare how many students have each eye color. While a pictograph is also possible, if there are many different eye colors in the class, it would take up a lot of space to graph it this way.

74. **Which of the following skills would a student develop first?**

    A. Understanding place value
    B. Recognizing number patterns
    C. Counting objects
    D. Solving number problems

Answer C: Counting objects

As with the phonemic awareness skills in reading, number sense is the foundation upon which all future math topics will be built. While in this beginning stage, children will be able to identify how many objects are in a group.

75. **Maddie is a first grade teacher who understands the importance of including the family when providing instruction. She wants to take several steps to provide families with a connection to what the students are doing in her math class. Which of the following is NOT a strategy she could incorporate?**

    A. Including a math portion in her regular newsletter
    B. Incorporating manipulatives into her math lessons
    C. Translating math homework into the native language of the students in her classroom
    D. Having a family math night at school

Answer B: Incorporating manipulatives into her math lessons

While incorporating manipulatives into her curriculum is an excellent strategy, which should take place in every math classroom, it does not promote the inclusion of family into the curriculum.

76. **George has successfully mastered his basic addition facts. However, as his teacher presents more complex addition problems, it is obvious to him that George is lacking a basic understanding of the concept of addition. What would George's teacher be best to do to increase his basic understanding?**

    A.   Provide additional instruction with hands on materials
    B.   Have George practice his addition facts more frequently
    C.   Have George complete more challenging addition problems
    D.   Provide George with remediation

Answer A: Provide additional instruction with hands on materials

When students have the time to explore and build their own constructs using concrete objects, they are able to make more generalizations. Students may be able to memorize pieces of rote information, but without the foundational exposure to hands on materials they may not be able to demonstrate these generalizations. It is the role of the teacher to take the time to provide these opportunities.

77. **Carrie approaches her teacher after class and expresses her personal frustration with math and her feeling that she will never get it. Which of the following is NOT a suitable method Carrie's teacher can utilize to improve Carrie's feelings about math?**

    A.   Incorporating some of Carrie's specific interests into math lessons
    B.   Holding Carrie to high expectations
    C.   Sharing with Carrie her own struggles and dislike for math
    D.   Providing Carrie with extra positive reinforcement and encouragement

Answer C: Sharing with Carrie her own struggles and dislike for math

While it may seem to be a bonding experience to share your own personal struggles and dislike for the subject with a student who feels the same way, it is important for the teacher to maintain excitement and enthusiasm for the subject. Carrie's teacher would be better to share positive aspects about how math as affected her life, than to share any negative feelings. Building a positive excitement and interest in the subject is an important part of teaching.

78. **The principal walks into your classroom during math class. He sees your students making cake mixtures. Later, the principal questions your lesson. What would be the best explanation for your lesson?**

    A.   The students earned a reward time and it was free choice.
    B.   You were teaching the students how math is used in real-life situations.
    C.   You had paperwork to complete and needed the time to complete it.
    D.   It kept the students interested in math and prevented boredom.

Answer B: You were teaching the students how math is used in real-life situations.

Providing the students with the opportunity to explore how math is around them and how it is utilized in everyday experiences is important. As students identify and realize the importance of the skills being learned to their lives at home, they will become more involved in the learning, as it has new and better value for them.

79. **What is a large, rotating, low-pressure system accompanied by heavy precipitation and strong winds known as?**

    A.   A hurricane
    B.   A tornado
    C.   A thunderstorm
    D.   A tsunami

Answer A: A hurricane

Hurricanes are storms that develop when warm, moist air carried by trade winds rotates around a low-pressure "eye". These form a large, rotating, low-pressure system and are accompanied by heavy precipitation and strong winds. They are also known as tropical cyclones or typhoons.

80. **What does a primary consumer most commonly refer to?**

    A. Herbivore
    B. Autotroph
    C. Carnivore
    D. Decomposer

Answer A: Herbivore

Autotrophs are the primary producers of the ecosystem. Producers mainly consist of plants. Primary consumers are the next trophic level. The primary consumers are the herbivores that eat plants or algae. Secondary consumers are the carnivores that eat the primary consumers. Tertiary consumers eat the secondary consumer. These trophic levels may go higher depending on the ecosystem.

81. **Airplanes generate pressure and remain balanced by:**

    A. Fast air movement over wings and slow movement under wings
    B. Slow air movement over wings and fast movement under wings
    C. Air movement that is equal above and below wings
    D. Air movement that only occurs over the wings

Answer A: Fast air movement over wings and slow movement under wings

Airplanes or fixed-wing aircraft are heavier than aircraft that utilize the laws of physics to achieve flight. As the aircraft is propelled forward by thrust from the engines, air moves faster over the top of the wings and slower under the bottom. The slower airflow beneath the wing generates more pressure, while the faster airflow above generates less. This difference in pressure results in upward lift.

82. **The breakdown of rock due to acid rain is an example of:**

    A. Physical weathering
    B. Frost wedging
    C. Chemical weathering
    D. Deposition

Answer C: Chemical weathering

The breaking down of rocks at or near to the Earth's surface is known as weathering. Chemical weathering is the breaking down of rocks through changes in their chemical composition. The breakdown of rock due to acid rain is an example of chemical weathering.

83. **What is the last step in the scientific method?**

    A. Pose a question
    B. Draw a conclusion
    C. Conduct a test
    D. Record data

Answer B: Draw a conclusion

The steps in the scientific method, in order, are: pose a question, form a hypothesis, conduct a test, observe and record data, and draw a conclusion.

84. Which term best describes Newton's universal gravitation?

    A.   Theory
    B.   Hypothesis
    C.   Inference
    D.   Law

Answer D: Law

A hypothesis is an unproved theory or educated guess followed by research to best explain a phenomenon. A theory is the formation of principles or relationships, which have been verified and accepted. It is a proven hypothesis. A law is an explanation of events that occur with uniformity under the same conditions, such as laws of nature or laws of gravitation.

85. When teaching science, which of the following is a method of focusing on students' intrinsic motivation?

    A.   Adapting the lessons to students' interests
    B.   Providing regular feedback
    C.   Supplying rewards for the highest achievers
    D.   Having regular science tests

Answer A: Adapting the lessons to students' interests

Teachers can focus on students' intrinsic motivation through adapting the tasks to students' interests, providing opportunities for active response, including a variety of tasks, providing rapid feedback, incorporating games into the lesson, and allowing students the opportunity to make choices, create, and interact with peers.

86. What does geography include the study of?

    A.   Location
    B.   Distribution of living things
    C.   Distribution of the earth's features
    D.   All of the above

Answer D: All of the above

Geography involves studying location and how living things and earth's features are distributed throughout the earth. It includes where animals, people, and plants live and the effects of their relationship with earth's physical features.

87. **Economics is the study of how a society allocates its scarce resources to satisfy:**

   A.   Unlimited and competing wants
   B.   Limited and competing wants
   C.   Unlimited and cooperative wants
   D.   Limited and cooperative wants

Answer A: Unlimited and competing wants

Economics is the study of how a society allocates its scarce resources to satisfy what are basically unlimited and competing wants. A fundamental fact of economics is that resources are scarce and that wants are infinite.

88. **The two elements of a market economy are:**

   A.   Inflation and deflation
   B.   Supply and demand
   C.   Cost and price
   D.   Wants and needs

Answer B: Supply and demand

A market economy is based on supply and demand. Demand is based on consumer preferences and satisfaction and refers to the quantities of a good or service that buyers are willing and able to buy at different prices during a given period of time. Supply is based on costs of production and refers to the quantities that sellers are willing and able to sell at different prices during a given period of time.

89. **Who has the power to veto a bill that has passed the House of Representatives and the Senate?**

   A.   The President
   B.   The Vice President
   C.   The Speaker of the House
   D.   Any member of Congress

Answer A: The President

Once a bill receives final approval by a conference committee, it is signed by the Speaker of the House and the Vice President, who is also the President of the Senate, and sent to the President for consideration. The President may either sign the bill or veto it. If he vetoes the bill, his veto may be overruled if two-thirds of both the Senate and the House vote to do so. Once the President signs it the bill becomes a law.

90. **Which part of a map shows the relationship between a unit of measurement on the map versus the real world measure on the Earth?**

     A.   Scale
     B.   Title
     C.   Legend
     D.   Grid

Answer A: Scale

The scale of a map is used to show the relationship between a unit of measurement on the map versus the real world measure on the Earth.

91. **What is the most important focus in developing social studies skills during the early years?**

     A.   Recalling facts
     B.   Understanding statistics
     C.   Discussing ideas
     D.   Memorizing rights and responsibilities

Answer C: Discussing ideas

The early years of childhood education is important in shaping the values of a democracy and preparing students for citizenship in later life. Social studies begin the exploration of the processes, rights and freedoms of a democracy. Early in a child's education they begin to learn cooperation, tolerance, and sharing. During the early years, the recalling of factual information is not as important as encouraging discussion and exploration of different perspectives.

92. **What is one of the ten essential themes identified by the National Council for Social Studies?**

    A.   Culture
    B.   Lifestyle
    C.   Population
    D.   Democracy

Answer A: Culture

The National Council for Social Studies identifies 10 themes essential to social science instruction. These are:
1. Culture
2. Time, Continuity and Change
3. People, Places and Environments
4. Individual development and identity
5. Individuals, Groups and Institutions
6. Power, Authority and Governance
7. Production, Distribution and Consumption
8. Science, Technology and Society
9. Global Connections
10. Civic Ideals and Practices

93. **Which subject would a color wheel most likely be used for?**

    A.   Visual arts
    B.   Music
    C.   Movement
    D.   Drama

Answer A: Visual arts

A color wheel is an important tool in teaching students visual arts. It is used to teach students about primary colors and secondary colors. It is also used to help students learn about mixing colors.

94. **A student art sample book would include cotton balls and sand paper to represent:**

   A. Color
   B. Lines
   C. Texture
   D. Shape

Answer C: Texture

Texture refers to the way something feels because of the tactile quality of its surface. An art sample book can include materials such as cotton balls and sand paper as examples of different textures.

95. **Which terms refers to the arrangement of one or more items so that they appear symmetrical or asymmetrical?**

   A. Balance
   B. Contrast
   C. Emphasis
   D. Unity

Answer A: Balance

The principles of visual are that students should be introduced to include abstract, background, balance, contrast, emphasis, sketch, texture, and unity. Balance refers to the arrangement of one or more elements in a work of art so that they appear symmetrical or asymmetrical in design and proportion.

96. **The four principles of modern dance are substance, form, metakinesis, and:**

   A. Dynamism
   B. Function
   C. Space
   D. Performance

Answer A: Dynamism

Modern dance is a type of dance where the focus is on expressing opposites, such as fast-slow or contract-release. Modern dance is based on four principles. These are substance, form, metakinesis, and dynamism.

97. **What should the arts curriculum for early childhood avoid?**

   A. Judgment
   B. Open expression
   C. Experimentation
   D. Discovery

Answer A: Judgment

The arts curriculum for early childhood should focus on the experimental and discovery aspects of the arts. The emphasis should be on creative processes with little judgment and criticism should be minimal.

98. **What would the viewing of a dance company performance be most likely to promote?**

   A. Critical-thinking skills
   B. Appreciation of the arts
   C. Improvisation skills
   D. Music vocabulary

Answer B: Appreciation of the arts

Live performances are an important part of learning arts and help to develop aesthetic appreciation of the arts. A dance company performance is one example of a live performance that students could attend.

99. **In which subject is it most important for students to work with costumes and props?**

   A. Visual arts
   B. Music
   C. Movement
   D. Drama

Answer D: Drama

When studying drama, students should experience working with props and performing in costume. These can both help students act out experiences and tend to increase creativity.

100. **According to Charles Fowler, why is it important for arts to be incorporated into the teaching of other subject areas?**

   A.   It reduces loss of interest in the subject.
   B.   It enhances the likelihood that students will retain the information.
   C.   It provides a three dimensional view of the subject.
   D.   It encourages the development of personal connections with the subject.

Answer C: It provides a three dimensional view of the subject.

Charles Fowler has argued that the best schools also have the best arts programs. According to Fowler, integrating arts with other subject areas gives a more complete view of the subject. Students then gain a more three dimensional understanding of the subject.

SAMPLE TEST

DIRECTIONS: Read each item and select the best response.

1. **All of the following are common types of narratives EXCEPT:**

   (Rigorous) (Skill 1.1)

   A. Legends

   B. Short stories

   C. Poems

   D. Memoirs

2. **Which of the following is an example of nonfiction literature?**

   (Average Rigor) (Skill 1.2)

   A. Letters

   B. Biographies

   C. Journals

   D. All of the above

3. **Which is NOT a true statement concerning an author's literary tone?**

   (Rigorous) (Skill 1.2)

   A. Tone is partly revealed through the selection of details.

   B. Tone is the expression of the author's attitude toward his/her subject.

   C. Tone in literature is usually satiric or angry.

   D. Tone in literature corresponds to the tone of voice a speaker uses.

4. **Alliteration is a type of poetry where:**

    (Average Rigor) (Skill 1.3)

    A. The words used (*Pow, Zap, etc...*) evoke meaning by their sounds.

    B. The final consonant sounds are the same, but the vowels are different.

    C. The vowel sound within a word matches the vowel sound within a   nearby word, but the surrounding consonant sounds are different (Ex. *J*une and T*une*).

    D. The initial sound of a word, beginning in either a consonant of a vowel, in repeated in succession (Ex. *P*eople who *p*en *p*oetry).

5. **Which of the following are examples of research materials that are available to use?**

    (Easy) (Skill 1.4)

    A. Encyclopedias

    B. Internet search engines

    C. Card catalogues

    D. All of the above

6. **Which of the following is NOT a strategy of teaching reading comprehension?**

    (Rigorous) (Skill 2.1)

    A. Summarization

    B. Utilizing graphic organizers

    C. Manipulating sounds

    D. Having students generate questions

7. **All of the following are examples of transitional phrases EXCEPT:**

    (Easy) (Skill 2.2)

    A. The

    B. However

    C. Furthermore

    D. Although

8. **Which aspect of language is innate?**

   (Rigorous) (Skill 3.1)

   A. Biological capability to articulate sounds understood by other humans

   B. Cognitive ability to create syntactical structures

   C. Capacity for using semantics to convey meaning in a social environment

   D. Ability to vary inflections and accents

9. **Which of the following indicates that a student is a fluent reader?**

   (Easy) (Skill 3.1)

   A. Reads texts with expression or prosody

   B. Reads word-to-word and haltingly

   C. Must intentionally decode a majority of the words

   D. In a writing assignment, sentences are poorly-organized structurally

10. **Which of the following is NOT a characteristic of a fable?**

    (Average Rigor) (Skill 3.2)

    A. Animals that feel and talk like humans

    B. Happy solutions to human dilemmas

    C. Teaches a moral or standard for behavior

    D. Illustrates specific peoples or groups without directly naming them

11. **Which of the following is a ballad?**

    (Average Rigor) (Skill 3.2)

    A. "The Knight's Tale"

    B. *Julius Ceasar*

    C. *Paradise Lost*

    D. "The Rime of the Ancient Mariner"

12. **Which of the following is an epic?**

(Rigor) (Skill 3.2)

A. *On the Choice of Books*

B. *The Faerie Queene*

C. *Northanger Abbey*

D. *A Doll's House*

13. **The children's literature genre came into its own in the:**

(Average Rigor) (Skill 3.2)

A. Seventeenth century

B. Eighteenth century

C. Nineteenth century

D. Twentieth century

14. **To decode is to:**

(Easy) (Skill 3.3)

A. Construct meaning

B. Sound out a printed sequence of letters

C. Use a special code to decipher a message

D. None of the above

15. **To encode means that you:**

(Easy) (Skill 3.3)

A. Decode a second time

B. Construct meaning from a code

C. Change message into symbols

D. None of the above

16. **All of the following are true about phonological awareness EXCEPT?**

(Average Rigor) (Skill 3.3)

A. It may involve print.

B. It is a prerequisite for spelling and phonics.

C. Development of phonological skills may begin during the pre-kindergarten years.

D. Students have the ability to recognize the sounds of spoken language.

17. **Effective reading and comprehension requires:**

(Rigorous) (Skill 3.3)

A. Encoding

B. Decoding

C. Both A and B

D. Neither A nor B

18. **Which of the following is an opinion?**

    (Easy) (Skill 3.4)

    A. The sky is blue.

    B. Albany is the capital of New York State.

    C. A dog is the best pet to have.

    D. Humans breathe.

19. **Which of the following is a fact?**

    (Easy) (Skill 3.4)

    A. It's going to rain.

    B. John is a liar.

    C. Joe said he believes John is a liar.

    D. The world is going to the dogs.

20. **A sixth-grade science teacher has given her class a paper to read on the relationship between food and weight gain. The writing contains signal words such as "because," "consequently," "this is how," and "due to." This paper has which text structure?**

    (Average Rigor) (Skill 3.4)

    A. Cause & effect

    B. Compare & contrast

    C. Description

    D. Sequencing

21. **Which of the following is a valid conclusion?**

    (Rigorous) (Skill 3.4)

    A. Based on the evidence, I believe John Jones stole the car.

    B. I suspect that John Jones stole the car.

    C. John Jones looks guilty, so he must have stolen the car.

    D. Of the two suspects, John Jones cynical expression makes me think he's guilty.

22. **All of the following are correctly capitalized EXCEPT:**

    (Rigorous) (Skill 4.1)

    A. Queen Elizabeth

    B. Congressman McKay

    C. commander Alger

    D. the president of the United States

23. **The arrangement and relationship of words in sentences or sentence structure best describes:**

    (Average Rigor) (Skill 4.2)

    A. Style

    B. Discourse

    C. Thesis

    D. Syntax

24. **Orthography is:**

    (Rigorous) (Skill 4.3)

    A. The study of word structure.

    B. A method of representing a spoken language through the use of written symbols.

    C. The complete set of related word-forms associated with a given lexeme.

    D. A process of word-formation that involves combining complete word-forms into a single compound form.

25. **If a student has a poor vocabulary, the teacher should recommend that:**

    (Average Rigor) (Skill 4.5)

    A. The student read newspapers, magazines, and books on a regular basis.

    B. The student enroll in a Latin class.

    C. The student write the words repetitively after looking them up in a dictionary.

    D. The student use a thesaurus to locate synonyms and incorporate them into his/her vocabulary.

26. A simile is:

    (Average Rigor) (Skill 4.6)

    A. A direct comparison between two things.

    B. An indirect comparison between two things.

    C. When human characteristics are applied to things that are not human, such as animals.

    D. Deliberate exaggeration for effect or comic effect.

27. A student has written a paper with the following characteristics: written in first person; characters, setting, and plot; some dialogue; and events organized in chronological sequence with some flashbacks. In what genre has the student written?

    (Easy) (Skill 5.1)

    A. Expository writing

    B. Narrative writing

    C. Persuasive writing

    D. Technical writing

28. The use of steroids in professional baseball is ruining the sport. Which of the following does NOT support this thesis?

    (Rigorous) (Skill 5.1)

    A. Steroids are performance enhancers and give players who take steroids an unfair advantage.

    B. Steroids are physically harmful to the players.

    C. Steroids make baseball more exciting because more players hit home runs.

    D. Kids in high school and college are taking steroids because they want to give themselves a better shot to make it into the major leagues.

29. Which of the following is NOT a technique of prewriting?

    (Average Rigor) (Skill 5.2)

    A. Clustering

    B. Listing

    C. Brainstorming

    D. Proofreading

30. When students present information orally, they should keep the following in mind:

(Average Rigor) (Skill 5.4)

A. Volume

B. Pace

C. Body language

D. All of the above

31. Deductive reasoning is:

(Average Rigor) (Skill 6.1)

A. The process of finding a pattern from a group of examples.

B. The process of arriving at a conclusion based on other statements that are known to be true.

C. Both A and B

D. Neither A nor B

32. Find the inverse of the following statement: If I like dogs, then I do not like cats.

(Rigorous) (Skill 6.4)

A. If I like dogs, then I do like cats.

B. If I like cats, then I like dogs.

C. If I like cats, then I do not like dogs.

D. If I do not like dogs, then I like cats.

33. Find the converse of the following statement: If I like math, then I do not like science.

(Average Rigor) (Skill 6.4)

A. If I do not like science, then I like math.

B. If I like math, then I do not like science.

C. If I do not like math, then I do not like science.

D. If I like math, then I do not like science.

34. Which of the following is an irrational number?

(Rigorous) (Skill 7.1)

A. .36262626262…

B. 4

C. 8.2

D. -5

35. The number "0" is a member of all the following groups of numbers EXCEPT:

(Rigorous) (Skill 7.1)

A. Whole numbers

B. Real numbers

C. Natural numbers

D. Integers

36. The order of mathematical operations is done in the following order:

(Average Rigor) (Skill 7.2)

A. Simplify inside grouping characters such as parentheses, brackets, square root, fraction bar, etc.; multiply out expressions with exponents; do multiplication or division, from left to right; do addition or subtraction, from left to right.

B. Do multiplication or division, from left to right; simplify inside grouping characters such as parentheses, brackets, square root, fraction bar, etc.; multiply out expressions with exponents; do addition or subtraction, from left to right.

C. Simplify inside grouping characters such as parentheses, brackets, square root, fraction bar, etc.; do addition or subtraction, from left to right; multiply out expressions with exponents; do multiplication or division, from left to right.

D. None of the above

37. An item that sells for $375 is put on sale at $120. What is the percent of decrease?

    (Average Rigor) (Skill 7.4)

    A. 25%

    B. 28%

    C. 68%

    D. 34%

38. 4,087,361 What number represents the ten-thousandths place?

    (Easy) (Skill 7.6)

    A. 4

    B. 6

    C. 0

    D. 8

39. 0.16 is equivalent to:

    (Average Rigor) (Skill 7.7)

    A. 16

    B. 16%

    C. 16/10

    D. 1.6

40. What is the greatest common factor of 16, 28, and 36?

    (Easy) (Skill 7.8)

    A. 2

    B. 4

    C. 8

    D. 16

41. What is the least common multiple of 18 and 24?

    (Easy) (Skill 7.8)

    A. 48

    B. 72

    C. 108

    D. 64

42. Which is the better buy, 10 items for $2.56 or 8 items for $2.46?

    (Rigorous) (Skill 7.9)

    A. 10 items for $2.56

    B. 8 items for $2.46

    C. Both are equally good deals

    D. There is no better buy.

43. Two mathematics classes have a total of 410 students. The 8:00 am class has 40 more than the 10:00 am class. How many students are in the 10:00 am class?

(Average rigor) (Skill 7.9)

A. 123.3

B. 370

C. 185

D. 330

44. What is the absolute value of the number -5?

(Rigorous) (Skill 7.12)

A. -5

B. 10

C. 1/5

D. 5

45. Which of the following is an example of the associative property?

(Average Rigor) (Skill 8.2)

A. a (b + c) = ab + bc

B. a + 0 = a

C. (a + b) + c = a + (b + c)

D. a + b = b + a

46. Two kids are selling lemonade on the side of the road and want to raise at least $320. If the materials needed (lemons, pitcher, table, etc.) to run a lemonade stand costs $15, how many glasses of lemonade will they need to sell if each glass costs $6?

(Rigorous) (Skill 8.6)

A. 210 glasses

B. 61 glasses

C. 74 glasses

D. 53 glasses

47. 3x + 2y = 12

12x + 8y = 15

Solve for x and y.

(Average Rigor) (Skill 8.6)

A. All real numbers

B. x = 4, y = 4

C. x = 2, y = -1

D. None of the above

48. **Three-dimensional figures in geometry are called:**

   (Rigorous) (Skill 9.1)

   A. Solids

   B. Cubes

   C. Polygons

   D. Blocks

49. **If a right triangle has legs with the measurements of 3 cm and 4 cm, what is the measure of the hypotenuse?**

   (Average Rigor) (Skill 9.2)

   A. 6 cm

   B. 1 cm

   C. 7 cm

   D. 5 cm

50. **If a right triangle has a hypotenuse of 10 cm and one leg of 6 cm, what is the measure of the other leg?**

   (Average Rigor) (Skill 9.2)

   A. 7 cm

   B. 5 cm

   C. 8 cm

   D. 9 cm

51. **What is a translation?**

   (Rigorous) (Skill 9.3)

   A. To turn a figure around a fixed point.

   B. The object has the same shape and same size, but figures face in different directions.

   C. To "slide" an object a fixed distance in a given direction.

   D. The transformation that "shrinks" or "makes it bigger."

52. **A tetrahedron consists of the following:**

   (Rigorous) (Skill 9.5)

   A. 4 equilateral triangles

   B. 6 squares

   C. 12 regular pentagons

   D. 8 equilateral triangles

53. **What measures could be used to report the distance traveled in walking around a track?**

    (Easy) (Skill 9.6)

    A. Degrees

    B. Square meters

    C. Kilometers

    D. Cubic feet

54. **3 km is equivalent to:**

    (Easy) (Skill 9.6)

    A. 300 cm

    B. 300 m

    C. 3000 cm

    D. 3000 m

55. **The mass of a cookie is closest to:**

    (Easy) (Skill 9.6)

    A. 0.5 kg

    B. 0.5 grams

    C. 15 grams

    D. 1.5 grams

56. **If the radius of a right circular cylinder is doubled, how does its volume change?**

    (Rigorous) (Skill 9.6)

    A. No change

    B. Also is doubled

    C. Four times the original

    D. Pi times the original

57. **10 cups = _____ quarts?**

    (Average Rigor) (Skill 9.6)

    A. 2 quarts

    B. 1 quart

    C. 3.5 quarts

    D. 2.5 quarts

58. **In similar polygons, if the perimeters are in a ratio of x:y, the sides are in the ratio of?**

    (Average Rigor) (Skill 9.6)

    A. m : y

    B. $x^2 : y^2$

    C. 2x : y

    D. 1/2x : y

59. **Find the area of a rectangle if you know that the base is 8 cm and the diagonal of the rectangle is 8.5 cm:**

    (Rigorous) (Skill 9.8)

    A. 24 cm²

    B. 30 cm²

    C. 18.9 cm²

    D. 24 cm

60. **The volume is:**

    (Easy) (Skill 9.8)

    A. Area of the faces excluding the bases

    B. Total area of all the faces, including the bases

    C. The number of cubic units in a solid

    D. The measure around the object

61. **What is the area of a square whose side is 13 feet?**

    (Rigorous) (Skill 9.8)

    A. 169 feet

    B. 169 square feet

    C. 52 feet

    D. 52 square feet

62. **A boat travels 30 miles upstream in three hours. It makes the return trip in one and a half hours. What is the speed of the boat in still water?**

    (Average Rigor) (Skill 9.9)

    A. 10 mph

    B. 15 mph

    C. 20 mph

    D. 30 mph

63. **All of the following are examples of obtuse angles EXCEPT:**

    (Average Rigor) (Skill 9.10)

    A. 110 degrees

    B. 90 degrees

    C. 135 degrees

    D. 91 degrees

64. Given the formula d=rt, (where d = distance, r = rate, and t = time), calculate the time required for a vehicle to travel 585 miles at a rate of 65 miles per hour.

(Average Rigor) (Skill 9.11)

A. 8.5 hours

B. 6.5 hours

C. 9.5 hours

D. 9 hours

65. Given a drawer with 5 black socks, 3 blue socks, and 2 red socks, what is the probability that you will draw two black socks in two draws in a dark room?

(Rigorous) (Skill 10.4)

A. 2/9

B. 1/4

C. 17/18

D. 1/18

66. Suppose you have a bag of marbles that contains 2 red marbles, 5 blue marbles, and 3 green marbles. If you replace the first marble chosen, what is the probability you will choose 2 green marbles in a row?

(Average Rigor) (Skill 10.4)

A. 2/5

B. 9/100

C. 9/10

D. 3/5

67. Suppose you have a bag of marbles that contains 4 red marbles, 6 blue marbles, and 2 green marbles. If you do not replace the first marble chosen, what is the probability you will choose 2 blue marbles in a row?

(Rigorous) (Skill 10.4)

A. 36/144

B. 1/4

C. 5/22

D. 30/132

68. In probability, the sample space represents:

(Average Rigor) (Skill 10.5)

A. An outcome to an experiment

B. A list of all possible outcomes of an experiment.

C. The amount of times you must flip a coin.

D. The amount of room needed to conduct an experiment.

69. Permutation is:

(Rigorous) (Skill 10.5)

A. The number of possible arrangements, without repetition, where order of selection is not important.

B. The number of possible arrangements, with repetition, where order of selection is not important

C. The number of possible arrangements of items, without repetition, where order of selection is important.

D. The number of possible arrangements of items, with repetition, where order of selection is important.

70. If given the question "How many different ways can you arrange a committee of three people?" what type of probability is this?

(Rigorous) (Skill 10.5)

A. Sample space

B. Permutation

C. Fundamental counting principle

D. Combination

71. Corporate salaries are listed for several employees. Which would be the best measure of central tendency?

(Average Rigor) (Skill 10.10)

$24,000	$24,000
$26,000	$28,000
$30,000	$120,000

A. Mean

B. Median

C. Mode

D. No difference

72. **Given the following numbers, find the median:**

    (Rigorous) (Skill 10.10)

    25, 18, 16, 45, 10, 27

    A. 21.5

    B. 25

    C. 18

    D. There is no median

73. **Given the following numbers, find the mode:**

    (Rigorous) (Skill 10.10)

    14, 5, 16, 7, 18, 15, 3

    A. 5

    B. 14

    C. 18

    D. There is no mode

74. **Which landform supports the majority of the world's people?**

    (Rigorous) (Skill 11.2)

    A. Mountains

    B. Plains

    C. Plateaus

    D. Hills

75. **All of the following are oceans EXCEPT:**

    (Easy) (Skill 11.2)

    A. Pacific

    B. Atlantic

    C. Mediterranean

    D. Indian

76. **The theory of "sea floor spreading" explains** _____

    (Average Rigor) (Skill 11.2)

    A. The shapes of the continents.

    B. How continents got named.

    C. How continents move apart.

    D. How continents sink to become part of the ocean floor.

77. **Which term best defines the customs, traditions, and arts of a group of people?**

    (Easy) (Skill 11.3)

    A. Culture

    B. Democracy

    C. Interdependence

    D. Geography

78. All of the following are natural resources EXCEPT:

(Average Rigor) (Skill 11.4)

A. Trees

B. Coal

C. Fish

D. Paper

79. All of the following are examples of why the first known civilizations developed by water EXCEPT:

(Average Rigor) (Skill 12.1)

A. Rivers provided water, which both the humans and animals needs.

B. Rivers allowed the settlers to travel so they could trade goods.

C. The rivers attracted animals so hunters had a continuous supply of food.

D. The rivers overflowed, which left a deposit of very rich soil.

80. Which civilization invented the wheel?

(Rigorous) (Skill 12.1)

A. Egyptians

B. Romans

C. Assyrians

D. Sumerians

81. What is the "Pax Romana"?

(Rigorous) (Skill 12.1)

A. Long period of peace enabling free travel and trade, spreading people, cultures, goods, and ideas all over the world

B. A period of war where the Romans expanded their empire

C. The Roman government

D. A time where the government was over-ruled

82. Who wrote the *Iliad* and the *Odyssey*?

(Rigorous) (Skill 12.2)

A. Aristotle

B. Homer

C. Pythagoras

D. Herodotus

83. The "divine right" of kings was the key political characteristic of:

(Rigorous) (Skill 12.4)

A. The Age of Absolutism

B. The Age of Reason

C. The Age of Feudalism

D. The Age of Despotism

84. Which one of the following would not be considered a result of World War II?

(Average Rigor) (Skill 12.6)

A. Economic depressions and slow resumption of trade and financial aid

B. Western Europe was no longer the center of world power

C. The beginnings of new power struggles not only in Europe but in Asia as well

D. Territorial and boundary changes for many nations, especially in Europe

85. The cold war involved which two countries who both emerged as world powers?

(Rigorous) (Skill 12.6)

A. China and Japan

B. United States and the Soviet Union

C. England and Brazil

D. Afghanistan and the United States

86. What was the long-term importance of the Mayflower Compact?

(Rigorous) (Skill 13.1)

A. It established the foundation of all later agreements with the Native peoples.

B. It established freedom of religion in the original English colonies.

C. It ended the war in Europe between Spain, France and England.

D. It established a model of small, town-based government that was adopted throughout the New England colonies.

87. **Which one of the following is not a reason why Europeans came to the New World?**

    (Average Rigor) (Skill 13.1)

    A. To find resources in order to increase wealth.

    B. To establish trade.

    C. To increase a ruler's power and importance.

    D. To spread Christianity.

88. **The year 1619 was memorable for the colony of Virginia. Three important events occurred, resulting in lasting effects on U.S. history. Which one of the following is not one of events?**

    (Rigorous) (Skill 13.1)

    A. Twenty African slaves arrived.

    B. The London Company granted the colony a charter making it independent.

    C. The colonists were given the right by the London Company to govern themselves through representative government in the Virginia House of Burgesses.

    D. The London Company sent to the colony 60 women who were quickly married, establishing families and stability in the colony.

89. **The belief that the United States should control all of North America was called:**

    (Easy) (Skill 13.1)

    A. Westward Expansion

    B. Pan Americanism

    C. Manifest Destiny

    D. Nationalism

90. **All of the following were causes of the American Revolution EXCEPT:**

(Average Rigor) (Skill 13.2)

A. The Tea Act of 1773

B. The Stamp Act

C. The colonists were forced to house English troops

D. The colonists wanted more schools

91. **The English placed taxes on the colonies for two reasons, what were they?**

(Easy) (Skill 13.2)

A. To generate revenue

B. To gain control over the colonists

C. A only

D. Both A and B

92. **The first real party organization developed soon after the inauguration of Washington as President. It included which of the following:**

(Rigorous) (Skill 13.3)

A. Democrats

B. Republicans

C. Nationalists

D. All of the above

93. **The Westward expansion occurred for a number of reasons; however, the most important reason was:**

(Average Rigor) (Skill 13.3)

A. Colonization

B. Slavery

C. Independence

D. Economics

94. During the 1920s, the United States almost completely stopped all immigration. One of the reasons was:

(Rigorous) (Skill 13.3)

A. Plentiful, cheap unskilled labor was no longer needed by industrialists

B. War debts from World War I made it difficult to render financial assistance

C. European nations were reluctant to allow people to leave since there was a need to rebuild populations and economic stability

D. The United States did not become a member of the League of Nations

95. Which war took the most American lives in American history?

(Easy) (Skill 13.3)

A. The Civil War

B. The Revolutionary War

C. World War I

D. World War II

96. The economic collapse of the United States in 1929 is known as the:

(Easy) (Skill 13.4)

A. Cold War

B. New Deal

C. Unhappy times

D. Great Depression

97. A communistic government is:

(Average Rigor) (Skill 14.2)

A. A government that is ruled by one individual or a small group of individuals.

B. A government with a legislature, usually involving a multiplicity of political parties and often coalition politics.

C. A political system characterized by the ideology of class conflict and revolution and that the product of all the people is shared by each and every person.

D. A political system that values conflict and revolution with a central political control that allows for private ownership of the means of production.

98. **The Bill of Rights consists of which Amendments?**

    (Average Rigor) (Skill 14.3)

    A. Amendments 1-5

    B. Amendments 1-10

    C. Amendments 1 and 2

    D. Amendments 1-22

99. **All of the following are rights that are granted by the Bill of Rights EXCEPT:**

    (Rigorous) (Skill 14.4)

    A. Freedom of religion.

    B. No cruel or unusual punishment allowed.

    C. Right for a free education.

    D. Security from the quartering of troops in homes.

100. **Social skills and values developed by activity include all of the following EXCEPT:**

     (Average Rigor) (Skill 15.1)

     A. Winning at all costs

     B. Making judgments in groups

     C. Communicating and cooperating

     D. Respecting rules and property

101. **The "sense of who one is" in a society refers to:**

     (Average Rigor) (Skill 15.1)

     A. Cultural identity

     B. Population identity

     C. Anthropology

     D. Cultural bias

102. **Activities that enhance team socialization include all of the following EXCEPT:**

     (Easy) (Skill 15.2)

     A. Basketball

     B. Soccer

     C. Golf

     D. Volleyball

103. **Cultural diffusion is:**

(Rigorous) (Skill 15.2)

A. The process that individuals and societies go through in changing their behavior and organization to cope with social, economic and environmental pressures.

B. The complete disappearance of a culture.

C. The exchange or adoption of cultural features when two cultures come into regular direct contact.

D. The movement of cultural ideas or materials between populations independent of the movement of those populations.

104. **An economist might engage in which of the following activities?**

(Easy) (Skill 16.2)

A. An observation of the historical effects of a nation's banking practices

B. The application of a statistical test to a series of data

C. Introduction of an experiment factor into a specified population to measure the effect of the factor

D. An economist might engage in all of these

105. **The following are factors of production EXCEPT:**

(Rigorous) (Skill 16.3)

A. Labor

B. Entrepreneurship

C. Land

D. Income

106. **The most abundant gas in the atmosphere is:**

    (Rigorous) (Skill 17.1)

    A. Oxygen

    B. Nitrogen

    C. Carbon dioxide

    D. Methane

107. **Which of the following types of rock are made from magma?**

    (Rigorous) (Skill 17.2)

    A. Fossils

    B. Sedimentary

    C. Metamorphic

    D. Igneous

108. **Which of the following is the best definition for 'meteorite'?**

    (Rigorous) (Skill 17.4)

    A. A meteorite is a mineral composed of mica and feldspar.

    B. A meteorite is material from outer space that has struck the earth's surface.

    C. A meteorite is an element that has properties of both metals and nonmetals.

    D. A meteorite is a very small unit of length measurement.

109. **What cell organelle contains the cell's stored food?**

    (Rigorous) (Skill 18.1)

    A. Vacuoles

    B. Golgi Apparatus

    C. Ribosome

    D. Lysosome

110. **Identify the correct sequence of organization of living things from lower to higher order:**

    (Rigorous) (Skill 18.1)

    A. Cell, Organelle, Organ, Tissue, System, Organism

    B. Cell, Tissue, Organ, Organelle, System, Organism

    C. Organelle, Cell, Tissue, Organ, System, Organism

    D. Organelle, Tissue, Cell, Organ, System, Organism

111. **Which kingdom is comprised of organisms made of one cell with no nuclear membrane?**

    (Average Rigor) (Skill 18.1)

    A. Monera

    B. Protista

    C. Fungi

    D. Algae

112. **Heterozygous refers to:**

    Average Rigor) (Skill 18.2)

    A. Having 2 dominant genes

    B. Having 2 recessive genes

    C. Having neither a recessive nor a dominant gene

    D. Having 1 recessive gene and 1 dominant gene

113. **Which of the following is the most accurate definition of a nonrenewable resource?**

    (Average Rigor) (Skill 18.5)

    A. A nonrenewable resource is never replaces once used.

    B. A nonrenewable resource is replaced on a timescale that is very long relative to human life spans.

    C. A nonrenewable resource is a resource that can only be manufactured by humans.

    D. A nonrenewable resource is a species that has already become extinct.

114. **The following are examples of chemical reactions EXCEPT:**

(Average Rigor) (Skill 19.1)

A. Melting ice into water

B. Dissolving a seltzer tablet in water

C. Using a fire-cracker

D. Burning a piece of plastic

115. **The transfer of heat by electromagnetic waves is called _____:**

(Easy) (Skill 19.2)

A. Conduction

B. Convection

C. Phase change

D. Radiation

116. **Which is the correct order of methodology?**

(Average Rigor) (Skill 20.2)

1. Collecting data

2. Planning a controlled experiment

3. Drawing a conclusion

4. Hypothesizing a result

5. Re-visiting a hypothesis to answer a question

A. 1,2,3,4,5

B. 4,2,1,3,5

C. 4,5,1,3,2

D. 1,3,4,5,2

117. **In an experiment measuring the growth of bacteria at different temperatures, what is the independent variable?**

(Rigorous) (Skill 22.3)

A. Number of bacteria

B. Growth rate of bacteria

C. Temperature

D. Size of bacteria

118. All of the following professions are classified under 'earth sciences' EXCEPT:

(Average Rigor) (Skill 22.4)

A. Geologist

B. Meteorologist

C. Seismologist

D. Biochemist

119. Which of the following is a correct explanation for scientific evolution?

(Rigorous) (Skill 23.1)

A. Giraffes need to reach higher leaves to eat, so their necks stretch. The giraffe babies are then born with longer necks. Eventually, there are more long-necked giraffes in the population.

B. Giraffes with longer necks are able to reach more leaves, so they eat more and have more babies than other giraffes. Eventually, there are more long-necked giraffes in the population.

C. Giraffes want to reach higher for leaves to eat, so they release enzymes into their bloodstream, which in turn causes fetal development of longer-necked giraffes. Eventually, there are more long-necked giraffes in the population.

D. Giraffes with long necks are more attractive to other giraffes, so they get the best mating partners and have more babies. Eventually, there are more long-necked giraffes in the population.

120. The advancement of understanding in dealing with human beings has led to a number of interdisciplinary areas. Which of the following interdisciplinary studies would NOT be considered under the social sciences?

(Average Rigor) (Skill 23.3)

A. Molecular biophysics

B. Peace studies

C. African-American studies

D. Cartographic information studies

Answer Key

1.	C	31.	C	61.	B	91.	D
2.	D	32.	D	62.	B	92.	D
3.	B	33.	A	63.	B	93.	D
4.	D	34.	A	64.	D	94.	A
5.	D	35.	C	65.	A	95.	A
6.	C	36.	A	66.	B	96.	D
7.	A	37.	C	67.	C	97.	C
8.	A	38.	D	68.	B	98.	B
9.	A	39.	B	69.	C	99.	C
10.	D	40.	B	70.	D	100.	A
11.	D	41.	B	71.	A	101.	A
12.	B	42.	A	72.	A	102.	C
13.	B	43.	C	73.	D	103.	D
14.	A	44.	D	74.	B	104.	D
15.	C	45.	C	75.	C	105.	D
16.	A	46.	B	76.	C	106.	B
17.	C	47.	D	77.	A	107.	D
18.	C	48.	A	78.	D	108.	B
19.	C	49.	D	79.	B	109.	A
20.	A	50.	C	80.	D	110.	C
21.	A	51.	C	81.	A	111.	A
22.	C	52.	A	82.	B	112.	D
23.	D	53.	C	83.	A	113.	B
24.	B	54.	D	84.	A	114.	A
25.	A	55.	C	85.	B	115.	D
26.	A	56.	C	86.	D	116.	B
27.	B	57.	D	87.	B	117.	C
28.	C	58.	A	88.	B	118.	D
29.	D	59.	A	89.	C	119.	B
30.	D	60.	C	90.	D	120.	A

Rigor Table

	Easy	Average Rigor	Rigorous
	%20	**%40**	**%40**
Question #	5, 7, 9, 14, 15, 18, 19, 27, 38, 40, 41, 53, 54, 55, 60, 75, 77, 89, 91, 95, 96, 102, 104, 115	2, 4, 10, 11, 13, 16, 20, 23, 25, 26, 29, 30, 31, 33, 36, 37, 39, 43, 45, 47, 49, 50, 57, 58, 62, 63, 64, 66, 68, 71, 76, 78, 79, 84, 87, 90, 93, 97, 98, 100, 101, 111, 112, 113, 114, 116, 118, 120	1, 3, 6, 8, 12, 17, 21, 22, 24, 28, 32, 34, 35, 42, 44, 46, 48, 51, 52, 56, 59, 61, 65, 67, 69, 70, 72, 73, 74, 80, 81, 82, 83, 85, 86, 88, 92, 94, 99, 103, 105, 106, 107, 108, 109, 110, 117, 119

Rationales with Sample Questions

1.   **All of the following are common types of narratives EXCEPT:**

(Rigorous) (Skill 1.1)

A. Legends

B. Short stories

C. Poems

D. Memoirs

Answer: C

Poems

Poems are not narratives; however legends, short stories, and memoirs are.

2.   **Which of the following is an example of nonfiction literature?**

(Average Rigor) (Skill 1.2)

A. Letters

B. Biographies

C. Journals

D. All of the above

Answer: D

All of the above

All of these are examples of nonfiction literature.

3. **Which is NOT a true statement concerning an author's literary tone?**

(Rigorous) (Skill 1.2)

A. Tone is partly revealed through the selection of details.

B. Tone is the expression of the author's attitude toward his/her subject.

C. Tone in literature is usually satiric or angry.

D. Tone in literature corresponds to the tone of voice a speaker uses.

Answer: B

Tone in literature corresponds to the tone of voice a speaker uses.

Tone in literature conveys a mood and can be as varied as the tone of voice of a speaker (e.g., sad, nostalgic, whimsical, angry, formal, intimate, satirical, sentimental, etc).

4. **Alliteration is a type of poetry where:**

(Average Rigor) (Skill 1.3)

A. The words used (*Pow, Zap,* etc...) evoke meaning by their sounds.

B. The final consonant sounds are the same, but the vowels are different.

C. The vowel sound within a word matches the vowel sound within a nearby word, but the surrounding consonant sounds are different (Ex. *June* and *Tune*).

D. The initial sound of a word, beginning in either a consonant of a vowel, in repeated in succession (Ex. *People* who *pen poetry*).

Answer: D

The initial sound of a word, beginning in either a consonant of a vowel, in repeated in succession (Ex. *People* who *pen poetry*).

Alliteration is the repetition of a consonant or a vowel within poetry.

5. **Which of the following are examples of research materials that are available to use?**

(Easy) (Skill 1.4)

A. Encyclopedias

B. Internet search engines

C. Card catalogues

D. All of the above

Answer: D

All of the above

Encyclopedias, Internet search engines (Google, aol,), and card catalogues can all be used for research purposes.

6. **Which of the following is NOT a strategy of teaching reading comprehension?**

(Rigorous) (Skill 2.1)

A. Summarization

B. Utilizing graphic organizers

C. Manipulating sounds

D. Having students generate questions

Answer: C

Manipulating sounds

Comprehension simply means that the reader can ascribe meaning to text. Teachers can use many strategies to teach comprehension, including questioning, asking students to paraphrase or summarize, utilizing graphic organizers, and focusing on mental images.

7. **All of the following are examples of transitional phrases EXCEPT:**

(Easy) (Skill 2.2)

A. The

B. However

C. Furthermore

D. Although

Answer: A

The

The word "the" is not a traditional word. "However," "furthermore," and "although" are all transitional words.

8. **Which aspect of language is innate?**

(Rigorous) (Skill 3.1)

A. Biological capability to articulate sounds understood by other humans

B. Cognitive ability to create syntactical structures

C. Capacity for using semantics to convey meaning in a social environment

D. Ability to vary inflections and accents

Answer: A

Biological capability to articulate sounds understood by other humans

Language ability is innate, and the biological capability to produce sounds lets children learn semantics and syntactical structures through trial and error. Linguists agree that language is a vocal system of word symbols that enable a human to communicate his/her feelings, thoughts, and desires to other human beings.

9. **Which of the following indicates that a student is a fluent reader?**

   (Easy) (Skill 3.1)

   A. Reads texts with expression or prosody

   B. Reads word-to-word and haltingly

   C. Must intentionally decode a majority of the words

   D. In a writing assignment, sentences are poorly-organized structurally

   Answer: A

Reads texts with expression or prosody.

The teacher should listen to the children read aloud, but there are also clues to reading levels in their writing.

10. **Which of the following is NOT a characteristic of a fable?**

    (Average Rigor) (Skill 3.2)

    A. Animals that feel and talk like humans

    B. Happy solutions to human dilemmas

    C. Teaches a moral or standard for behavior

    D. Illustrates specific peoples or groups without directly naming them

    Answer: D

Illustrates specific people or groups without directly naming them.

A fable is a short tale with animals, humans, gods, or even inanimate objects as characters. Fables often conclude with a moral, delivered in the form of an epigram (a short, witty, and ingenious statement in verse). Fables are among the oldest forms of writing in human history: it appears in Egyptian papyri of c 1500 BCE. The most famous fables are those of Aesop, a Greek slave living in about 600 BCE. In India, the Pantchatantra appeared in the third century. The most famous modern fables are those of seventeenth century French poet Jean de La Fontaine.

11. **Which of the following is a ballad?**

    (Average Rigor) (Skill 3.2)

    A. "The Knight's Tale"

    B. *Julius Caesar*

    C. *Paradise Lost*

    D. "The Rime of the Ancient Mariner"

    Answer: D

"The Rime of the Ancient Mariner"

"The Knight's Tale" is a Romantic poem from the longer *Canterbury Tales* by Chaucer. *Julius Caesar* is a Shakespearian play. *Paradise Lost* is an epic poem in blank verse. A ballad is an *in media res* story told or sung, usually in verse and accompanied by music, and usually with a refrain. Typically, ballads are based on folk stories

12. **Which of the following is an epic?**

    (Rigor) (Skill 3.2)

    A. *On the Choice of Books*

    B. *The Faerie Queene*

    C. *Northanger Abbey*

    D. *A Doll's House*

    Answer: B

The Faerie Queene

An epic is a long poem, usually of book length, reflecting the values of the society in which it was produced. *On the Choice of Books* is an essay by Thomas Carlyle. *Northanger Abbey* is a novel written by Jane Austen, and *A Doll's House* is a play written by Henrik Ibsen.

13. **The children's literature genre came into its own in the:**

    (Average Rigor) (Skill 3.2)

    A. Seventeenth century

    B. Eighteenth century

    C. Nineteenth century

    D. Twentieth century

    Answer: B

Eighteenth century

In the seventeenth Century, authors such as Jean de La Fontaine and his *Fables*, Pierre Perreault's *Tales*, Mme d'Aulnoye's Novels based on old folktales and Mme de Beaumont's *Beauty and the Beast* all created a children's literature genre. In England, Perreault was translated, and a work allegedly written by Oliver Smith, *The Renowned History of Little Goody Two Shoes*, also helped to establish children's literature in England.

14. **To decode is to:**

    (Easy) (Skill 3.3)

    A. Construct meaning

    B. Sound out a printed sequence of letters

    C. Use a special code to decipher a message

    D. None of the above

    Answer: A

Construct meaning

Word analysis (phonics or decoding) is the process readers use to figure out unfamiliar words based on written patterns. Decoding is the process of constructing meaning of an unknown word.

15. **To encode means that you:**

    (Easy) (Skill 3.3)

    A. Decode a second time

    B. Construct meaning from a code

    C. Change message into symbols

    D. None of the above

    Answer: C

Change messages into symbols

Encoding involves changing a message into symbols.

16. **All of the following are true about phonological awareness EXCEPT?**

    (Average Rigor) (Skill 3.3)

    A. It may involve print.

    B. It is a prerequisite for spelling and phonics.

    C. Development of phonological skills may begin during the prekindergarten years.

    D. Students have the ability to recognize the sounds of spoken language.

    Answer: A

It may involve print.

The key word here is EXCEPT, which will be highlighted in upper case on the test as well. All of the options are correct aspects of phonological awareness except the first one, A, because phonological awareness DOES NOT involve print.

17.   **Effective reading and comprehension requires:**

(Rigorous) (Skill 3.3)

A. Encoding

B. Decoding

C. Both A and B

D. Neither A nor B

Answer: C

Both A and B

Reading comprehension requires that the reader learn the code within which a message is written and be able to decode it to get the message.

18.   **Which of the following is an opinion?**

(Easy) (Skill 3.4)

A. The sky is blue.

B. Albany is the capital of New York State.

C. A dog is the best pet to have.

D. Humans breathe.

Answer: C

A dog is the best pet to have.

An opinion is a subjective evaluation based upon personal bias.

19. **Which of the following is a fact?**

(Easy) (Skill 3.4)

A. It's going to rain.

B. John is a liar.

C. Joe said he believes John is a liar.

D. The world is going to the dogs.

Answer: C

Joe said he believes John is a liar.

The only answer that is a fact is C. Joe said he believes John is a liar. It's a fact that he said it, even though what he said may not be a fact.

20. **A sixth-grade science teacher has given her class a paper to read on the relationship between food and weight gain. The writing contains signal words such as "because," "consequently," "this is how," and "due to." This paper has which text structure?**

(Average Rigor) (Skill 3.4)

A. Cause & effect

B. Compare & contrast

C. Description

D. Sequencing

Answer: A

Cause & effect

Cause and effect is the relationship between two things when one thing makes something else happen. Writers use this text structure to show order, inform, speculate, and change behavior. This text structure uses the process of identifying potential causes of a problem or issue in an orderly way.

21. Which of the following is a valid conclusion?

(Rigorous) (Skill 3.4)

A. Based on the evidence, I believe John Jones stole the car.

B. I suspect that John Jones stole the car.

C. John Jones looks guilty, so he must have stolen the car.

D. Of the two suspects, John Jones cynical expression makes me think he's guilty.

Answer: A

Based on the evidence, I believe John Jones stole the car.

Valid conclusions are based on evidence.

22. All of the following are correctly capitalized EXCEPT:

(Rigorous) (Skill 4.1)

A. Queen Elizabeth

B. Congressman McKay

C. commander Alger

D. the president of the United States

Answer: C

commander Alger

If the statement read "Alger the commander" then commander would not need to be capitalized; however, because commander is the title it is capitalized.

23. **The arrangement and relationship of words in sentences or sentence structure best describes:**

    (Average Rigor) (Skill 4.2)

    A. Style

    B. Discourse

    C. Thesis

    D. Syntax

    Answer: D

Syntax

Syntax is the grammatical structure of sentences.

24. **Orthography is:**

    (Rigorous) (Skill 4.3)

    A. The study of word structure.

    B. A method of representing a spoken language through the use of written symbols.

    C. The complete set of related word-forms associated with a given lexeme.

    D. A process of word-formation that involves combining complete word-forms into a single compound form.

    Answer: B

A method of representing a spoken language through the use of written symbols.

By definition, orthography is using written symbols to represent spoken language.

25. **If a student has a poor vocabulary, the teacher should recommend that:**

(Average Rigor) (Skill 4.5)

    A. The student read newspapers, magazines, and books on a regular basis.

    B. The student enroll in a Latin class.

    C. The student write the words repetitively after looking them up in a dictionary.

    D. The student use a thesaurus to locate synonyms and incorporate them into his/her vocabulary.

    Answer: A

The student should read newspapers, magazines, and books on a regular basis.

It is up to the teacher to help the student to choose reading material, but the student must be able to choose where he/she will search for the reading pleasure indispensable for enriching vocabulary.

26. **A simile is:**

(Average Rigor) (Skill 4.6)

    A. A direct comparison between two things.

    B. An indirect comparison between two things.

    C. When human characteristics are applied to things that are not human, such as animals.

    D. Deliberate exaggeration for effect or comic effect.

    Answer: A

A simile is when there is a direct comparison between two things. For example: "The boy was as red as a lobster."

27. **A student has written a paper with the following characteristics: written in first person; characters, setting, and plot; some dialogue; and events organized in chronological sequence with some flashbacks. In what genre has the student written?**

   (Easy) (Skill 5.1)

   A. Expository writing

   B. Narrative writing

   C. Persuasive writing

   D. Technical writing

   Answer: B

Narrative writing

These are all characteristics of narrative writing. Expository writing is intended to give information such as an explanation or directions; in it, the information is logically organized. Persuasive writing gives an opinion in an attempt to convince the reader that this point-of-view is valid. It also tries to persuade the reader to take a specific action. The goal of technical writing is to clearly communicate a select piece of information to a targeted reader or group of readers.

28.   "The use of steroids in professional baseball is ruining the sport."
       Which of the following does NOT support this thesis?

       (Rigorous) (Skill 5.1)

       A. Steroids are performance enhancers and give players who take
           steroids an unfair advantage.

       B. Steroids are physically harmful to the players.

       C. Steroids make baseball more exciting because more players hit home
           runs.

       D. Kids in high school and college are taking steroids because they want
           to give themselves a better shot to make it into the major leagues.

       Answer: C

Steroids make baseball more exciting because more players hit home runs.

The thesis speaks negatively about steroids in the sport of baseball, while choice
C is a positive statement about steroids. Because of this, choice C does not
support the thesis.

29.   Which of the following is NOT a technique of prewriting?

       (Average Rigor) (Skill 5.2)

       A. Clustering

       B. Listing

       C. Brainstorming

       D. Proofreading

       Answer: D

Proofreading

Proofreading cannot be a method of prewriting, since it is done on already written
texts only.

30. **When students present information orally, they should keep the following in mind:**

    (Average Rigor) (Skill 5.4)

    A. Volume

    B. Pace

    C. Body language

    D. All of the above

    Answer: D

All of the above

When students are presenting information orally, they should be aware of the volume of their voice, the pace in which they speak, and their body language.

31. **Deductive reasoning is:**

    (Average Rigor) (Skill 6.1)

    A. The process of finding a pattern from a group of examples.

    B. The process of arriving at a conclusion based on other statements that are known to be true.

    C. Both A and B

    D. Neither A nor B

    Answer: C

Both A and B

Deductive reasoning moves from a generalization or set of examples to a specific instance or solution.

32. **Find the inverse of the following statement: If I like dogs, then I do not like cats.**

    (Rigorous) (Skill 6.4)

    A. If I like dogs, then I do like cats.

    B. If I like cats, then I like dogs.

    C. If I like cats, then I do not like dogs.

    D. If I do not like dogs, then I like cats.

    Answer: D

If I do not like dogs, then I like cats.

When you take the inverse of the statement you negate both statements. By negating both statements you take the opposite of the original statement.

33. **Find the converse of the following statement: If I like math, then I do not like science.**

    (Average Rigor) (Skill 6.4)

    A. If I do not like science, then I like math.

    B. If I like math, then I do not like science.

    C. If I do not like math, then I do not like science.

    D. If I like math, then I do not like science.

    Answer: A

If I do not like science, then I like math.

When finding the converse of a statement you take the second part of the statement and reverse it with the first part of the statement. In other words, you reverse the statements.

34. **Which of the following is an irrational number?**

    (Rigorous) (Skill 7.1)

    A. .36262626262…

    B. 4

    C. 8.2

    D. -5

    Answer: A

.362626262626…

Irrational numbers are numbers that can not be made into a fraction. This number cannot be made into a fraction so it must be irrational.

35. **The number "0" is a member of all the following groups of numbers EXCEPT:**

    (Rigorous) (Skill 7.1)

    A. Whole numbers

    B. Real numbers

    C. Natural numbers

    D. Integers

    Answer: C

Natural numbers

The number zero is a member of the whole numbers, real numbers, and integers, but the natural numbers (also known as the counting numbers) start with the number one, not zero.

36. **The order of mathematical operations is done in the following order:**

   (Average Rigor) (Skill 7.2)

   A. Simplify inside grouping characters such as parentheses, brackets, square root, fraction bar, etc.; multiply out expressions with exponents; do multiplication or division, from left to right; do addition or subtraction, from left to right.

   B. Do multiplication or division, from left to right; simplify inside grouping characters such as parentheses, brackets, square root, fraction bar, etc.; multiply out expressions with exponents; do addition or subtraction, from left to right.

   C. Simplify inside grouping characters such as parentheses, brackets, square root, fraction bar, etc.; do addition or subtraction, from left to right; multiply out expressions with exponents; do multiplication or division, from left to right.

   D. None of the above

   Answer: A

Simplify inside grouping characters such as parentheses, brackets, square root, fraction bar, etc.; multiply out expressions with exponents; do multiplication or division, from left to right; do addition or subtraction, from left to right.

When facing a mathematical problem that requires all mathematical properties to be performed first, you do the math within the parentheses, brackets, square roots, or fraction bars. Then you multiply out expressions with exponents. Next, you do multiplication or division. Finally, you do addition or subtraction.

37.   An item that sells for $375 is put on sale at $120. What is the percent of decrease?

   (Average Rigor) (Skill 7.4)

   A. 25%

   B. 28%

   C. 68%

   D. 34%

   Answer: C

68%

In this problem you must set up a cross-multiplication problem. You begin by placing X/100 to represent the variable you are solving for and it being over 100% and then you place 120/375 to represent the new price over the original price. Once you cross multiply you will get 68, which is the percent decrease the item is selling for.

38.   4,087,361 What number represents the ten-thousandths place?

   (Easy) (Skill 7.6)

   A. 4

   B. 6

   C. 0

   D. 8

   Answer: D

8

The ten-thousandths place is the number 8 in this problem.

39. **0.16 is equivalent to:**

(Average Rigor) (Skill 7.7)

A. 16

B. 16%

C. 16/10

D. 1.6

Answer: B

16%

0.16 is equivalent to 16% because 16% is 16/100.

40. **What is the greatest common factor of 16, 28, and 36?**

(Easy) (Skill 7.8)

A. 2

B. 4

C. 8

D. 16

Answer: B

4

The smallest number in this set is 16; its factors are 1, 2, 4, 8, and 16. 16 is the largest factor, but it does not divide into 28 or 36. Neither does 8. 4 does factor into both 28 and 36.

41. **What is the least common multiple of 18 and 24?**

    (Easy) (Skill 7.8)

    A. 48

    B. 72

    C. 108

    D. 64

    Answer: B

72

The answer is 72 because it is a multiple of both 18 and 24.

42. **Which is the better buy, 10 items for $2.56 or 8 items for $2.46?**

    (Rigorous) (Skill 7.9)

    A. 10 items for $2.56

    B. 8 items for $2.46

    C. Both are equally good deals

    D. There is no better buy

    Answer: A

10 items for $2.56

10 items for $2.56 is the better deal because each item is less per item then if you were to get 8 items for $2.46.

43. **Two mathematics classes have a total of 410 students. The 8:00 am class has 40 more than the 10:00 am class. How many students are in the 10:00 am class?**

    (Average rigor) (Skill 7.9)

    A. 123.3

    B. 370

    C. 185

    D. 330

    Answer: C

185

Let x = # of students in the 8 am class and x – 40 = # of students in the 10 am class. So there are 225 students in the 8 am class, and 225 – 40 = 185 in the 10 am class, which is answer C.

44. **What is the absolute value of the number -5?**

    (Rigorous) (Skill 7.12)

    A. -5

    B. 10

    C. 1/5

    D. 5

    Answer: D

5

The absolute value is how far on a number line the number is from zero.

45. **Which of the following is an example of the associative property?**

    (Average Rigor) (Skill 8.2)

    A. a (b + c) = ab + bc

    B. a + 0 = a

    C. (a + b) + c = a + (b + c)

    D. a + b = b + a

    Answer: C

(a + b) + c = a + (b + c)

The associative property is when the parentheses of a problem are switched.

46. **Two kids are selling lemonade on the side of the road and want to raise at least $320. If the materials needed (lemons, pitcher, table, etc.) to run a lemonade stand costs $15, how many glasses of lemonade will they need to sell if each glass costs $6?**

    (Rigorous) (Skill 8.6)

    A. 210 glasses

    B. 59 glasses

    C. 74 glasses

    D. 53 glasses

    Answer: B

61 glasses

To complete this problem you must make a problem that includes a variable. You start with how much the materials cost since that number must be included due to the fact the materials set the kids back. Also, since each glass is $6 you will have to multiply that number by X, which represents how many glasses need to be sold. Finally, you must incorporate how much the kids want to make, which is $320. The statement should look like 6x − 15 = 320.

47.   3x + 2y = 12

        12x + 8y = 15

        Solve for x and y.

        (Average Rigor) (Skill 8.6)

        A. All real numbers

        B. x = 4, y = 4

        C. x = 2, y = -1

        D. None of the above

        Answer: D

None of the above

Multiplying the top equation by -4 and adding results in the equation 0 = -33. Since this is a false statement, the correct choice is the null set.

48.   **Three-dimensional figures in geometry are called:**

        (Rigorous) (Skill 9.1)

        A. Solids

        B. Cubes

        C. Polygons

        D. Blocks

        Answer: A

Solids

Three-dimensional figures are referred to as solids.

49. **If a right triangle has legs with the measurements of 3 cm and 4 cm, what is the measure of the hypotenuse?**

    (Average Rigor) (Skill 9.2)

    A. 6 cm

    B. 1 cm

    C. 7 cm

    D. 5 cm

    Answer: D

5 cm

If you use the Pythagorean Theorem, you will get 5 cm for the hypotenuse leg.

50. **If a right triangle has a hypotenuse of 10 cm and one leg of 6 cm, what is the measure of the other leg?**

    (Average Rigor) (Skill 9.2)

    A. 7 cm

    B. 5 cm

    C. 8 cm

    D. 9 cm

    Answer: C

8 cm

If you use the Pythagorean Theorem, you will get 8 cm for the other leg of the triangle.

51.   What is a translation?

(Rigorous) (Skill 9.3)

A. To turn a figure around a fixed point.

B. The object has the same shape and same size, but figures face in different directions.

C. To "slide" an object a fixed distance in a given direction.

D. The transformation that "shrinks" or "makes it bigger."

Answer: C

To "slide" an object a fixed distance in a given direction.

A translation is when you slide an object a fixed distance, but do not change the size of the object.

52.   A tetrahedron consists of the following:

(Rigorous) (Skill 9.5)

A. 4 equilateral triangles

B. 6 squares

C. 12 regular pentagons

D. 8 equilateral triangles

Answer: A

4 equilateral triangles

A tetrahedron is 4 triangles that are all equilateral.

53. **What measures could be used to report the distance traveled in walking around a track?**

(Easy) (Skill 9.6)

A. Degrees

B. Square meters

C. Kilometers

D. Cubic feet

Answer: C

Kilometers

Degrees measure angles, square meters measure area, cubic feet measure volume, and kilometers measure length. Kilometers is the only reasonable answer.

54. **3 km is equivalent to:**

(Easy) (Skill 9.6)

A. 300 cm

B. 300 m

C. 3000 cm

D. 3000 m

Answer: D

3000 m

To change kilometers to meters, move the decimal 3 places to the right.

55. **The mass of a cookie is closest to:**

(Easy) (Skill 9.6)

A. 0.5 kg

B. 0.5 grams

C. 15 grams

D. 1.5 grams

Answer: C

15 grams

Science utilizes the metric system, and the unit of grams is used when measuring mass (the amount of matter in an object). A common estimation of mass used in elementary schools is that a paperclip has a mass of approximately one gram, which eliminates choices B and D, as they are very close to 1 gram. A common estimation of one kilogram is equal to one liter of water. Half of one liter of water is still much more than one cookie, eliminating choice A. Therefore, the best estimation for one cookie is narrowed to 15 grams, or choice C.

56. **If the radius of a right circular cylinder is doubled, how does its volume change?**

(Rigorous) (Skill 9.6)

A. No change

B. Also is doubled

C. Four times the original

D. Pi times the original

Answer: C

Four times the original

If the radius of a right circular cylinder is doubled, the volume is multiplied by four because in the formula, the radius is squared. Therefore, the new volume is 2 x 2 or four times the original.

57.   10 cups = _____ quarts?

(Average Rigor) (Skill 9.6)

A. 2 quarts

B. 1 quart

C. 3.5 quarts

D. 2.5 quarts

Answer: D

2.5 quarts

First, to do this problem you must know that 4 cups make up 1 quart. Now, you must set up an inequality. If 4 cups equals 1 quart, 10 cups equals _____ quarts. You must set up the following formula: 4 cup/1 quart = 10 cups/X quarts.

58.   **In similar polygons, if the perimeters are in a ratio of x:y, the sides are in the ratio of?**

(Average Rigor) (Skill 9.6)

A. m : y

B. $x^2 : y^2$

C. 2x : y

D. 1/2x : y

Answer: A

m : y

The sides are in the same ratio.

59.   Find the area of a rectangle if you know that the base is 8 cm and the diagonal of the rectangle is 8.5 cm:

(Rigorous) (Skill 9.8)

   A. 24 cm²

   B. 30 cm²

   C. 18.9 cm²

   D. 24 cm

   Answer: A

The answer is choice A because the base of the rectangle is also one leg of the right triangle, and the diagonal is the hypotenuse of the triangle. To find the other leg of the triangle you can use the Pythagorean Theorem. Once you get the other leg of the triangle, that also is the height of the rectangle. To get the area you perform the base times the height. The reason why the answer is A and not D is because area is measured in centimeters-squared, not just centimeters

60.   The volume is:

(Easy) (Skill 9.8)

   A. Area of the faces excluding the bases

   B. Total area of all the faces, including the bases

   C. The number of cubic units in a solid

   D. The measure around the object

   Answer: C

The number of cubic units in a solid

Volume refers to how much "stuff" can be placed within a solid. Cubic units is one of many things that can be placed within a solid to measure its volume.

61. **What is the area of a square whose side is 13 feet?**

    (Rigorous) (Skill 9.8)

    A. 169 feet

    B. 169 square feet

    C. 52 feet

    D. 52 square feet

    Answer: B

169 square feet

Area = length times width ($l \times w$)

Length = 13 feet

Width = 13 feet (square, so length and width are the same)

13 x 13 = 169

Area = square feet

Area is measured in square feet.

62. **A boat travels 30 miles upstream in three hours. It makes the return trip in one and a half hours. What is the speed of the boat in still water?**

(Average Rigor) (Skill 9.9)

A. 10 mph

B. 15 mph

C. 20 mph

D. 30 mph

Answer: B

15 mph

Let x = the speed of the boat in still water and c = the speed of the current.

	rate	time	distance
upstream	$x - c$	3	30
downstream	$x + c$	1.5	30

Solve the system:

$$3x - 3c = 30$$

$$1.5x + 1.5c = 30$$

63.   **All of the following are examples of obtuse angles EXCEPT:**

      (Average Rigor) (Skill 9.10)

      A. 110 degrees

      B. 90 degrees

      C. 135 degrees

      D. 91 degrees

      Answer: B

90 degrees

A 90 degree angle is not obtuse; it is a right angle.

64.   **Given the formula d=rt, (where d = distance, r = rate, and t = time), calculate the time required for a vehicle to travel 585 miles at a rate of 65 miles per hour.**

      (Average Rigor) (Skill 9.11)

      A. 8.5 hours

      B. 6.5 hours

      C. 9.5 hours

      D. 9 hours

      Answer: D

9 hours

We are given d = 585 miles and r = 65 miles per hour and $d = rt$. Solve for t. hours.

65.   Given a drawer with 5 black socks, 3 blue socks, and 2 red socks, what is the probability that you will draw two black socks in two draws in a dark room?

   (Rigorous) (Skill 10.4)

   A. 2/9

   B. 1/4

   C. 17/18

   D. 1/18

   Answer: A

2/9

In this example of conditional probability, the probability of drawing a black sock on the first draw is 5/10. It is implied in the problem that there is no replacement, therefore the probability of obtaining a black sock in the second draw is 4/9. Multiply the two probabilities and reduce to lowest terms.

66.   Suppose you have a bag of marbles that contains 2 red marbles, 5 blue marbles, and 3 green marbles. If you replace the first marble chosen, what is the probability you will choose 2 green marbles in a row?

   (Average Rigor) (Skill 10.4)

   A. 2/5

   B. 9/100

   C. 9/10

   D. 3/5

   Answer: B

9/100

When performing a problem where you replace the item you multiply the first probability fraction by the second probability fraction and replace the item when finding the second probability.

67. Suppose you have a bag of marbles that contains 4 red marbles, 6 blue marbles, and 2 green marbles. If you do not replace the first marble chosen, what is the probability you will choose 2 blue marbles in a row?

(Rigorous) (Skill 10.4)

A. 36/144

B. 1/4

C. 5/22

D. 30/132

Answer: C

5/22

When performing a problem where you do not replace the marble, you multiply the first probability by the second probability (which is one less because you have one less marble).

68. In probability, the sample space represents:

(Average Rigor) (Skill 10.5)

A. An outcome to an experiment

B. A list of all possible outcomes of an experiment.

C. The amount of times you must flip a coin.

D. The amount of room needed to conduct an experiment.

Answer: B

The sample space is all the possible outcomes that you can have for an experiment.

69. **Permutation is:**

(Rigorous) (Skill 10.5)

- A. The number of possible arrangements, without repetition, where order of selection is not important.

- B. The number of possible arrangements, with repetition, where order of selection is not important

- C. The number of possible arrangements of items, without repetition, where order of selection is important.

- D. The number of possible arrangements of items, with repetition, where order of selection is important.

Answer: C

By definition, permutation is the number of possible arrangements, without repeating items, where the order of the selection is important.

70. **If given the question "How many different ways can you arrange a committee of three people?" what type of probability is this?**

(Rigorous) (Skill 10.5)

- A. Sample space

- B. Permutation

- C. Fundamental counting principle

- D. Combination

Answer: D

Combination

When referring to a committee, the order does not matter because you can make a committee with a variety of people and switch their roles. When the order does not matter then it is a combination.

71. Corporate salaries are listed for several employees. Which would be the best measure of central tendency?

(Average Rigor) (Skill 10.10)

$24,000 $24,000 $26,000 $28,000 $30,000 $120,000

A. Mean

B. Median

C. Mode

D. No difference

Answer: A

Mean

The median provides the best measure of central tendency in this case, as the mode is the lowest number and the mean would be disproportionately skewed by the outlier $120,000.

72. Given the following numbers, find the median:

(Rigorous) (Skill 10.10)

25, 18, 16, 45, 10, 27

A. 21.5

B. 25

C. 18

D. There is no median

Answer: A

21.5

The median refers to the number that is in the middle. First, to find this number you must order the number from smallest to largest (or largest to smallest) and find the number in the middle. If there is an even amount of numbers you add the two numbers in the middle and divide by two.

73.   **Given the following numbers, find the mode:**

(Rigorous) (Skill 10.10)

14, 5, 16, 7, 18, 15, 3

A. 5

B. 14

C. 18

D. There is no mode

Answer: D

The mode refers to the number that shows up the most in a set of numbers. In this example there is no number that appears more than once, so there is no mode.

74.   **Which landform supports the majority of the world's people?**

(Rigorous) (Skill 11.2)

A. Mountains

B. Plains

C. Plateaus

D. Hills

Answer: B

Plains

Plains support the most people in the world.

75. **All of the following are oceans EXCEPT:**

(Easy) (Skill 11.2)

A. Pacific

B. Atlantic

C. Mediterranean

D. Indian

Answer: C

Mediterranean

The Mediterranean is a sea, which is smaller than an ocean and surrounded by land.

76. **The theory of "sea floor spreading" explains _____**

(Average Rigor) (Skill 11.2)

A. The shapes of the continents.

B. How continents got named.

C. How continents move apart.

D. How continents sink to become part of the ocean floor.

Answer: C

How continents move apart

In the theory of "sea floor spreading," the movement of the ocean floor causes continents to spread apart from one another. This occurs because crustal plates split apart, and new material is added to the plate edges. This process pulls the continents apart, or may create new separations; it is believed to have caused the formation of the Atlantic Ocean.

77. **Which term best defines the customs, traditions, and arts of a group of people?**

    (Easy) (Skill 11.3)

    A. Culture

    B. Democracy

    C. Interdependence

    D. Geography

    Answer: A

Culture

When dealing with customs, traditions, and the arts of a group of people only culture A makes sense. The other answers do not refer to people, so they are not logical answers to the question.

78. **All of the following are natural resources EXCEPT:**

    (Average Rigor) (Skill 11.4)

    A. Trees

    B. Coal

    C. Fish

    D. Paper

    Answer: D

Paper

A natural resource is something that is found in nature and though trees are found in nature, paper is not.

79. **All of the following are examples of why the first known civilizations developed by water EXCEPT:**

(Average Rigor) (Skill 12.1)

A. Rivers provided water, which both the humans and animals needs.

B. Rivers allowed the settlers to travel so they could trade goods.

C. The rivers attracted animals so hunters had a continuous supply of food.

D. The rivers overflowed, which left a deposit of very rich soil.

Answer: B

Rivers allowed the settlers to travel so they could trade goods.

There is no evidence that the *first* civilizations used water for trading purposes.

80. **Which civilization invented the wheel?**

(Rigorous) (Skill 12.1)

A. Egyptians

B. Romans

C. Assyrians

D. Sumerians

Answer: D

Sumerians

The ancient Sumerian civilization invented the wheel.

81. **What is the "Pax Romana"?**

(Rigorous) (Skill 12.1)

  A. Long period of peace enabling free travel and trade, spreading people, cultures, goods, and ideas all over the world

  B. A period of war where the Romans expanded their empire

  C. The Roman government

  D. A time where the government was over-ruled

  Answer: A

Long period of peace enabling free travel and trade, spreading people, cultures, goods, and ideas all over the world

The "Pax Romana" was a time when the Roman's were peaceful and wanted to spread their culture all over the world.

82. **Who wrote the *Iliad* and the *Odyssey*?**

(Rigorous) (Skill 12.2)

  A. Aristotle

  B. Homer

  C. Pythagoras

  D. Herodotus

  Answer: B

Homer

Homer is the author of both the *Iliad* and the *Odyssey*.

83. The "divine right" of kings was the key political characteristic of:

    (Rigorous) (Skill 12.4)

    A. The Age of Absolutism

    B. The Age of Reason

    C. The Age of Feudalism

    D. The Age of Despotism

    Answer: A

The Age of Absolutism

The "divine right" of kings was the key political characteristic of The Age of Absolutism and was most visible in the reign of King Louis XIV of France, as well as during the times of King James I and his son, Charles I. The divine right doctrine claims that kings and absolute leaders derive their right to rule by virtue of their birth alone. They see this both as a law of God and of nature.

84. Which one of the following would NOT be considered a result of World War II?

    (Average Rigor) (Skill 12.6)

    A. Economic depressions and slow resumption of trade and financial aid

    B. Western Europe was no longer the center of world power

    C. The beginnings of new power struggles not only in Europe but in Asia as well

    D. Territorial and boundary changes for many nations, especially in Europe

    Answer: A

Economic depressions and slow resumption of trade and financial aid

Following World War II, the economy was vibrant and flourished from the stimulant of war and an increased dependence of the world on United States industries. Therefore, World War II didn't result in economic depressions and slow resumption of trade and financial aid.

85. **The cold war involved which two countries who both emerged as world powers?**

(Rigorous) (Skill 12.6)

A. China and Japan

B. United States and the Soviet Union

C. England and Brazil

D. Afghanistan and the United States

Answer: B

United States and the Soviet Union

After World War II, the United States and the Soviet Union constantly competed in space exploration and the race to develop nuclear weapons.

86. **What was the long-term importance of the Mayflower Compact?**

(Rigorous) (Skill 13.1)

A. It established the foundation of all later agreements with the Native peoples.

B. It established freedom of religion in the original English colonies.

C. It ended the war in Europe between Spain, France and England.

D. It established a model of small, town-based government that was adopted throughout the New England colonies.

Answer: D

Before setting foot on land in 1620, the Pilgrims aboard the Mayflower agreed to a form of self-government by signing the Mayflower Compact. The Compact served as the basis for governing the Plymouth colony for many years and set an example of small, town-based government that would proliferate throughout New England. The present day New England town meeting is an extension of this tradition. This republican ideal was later to clash with the policies of British colonial government

87. **Which one of the following is NOT a reason why Europeans came to the New World?**

(Average Rigor) (Skill 13.1)

A. To find resources in order to increase wealth.

B. To establish trade.

C. To increase a ruler's power and importance.

D. To spread Christianity.

Answer: B

To establish trade.

When the Europeans came to the New World they were not concerned to establish trade: they wanted to increase their wealth and influence across seas.

88.   **The year 1619 was memorable for the colony of Virginia. Three important events occurred, resulting in lasting effects on U.S. history. Which one of the following is not one of events?**

(Rigorous) (Skill 13.1)

A. Twenty African slaves arrived.

B. The London Company granted the colony a charter making it independent.

C. The colonists were given the right by the London Company to govern themselves through representative government in the Virginia House of Burgesses.

D. The London Company sent to the colony 60 women who were quickly married, establishing families and stability in the colony.

Answer: B

The London Company granted the colony a charter making it independent.

In the year 1619, the Southern colony of Virginia had an eventful year, including the first arrival of twenty African slaves, the right to self-governance through representative government in the Virginia House of Burgesses (their own legislative body), and the arrival of sixty women sent to marry and establish families in the colony. The London Company did not, however, grant the colony a charter in 1619.

89. **The belief that the United States should control all of North America was called:**

(Easy) (Skill 13.1)

A. Westward Expansion

B. Pan Americanism

C. Manifest Destiny

D. Nationalism

Answer: C

Manifest Destiny

The belief that the United States should control all of North America was called C Manifest Destiny. This idea fueled much of the violence and aggression towards those already occupying the lands such as the Native Americans. Manifest Destiny was certainly driven by sentiments of D nationalism and gave rise to A westward expansion.

90. **All of the following were causes of the American Revolution EXCEPT:**

(Average Rigor) (Skill 13.2)

A. The Tea Act of 1773

B. The Stamp Act

C. The colonists were forced to house English troops

D. The colonists wanted more schools

Answer: D

The colonists wanted more schools

The colonists were not concerned about the amount of schools they had, and it was not a factor of the American Revolution.

91.   **The English placed taxes on the colonies for two reasons, what were they?**

   (Easy) (Skill 13.2)

   A. To generate revenue

   B. To gain control over the colonists

   C. A only

   D. Both A and B

   Answer: D

Both A and B

The English placed taxes on the colonies to both generate revenue and gain control over the colonists.

92.   **The first real party organization developed soon after the inauguration of Washington as President. It included which of the following:**

   (Rigorous) (Skill 13.3)

   A. Democrats

   B. Republicans

   C. Nationalists

   D. All of the above

   Answer: D

All of the above

Washington's cabinet included people of both factions. Hamilton was the leader of the Nationalists (the Federalist Party), and Jefferson was the spokesman for the Anti-Federalists, later known as Republicans, Democratic-Republicans, and finally Democrats.

93. **The Westward expansion occurred for a number of reasons; however, the most important reason was:**

(Average Rigor) (Skill 13.3)

A. Colonization

B. Slavery

C. Independence

D. Economics

Answer: D

Economics

Westward expansion occurred for a number of reasons, the most important being economic.

94. **During the 1920s, the United States almost completely stopped all immigration. One of the reasons was:**

(Rigorous) (Skill 13.3)

A. Plentiful, cheap unskilled labor was no longer needed by industrialists

B. War debts from World War I made it difficult to render financial assistance

C. European nations were reluctant to allow people to leave since there was a need to rebuild populations and economic stability

D. The United States did not become a member of the League of Nations

Answer: A

Plentiful, cheap unskilled labor was no longer needed by industrialists

The primary reason that the United States almost completely stopped all immigration during the 1920s was because their once much needed cheap, unskilled labor jobs, made available by the once booming industrial economy, were no longer needed. This had much to do with the increased use of machines to do the work once done by cheap, unskilled laborers.

95. **Which war took the most American lives in American history?**

(Easy) (Skill 13.3)

A. The Civil War

B. The Revolutionary War

C. World War I

D. World War II

Answer: A

The Civil War

In the Civil War, it was Americans fighting Americans, so the casualties were astronomical and more than the Revolutionary War, and both World War I and World War II.

96. **The economic collapse of the United States in 1929 is known as the:**

(Easy) (Skill 13.4)

A. Cold War

B. New Deal

C. Unhappy times

D. Great Depression

Answer: D

Great Depression

The economic collapse of the United States in 1929 was known as the Great Depression.

97.   **A communistic government is:**

(Average Rigor) (Skill 14.2)

A. A government that is ruled by one individual or a small group of individuals.

B. A government with a legislature, usually involving a multiplicity of political parties and often coalition politics.

C. A political system characterized by the ideology of class conflict and revolution and that the product of all the people is shared by each and every person.

D. A political system that values conflict and revolution with a central political control that allows for private ownership of the means of production.

Answer: C

A political system characterized by the ideology of class conflict and revolution and that the product of all the people is shared by each and every person.

By definition, answer C is the correct definition of a communistic government. Choice C and choice D are different because choice D states that the citizens are allowed to have private ownership, while in choice C, the citizens are not allowed private ownership.

98.   **The Bill of Rights consists of which Amendments?**

(Average Rigor) (Skill 14.3)

A. Amendments 1-5

B. Amendments 1-10

C. Amendments 1 and 2

D. Amendments 1-22

Answer: B

Amendments 1-10

The Bill of Rights consists of the first 10 amendments.

99. **All of the following are rights that are granted by the Bill of Rights EXCEPT:**

    (Rigorous) (Skill 14.4)

    A. Freedom of religion.

    B. No cruel or unusual punishment allowed.

    C. Right for a free education.

    D. Security from the quartering of troops in homes.

    Answer: C

Right for a free education.

The right for a free education is not one of the 10 Bill of Rights.

100. **Social skills and values developed by activity include all of the following EXCEPT:**

    (Average Rigor) (Skill 15.1)

    A. Winning at all costs

    B. Making judgments in groups

    C. Communicating and cooperating

    D. Respecting rules and property

    Answer: A

Winning at all costs

Winning at all costs is not a desirable social skill. Instructors and coaches should emphasize fair play and effort over winning. Answers B, C, and D are all positive skills and values developed in physical activity settings.

101. The "sense of who one is" in a society refers to:

(Average Rigor) (Skill 15.1)

A. Cultural identity

B. Population identity

C. Anthropology

D. Cultural bias

Answer: A

Cultural identity

When thinking of "who one is," think of identity. If thinking of identity in a society or culture, that would extend to include cultural identity.

102. Activities that enhance team socialization include all of the following EXCEPT:

(Easy) (Skill 15.2)

A. Basketball

B. Soccer

C. Golf

D. Volleyball

Answer: C

Golf

Golf is mainly an individual sport. Though golf involves social interaction, it generally lacks the team element inherent in basketball, soccer, and volleyball.

103. **Cultural diffusion is:**

(Rigorous) (Skill 15.2)

A. The process that individuals and societies go through in changing their behavior and organization to cope with social, economic and environmental pressures.

B. The complete disappearance of a culture.

C. The exchange or adoption of cultural features when two cultures come into regular direct contact.

D. The movement of cultural ideas or materials between populations independent of the movement of those populations.

Answer: D

The movement of cultural ideas or materials between populations independent of the movement of those populations.

By definition, cultural diffusion is the movement of cultural ideas or materials between populations independent of the movement of those populations.

104. **An economist might engage in which of the following activities?**

(Easy) (Skill 16.2)

A. An observation of the historical effects of a nation's banking practices

B. The application of a statistical test to a series of data

C. Introduction of an experiment factor into a specified population to measure the effect of the factor

D. An economist might engage in all of these

Answer: D

An economist might engage in all of these

Economists use statistical analysis of economic data, controlled experimentation, and historical research in their field of social science.

105. **The following are factors of production EXCEPT:**

(Rigorous) (Skill 16.3)

A. Labor

B. Entrepreneurship

C. Land

D. Income

Answer: D

Income

Income is not a factor of production. However, it would be a possible factor of demand.

106. **The most abundant gas in the atmosphere is:**

(Rigorous) (Skill 17.1)

A. Oxygen

B. Nitrogen

C. Carbon dioxide

D. Methane

Answer: B

Nitrogen

Nitrogen accounts for 78.09 percent of the atmosphere, oxygen 20.95 percent, carbon dioxide 0.03 percent, and methane does not make up any of the atmosphere.

107. **Which of the following types of rock are made from magma?**

(Rigorous) (Skill 17.2)

A. Fossils

B. Sedimentary

C. Metamorphic

D. Igneous

Answer: D

Igneous

Metamorphic rocks are formed by high temperatures and great pressures. Fluid sediments are transformed into solid sedimentary rocks. Only igneous rocks are formed from magma.

108. **Which of the following is the best definition for 'meteorite'?**

(Rigorous) (Skill 17.4)

A. A meteorite is a mineral composed of mica and feldspar.

B. A meteorite is material from outer space that has struck the earth's surface.

C. A meteorite is an element that has properties of both metals and nonmetals.

D. A meteorite is a very small unit of length measurement.

Answer: B

A meteorite is material from outer space that has struck the earth's surface.

Meteoroids are pieces of matter in space, composed of particles of rock and metal. If a meteoroid travels through the earth's atmosphere, friction causes burning and a "shooting star" (i.e., a meteor). If the meteor strikes the earth's surface, it is known as a meteorite. Note that although the suffix –ite often means a mineral, answer A is incorrect. Answer C refers to a "metalloid" rather than a "meteorite," and answer D is simply a misleading pun on "meter."

109. What cell organelle contains the cell's stored food?

(Rigorous) (Skill 18.1)

A. Vacuoles

B. Golgi Apparatus

C. Ribosome

D. Lysosome

Answer: A

Vacuoles

In a cell, the subparts are called organelles. Of these, the vacuoles hold stored food (and water and pigments). The Golgi Apparatus sorts molecules from other parts of the cell; the ribosomes are sites of protein synthesis; and the lysosomes contain digestive enzymes.

110. Identify the correct sequence of organization of living things from lower to higher order:

(Rigorous) (Skill 18.1)

A. Cell, Organelle, Organ, Tissue, System, Organism

B. Cell, Tissue, Organ, Organelle, System, Organism

C. Organelle, Cell, Tissue, Organ, System, Organism

D. Organelle, Tissue, Cell, Organ, System, Organism

Answer: C

Organelle, Cell, Tissue, Organ, System, Organism

Organelles are parts of the cell; cells make up tissue, which makes up organs. Organs work together in systems (e.g., the respiratory system), and the organism is the living thing as a whole.

111. **Which kingdom is comprised of organisms made of one cell with no nuclear membrane?**

    (Average Rigor) (Skill 18.1)

    A. Monera

    B. Protista

    C. Fungi

    D. Algae

    Answer: A

Monera

To answer this question, first note that algae are not a kingdom of their own. Some algae are in Monera, the kingdom that consists of unicellular prokaryotes with no true nucleus. Protista and Fungi are both eukaryotic, with true nuclei, and are sometimes multi-cellular. Therefore, the answer is A.

112. **Heterozygous refers to:**

    (Average Rigor) (Skill 18.2)

    A. Having 2 dominant genes

    B. Having 2 recessive genes

    C. Having neither a recessive nor a dominant gene

    D. Having 1 recessive gene and 1 dominant gene

    Answer: D

Having 1 recessive gene and 1 dominant gene

Heterozygous means to have 1 recessive gene and 1 dominant gene, so the correct answer is A.

113.   **Which of the following is the most accurate definition of a
nonrenewable resource?**

(Average Rigor) (Skill 18.5)

A. A nonrenewable resource is never replaces once used.

B. A nonrenewable resource is replaced on a timescale that is very long
relative to human life spans.

C. A nonrenewable resource is a resource that can only be manufactured
by humans.

D. A nonrenewable resource is a species that has already become
extinct.

Answer: B

Renewable resources are those that are renewed, or replaced, in time for
humans to use more of them. Examples include fast-growing plants, animals, or
oxygen gas. (Note that while sunlight is often considered a renewable resource,
it is actually a nonrenewable but extremely abundant resource.) Nonrenewable
resources are those that renew themselves only on very long timescales, usually
geologic timescales. Examples include minerals, metals, or fossil fuels.

114.   **The following are examples of chemical reactions EXCEPT:**

(Average Rigor) (Skill 19.1)

A. Melting ice into water

B. Dissolving a seltzer tablet in water

C. Using a fire-cracker

D. Burning a piece of plastic

Answer: A

Melting ice into water

When you melt ice there is no chemical reaction. Ice and water have the same
chemical make-up.

115. **The transfer of heat by electromagnetic waves is called _____ :**

(Easy) (Skill 19.2)

A. Conduction

B. Convection

C. Phase change

D. Radiation

Answer: D

Radiation

Heat transfer via electromagnetic waves (which can occur even in a vacuum) is called radiation. Heat can also be transferred by direct contact (conduction), by fluid current (convection), and by matter changing phase, but these are not relevant here.

116. Which is the correct order of methodology?

(Average Rigor) (Skill 20.2)

1. Collecting data

2. Planning a controlled experiment

3. Drawing a conclusion

4. Hypothesizing a result

5. Re-visiting a hypothesis to answer a question

    A. 1,2,3,4,5

    B. 4,2,1,3,5

    C. 4,5,1,3,2

    D. 1,3,4,5,2

    Answer: B

4, 2, 1, 3, 5: Hypothesizing a result, planning a controlled experiment, collecting data, drawing a conclusion, and re-visiting a hypothesis to answer a question.

The scientific method is a very structured way to create valid theories and laws. All methodologies must follow this specific, linear plan.

117. **In an experiment measuring the growth of bacteria at different temperatures, what is the independent variable?**

(Rigorous) (Skill 22.3)

A. Number of bacteria

B. Growth rate of bacteria

C. Temperature

D. Size of bacteria

Answer: C

Temperature

To answer this question, recall that the independent variable in an experiment is the entity that is changed by the scientist in order to observe the effects (the dependent variable). In this experiment, temperature is changed in order to measure growth of bacteria, so C is the answer. Note that answer A is the dependent variable, and neither B nor D is directly relevant to the question.

118. **All of the following professions are classified under 'earth sciences' EXCEPT:**

(Average Rigor) (Skill 22.4)

A. Geologist

B. Meteorologist

C. Seismologist

D. Biochemist

Answer: D

Biochemist

A geologist, meteorologist, and seismologist all work with phenomena that are earth related. A biochemist deals with objects that are living.

119. **Which of the following is a correct explanation for scientific evolution?**

(Rigorous) (Skill 23.1)

A. Giraffes need to reach higher leaves to eat, so their necks stretch. The giraffe babies are then born with longer necks. Eventually, there are more long-necked giraffes in the population.

B. Giraffes with longer necks are able to reach more leaves, so they eat more and have more babies than other giraffes. Eventually, there are more long-necked giraffes in the population.

C. Giraffes want to reach higher for leaves to eat, so they release enzymes into their bloodstream, which in turn causes fetal development of longer-necked giraffes. Eventually, there are more long-necked giraffes in the population.

D. Giraffes with long necks are more attractive to other giraffes, so they get the best mating partners and have more babies. Eventually, there are more long-necked giraffes in the population.

Answer: B

Organisms with a life/reproductive advantage will produce more offspring. Over many generations, this changes the proportions of the population. In any case, it is impossible for a stretched neck A or a fervent desire C to result in biologically mutated baby. Although there are traits that are naturally selected because of mate attractiveness and fitness D, this is not the primary situation here, so answer B is the best choice.

120. The advancement of understanding in dealing with human beings has led to a number of interdisciplinary areas. Which of the following interdisciplinary studies would NOT be considered under the social sciences?

(Average Rigor) (Skill 23.3)

A. Molecular biophysics

B. Peace studies

C. African-American studies

D. Cartographic information studies

Answer: A

Molecular biophysics

Molecular biophysics is an interdisciplinary field combining the fields of biology, chemistry, and physics. These are all natural sciences, and not social sciences

XAMonline, INC. 21 Orient Ave. Melrose, MA 02176

Toll Free number 800-509-4128

TO ORDER Fax 781-662-9268 OR www.XAMonline.com

WEST SERIES

PO#   Store/School:

Address 1:

Address 2 (Ship to other):

City, State Zip

Credit card number_____-_____-_____-_____   expiration_____

EMAIL _____

PHONE   **FAX**

ISBN	TITLE	Qty	Retail	Total
978-1-58197-550-5	WEST-B Basic Skills			
978-1-58197-564-2	WEST-E Biology 0235			
978-1-58197-565-9	WEST-E Chemistry 0245			
978-1-58197-566-6	WEST-E Designated World Language: French Sample Test 0173			
978-1-58197-557-4	WEST-E Designated World Language: Spanish 0191			
978-1-58197-558-1	WEST-E Elementary Education 0014			
978-1-58197-554-3	WEST-E English Language Arts 0041			
978-1-58197-551-2	WEST-E General Science 0435			
978-1-58197-559-8	WEST-E Health & Fitness 0856			
978-1-58197-560-4	WEST-E Library Media 0310			
978-1-58197-555-0	WEST-E Mathematics 0061			
978-1-58197-556-7	WEST-E Middle Level Humanities 0049, 0089			
978-1-58197-568-0	WEST-E Physics 0265			
978-1-58197-563-5	WEST-E Reading/Literacy 0300			
978-1-58197-552-9	WEST-E Social Studies 0081			
978-1-58197-553-6	WEST-E Special Education 0353			
978-1-58197-567-3	WEST-E Visual Arts Sample Test 0133			
	SUBTOTAL		Ship	$8.25
	FOR PRODUCT PRICES VISIT WWW.XAMONLINE.COM		**TOTAL**	

Printed in the United States
114274LV00003B/166/P